VIOLENCE AND NONVIOLE

Conceptual Excursions into Phantom Opposites

Through an original and close reading of the key literature regarding both revolutionary violence and nonviolence, this book collapses these two widely assumed mutually exclusive concepts. By revealing that violence and nonviolence are in fact braided concepts arising from human action, Peyman Vahabzadeh demonstrates that in many cases actions deemed to be either violent or nonviolent might actually produce outcomes that are essentially the same.

Vahabzadeh offers a conceptual phenomenology of both the key thinkers and theorists of revolutionary violence and the various approaches to nonviolence. Arguing that violence is inseparable from civilizations, *Violence and Nonviolence* concludes by making a number of original conceptualizations regarding the relationship between violence and nonviolence, exploring the possibility of a nonviolent future, and proposing to understand the relationship between the two concepts as concentric, not opposite.

PEYMAN VAHABZADEH is a professor of sociology at the University of Victoria.

Violence and Nonviolence

*Conceptual Excursions into
Phantom Opposites*

PEYMAN VAHABZADEH

UNIVERSITY OF TORONTO PRESS
Toronto Buffalo London

© University of Toronto Press 2019
Toronto Buffalo London
utorontopress.com
Printed in Canada

ISBN 978-1-4875-0417-5 (cloth)
ISBN 978-1-4875-2318-3 (paper)

∞

Printed on acid-free, 100% post-consumer recycled paper with
vegetable-based inks.

___

Library and Archives Canada Cataloguing in Publication

Vahabzadeh, Peyman, 1961–, author
Violence and nonviolence : conceptual excursions into phantom opposites /
Peyman Vahabzadeh.

Includes bibliographical references and index.
ISBN 978-1-4875-0417-5 (cloth). ISBN 978-1-4875-2318-3 (paper)

1. Violence.   2. Nonviolence.   I. Title.

HM1116.V34 2019   303.6   C2018-904973-1

___

This book has been published with the help of a grant from the Federation
for the Humanities and Social Sciences, through the Awards to Scholarly
Publications Program, using funds provided by the Social Sciences and
Humanities Research Council of Canada.

University of Toronto Press acknowledges the financial assistance to its
publishing program of the Canada Council for the Arts and the Ontario
Arts Council, an agency of the Government of Ontario.

Canada Council
for the Arts

Conseil des Arts
du Canada

ONTARIO ARTS COUNCIL
CONSEIL DES ARTS DE L'ONTARIO

an Ontario government agency
un organisme du gouvernement de l'Ontario

Funded by the   Financé par le
Government   gouvernement
of Canada   du Canada

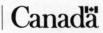

Canadä

MIX
Paper from
responsible sources
FSC® C016245

for Emile
the light of my eyes

To the question, What is to be done? when raised together with the question, What is being? a radical phenomenologist can only respond: dislodge all vestiges of a teleocratic economy from their hideouts—in common sense as much as in ideology—and thereby liberate things from the "ordinary concept" which "captures" them under ultimate representations.

Reiner Schürmann, *Heidegger on Being and Acting*

Contents

Acknowledgments

This book simmered for a long time while I pondered violence and wondered about the possibility of acting and living in nonviolent ways. Increasingly, violence and nonviolence lost their contrariness in my meditations, and my book, *Exilic Meditations: Essays on A Displaced Life* (2012), paved the way for rethinking (non)violence. The ideas of this book gradually emerged through three Directed Readings courses I taught and the dialogues I had with my doctoral students at the University of Victoria. So, I am grateful to Laurel Collins and Rebeccah Nelems whose challenging questions regarding violence, nonviolence, human action, and the possibility of changing this unjust world kept me searching for answers. My thanks also go to my students in the Cultural, Social, and Political Thought (CSPT) Core Seminar (2015–16), and in particular to Veronica (Wrenna) Robertson, who offered insightful observations. Of particular mention are two retreat symposia to which I was invited by the Institute for the Humanities at Simon Fraser University on "Violence and Its Alternatives" (2003) and "Exile" (2012), on Bowen Island in British Columbia. The feedback I received on my presentations at these symposia sharpened my thinking. Parts of chapters 1 and 2 of this book were presented in a public lecture to which I was invited by the Institute for the Humanities at Simon Fraser University (13 March 2015). I thank the audience at this event for their formidable questions and perceptive comments. I would like to thank Ian Angus and Samir Gandesha for their reflections. I am indebted to my first mentor in sociology, Matthew Speiers, for introducing me to peace research literature and Johan Galtung. Thanks also to Jerry Zaslove for generously offering several insightful comments. I am indebted to Victoria Tahmasebi-Birgani, whose intervention brought this book closer to publication. I would like to thank

Karin Renee O'Leary, Megan Spencer, and Sara Naderi for their assistance with certain components of this research. Last but not least, I am grateful to Douglas Hildebrand, Jennifer DiDomenico, Jodi Lewchuk, Breanna Muir, Robin Studniberg, and Lisa Jemison for their professionalism and support throughout the review and publication process. Parts of chapters 2 and 3 have been published in *Heathwood Journal of Critical Theory* 1(1) (September 2015) and a section of chapter 5 in *Journal for Cultural and Religious Theory* 6(2) (Spring 2005). I thank these journals for their permission to republish my articles in this book.

Once again, this book has emerged through the loving support of my son, Emile, and my long-time exilic companion, Giti. I have had numerous "casual" conversations with her on the subject. My source of inspiration and teacher of nonviolence, Giti taught me that nonviolence is materialized only through unconditional generosity, hospitality, and forgiveness, as these human qualities extend one's life into that of others without imposition, and that the rigid and widely held opposition between violence and nonviolence – the exposition and critique of which being the central thesis of this book – is either an academic's fancy or a symptom of living a privileged life, and that life is irreducible to neither.

VIOLENCE AND NONVIOLENCE

Conceptual Excursions into Phantom Opposites

Introduction: Back to Violence

The critique of violence is the philosophy of its history.

> Benjamin, "Critique of Violence" (1996, 251)

We can also say now that history is from the start nothing other than the vital movement of the coexistence and the interweaving of original formations and sedimentations of meaning.

> Husserl, *The Crisis of European Sciences and Transcendental Phenomenology* (1970, 371)

This study offers a controversial thesis: it critically probes and exposes the apocryphal mutual exclusivity of violence and nonviolence within existing theoretical and philosophical approaches. The thesis of this book can be summarized as follows: properly understood, violence and nonviolence are originally revealed in human action (and subsequently manifested in institutionalized activities and through legal and/or administrative procedures) within the epochal and structural ambits that contain us. These epochs can be identified by their hegemonic–epistemic principles of intelligibility that are in the air we breathe. *Human activity in every epoch is normatively aligned with these principles.* It is *action* alone (as opposed to task-oriented activity) that simultaneously opens up certain possibilities and forecloses on others. Consequently, *violence and nonviolence are never pure moments.* The distinction between violence and nonviolence cannot be positively and objectively ascertained, and thus, theoretically, the now fashionable *opposition* of violence to nonviolence remains theoretically untenable and indicative of Manichaean thinking. This binary is generally achieved through self-righteous moralizing about, or utilitarian

approaches to, nonviolence, or – to look at the flip side of the proverbial coin – through the (decontextualized) demonization of violence.
In both cases, human action is perceived in pure, ideal, and decontextualized modes and corresponding categorical typologies, unaffected by
the horizons of intelligibility of action, forces of circumstance, and/or
the need to preserve human and non-human life. This book therefore
launches a conceptual phenomenology of the concepts of violence
and nonviolence through a close and meticulous reading of the key
treatises on revolutionary violence and on various strands of nonviolence as well as the important contributions pertaining to them. The
book begins with the "hypothesis of the ontological primacy of violence" and argues, in its conclusion, for "ontological concentricity of
(non)violence."

A recent book problematizes the "naturalistic" justifications for violence
and, linking nonviolence to the search for moral truth in Eastern religions, essentializes nonviolence, equating it with the political-democratic
code (Jahanbegloo 2014, 1–10). This approach works fine insofar as
readers have already subscribed to certain moral codes as absolute Truth.
Treatises like this assume that the marker(s) between violence and nonviolence are epistemologically knowable in advance. That is why advocates
of nonviolence appeal so readily to moral principles: morality provides
the most convenient (and most rigid) epistemological marker when it
comes to the convoluted fields of action. By contrast, another recent
study problematizes the said binary, offering a conceptual history that
traces nonviolence to the early-nineteenth-century United States and the
emergence of Christian pacifism and abolitionism (Losurdo 2015, 7–19).
It claims to demystify nonviolence by offering an interesting but selective
social and political history behind the long tradition of nonviolence (and
biographies of nonviolent preachers and practitioners). It ends up offering conjectural and decontextualized analyses by *a priori* separating violence from nonviolence as opposite categories, portraying nonviolence
as capitulation and as an apology for the status quo and the powers that
be, the so-called "Great Game" – that is, the "proclamation of the ideal of
non-violence goes hand in hand with celebration of the West, which has
erected itself into custodian of the moral conscience of humanity and, as
a result, considers itself authorized to practice destabilization and coups
d'état, as well as embargoes and 'humanitarian' wars, in every part of the

world." In contrast to Gandhian belief, "*Satyagraha* has now been turned into its opposite: it has been transformed from a 'truth force' into an original force for manipulation" (2015, 203; emphasis in original). Thus, waving "the flag of non-violence has now become a key element in this Great Game" (2015, 183) and "a key element in psychological warfare and the Great Game" (2015, 170). It is true that intelligence apparatuses of Western imperialism nowadays promote open and nonviolent movements over militant resistance (because the former are easier to manipulate and crush). It has become a sad reality that powers that be rally behind nonviolent resistance around the world to conceal their imperialist motives under the banner of democracy. In making these observations, Domenico Losurdo is certainly correct. But these undeniable facts cannot justify interpreting the long tradition of nonviolence as the historic trajectory of (seemingly inevitable) co-option and assimilation: if anything, in order to serve present-day global progressive movements and aid the activists with conceptual tools that empower them in the face of the militaristic machinery of repression, today we need more serious analyses of violence and nonviolence and their links to collective action. The aforesaid positions apropos nonviolence point to serious misunderstandings: this book will show that nonviolence involves deploying force and applying pressure on a repressive adversary, but in ways different from violence.

In contrast to the aforesaid approaches, this book probes violence and nonviolence on more sophisticated conceptual levels. As a phenomenologist, I cannot adhere to truisms because I question whether *any* knowledge is pregiven. I argue that the distinction between violence and nonviolence – a distinction that always constitutes a *knowledge claim* – is always already present in any concrete condition under which an actor meets an adversary, but that this distinction does not necessarily lead to the *opposition* of violence and nonviolence. The *distinction remains because it is always time- and context-specific* and thus only established in the circumstances at hand. On the contrary, *the opposition gestures towards timelessness*: it decides once and for all, and for past and future generations, how to perceive and partake in action. The existing and commonly held categorical distinctions between violent and nonviolent modalities of action report a fact of knowledge according to the sensibilities of our common era of reigning principles of democratic citizenship and human rights under increasingly militarized states. Principles like citizenship, democracy, and rights need not be abandoned. Indeed, they should be defended, for they allow legal, political, and cultural bases for victims of violence to fight back against their abusers and rulers. However, these categories have resulted in pervasive artefacts – in uncritical cultural worship or demonization – which themselves are the result of the essentializing, substantiating, and, most importantly, *reifying* of both violence and nonviolence. Here, the term "reification" is understood à la Georg Lukács (1971): an object is reified when it is detached from the socialized relations in which it originated so as to seem freestanding. Reified and objectified concepts then acquire a life of their own, concealed from critical inquiry. Violence is commonly reified by measuring the acts of violence in terms of pre-existing categories that impede us from inquiring into the conditions from which violent acts emerge. These reified concepts are increasingly detached from that which enables *action*: *liberation*, or in other words, defence of one's *dignity* and the *authentication* of one's (individual and collective) existence against the position of enforced residence within an imposed (i.e., unfree, inauthentic) world. Seeking the origins of this opposition will generate new insights with regard to the pervasiveness of violence, even and indeed *especially* in what is commonly deemed to be nonviolence. One of my major concerns is therefore to *rethink the ways in which we can or (cannot) refrain from reproducing violence* in ever new manifestations born out of cultural grounds as well as the structures of injustice and exploitation that enable and justify such manifestations, sometimes even under the banner of nonviolence.

Today, nonviolence enjoys the enthusiastic backing of influential spiritual leaders, philosophers, theologians, and activists, all of whom are rallying to the cause. Movements with nonviolent components have achieved measurable advances for their participants. However, nonviolence has also been propagated by corporate media as well as by those wielding political power – by the ruling elites, who know that repressing nonviolent movements is far less messy, costly, and surgical than repressing violent ones. Often, promoting nonviolence has had the effect of stifling meaningful transformation and radical rethinking and action in relation to structural inequalities and various injustices, as well as delivering social movements to the fields of "dissent management" by the state. The recent media circuses surrounding four African Americans killed by police in the United States – the choking of Eric Garner in New York City in July 2014; the fatal shooting of eighteen-year-old Michael Brown in Ferguson, Missouri, in August 2014; the death of Freddie Gray while in police custody in Baltimore, Maryland, in April 2015; and the fatal shooting of Keith Lamont Scott in Charlotte, North Carolina, in September 2016 – are cases in point. In the wake of the massive protests and riots these cases ignited, Baltimore city officials and state governors steadfastly called for calm. Baltimore politicians, in particular, called on the people to remain peaceful and "nonviolent." In response, Ta-Nehisi Coates rightly identified these politicians' and police chiefs' calls for "nonviolence as compliance":

> When nonviolence is preached as an attempt to evade the repercussions of political brutality, it betrays itself. When nonviolence begins halfway through the war with the aggressor calling time out, it exposes itself as a ruse. When nonviolence is preached by the representatives of the state, while the state doles out heaps of violence to its citizens, it reveals itself to be a con. And none of this can mean that rioting or violence is "correct" or "wise," any more than a forest fire can be "correct" or "wise." Wisdom isn't the point tonight. Disrespect is. In this case, disrespect for the hollow law and failed order that so regularly disrespects the community. (Coates 2015)

Coates is certainly right. Let the reader know that this is precisely the kind of nonviolence that I disavow in this book; instead, I advocate a form of transformative nonviolence close in spirit to Gandhi's "nonviolence of the brave."

Prominent thinkers of our time who take nonviolence for granted are, at the very best, offering political, logistical, or ethical arguments as to why violence should be avoided. They claim theoretical allegiances to critical theory, deconstruction, various post-structuralist ethics, garden-variety spiritualisms, or Gandhian thought, but in their hearts and despite their rhetoric, they remain uncritical in that they are unable to defend their advocacy for nonviolence without founding it on the pregiven evil of violence. This error stems from an assumed Manichaean binary between violence and nonviolence. I advocate nonviolence, but not without theoretically (*rather than* morally) qualifying my position. In addition, unlike other advocates of nonviolence, I expressly refrain from advancing my position as one of universal validity: the social, political, and historic *contexts will judge the applicability of my position.*

In this book, therefore, I do not take the much-too-easy position of advocating nonviolence without properly justifying and situating my arguments. Neither do I take violence and nonviolence as received concepts. For me, *critique of violence does not automatically yield an affirmation of nonviolence,* as I do not subscribe to proof by negation. I refuse to use utility (i.e., reduction of harm) as a justifiable end that apparently necessitates just means – nonviolence. I do not accept politics as

essentially nonviolent. Thus, besides providing conceptual grounds for
understanding violence and nonviolence, I take the unpopular but necessary position that *violence and nonviolence significantly overlap*, albeit to
varying degrees and depending on the context, and that, furthermore,
the two often share modes or aspects within action. Human action is always the
nodal point from which both violence and nonviolence can arise and
through which violence and nonviolence meet and even challenge each
other. Human collective action has always oscillated between violence
and nonviolence, and that being so, human action, in any historically
specific manifestation, cannot be viewed as purely violent or nonviolent. In this book, the term "(non)violence" *signifies simultaneously the
two concepts of nonviolence and violence, the overlap of the two, and the lack of a
positive and ascertainable distinction between the two.* This book invites readers to question common notions of violence and nonviolence and to set
the conceptual bar higher in understanding this complex, age-old phenomenon. It brings to light its central thesis through phenomenology
and phenomenologically enabled interpretations of the key literature
pertaining to the subject. Since I take the position that violence and
nonviolence are not mutually exclusive (at least not without qualification), I argue that we need to understand the possibilities and limitations of both violence and nonviolence and try thereby to conceptually
and practically situate action in the contemporary human world. This
book proposes that if there is to be advocacy for nonviolence, it should
be *qualified* advocacy.

The World We Have Inherited

As members of today's collective humanity sharing a common destiny in
this age of globalization and technological Enframing (following Heidegger), we have emerged from a postcolonial age of national liberation, anti-colonial wars, civil rights movements, and cultural rebellion
(during the 1960s). During that age, as Fredric Jameson cogently states,
"for a time, everything was possible … this period, in other words, was a
moment of a universal liberation" (1988, 207). Without question, humanity in general has challenged some age-old and rampant injustices and
discriminations and has gained, to varying degrees and in different parts
of the world, some improvements. These gains are best revealed in relation to the challenges that contemporary social movements continue to
pose to the status quo – in the realms of gender, sexuality, workers' rights,
and indigenous and minority rights, to name a few. Yet oftentimes these

achievements seem meagre in relation to undying structures of injustice – structures that remain as pervasive and powerful as ever, often by masking themselves with various hegemonic gestures of necessity or naturalistic justifications for their inevitability. States remain violent and aggressive even in democratic societies that respect citizen and human rights. Judging from the new assault by neoliberal capitalism and by neoconservative states of assorted shades that are implementing neoliberal social policies at home or even half a world away through regime change, the installation of puppet governments, and practices of global exceptionalism, violence has in fact become increasingly systemic, calculated, clinical, and hubristic. A sober examination tells us that the most prominent feature of today's systemic violence is that this violence is being concealed! Systemic violence is wrapped in the sacred veils of security, necessity, inevitability, progress, and even welfare. Examples abound: rampant (digital) surveillance, the criminalization of activism, (anti-)refugee policies, so-called humanitarian interventions, drone warfare, and – perhaps most invisible of all – labour sweatshops in the global South.

By the early 1980s, a neoconservative backlash – epitomized by the rise to power of Margaret Thatcher in the Britain and Ronald Reagan in the United States – had set out to dismantle the gains of the movements that originated in the 1960s among welfare state liberals and social democrats in the West. A shift in the public discourse about "fiscal responsibility" veiled the true, *violent* mechanisms of neoliberal cutbacks, which aimed to privatize public services and do away with the postwar promise of a "social safety net." The ruling elite of global financial capitalism had turned its attention to extracting profit from (welfare state) social services. As world resources begin to shrink, capitalist expansion has reversed course in order to extract from the "inside." The global financial crisis of 2008 is the most visible manifestation of this. And all of this was justified by resort to camouflaged rhetoric. In the words of Gérard Duménil and Dominique Lévy, "the rules whose imposition define neoliberalism are generally designated euphemistically as 'market' rules, avoiding the direct reference to capital" (2004, 2).

The collapse of the Soviet Union and "actually existing socialism" – euphorically but transiently celebrated by Francis Fukuyama as the "end of history" (1992) – did not quite ensure unrivalled world domination for the United States and its allies. The "end of history" must be understood properly as representing Hegel's Eurocentric conception of world history as the Spirit (*Geist*) externalizing itself, actualizing its potentials, as an expression of its immanent "impulse of *perfectibility*" (Hegel, 1991, 54;

emphasis in original). The Spirit expands its rational freedom (1991, 47, 55, 65) and resides within the state as its objective embodiment (1991, 47). In terms of this philosophy, the Other – notably Africa and Latin America but also Asia – is understood as merely the signifiers of a lack (1991, 71), and the Orient (which for Hegel started east of the Danube!) trails (read: should trail) the West (of Europe) in Hegel's "choo-choo train theory of a world history" (Dabashi 2007, 205). According to this normative (and Eurocentric) theory (which is not without humour), the Other is allowed to participate in this world-historical game only provided that it will assimilate to the self-acclaimed Self. Kamran Matin exposes how Eurocentrism's "internalist" logic informs its approach to historical heterogeneity of societal constitutions (Matin 2013, 144). My study hopes to show how such normativity is at the root of much of the violence we face today. No wonder, then, that the superpower that survived the Cold War enjoyed telling itself it was the embodiment of world history and was always more than willing to impose its will on the rest of the world. But it turned out that Samuel Huntington's notion of world domination by the American ruling class was problematic; actually at hand was a "clash of civilizations" (Huntington 1996). For Fukuyama, the West had emerged as triumphant and it was now time for the world to become America (well, its satellite)! For Huntington, America was superior to the rest of the world, so it inevitably was going to outdo the others. Global capitalism and smart foreign policy were the primary means for the first approach; militarism and unilateralism were the primary means for the second.

To complete the picture, China has turned the Americans' dream of leading the world economy into a nightmare; it has shown itself to be a robust economic rival to America, far outpacing the G8 countries in GDP growth (in 2011, China's GDP stood at 9.3%, while those of the "Group of 8" ranged between –0.7% and 4.3%) (World Bank 2013). Moreover, the euphoria that followed the collapse of the Soviet Union had not quite faded when garden-variety Islamic fundamentalisms began to challenge Western hegemony in Asia and Africa, often with rabid violence, within countries destabilized by US-led interventionism. The Project for the New American Century (now seemingly dormant) expresses the worries of American neoconservatives and is meant to influence foreign and domestic policy in order to maintain and expand zones of US influence. Western powers' unilateralism in the Middle East and North Africa – the invasions of Iraq and Afghanistan, as well as the mortal assault on Kaddafi's Libya and Assad's Syria in the name of liberating these countries – must be viewed in this context. Domestically, various security and "anti-terrorism" laws have made it legal for Western nations to turn democratic societies into surveillance societies, impede progressive social change, and produce a generation of meek, hegemonized citizens. We are now on the doorstep of societies in which security or intelligence drones are a common sight everywhere, flying above our homes, roads, and public venues, extracting information and engaging in crowd control (*Russia Today* 2013). The police are being militarized, laws are being passed to allow intrusive monitoring, and intelligence agencies are being expanded – all out of sight of the public, despite freedom-of-information laws. States are repressing activists by invoking "security" or "terrorism" clauses in the "global civil war" (Agamben 2005, 2). Lo and behold: "Political linguistics: armor of the Establishment" (Marcuse 1969, 73). As a result, human collective action – the source of the liberties and civil and human rights that some of us enjoy today in various manifestations, such as protests, demonstrations, strikes, marches, occupations, and roadblocks – is increasingly being criminalized. Stronger limits are being imposed on civic spaces for action. In this context, argues Giorgio Agamben, the "state of exception" is becoming "the dominant paradigm of government" (2005, 2). The state is unnerved by undecidability – that undeniable fact of life – and thus bestows upon itself an existence that is outside the law yet part of society (2005, 35). To use the imagery proposed by Hannah Arendt, we have all become potential "stateless" persons as the spectre of the "end of rights of [hu]man" looms large (1958b, 267–302).

This has enormously raised the pressure on activism: the existing liberal-democratic, global capitalist system encourages people to "change the system from within" by pointing at the rewards for becoming yet another reformist cog in the existing monstrous system – this, even while collective action is prohibited and criminalized and a heavy human price is imposed on activists. From the point of view of the powerful, collective action – citizens' responses to perceived injustices – is criminal. Herbert Marcuse was right when he averred, "In accord with established law and order not the crimes but the attempt to stop them is condemned and punished as a crime; thus it is judged by the very standards which the action indicts" (1969, 73). Under these conditions, the pressure on activism is amplified; collective action sets out to challenge the injustices safeguarded by laws that are "enforceable," which means the laws are implemented through violent means to protect certain ends and justified through corporate mass media and by means of popular, numbing

amusements that produce the "one-dimensional society" (Marcuse 1964);
yet simultaneously, activists largely refuse to partake in counter-violence
against the violence of the law and the state, mainly because they do not
see politics as a means to an end. Thus, contemporary activists by and
large refuse to partake in violence as they try to bring about a more just
future. The result is an agonizing situation for activism: the masses have
become politically indifferent in vast areas of the world – a stunning
indifference despite declining conditions of human sustainability – as
a result of the hegemonic inculcation of the exploited masses, or stun-
ningly repressive regimes, or both. It seems that visionary activism for a
better future has become the imperilling preoccupation of a minority.

These reflections are meant to offer a summary of our immediate historical context in a painful nutshell. The above quick sketch of
our global, shared destiny shows how rampant and commonplace, yet
increasingly veiled, violence has become. In this context, it is inevitable
that we rethink violence as well as human collective action and activism. The growing restrictions imposed on activism by those who own
the means to control it call for a renewed understanding of (non)vio-
lence, a task to which this book is dedicated. In the face of rampant
social, political, class, gender, sexual, racial, and ecological injustices,
on the one hand, and unilateralism and exceptionalism (both breeding
unending violence), on the other, we must inquire about the *ontological*
pregivenness of violence beyond the historically specific, locatable, and
identifiable *ontic* cases and causes. This is a daunting task and taking it
up requires humility: this book is only a humble attempt at answering
the piercing question of *action* in relation to violence and nonviolence.
This study hopes to find approximations to the relations between these
two concepts.

Recollective Thoughts on (Non)Violence

The ideas in this book have been simmering for a long time. When the
book finally emerged in its present shape, it struck me that perhaps the
general idea behind it – that violence and nonviolence are not pure
moments, nor are they mutually exclusive – was rooted in my life-altering
experience as a young revolutionary who played a very small role in the
fateful months of 1978–79 that led to the overthrow of the US-backed
Pahlavi regime of the Shah Mohammad Reza Pahlavi. The Iranian Revolution was a popular revolt by any standard – women and men, young
and old, Muslim, non-Muslim, and secular, indeed people from all walks

of life, converged to make it happen. It contained elements of postcolonial national self-assertion, and its outcome, a repressive Islamic Republic, had nothing to do with the broad diversity of participants – in terms of demographics (youth, women, workers, peasants, urban poor, the traditional bazaar sector, and the educated middle class), ideological tendencies (various traditional Shi'is, Marxists, nationalists, and radical Muslims), or sociocultural roots (traditional, urban and modern, secular, or religious) – in the continued nationwide protest movement that gradually exhausted the Shah's regime and led to its demise (see Dabashi 2007). History is written by the victors, and as such, we do not often hear about the diversity of visions for a future Iran that streamed through the streets of Tehran and other major cities. In 2005, twenty-five years after the revolution, accomplished photojournalist Akbar Nazemi (2005) held an impressive photography exhibit at Presentation House Gallery in North Vancouver, British Columbia, where he displayed hundreds of pictures he had taken as a photojournalist during the 1978–79 street protests. Those photographs showed how people from all walks of life with diverse demands participated in the revolution. They bore little resemblance to the monolithic images of the revolution broadcast over Iranian and Western media alike. We will see why the initial symptom of violence is the reduction or elimination of diversity. To understand what happened in 1979 in Iran, I think it is useful to maintain the conceptual distinction between "revolt" and "revolution" proposed by Michel Foucault. Although Foucault was blind to the diverse secular forces participating in the revolution and seemed fascinated by its anti-colonial, "Islamic" character (Dabashi 2016, 165–6), his distinction remains useful. The "revolution" – with the added qualification of "Islamic" – justified and historicized the people's revolt against monarchical dictatorship. "In repatriating revolt, one has claimed to have manifested its truth and to have brought it to its real issue. A marvellous and formidable promise. Certain people will say that the revolt has found itself colonized by realpolitik" (Foucault and Bernauer 1981, 6). The "repatriation" has long clouded our view of the diversity of movements that led to the revolution. That popular revolt, a unique political experience in which I participated, has been occulted by a might-seeking revolution in which I played no part.

I recall that the popular and massive protest movement of 1978 was plainly nonviolent. As if bound by an unwritten commitment, the protesters adhered to nonviolence, even in the face of violent crackdown and shootings by the police and the military. In the corporate, mainstream media, the Iranian Revolution has not been represented as nonviolent; but its nonviolent character has been the subject of a documentary film (Fazeli 2013). Sporadic armed operations by Marxist and Muslim guerrillas did not really affect the attitude of the protesters; in fact, the former only accentuated the latter. In desperate situations when cornered by the police, the protesters did no more than throw rocks in self-defence, and then only rarely. Ayatollah Khomeini often threatened to order the protesters to launch a Jihad (to be understood, in this context, as a revolutionary uprising) against the regime, as if the people on the streets were his mindless followers. The protesters' slogan in 1978–79 captures the nonviolent character of the Revolution: "Blood is victorious over the Sword." This slogan reveals how the participants in the mass rallies overcame their formidable oppressor, a regime backed by Western powers: hundreds of protesters died demanding liberation and self-rule. I was seventeen at the time, and I remember leaving my home to join the street protests knowing that I might not return. And I felt good about it: What could be more honourable than losing my life to a cause greater than my own life without resorting to violence? At that time, I had not yet read Gandhi. I recall it to be a spiritual moment of submission to fate, one that (as I reflected decades later) was a precondition for becoming a historical individual. The revolt was indeed Gandhian in spirit: it was essentially *confrontational* while generally refraining from violence, and this process emerged at the grassroots intuitively, largely without the guidance of the Islamists. The 10–11 February 1979 popular armed uprising, inadvertently launched by mutinous Air Force technicians and supported by the Marxist People's Fadai Guerrillas (and then other underground groups), was not planned by Ayatollah Khomeini and his Revolutionary Council: it came as a surprise to them (Vahabzadeh 2010, 58–9; Keddie 1981, 257) and conclusively overthrew the regime. While the cities of Iran were sites of a popular uprising, the Ayatollah became frightened and declared that he had not yet ordered a Jihad (he was secretly negotiating with the Americans and the Imperial Army for a peaceful transition). Post-revolutionary propaganda would exaggerate the number of casualties of 1978–79 astronomically (it claimed that 70,000 died during the 1978–79 uprising, as opposed to the carefully recorded deaths of 2,781 in the same period) in order to amplify the brutality of the regime and exaggerate the revolutionaries' determination. These falsified numbers served as psychological leverage that later legitimized among the uneducated and displaced masses the post-revolutionary regime's repression of the protests against the new government (see Baghi n.d). Put differently, revolutionary propaganda fabricated an epic depiction of the revolution involving enormous casualties in order to prove that the fallen regime had been fiendishly violent and to build a sense of righteousness extracted from the long-held Shi'i discourse of martyrdom.

The Iranian Revolution was indeed a triumph of blood over the sword: it was a victory of flowers over guns. In organized protests (as opposed to spontaneous ones), each of us would place a long-stemmed carnation in the barrel of a soldier's G3 assault rifle, kissing him, calling him "brother," and offering him water or sweets. The February uprising was a visible *historical moment of liberation*; from the perspective of Frantz Fanon, it marked the (re)birth of a people. The armed uprising in February 1979 could not overshadow the long nonviolent movement that preceded it and that exhausted the regime politically, economically, and in terms of its supporters' morale. But neither can we dismiss that armed uprising as an "exception" to nonviolent rule: the former was integral to the latter. Clearly, then, while the Iranian Revolution was a nonviolent movement, violent actions (including the February uprising) were integral to it, however marginally. The revolution of 1978–79 stood out as Iran's Gandhian moment. Thirty years later, in 2009, a massive ten-month-long movement known as the Green Movement rocked the country as Iranians poured onto the streets protesting against rigged presidential elections. This time, too, they reminded the world of a gentle yet persevering nation. Inspiring the uprisings that were later dubbed as the Arab Spring (see Vahabzadeh 2014; Dabashi 2007; Hashemi and Postel 2010), the Green Movement eventually succumbed to the protracted and brutally surgical repression of the state. But it showed a historically significant point: the liberatory nonviolence of 1979 had been transformed into the civil rights nonviolence in 2009. In short, within thirty years Iranians had moved from Mahatma Gandhi to Martin Luther King, Jr.! *The epochal discourse had changed; the modality of action had remained constant.*

Still, the question is not fully formed. The outcome of the revolution, with the continued consolidation of power in Tehran over a society that has always been irreducibly pluralistic, dynamic, and ahead of its rulers, has made incessant international headlines since 1979. Here I do not wish to dwell on the rampant violence that has reigned over the country since 1979, though I am obliged to sadly acknowledge it. Rather, I want to point out that above and beyond the reign of terror in the 1980s and the continued repression of civil society (particularly the Green Movement of 2009), there are invisible forms of violence that arose from the nonviolent Iranian Revolution: it was the *violence of institutional displacement* – a violence arising from economic (a *nomos*, law, reigning over an *eco-*, milieu) phenomenalization (which I will explain in chapter 1), in a manner that will be illuminated by a phenomenological reading of the pioneer work of George Sorel on violence (chapter 3). This form of violence involves displacement of cultural, social, economic, and moral elements with the result that, as we say in Persian, "nothing [stays] in its place." So for me, the Iranian Revolution provides a historical case of nonviolent action leading to liberation and to the (re)birth of a people who, by virtue of constituting a new regime, enabled structural, institutional, and "economic" violence on a national scale. In short, it fascinates me that nonviolence can breed and lead to violence. Reflections on this formative experience pointed me to the central thesis of this book.

Violence and nonviolence can only arise as a *possibility* in the shadow of the Other and as an attempt at excluding the Other from the *shared* and simultaneously *contested* field of action. As a principle, I personally advocate nonviolence, but the experience of those revolutionary years taught me that the distinction between violence and nonviolence is never absolutely clear. Nor can I extract my advocacy of nonviolence from self-acclaimed, self-righteous moral superiority (popular nowadays because it is rigid and self-serving) or from the liberal, rights-based position that hides the institutional and structural violence embedded in modern-day democracies (see Vahabzadeh 2003, 103–40). I will subsequently argue that if we accept the lack of a clear epistemological distinction between violence and nonviolence, we will need to seriously acknowledge its theoretical consequences. I know that my statements sound strange for a treatise that ultimately advocates nonviolence, but it is precisely in light of this indistinctness that the book offers new, phenomenological readings of a specific genealogy of the literature pertaining to violence and nonviolence.

It has been my intention to bring together the major tenets of primarily European sources pertaining to questions of violence and nonviolence as foundational moments. In dealing with the question of nonviolence, however, I found a vast and practically unworkable literature. Naturally, not everything that has been written on violence and nonviolence is theoretically pertinent to this study. Considerable volumes in these fields are empirical and can be used in studies pertaining to public policy, advocacy networks, educational reforms, or legal studies – all of which are valuable in their own right. The theoretical approach of this work therefore necessitates engaging only with select numbers of works on the theme. These selections are not arbitrary: they are among the foundational works on this theme, and when we read them phenomenologically, we find that they are permeated with uneasy conceptual relations between violence and nonviolence. Setting myself the unenviable task of dislodging the historically sedimented meanings associated with the two concepts, à la Benjamin and Husserl (in the epigraphs above), I acknowledge that the thesis of this book is controversial and that in order to fit my arguments into book format, I have had to exclude many potentially fruitful trajectories. I hope to attend to what has been excluded from this treatise in subsequent works.

Caveat Lector

I mean for this book to provide a phenomenologically informed theoretical framework for analysing violence and nonviolence. I imagine that every reader of this book is aware of the vast literature pertaining to these themes. My work makes no claim or attempt to offer any comprehensive account of the relevant literature in any shape or form. My subsequent readings of the theorists and practitioners of violence or nonviolence are deeply phenomenological; these readings are offered in order to advance a new understanding of the relationship between violence and nonviolence. The treatises and ideas I analyse here of course invite even more diverse readings than acknowledged here.

Jerry Zaslove (2015a) has observed that this book's approach attempts to look violence in the eye – an act that invites a psychoanalytical approach to the issue of violence, especially in terms of aggression and the fear that dwells in each us from childhood onwards. Ken Seigneurie (2015) has also remarked that the claim, made in chapter 7, that conceptually speaking nonviolence is a twentieth-century invention (despite its long history) – which implies that the contemporary concept of violence is also fairly new – needs historicization, which in turn necessitates a conceptual history of both violence and nonviolence. These are two formidable strategies that need to be undertaken in future research; alas, I need to exclude them from the present study in order to retain its focus.

Finally, this book is not the work of a detached scholar; there is rather something deeply personal about my conceptual excursions. My readings and interpretations are admittedly "accented" – as *I think with an accent* (Vahabzadeh 2012a) – and only thus proceeding. I hope this book will negotiate the nexus between my particular (even personal) and accented approach and a certain, cautious claim to the general applicability of what I theoretically submit here.

Critical Note on the Approach

Aiming to deconstruct one of the most unquestioned metaphysical
assumptions of our time, this book offers a *conceptual phenomenology* of
violence and nonviolence as (supposedly) opposite terms. In doing so, I
start with the foundational theoretical works in established phenomenological literature that pertains to violence, beginning with Martin Heidegger, and then work my way up to the concluding propositions that, I
hope, constitute original contributions. As such, what I offer throughout
the chapters as my particular contributions arise from my engagements
with, and reinterpretations of, these foundational analyses and propositions. I believe that any other approach would render my arguments
and propositions theoretically shaky, if not arbitrary, since my proposed
concepts cannot be properly situated without these foundational works.
This approach allows me *to move from the obvious to the hidden.* Of course,
"[w]hat is hidden and distant from us is the most obvious, that which
is taken for granted and unnoticed because of its intimate familiarity"
(Marder 2013, 32). That which is hidden – the central thesis of this book –
is concealed because it has been encrypted, and my work attempts a
phenomenological decryption of the relationship between violence and
nonviolence. When discussing my approach, I often ask my interlocutor
to think of certain key concepts as catalysts of the sort used in chemistry:
a catalyst is a substance that won't be present in the outcome of a chemical reaction, but without its presence in the process, the desired reaction
among other substances will not take place. I hope the reader will recognize the merits of the conceptual catalysts in this book.

Our Conceptual Journey

This book has been greatly inspired by radical phenomenology of Reiner
Schürmann. A phenomenological approach inspired by Schürmann runs
through the whole book; serving as a hermeneutical master key, it enables
a specific deconstructive reading of the literature in the field. Chapter 1
constructs a foundational radical phenomenological approach to violence and thereby to nonviolence, beginning with Heidegger's linking
of metaphysics to violence. While dwelling in Schürmann's philosophy,
the chapter also benefits from the philosophies of Gianni Vattimo and
Hannah Arendt, offering preparatory conceptualizations of violence and
nonviolence, proposing a hermeneutic of violence in relation to human
action and liberation. In light of these foundational works, chapter 2

offers key phenomenological reflections on the concepts of violence and nonviolence in terms of humans' relationship to their world(s). Chapter 3 offers close readings of the seminal works of George Sorel, Walter Benjamin, and Jacques Derrida regarding the complexities of liberation in relation to (non)violence. This chapter paves the way for further reflections on liberation through the works of Frantz Fanon, Hannah Arendt, Giorgio Agamben, and Ernesto Laclau in chapter 4, which specifically addresses the constitution of a new "people" as the nonviolent emerging of political beings through acts of emancipation or liberation. Then a short interregnum sets the stage for the rest of the book, which critically examines four categorical approaches to nonviolence. Chapter 5 critically revisits the argument championed by Gene Sharp that hinges on the logistical necessity of nonviolence under repressive conditions. Chapter 6 closely re-examines the argument in favour of nonviolence from the vantage point of utility, laid out mainly – and meticulously – by Johan Gultang in his seminal works, which conceptually link nonviolence to social justice. Chapter 7 engages with key moral and ethical arguments for nonviolence in the works of Leo Tolstoy, David Henry Thoreau, Arendt, and Judith Butler. Chapter 8 provides a close reading of Mahatma Gandhi, exploring issues pertaining to the politics of nonviolence. The Conclusion offers new postulates pertaining to the theme of this book.

1
Towards a Radical
Phenomenology of (Non)Violence

The rootedness of the ego in my autonomy blocks forever the attempts to exile evil outside of my acts where I am most myself. It is impossible, after the critical turn, to ascribe it to entitative givens ... These are so many attempts to objectify evil, as if it could be tracked down in some arrangement of beings. Where is evil? The metaphysical genius in us looks everywhere, except in our rational will.

Schürmann, *Broken Hegemonies* (2003, 477)

A few exceptions aside, through popular media and theoretical works alike, violence has been rendered a *reified* concept in that the positivist and *a priori* distinctions (as in the law and moral discourses) between violence and nonviolence define what they name "violence" prior to its emergence in action and regardless of its context(s). While distinctions between violence and nonviolence are common sense and often useful, they impede us from probing (non)violence and thus from a proper understanding of what is at issue in that very distinction. Phenomeno-logically and à la Heidegger (viz., Heidegger's critique of metaphysics in mistaking *beings*, entities, for *Being* as such, the matter of philosophy), the said *a priori* distinction(s) mistake(s) that which is violent for violence proper, and as such they try to explain the *essence* of violence through the existing, concrete violent *acts*. The recognition of violence in an act – whether, to name a few cases, it is genocide, a revolutionary purge, rape, or police brutality – attests to what I call the *epistemological a priori*, which is by and large a product of the internalization of values, customs, or legal codes, which enable us to react to the agreed-upon manifestations of violence but which often hinder us from recognizing emerging, subtle forms of violence. This study offers a phenomenological examination of (non)violence – one that is primarily influenced by Reiner Schürmann (1941–1993) and his distinct engagement with the phenomenological tradition, Heidegger above all. He calls his approach *radical* or *temporal phenomenology*. As with my previous studies (Vahabzadeh 2003; 2010), Schürmann's philosophical watershed informs the approach this book takes, enabling a deconstructive gaze by allowing me to step back from the phenomena to the specific nexus of the contexts in which they become possible. Schürmann's work has certain affinities with several trends in contemporary Continental thought: Derrida's deconstruction, Lyotard's concept of *différend*, Foucault's conceptualizations of power, subject, and governmentality, aspects of Deleuze and Guattari, and certain conceptual trajectories in Arendt, in addition to the works of post-Heideggerians Werner Marx and Gianni Vattimo (see Vahabzadeh 2009). Since Schürmann, a maverick philosopher, is not a "household" philosophical name, this chapter offers a brief overview of his thought and then *constructs* a phenomenological theory of violence based on his thought. This theory is enriched with contributions by Arendt and Vattimo. I think that in suspending positive and *a priori* distinctions (between violence and non-violence and through what I later call "algorithmic thinking"), my phenomenology will be worthy of the qualifier "radical."

Metaphysics of Violence, Violence of Metaphysics

Heidegger submitted that the (European) history of metaphysics, from Aristotle to Hegel, was that of oblivion of Being in which the question of Being was "camouflaged" (Marx 1971; Heidegger 1996, 1; Schürmann 2003). Due to the withdrawal of Being, the philosophers mistook beings (entities and existents) for Being as such, thereby asserting the "first principles" from which subsequent philosophical principles were to be extracted. Following Heidegger, Schürmann proposes the "hypothesis of metaphysical closure," according to which – given the epochal transmutation at our historic juncture when "time is out of joint" (Hamlet) – for the first time in history, it has become possible for us to think beyond metaphysics and its principles. Schürmann (2003) reinterprets the history of metaphysics as the rise and demise of the principles governing *epochal hegemonies* founded on (hegemonic) first principles and their practical and scholastic enactments that rendered these principles intelligible and matters of fact. As such, history is understood not as a succession of unfolding, progressive periods endowed with an underlying logic (economy, race, or morals) or as an eschatological or monistic

movement animated by a supreme and transcendent *Geist*. On the contrary, history is viewed by radical phenomenology in terms of epochs that
are governed by a founding First or *arché*. An *arché* signifies a *beginning* –
a founding moment that dominates an entire subsequent era, or put
differently, an inceptive point (of an epoch), simultaneously founding
and founded upon a *principle*. This "supreme" principle is nonetheless
rooted in a humble, particular experience, but it expands to govern the
state of affairs of each subsequent epoch. An *arché*, therefore, contains
and puts in operation the epochal code of intelligibility that Schürmann calls *principium*. A *principium* is legitimated by sets of *injunctions*
that justify its application. Schürmann calls these injunctions *princeps*
(the prince) – that is, the authority that upholds the supreme principle
(Schürmann 1990, 97–154). Bound together, *principium–princeps* (principle–authority) marks the founding of an epochal–regional public life
and gives rise to an epochal–political regime, which Schürmann explains
through his reading of the puma-shaped, Inca city of Cusco in today's
Peru (1990, 26–9). The principle-authority pair establishes the Truth of
an age in its specific epochal modality. Thus the "epochal constellations
of Truth" are born. In addition to *principium–princeps*, there is a third concept, *Ursprung*, the "surging forth of presence" (Schürmann 1981, 247),
through which, strictly speaking, the "ontological difference" (between
Being and beings or entities) is temporalized (between present, or an
actual, and presence, or the event of actualization). *Ursprung* enables (in
non-causal terms) new modalities of phenomenal presentness and new
constellations of Truth, and it allows us to view the fall and demise of the
existing constellations of Truth and the hegemonic principles governing the doable and intelligible not as matters of dialectical opposition,
but rather as matters of hegemonies that are broken from the inside by
virtue of the founding act, *arché*, which always remains at variance with
itself (I will return to this shortly). Stated simply, the principle–authority
pair (*principium–princeps*) holds phenomena and entities within a certain
domain of intelligibility and actuality, which following Michel Foucault
we may call a "regime of Truth." The "surging forth" (*Ursprung*) points
to how such regimes of Truth fall and how dominant truths change. The
reason for such changes is the founding principle itself (*arché*), which in
giving birth to an entire new epoch also activates the seeds of its future
demise.

Together, *arché* and *principium–princeps* shape the mode of theory and
practice in a given age. At its apogee, when it rules virtually uncontested,
the twofold origination of an epoch permeates every aspect of life to the

extent that almost all that one does and perceives, comprehends and contemplates, imagines and desires, is but a disclosure of the originative–hegemonic terms. In Schürmann's words: "Epochal principles are always ontic givens. Each of them opens modalities of possible interaction and forecloses on others. An epoch, then, is 'reduced' to the way things, words, and actions are mutually present in it" (1990, 81). It is because of such modalities that scholar and layperson alike are able to distinguish, relatively clearly and without considerable effort or esoteric abstruseness, between the ancient, medieval, and modern humanities (and historical periods). Not having access to the proper science, the genius Renaissance inventor could only imagine humans flying (perhaps by imagining that human arms were potential wings); conversely, for a country today to feed its population using the wooden plough seems rather a romantic fancy bereft of reason and practicality. The former constitutes a futuristic dream (the notion precedes the science); the latter represents a nostalgic dream (science is shunned in order to return to innocence). Yet both are "dreams." We are always situated in a particular structural totality of the possible and doable that can be genealogically traced back – through phenomenology of history – to the institutive moment(s) of our age.

Furthermore, the fact that we are able to distinguish between past historical periods suggests that epochal principles have their periods of institution, zenith, and destitution. Thus the seed of destruction of an epoch is planted in that epoch at the moment of its foundation (see Arendt below). Yet an epoch's rise, reign, and ruin do not fall into neatly ascertainable periods. There are, of course, exceptional historical situations in which the sweeping power of an apocalyptic historic turn displaces human (and non-human) life in its entirety and brings each and every hitherto meaningful practice, order, and thing to face its own inevitable, tragic "deworldedness." Colonialism is a case in point, and the Spanish conquest of the Inca Empire exemplifies an imposed, apocalyptic epochal transmutation (Schürmann 1990, 26–29). I will return to this case, for it exemplifies what I call "phenomenal violence" – a rampant but also elusive and thus largely untheorized genus of violence that manifests itself through events of *deworlding* and *reworlding* (see chapter 2). These dramatic intercultural cases aside, it is often the case intraculturally that the epochs are instituted through the initially inconspicuous Firsts – that is, through specific acts that gradually translate into a principle (*principium*) that rises to the governing principle during an era, before ceding a long, slow period of destitution. Indeed, the death of a principle "usually takes disproportionately more time than its reign"

(1990, 29). The surging forth of presence (*Ursprung*) enables the existing phenomenal arrangements, their meanings and our theorizations about them, to reappear in a recognizably different modality. Interestingly, this is why, while we are able to distinguish between ancient, medieval, and modern epochs within European humanity, the positivist's attributing the moment of rise or ruin of each epoch to any single event remains forever contestable. It is through the genealogy of the principles of an epoch that we can archaeologically arrive at the epochal First command (*archê*). In many cases, epochal principles are declared as if there was only one principle or one moment of foundation. This error arises from the historical distance between the observer and the originative moment. It is also a result of subsuming several founding principles under one formidable grand principle. The identification of these (plural) Firsts is the task of those who would phenomenologically deconstruct epochs. Precisely herein rests the "revolutionary" task of radical phenomenology: "a phenomenology that deconstructs the epochs 'changes the world' because it reveals the withering away of these principles" (1990, 11). Knowledge about hegemonic principles is knowledge with inescapable social and political consequences. So in discussing the epochal, and thus structural and predicative, roots of violence in this study, we need to critically probe how a founding First is transformed into a hegemonic, governing principle. Much of the violence to which we are subjected is overlooked because matter-of-factness reigns over our acting and being in various shapes of "normalcies" as well as normative–utilitarian and biopolitical expectations of human and non-human existence.

In *Broken Hegemonies*, Schürmann offers an erudite and compelling reinterpretation of Western philosophy in terms of the rises (maximizations) and demises (singularizations) of the hegemonic fantasms. The "rise" is associated with natality (Arendt), the "demise" with mortality (Heidegger). This "ultimate double-bind" allows us to see action in terms of the vital expansion that follows an event of *natality* – in human terms, simply the birth of an individual, or initiating a course of action, or starting a business – that will inevitably meet its own decline in the final eventuation of *mortality* – simultaneously as a life's *accomplishment* and as sheer (physical) *diminishing* and the dying body. These are ultimate conditions in that they are "not determined by some yet more originative condition" (Schürmann 1993, 204). Natality and mortality do not simply designate the two poles that bracket life (biological or historical coming-into-being); rather, these poles present themselves in the form of *strife* between actuality and possibility that is present within every act.

Caught between these two poles, action marks the manifestation of *temporality*, which is where, for Arendt, the capacity for *experiencing human freedom in terms of political life* resides. Let me quote Arendt at length:

> What usually remains intact in the epochs of petrification and foreordained doom is the faculty of freedom itself, the sheer capacity to begin, which animates and inspires all human activities and is the hidden source of production of all great and beautiful things. But so long as this source remains hidden, freedom is not a worldly, tangible reality; that is, it is not political. Because the source of freedom remains present even when political life has become petrified and political action impotent to interrupt automatic processes, freedom can so easily be mistaken for an essentially nonpolitical phenomenon; in such circumstances, freedom is not experienced as a mode of being with its own kind of "virtue" and virtuosity, but as a supreme gift which only man, of all earthly creatures, seems to have received, of which we can find traces and signs in almost all his activities, but which, nevertheless, develops fully only when action has created its own worldly space where it can come out of hiding, as it were, and make its appearance. (Arendt 1969, 169)

So understood, acting is the unique human capacity that enables bringing something new into this world. In other words, the possibility of the new is tied to the human capacity to act. Freedom, for Arendt, cannot be non-political. That something new can arise from action can be called a "miracle," but it is a miracle within human reach (1969, 169). The "subversive" aspect of action is present in the above excerpt: even when an order is present and fully institutionalized, it is possible to bring *to* it, and *within* it, something new that may potentially undo the existing order. My reading of Arendt leads to this: action founds and assimilates (Schürmann's *archê*); action also subverts and liberates (Schürmann's *Ursprung*). Natality has the power to simultaneously achieve either and both. Mind you: natality is at variance with itself, and to explain this, Schürmann adopts Lyotard's concept of *différend*. This point is important for our upcoming discussion on violence. We should note, therefore, that for Schürmann, the question of natality and foundational principles is internally connected to the history of Western metaphysics (Heidegger), while for Arendt, natality represents the energy that inevitably expands and founds: "the act of foundation inevitably develops its own stability and permanence, and authority in this context is nothing more or less than a kind of necessary 'augmentation' by virtue of which all innovations and changes remain tied back to the foundation which, at the same time, they augment and increase" (1963, 202). *Homo natalis* always remains *Homo politicus*. Natality, in expanding and initiating, *appropriates*, whereas mortality, in bringing to closure, *expropriates* (Schürmann). For Schürmann, natality attaches itself to one representation and relativizes others, and thus the acting that grows into a foundational act denies, and sends into oblivion, its own singular and thus plural origins, by justifying its arising to some transhistorical and metatheoretical fantasm (good, divine, or necessary). The Heideggerian streak in Arendt and Schürmann is evident, although they both deploy a "political turn" in reinterpreting Heidegger, and although there is vivid departure on Arendt's part from the history of metaphysics that she factors out when analysing human freedom and political life.

Schürmann argues that until the exposure (and inevitably, "critique") of metaphysics by Heidegger, Western philosophy had been guided by the metaphysical tendency to maximize singular experiences: Greek *arché*, Neoplatonic *hen* (One), Latin *natura*, and modern *ego cogito* (the knowing subject). In each age the philosopher sought an ultimacy in an original, singular experience and maximized the singular experience by extending it and instituting laws and imposing norms upon the vast divergent aspects of life. The law, as maximization, is anchored to an "ultimate referent" (Schürmann 1990, 8; 148): *arché*, *natura*, God, rational animal. Schürmann calls these justifications "fantasms," by which he referred to the philosopher's desire to extract continuity from an original, humble event, seeking in that event the principle of duplicable, exercisable happiness and inner security, "a continuity that extends the principle of internal consolation into a principle of public consolidation" (Schürmann 2003, 192). However, the original, *archic* event is rather *an-archic* in its natality, in its appearing in this world as something *new*, and in its offering energy and possibilities. Therefore the *archic* rendition of this otherwise humble, *an-archic* event can only be the handiwork of the philosopher who is shaken to the core by life's untamable contingencies and who thus seeks consolation in face of the prospect of the mortality of all beings, of ruined civilizations and impoverished philosophies, of the mind-boggling prospect of "anarchy" when the city can no longer be consolidated under the Prince (*princeps* or authority). By virtue of instituting First Principles, philosophy becomes "the discourse that seeks to best safeguard the originary phenomena" (2003, 15).

While the maximization of an original event (and the mode of knowledge it produces) beyond its native–regional appearance is due to the expansive power of natality – which by virtue of the philosopher's intervention institutes laws, norms, and hegemonies – *singularization* slips under the foundations of the edified hegemony of universal laws like a stealth undertow, thanks to mortality. "The singular point of departure from which the law arises, a singularization, will fracture from within the universal endowed with the force of obligation" (2003, 343). When we speak of "broken hegemonies," we must understand the breakdown not as a consequence of a thetic opposition, and not as an impact of an agent's war of liberation, but rather as a fracturing of hegemonies from within. If maximization represents an inflated absolutization of a "relational given," then "transgressive strategies" can "topple a hegemony" – but this is not due to the subject's rational choice. Instead, singularizations and temporalization allow the actor to act according to the possibilities for openings that reside within the existing "regimes of Truth" (see 2003, 222). Natality opens up the possibility for expansion and institution, but it is also inevitably headed for its inevitable demise. Simon Critchley's description seems useful here: "The epoch of metaphysics, like a dying star, is at its point of exhaustion, a point from which, paradoxically, it swells like a red giant to extend its domination and comprehend all resistance, ethical, political, or otherwise" (1999, 89). Humans and all they create are born towards death, but the metaphysician adamantly disregards this and "sends into oblivion" (Heidegger) our being-towards-death.

Thus, in a phenomenology of violence whose point of departure is institutionalized, normative maximizations we must understand that *every genealogy of institution is simultaneously a necrology of destitution.* Following Schürmann's description, if we regard the "ultimate double-binds" as "two incongruent clusters of attraction-natality-maximization-appropriation and withdrawal-mortality-singularization-expropriation, then the denial of this whole second cluster as well as the exaltation of attractive, maximally normative theses[:] [t]hese then are *conditions of evil* other than ethical or moral" (2003, 626; emphasis added). In our age, this supreme, metaphysical maximization shows itself in what Heidegger calls "technological Enframing" or *Ge-stell* (1977, 20–3), in which existents, humans included, are "standing-reserve" (*Bestand*) and reduced to resource (Heidegger 1977, 17). As a quick detour, let us be reminded that as early as the summer of 1935, when he delivered a lecture course on metaphysics, Heidegger had considered the relationship between metaphysics and *Gewalt* (violence, force). Relevant for our discussion here, Heidegger points out, through his interpretation of the

Sophocles's *Antigone*, that the "human being is, in *one* word, *to deinota-ton*, the uncanniest" (2000, 159; emphasis in original). Here, Heidegger argues, *Deinon* refers to the terrible overwhelming that belongs to the sway of *phusis* – that is, to the "emerging forth" – which the Latins, Heidegger argues, mistranslated as *Natur*, Nature (2000, 14–15). "*Phusis* is Being itself" (Heidegger 2000, 15). Thus to Being belongs *das Walten*, the sway (and *walten*, to govern, to dominate), indeed the overwhelming sway. *Deinon* also denotes the "violence-doing" (*gewalt-tätigkeit*) of the human *Dasein*, a violence that belongs to the human *Dasein* – the one that needs to use violence. Here we can see how the implied waywardness and arbitrariness of the English word "violence" does not exist in the German *Gewalt*, much less in Heidegger's situating the human *Dasein* between the overwhelming sway of the mode of appearances of beings and the violence-doing of humans "in response" to the former. The latter renders humans *unheimlich* – uncanny, unhomely. As such, "*technē* characterizes the *deinon*, the violence-doing, in its decisive basic trait" (2000, 170). This is why my phenomenology of violence cannot but start from violence as ontological constitution of humanity, which leads to my hypothesis of the "ontological primacy of violence" (chapter 2).

This specific *technological* mode of "unconcealment" (*alétheia*) of form of "reductive violence," as a matter-of-factness of utility and productivity, is illuminating:

> The forester who, in the wood, measures the felled timber and to all appearances walks the same forest path in the same way as did his grandfather is today commanded by profit-making in the lumber industry, whether he knows it or not. He is made subordinate to the orderability of cellulose, which for its part is challenged forth by the need for paper, which is then delivered to newspapers and illustrated magazines. The latter, in their turn, set public opinion to swallowing what is printed, so that a set configuration of opinion becomes available on demand. (Heidegger 1977, 18)

The passage is as profound as it seems obvious to anyone who can see beyond the "veil of illusion" (Tolstoy). Philosophy rigorously sets the principles – and the laws governing over the city and upheld by the Prince – which we already tacitly "know." For Schürmann, *Ge-stell* presents to us the *epochal–structural violence*, the violence that permeates life under the existing "economy of presence" (1990, 288–9). This violence expresses itself in the predicative language in which acts and states are assigned purposes or are justified in terms of some fictional and pre-existing validation. The final product, as mentioned, is today's biopolitical society, one that, long before it was "discovered" by Michel Foucault, was inspired by Taylorism as well as by the artistic movement known as *Futurism*, and that was proposed in 1922 through the young Bolshevik state's utopian "biomechanics" (Žižek 2008, 212). That same image would be evoked decades later, rooted in entirely different concerns, in Donna Haraway's "cyborg" as the existent in which the liminality of human and machine remains ambiguous and contested (1991). Biomechanics envisioned a fully enframed humanity that would bring historical materialism to its inevitable dialectical mechanism through the human faculty of fabricating, but in such a way as to encompass human life in its entirety around the order of the machine – a society depicted so compellingly in Yevgeny Zamyatin's *We* (1921), the forgotten precursor of the twentieth-century dystopian genre (Aldus Huxley's *Brave New World*, George Orwell's *1984*, Ray Bradbury's *Fahrenheit 451*, and, more recently, the *Matrix* trilogy). Creating a cyborg remained an obsession for Soviet cyberneticists after the Second World War. If you think this is a long-gone utopian delusion, consider the automated manufacturers of our age, the Taylorist, algorithmic surveillance of our production and communication, the machine-like regimentation of human activity in sweatshops, and the violation of that which is most sacred to us and key to our survival, food, through its industrialized production based on GMOs, a process that imperils the future of known life on earth. Obviously, the violence that is ingrained in society through the epochal biomechanicization of life has the reduction of biodiversity attached to it, but it is also designed to unfetter humans from their human needs, that is, from their proper place on earth.

With the historic-structural relations between metaphysics and violence laid down, let us now turn to my *first set of phenomenological propositions regarding violence*.

A Tripartite Phenomenology of Violence

Schürmann's radical phenomenological engagement with the question of violence involves reactivating the origins of violence by stepping back from the common notion to the "conditions of evil" – the conditions that are not moral or ethical. By rearranging certain components of Schürmann's thought, I offer three interrelated concepts: *structural, hubristic*, and *institutional (or systemic)* violence. This tripartite conceptualization clearly indicates my own interpretation of Schürmann's philosophy. I will show how this tripartite concept of violence is informed by the ultimate

double-binds of natality (maximization and appropriation) and mortality (singularization and expropriation) and thus shows violence's ontological constitution.

(a) *Structural violence.* Let us begin with Schürmann's take on *evil* not as
the common biblical notion or philosophical concept – the latter being
the subject of a serious study (Bernstein 2002). The subject of considerable disagreement, "evil" is too generic a concept to yield theoretical
precision. Schürmann's concept of the "conditions of evil" is a phenomenological one rather than ethical or moral (2003, 621). The concept
enables us "to learn more deeply about the conditions of sufferings that
humans have inflicted upon themselves on a small and grand scale. The natural metaphysician in us might scoop up those conditions – the plural must
not be effaced – with one stroke of the shovel and summarily call them
evil" (Schürmann 2003, 621; emphasis added). The connection between
violence and the double-ultimates – natality and mortality – and thus life
itself now becomes clear. First, let us recall the *strife* within acting – the
universalizing trend of birth and the singularizing trait of death (these
are not a binary). Natality enables "the archic trait, prompts us toward
new commencements and sovereign commandments. It makes us mag-
nify norms and principles," whereas mortality "always wrests us from the
world of such archic referents. It is the singularizing, dispersing, desolat-
ing, evicting, dephenomenalizing, exclusory trait" (2003, 624). Thought
of in this way, evil moves against singularity, which the phantasmagorical
referents of an age, risen to be hegemonic and thus received (mostly) as
matters-of-fact, cannot dominate:

> Evil comes in an incredible move, when one cuts off singularization; when
> one blinds oneself against it; when, in the name of a jealous fantasm that
> subsumes everything that can become a phenomenon, one strikes a decisive
> blow – a fantasm that henceforth will command exclusive allegiance, that
> will integrate making, doing, and knowing in a masterable arrangement,
> and in this sense appropriates the world; when we deny the expropriation
> that wrests us from this world. (2003, 622)

The conditions of evil, therefore, are to be sought in maximization(s)
in the name of a *fantasmic but operative* idea, logos, or promise – in short,
a dominant referent – that subsumes under its expansive, universalizing rule(s) phenomena within its reach according to its normative measures and expectations. From this arise the structures of domination that
rivet phenomena, humans included, to preordained positions. These

structures often seem ageless: think of patriarchy, heteronormativity, or caste. With respect to the "two incongruent clusters of attraction-natality-maximization-appropriation and withdrawal-mortality-singularization-expropriation, then the denial of this whole second cluster as well as the exaltation of attractive, maximally normative theses … [constitute the] conditions of evil other than ethical or moral" (2003, 626). In short, the *conditions* of evil refer to the denial of the pull of mortality in favour of advancing the maximizing force of natality. Under our present epochal aegis, evil is conditioned by appropriating the world, allowing phenomena to appear *only* in normative ways prescribed by the extractive–exploitative global capitalist order policed by the equally normative state system, when the rainforest is reduced to projected cubic units of lumber; the river to a waterway and source of hydroelectric energy; and humans to *Homo faber*, the alienated (and increasingly impoverished) labourers who produce objects of profit or fetishized envy in a global economy of monstrous extraction and fiendish production. We commonly call "resistance" the singularizing moments of expropriating phenomena from aforesaid appropriative–normative modalities – resistances that are met with legal and/or extra-legal repression.

Stricto sensu, though, maximization alone does not constitute evil as such. The *denial* of the singularizing motion of mortality, the undertow that brings the dominant fantasms to their destitution, does: denial of mortality in favour of maximization, and denial of singularity in favour of appropriation (2003, 626). Note that denial does not mean negation: "denying a knowledge involves no such precursory normative thesis" (2003, 622). Universalization thrives when it denies its innermost singularizing force of mortality. The conditions of evil exist when the hegemonic referent, invigorated by the force of law and arising from the maximizing and appropriating power of natality – of the foundational gesture and archic expansion – denies the singularizing, expropriating power of mortality – of withdrawal from participation – and hides its denial through the "exaltation of attractive, maximally normative theses" (2003, 626). This constitutes the condition of evil other than ethics or morality.

In Christianity, evil is understood in terms of an irremediable lack, which renders evil ontologically ungraspable. Recall Christian teachings that hold that evil has no shape. In the common notion across many civilizational turns within Western history and through maximizing theses and normative powers, evil has been understood in terms of *dispossession*: being dispossessed of good (for the Greeks) or of self-consciousness (as

registered in the Enlightenment; see Kant) amounted to evil. In the face
of such *constructed* evil, the good posits itself as the law that exalts itself to
the supreme trope. Hence each law arises from the counter-movement
of that which is called "evil," and the law arises in denying evil only by
denying its denial, by hiding that the law is actually a "response" to the
lack (dispossession) of an essence, norm, or general will. A phenomenologist who suspends the legitimacy of the law within tacit, matter-of-
fact knowledge is able to see that the law legitimates itself by projecting
a spectral evil, as radical defect, from which the law, now positive Good
(as opposed to negative evil), excludes itself. Only thus can law appear
as self-sustaining, supreme, good, and only thus will the law enforce itself
through the formidable and punishing sword of the Prince and justify
its universalization in the name of a supreme referent. The law denies
that it has arisen from the denial of dispossession. The latter constitutes
a transgressive moment that the inevitable undertow of singularization
introduces to the maximization of the law. So the law ascends to be cer-
tified, legitimate violence. The law's denial of its *internal* undertow – a
denial that is the source of violence in law – in fact translates into denying that the law's acclaimed essence, norm, or general will, has no substance. The law conceals the fact that it can only arise as the signifier of
an irremediable lack; it projects the lack onto the Other wrought out as
evil simply because the latter stands out as the signifier of singularization
and dispossession.

The law, therefore, embodies a maximizing force, and that is why the
law must be *enforced*. Thus, the conditions of evil in the law amount to the
repression of the counter-law that arises everywhere and at every moment
from the untamable phenomenalization of life (2003, 625). The law's
claim to the good collapses and the unthinkable happens: "Evil in turn
gets maximized and introduced into the ultimate referent" (2003, 629).
Whence arises counter-violence in the face of the law. The counter-law
does not necessarily lead to emancipation of one kind or another. Singularizing a maximized referent potentially brings the law to its destitution,
but the singular also has within itself the force of maximization, thanks to
the "miraculous" power of natality. In Schürmann's judgment, though,
we should know better: "At first sight, nothing would seem more plau-
sible. Evil strips us of the good life, a just world, of love just as if it anticipated death. Accordingly, by paying attention to ordinary experience, we
know better than to exalt now this, now that, colossal referent and … to
put our trust in it" (2003, 623). Now the law's maximization pulls my life
activity into its devouring whirl and suddenly my life is oriented towards

the law: by virtue of being tied to a community, I participate, normatively and thoughtlessly, in the game whose rules are already set by the law (2003, 412). This law denies me as a genuine *actor*, renders me a *subject* partaking in its justification, and sculpts an *agent* of its enforcement out of my "miraculous" and mysterious, yet concrete and attainable, power of bringing something new, and potentially transgressive, to this world. This is how the law appropriates the singularizing "resistances" against it. Today's Hegelian–liberal celebration of the "politics of recognition" in the face of increasingly multicultural (read: multiversal) societies in the West (Taylor 1994) is a case in point. For indigenous populations around the world (and other groups), this recognition constitutes colonialism by other means (Coulthard 2014), and as such, politics represents the confluence of structural and institutional violence (see below). The law imposes equality as *isomorphism*. It renders us "equal" despite our differences by creating classes of people, categories of acts, and divisions of retributions and regulations through reductive sameness (*iso-*) that shapes (*-morphé*) the diversity of life according to the law's supreme referent (Schürmann 2003, 541). This referent, in turn, hides the *law's integrative violence* (2003, 539).

Theoretically, the law's universal reach is perpetually denied by its singular undertow, which requires the law to constantly revisit its source of legitimacy in the eyes of the governed. This is why the critical–phenomenological gaze requires us to revisit the law's humble archic origins in the collective experience of a historical community that attempts to renew the social contract – a moment of decision (indeed a decisive moment) that falls outside the law ("decision," from Latin *decidere*, to "determine"; literally, *de-*, "off," and *caedere*, "cut"). But according to history it is hardly the case that the law revisits its origins. If the law's denial of its own singular origins enables the manageable structuring of life according to the requirements of the supreme referent and in the form of normative biopolitics (Foucault) – not to mention imposition (enforceability) – then by virtue of my participation I unwittingly and tacitly submit to the law's maximizing appropriation. I deny my own singularity and deny myself openness to the singulars that at every moment gently beckon to me the possibility of seeing differently when things are expropriated from the normative hegemony of the law. Seeing things in their own terms, and thus unseeing things in their hegemonized mode, can only be possible when I shield my eyes from the law's hypnotizing projection. Arendt calls "thoughtlessness" the condition of being unaware of the consequences of one's action, which, in my terms, amounts to one's inability to unsee the law. "Thoughtlessness" provides an unsatisfactory English rendition of *Gedankenlosigkeit*, which denotes the *inability to think*, the (perpetual) condition in which I do not have the "soundless dialogue between me and myself" (Arendt 1972, 63). Arendt refers to the bureaucratic–administrative and matter-of-course proceduralism that renders thoughtlessness and evil interdependent (Arendt 1965, 288). While keeping me under the hegemonic construct that links me to the law, the justifications attached to the law – its "good," utility, or the security it (supposedly) provides – become irrelevant to my participation. These justifications make me feel secure in being on the law's side and in belonging to the community the law regulates. Because I have already internalized the law's expectations and normatively adjusted my life according to them, I become exempt from being "forced" into the law. Biopolitical rearrangements of activities are therefore essential to the law's hegemony. The bottom line is that I do participate in this regime as a docile subject. Of course, I may realize in utter shock one day that the laws to which I have lent allegiance have nothing to do with the good, utility, or security.

The appropriate designation for this complex, interlocked, and ageless web of violence, I propose, is "structural violence."

(b) *Hubristic violence.* This is where violence reveals itself most vividly, in the human acts that *violate*. The Greeks invoked the word *hybris*, derived from *hyper*, or "beyond," when one overstepped one's measure (Schürmann 1984, 169). When by virtue of universalization and institutionalization, an entity totalizes that which surrounds it beyond its own humble emergence, it expands its being over that of the others. Hence hubristic violence is identified by its "regional" conditions. The law maximizes an original and thus particular experience to reshape life, modes of activity, and communication within a community. It creates its own "economy of presence," requiring life to appear in determinate ways. Now a law is no longer a law, strictly speaking; it is a frame, a *posure*, and a set-up (*Stellen*). Here we have a situation in which a will is imposed not by virtue of planned and deliberate decision (a conscious act); rather, the will simply imposes while emerging, by virtue of its birth, with the vigour of maximizing imposition within a structurally determined regulated life. The nuance is important: by removing the centrality of the subject (willing to impose), we can look at the imposition phenomenologically and structurally (the will imposes). "The Greek name for such *unrestrained self-imposition* is *hubris*" (Schürmann 1990, 189; emphasis added). War, rape, abuse, and the exploitation of humans and non-humans exemplify hubristic violence. The concept of *hubris* takes us closer to the very issue that guides our conceptual excursions into the ontological pervasiveness of violence:

> It is impossible to escape regional violence: the micro-violence through which a body organ asserts itself, the macro-violence through which a collectivity asserts itself ... Life sustains itself through claiming territory after territory ... Nevertheless, to go through life with one's eyes open means to see tragic denial shape the entire morphological scope of the law. Crossing through our public spheres, in particular the national, with one's eyes open is seeing that they maintain themselves at the cost of obliterating – if necessary, through extreme violence – the counter-law that I shall call ... the singularization to come. (Schürmann 1991, 218–19)

The hubris – as unrestrained self-imposition – that *emanates from life against life* can only be challenged through singularization, by actively participating in a life always at variance with itself, if we wish for such singularization not to become the next law due to the maximizing force embedded in every act and in every event of natality. Hubris is enabled by, and secondary to, natality. Phenomenologically, it is by virtue of birth – of expansive, universal demands of an otherwise humble life – that hubristic violence arises, although not every birth ends up repressing other births through self-imposition. A closer look reveals that domination comes from "conceptual objectification," when entities are pinned to an already established biopolitical pattern, when the tree *only* stands as timber to be harvested and lumber to be sold, and when humans *only* live to manufacture unnecessary goods, to be mobilized to elect the lesser evil once every few years, and to be amused by numbing tunnel vision when off-duty. "Today objectification by conceptualization has resulted in a generalized violence that is more destructive than wars" (Schürmann 1983a, 37).

(c) *Institutional violence.* This type of violence is "the gift of generalized production and administration" (Schürmann 1990, 60). It is generalized in its application and in producing isomorphic subjects, an effect it shares with the violence of the law. An elaboration is in order: the institutions arise from an original experience in which the need to respond to a historically and regionally specific – ontic – experience takes the form of an *archic* foundation; this move then enables the edification of an institution as the means of perpetuation and universalization of the particular response to the particular experience. So one might say, à la Werner Marx, that institutions arise from a *creative moment* – from a First that endures (Greek *arché* denotes both institution and perpetuation). But once in place, the First moves farther and farther away from the original experience that once "necessitated" and legitimized the institutive act. As the institutions age, they lose legitimacy because the conditions under which they emerged are likely long gone. These institutions must subsequently resort to force in order to pervade (Marx 1971, 167). From this arises the necessity of "law enforcement" and the state as (in Weber's famous definition) the "human community that (successfully) claims the *monopoly of the legitimate use of physical force* within a given territory" (Weber 1946, 78; emphasis in original). As the instrument of micro- and macro-regulation of daily life, institutional violence creates a *system.* The systemic violence of the military, the mental institution, the "iron cage" of bureaucracy (Weber), and the like is fastened to the institutional logic. To challenge violence, one needs to recall the economies that animate systemic violence at both micro and macro levels, giving it momentum, resources, and the laws that hide violence through legitimation. Though tied to this system, institutional violence is nonetheless best understood as a sign of aging, of being pulled towards singularization of death.

How is it that in this particular time of ours, the issue of violence has been brought to the fore with so much intellectual and public vigour? It is certainly not because the "rational animal" has become smarter or progressed morally. Rather, it is because at this epochal junction the possibility that principial economies of presence might wither away has been made manifest to some of us. As the governing principles of our age begin to wither away, they reveal themselves to some bewildered eyes. We begin to unsee what we have been seeing. Schürmann avers, "I have spoken of *destitution* to describe what happens to such a fantasm when it loses its force of law. *Diremption* signifies the loss of every hegemony – the possibility that we have been living for more than a century. In the destitutions and in diremption, the ultimate trait of mortality is manifested, along with the singularizing condition that manifests itself in everydayness as *dispossession*" (2003, 623; emphasis in original). It is *now* that we can bring back the question of violence, which is presented to us inevitably through the given and the ontic, and understand the question of violence properly, as *ontological* – that is, in terms of what we can do to avoid reverting to the *economies of violence.* This is how the question of the distinction between violence and nonviolence is viewed *ontologically* (chapter 2) and linked to acting and to liberation (chapter 3 and 4).

Before proceeding, though, we need to explore the proposed sociological–epistemological markers of violence and of overcoming it – through Vattimo and Arendt.

Healing and the Persisting Scars of Metaphysical Violence

In probing the relationship between metaphysics and violence, we must also consider the important contribution of Gianni Vattimo. As a post-Heideggerian, his work has certain important affinities with that of Schürmann (and Werner Marx) as well as serious disagreements (see Schürmann, 1984). Vattimo's approach to our contemporary historical junction is more "sociological," issue-related, and ontic, in that he offers engaged analyses of the metaphysical "stamps" that have been placed on concrete issues, practices, and institutions. À la Heidegger, for whom the end of metaphysics signifies the "end of philosophy" as the securer of foundational and governing principles, Vattimo redefines philosophy in terms of "sociological impressionism" (2004, 4) – that is, as thinking oriented towards identifying and exposing metaphysical impositions within ontic everyday social practices. He declares that "what belies metaphysics is its unfolding in presence as a totalizing realization" (Vattimo 2007, 409). He writes in the aftermath of the "decline of the West," announced by Heidegger (translating *Abendland* or Occident, literally as the "land of sunset"), a time when the presumption that there is a unitary direction in the history of Western humanity is withering away (Vattimo 2004, 21). This allows him to declare a "weak ontology" or "an ontology of the weakening of Being" (2004, 19) that is linked to certain ethics that are not invigorated by moral principles; rather, his ethics are enabled by the demise of universal principles and supreme values. The governing values and fundamental qualities of modernity – long taken to be universal and unshakable – have lost legitimacy in the face of the irreducible diversity of our age, an age characterized by the sociological facticity of social plurality and multiculturalism (2004, 67). In the absence of foundations, experience attains primacy (Vattimo 1991, 177). Under these conditions, when "all that is solid melts into air," our (post-metaphysical) ethics cannot be extracted from immutable principles; instead, they arise from negotiation and consensus (Vattimo 2004, 67). Thus, "ethics can never speak the language of hard proof" (2004, 48). The "ethics of finitude," therefore, amounts to the exclusion of violence (2004, 46), the reduction of pain, and replacing retribution with rehabilitation (2004, 71–7). As we shall see, pain is the existential marker of violence. In any case, this is how Vattimo's "weak thought" (*il pensiero debole*) revisits the question of the law.

Every law is the edified and coded enactment of a plea for justice arising from a humble event linked to an experience of injustice, in response to which a certain maximized legislation in the form of a law arises. Running *justice against the law* – that is, taking the law at every moment as it holds sway and is implemented in the form of sanctions and punishments back to the pre-edified impulse and experience of (in)justice – remains on par with Vattimo's post-metaphysical ethics and represents the "institutional" practice of those ethics. As the event that gives rise to normative fiats called law (the event does not "cause" the law), justice does not itself resemble a norm. Rather, it must be understood as the singular event behind every regime of laws – an archic moment without archic intentions (thus an-archic). The law can only "do justice" through interpretation (2004, 136). As interpretation, then, the law does not so much preside over "facts," and this is how the law in our transitional, postmodern age must be understood: just as philosophy aspired to grant us Truth and guarantee foundations but has now reached its point of consummation, so the law must be taken as based on, not Truth(s), but rather norms that are only representations of precedents or (more simply) interpretations of interpretations (Heidegger's *Verwindung*). As such, laws are not timeless and eternal but historically bound and subject to interpretive re-evaluations (2004, 136–8). Based on the factic (as opposed to factual) observation that in our age metaphysical solidities have lost their sway, Vattimo's approach tries to unmask the *non-justice in the law* through nihilistic interpretation (2004, 140). This is how he potentially turns Derridean *undecidability* into a springboard for acting against injustices that our laws embody. In practice, the unjust law forces foreclosure on human acting and being, and it imposes norms that have no essential reason for their application. To use Schürmann's terms, the law becomes the normative maximization that prohibits singulars from entering public life. Vattimo's approach to the law clearly arises from the same intellectual watershed as that of Schürmann's understanding of the law's integrative violence.

Vattimo follows Heidegger's reflections on the possibility of Western metaphysical history coming to a close: instead of overcoming (*Überwindung*) (reminiscent of Hegelian–Marxian dialectical history), there will be distortion (*Verwindung*) of metaphysics. In Vattimo's approach, since violence is a stamp of Western metaphysical history, the laws must be twisted and distorted (*Verwunden*) in order to reduce violence (2004, 147): not just the violence the law is set up (through injunctions) to prevent, but the violence the law itself commits and perpetuates – namely, in the form of punishment that defines our systems of retributive justice (2004, 148). Here is how Vattimo conceptualizes violence: "I use 'violence' to mean the peremptory assertion of an ultimacy that, like the ultimate metaphysical foundation (or the God of philosophers), breaks off dialogue and silences the interlocutor by refusing even to acknowledge the question 'why?'" (2004, 98). In fact, much as with Schürmann's reference to institutional violence and counter-violence, Vattimo argues that crime and punishment are external to each other (2004, 166–7). Since punishing the perpetrator cannot undo the violence committed against the victim, every form of punishment ultimately reflects (a desire for) vengeance (2004, 167). And since the reduction of violence is on Vattimo's agenda, punishment must be replaced with education, rehabilitation, and reform. The reduction of violence is a sign that metaphysical normativity is being distorted, and of a possible transition towards a postmetaphysical age characterized by healing (*Verwindung* also implies recovering from an illness). To achieve this end, a postmodern proceduralism should replace the law's metaphysical foundations, for if we agree that metaphysics is impoverished, then in the absence of stable substances that can function as foundations, ethics, law, and politics can only be procedural (2004, 155). Nonviolence, linked to justice, therefore opens the possibility of healing metaphysically inflicted injuries, though we will carry forever their scars as sad keepsakes of an age that we have a chance, at this historic junction, to transform.

The concept of "healing" in relation to Heideggerian thought is not without controversy. For one, Schürmann expressly rejects the idea of thinking Being outside of *strife* (1993, 208; 1984), although in my opinion Heidegger's thought invites both readings. This is an esoteric disagreement that is not totally relevant for my discussion; in my judgment, though, the two readings – healing as recovering while incorporating metaphysics, and strife as the future of Being – are not mutually exclusive. Anyhow, Vattimo offers a rare insight into how the question of metaphysical violence can be translated into concrete and sociological analyses that in turn enable possibilities for engaged, issue-related politics and generate new modalities of advocacy and activism. This level of translation of the ontological into the ontic is admirable, although not without its risks, but if anything is ever to result from our phenomenological inquiries, it

involve asking ourselves how we are to act at the perceived end of metaphysical violence (see Schürmann 1983b). Phenomenological inquiries
are therefore always already linked to the question of acting – a trajectory
that this work avows, but one that is not without its risks.

Vattimo offers sociological perspectives on a possible post-metaphysical
age; Arendt is more concerned about marking off violence from several
interchangeable terms in relation to power and life.

Power and the Instrumentality of Violence

In 1969 – during the revolutionary sixties – Hannah Arendt diverted
her attention to probing the essence of violence in light of the growing militancy within the student movement (the radicalization of Students for Democratic Society) and Civil Rights Movement (the growing
influence of the Black Panthers) in America, as well as among Third
World national liberation movements. She differentiates violence from
its seemingly synonymous terms – power, strength, force, and authority. *Power*, a key concept in Arendt's thinking, refers to acting "in concert," an ability that resides in humans (Arendt 1970, 44). In essence,
"power" captures the sociological concept of "collective action," but
with a key proviso: power allows a "people" to emerge (see chapter 2),
and as such, it marks the formative political moment that has its roots
in the human capacity of *natality*, of beginning a project and bringing
something new to this world (Arendt 1958a, 9). Arendt avers: "What
makes man a political being is his faculty of action; it enables him to get
together with his peers, to act in concert ... Philosophically speaking,
to act is the human answer to the condition of natality" (1970, 82; emphasis
added). If the collective (acting in concert) were to disappear, so would
power. Resembling Rousseau's "social pact," a decision made outside
the law (as, potentially, the origin of the law), power, in its most authentic form, reveals itself in those nascent historic moments when a people
collectively makes decisions for its future: in the town hall meetings
during the American War of Independence and the councils (or Soviets) during the Russian revolutions of 1905 and 1917 or in Hungary
in 1919 (Arendt 1970, 22; Bernstein 2013, 100). Arendt's concept of
power clearly has anarchistic and an-archic undertones. One could
decipher that power's institutionalization – a proceduralism that perpetuates power beyond the original councils – leads to the instrumen-
talization of power, linking power to violence in its systemic manner
discussed earlier.

Strength, for Arendt, always remains individual in character and refers to "the property inherent in an object or person" (Arendt 1970, 44). Strength is an added quality of sorts, like one's physical strength in tackling a demanding weight or a formidable opponent. One can infer that strength can be present by virtue of predisposition (an object's design or an individual's genetic make-up) – or through "strengthening" (as in the cases of physical augmentation, structural reinforcement, team management, or skill acquisition). Due to its individuality, strength is always "overpowered by the many, who often will combine for no other purpose than to ruin the strength precisely because of its peculiar independence," and this is when *resentment* is acted out (1970, 44). The reference to Nietzsche's concept of *ressentiment* (Nietzsche 1967) – as "irrational," hateful (and destructive) energy of the weak against the strong, through which a certain morality is constructed to rationalize this devouring resentment – is clear. If strength appears in political life, phenomenologically it will remain "anti-power" in relation to human community, and it can only thus persist – as the pre- or post-political ruling, since strength, by virtue of its essence, is never connected to the political.

Force, as in coercion, is the concept closest to violence. Arendt reserves it for the determinants beyond our choice or power such as "the 'forces of nature' or the 'force of circumstances' (*la force des choses*), that is, to indicate the energy released by physical or social movements" (1970, 45). Force captures structural determinants or inescapable conditions within which we act and to which we respond. Force relates to the sociological concepts of structure and agency (Anthony Giddens) – a concept originating with Karl Marx: "Men make their own history, but they do not make it just as they please; they do not make it under circumstances chosen by themselves, but under circumstances directly encountered, given and transmitted from the past" (Marx 1963, 15). I submit that while force (as structural and historical determinant) *conditions* acting, the latter challenges the former to *re*condition itself. This is how acting pertains to opening possibilities, in general, and relates to democratic participation, in particular. Equally, the law is enforced because it is linked to the state and enjoys the "legitimate" use of violence. But having greater numbers of people "acting in concert" certainly adds to their social presence (and "strength") and amplifies their collective action in pushing the movement's demands through their reluctant lawmakers. Stated differently, collective action has the potential "property" of accumulating political weight and social intensity, and thus it can *re*condition the force(s) of condition. Force may therefore be a property of a situation we inexorably inherit, but it can also be cultivated for any specific purpose when humans act in concert. In short, force can equally lend itself to violence and to (nonviolent) "acting in concert" (see below).

Although this reading may be extraneous to Arendt's concept, I think it has an organic relationship to it. Thus, force can actually become a "property" of collective action when the latter circumscribes violence, limiting its ambit of exertion. In this case, we are not speaking of the *strength* of the many (acting in concert), trying to (physically) overwhelm violence. Nonviolence does have a coercive character too (see chapters 5 and 8). We can infer that in relation to power, one can always utilize the "added value" of force, since force remains essential to nonviolence, and one can also mobilize it to neutralize violence. Thus, force must be differentiated from counter-violence.

In relation to *authority*, "neither coercion nor persuasion is needed," for authority refers to "unquestioning recognition [of persons or institutions] by those who are asked to obey" (Arendt 1970, 45). Authority, following Weber, refers to the collective recognition of the legitimacy of power/force. While sources of authority may differ in nature, character, and outcome (in Weber, traditional, charismatic, and rational-legal types) they all pertain to political power.

This brings us to the key concept of *violence*. For Arendt the prime indicator of violence is its *instrumentality*, and it can be identified through its "implements" (1970, 4). "Phenomenologically, [violence] is close to strength, since the implements of violence, like all other tools, are designed and used for the purpose of multiplying natural strength until, in the last stage of their development, they can substitute for it" (1970, 46). Violence is not irrational (1970, 64), so its relation to political life needs clarification: political life is not "rational" in itself, although politics can be "rationalized" by justifying its ends.

> Violence, being instrumental by nature, is rational to the extent that it is effective in reaching the end that must justify it. And since when we act we never know with any certainty the eventual consequences of what we are doing, violence can remain rational only if it pursues short-term goals. Violence does not promote causes, neither history nor revolution, neither progress nor reaction; but it can serve to dramatize grievances and bring them to public attention. (1970, 79)

Still, violence cannot be properly understood without shedding light on its connection to human action.

Action is to be understood within Arendt's analysis of *vita activa*, the fundamental human activities that define "the basic conditions under which life on earth has been given" (Arendt 1958a, 7) to humans – labour, work, and action. In her signature conceptual taxonomy, Arendt defines *labour* in relation to *biological life* and in terms of "the activity which corresponds to the biological process of the human body, whose spontaneous growth, metabolism, and eventual decay are bound to the vital necessities produced and fed into the life process by labor. The human condition of labor is life itself" (1958a, 7). *Work*, on the other hand, pertains to the *artificially produced world*. Individual life dwells in this artificial world, which is intended to "outlast and transcend" any individual's life. Thus work corresponds "to the unnaturalness of human existence, which is not imbedded in, and whose mortality is not compensated by, the species' ever-recurring life cycle ... The human condition of work is worldliness" (1958a, 7). Lastly, the human condition of *action* is *plurality*. Action pertains to the activity between humans due "to the fact that men, not Man, live on the earth and inhabit the world" (1958a, 7). Plurality is *the* condition of political life and thus "acting in concert." Action is related to *natality* and bound by *mortality*. Natality corresponds to the fact that the outcome of action always lies beyond the imagination of the actor. Thus action is distinct from fabrication (work) in that the end product of action "can never be reliably predicted" (Arendt 1970, 4). Natality, in other words, gives action its *openness*, or stated more accurately, in every opening brought about by action there lies a trait of natality. Mortality – the fact that I have a life history – allows the individual life to arise from biological life (Arendt 1958a, 19). Thus, I add, *there are only two irrefutable, grounding facts in human life: that I was born and that I shall die.* The things that take place between these two non-binary poles are all primarily interpretations – as Nietzsche (in *Will to Power*, aphorism 481) via Vattimo averred: "there are no facts, only interpretations," and that is also an interpretation (Vattimo 1997, 105). Natality refers to a beginning that begets human life or a human life's project. Yet, one must not mistake mortality for the common notion of death (as a person's dying), for death remains outside of politics and can never find "an institutional, political expression" (Arendt 1970, 68).

Political life, for Arendt, arises from the confluence of action (*praxis*) and speech (*lexis*) (Arendt 1958a, 25) in that action makes possible and enlivens the new, while speech "reveals" the world to us. Power is achieved through *persuasion*, as politics can only arise from plurality and pertains only to freedom and power. In this respect, "violence is anti-political"

(Bernstein 2013, 84). Schürmann refines Arendt's phenomenological understanding and redefines the political as "situated in the confluence of words, things, and deeds" (Schürmann 1990, 81); to Arendt's conception he adds the element of constructs, implements, and institutions. This added factor has serious implications. The indeterminacy of actions' outcomes and the plurality of humans logically render the political consequences contingent. Persuasion is by definition fragile and needs to be maintained, via public debates among *diverse equals*, through further persuasion. *Freedom, then, is founded on abyss*. This is the key trait of power as "acting in concert," and it is also the essential reason why violence is sadly attached to power: violence, in its instrumentality and its integral connection to fabrication, guarantees results. In any case, writes Arendt, nothing "is more common than the combination of violence and power, nothing less frequent than to find them in their pure and therefore extreme form" (Arendt 1970, 46–7). Yet what separates the two is that power "needs no justification, being inherent in the very existence of political communities; what it does need is legitimacy ... Violence can be justifiable, but it never will be legitimate" (1970, 52). That said, violence is commonplace because of "the simple fact that no substitution for this final arbiter in international affairs has yet appeared on the political scene" (1970, 5). Properly understood, violence never leads to power; in fact violence can destroy power (1970, 53). Violence grows as power declines; indeed, it grows over power, replacing it and "substituting" for it, making violence indispensible (1970, 87). So power and violence stand as opposing concepts. If action is open-ended, and if by partaking in action the results of the act are never ensured, then violence is the means through which specific outcome(s) of the act are guaranteed. Violence guarantees results, of course, inasmuch as the future – which is by definition *open* – represents a projection of the present. Here, violence reveals its relation to fabrication: it produces the perceived end results or objects. "Action is irreversible, and a return to *status quo* in case of defeat is always unlikely. The practice of violence, like all action, changes the world, but the most probable change is to a more violent world" (1970, 80). That is why violence always introduces an "additional element of arbitrariness" (1970, 4). Perhaps, one can surmise, this is why for Arendt the council system represents a genuine manifestation of power, as the "only authentic outgrowth of the revolutionary tradition," a form of "participatory democracy" that never lasted due to the pressure to achieve preconceived political results for which violence proves efficient (1970, 22).

Arendt offers the epistemological means for identifying violence within political life. However, I need to critically revisit a few of her propositions.

Revisiting the Instrumentality of Violence

To pave the way for the upcoming discussions, I must offer a specific interpretation of Arendt's concept of violence. Arendt conceptualizes violence according to its instrumental character, identifying it (as opposed to power, force, strength, or authority) with its need for "implements" developed through technological revolutions and manifested through warfare (1970, 4). The distinction she makes between fabrication (work) and action is key here: violence is instrumental because it achieves results and guarantees their perpetuation, whereas action is open-ended due to natality and necessitates politics as form of genuine, participatory convergence of free women and men, who, because of their plurality, forge a body politic and thereby perpetuate the human community.

She observes that when left to themselves at times of revolution, people tend to create egalitarian and participatory grassroots councils for decision-making in order to forge a new social contract. The town hall meetings of the American Revolution and the workers' soviets of the Bolshevik Revolution exemplify the *genuine* springing forth of action. These councils became "spaces of freedom," unlike the parties, which offered "ready-made formulas" (Arendt 1963, 264). With regard to "acting together" (or power) in the "new revolutionary order," Bernstein observes that "the true legacy of the revolutionary spirit is the council system that spontaneously arises in every genuine revolution" (Bernstein 2013, 167). In contrast to this genuine and participatory mode of action with its intrinsic openness (in which power enables a new body politic to arise), there emerges the instrumentality of violence, which reduces human action to technologically mediated *inter*action, produced to achieve preconceived results. Here, my conceptual distinction between "action" (and actor) and "activity" (and activist) is useful. As I submitted in an earlier work, *activity* is a teleological practice – in which activity denotes participation in a more or less already sanctioned and ordained course of instrumental functionality and thus imposes closure on the future due to institutional calculative rationality; whereas *action* leads towards an open-ended futurity and is attuned to phenomenal modes of appearances as the world worlds (Vahabzadeh 2003, 177). Thus, *stricto sensu*, while intricately connected to action, violence denies and precludes action. Violence replaces action with fabrication, thus reducing action to activity by imposing closure on otherwise open futurity; it also transforms politics, properly understood, into reductive recruitment for the purpose of fabricating machines and managing institutions, exemplified by today's liberal parliamentary democracies. This evokes Schürmann's "institutional violence." The concept of "instrumentality" thus allows Arendt to distinguish between genuine human action – as the convergence of diverse equals, epitomized by the councils – and technicized activity of the agent represented by institutional, party, and ideological politics. Power is abandoned in the interest of instrumental management of the polity. A hegemonic violence thus masks power while successfully concealing its violent character under procedural rationality. State politics now amount to arithmetical-institutional manipulations of a representational game based on agenda-setting, "professional" consultations, and "solution" mongering.

In this context, the concept-referent "implement" in Arendt allows for an *epistemological indicator* of violence. Implements (in a broad sense) conceal the violent nature of this business of politics. Indeed, they are perceived to be legitimate signs of stability and practical means of perpetuating collective life in a predictable manner. The implements replace action (*praxis* as acting together) with functioning within the procedural machines – a sort of matter-of-fact working that hides the violent nature of the "service" it provides. Those who man this machine – bureaucrats, functionaries, planners, officers – are afflicted with "thoughtlessness" in that they are unable to recognize the monstrous machine they help run. These humans are reduced to the resources used up within the orderability of the machine, as Heidegger would say. In this sense, Arendt's proposed (and controversial) "banality of evil" glows in a new light. Evil becomes banal through the daily toil of enhancing bureaucratic proceduralism. Reflecting on Eichmann, Arendt observes: "when I speak of the banality of evil, I do so only on the strictly factual level, pointing to a phenomenon which stared one in the face at the trial … Except for an extraordinary diligence in looking out for his personal advancement, he had no motives at all. And this diligence in itself was in no way criminal … He *merely*, to put the matter colloquially, *never realized what he was doing*" (Arendt 1965, 287; emphasis in original). The interdependence of thoughtlessness and evil (1965, 288) is what perpetuates our technicized, capitalist, state-centric civilizations on the global scale, ruining the conditions of life for humans and non-humans, reducing existents first to calculable use and then to palpable, suffocating refuse. This interdependence renders ever more frightening the looking in the mirror by those who have overcome their daze of thoughtlessness. More unsettling, perhaps, is the thought of the Great Refusal.

Yet we need to engage with Arendt more critically: if power as acting in concert brings together diverse equals – through consensus and in a new human community – and if it thereby founds something new, then power, too, inevitably bears the seeds of violence. Unless that which is being founded through power emerges *ex nihilo*, there is no logical or actual possibility that something new won't emerge out of eradication, repression, annihilation, or decommissioning of an existing order, just or unjust, sustainable or not. The United States, for example, which emerged out of the nonviolent "acting in concert" epitomized in the town hall meetings during the American Revolution, was founded on the violence of occupation and dispossession imposed on the indigenous peoples. Arendt could have been more radical in her phenomenology, for it is clear that *since power founds by virtue of natality, it carries a certain family resemblance to violence*. Arendt identifies violence by its implements due to violence's instrumentality, but power, as nonviolent, is not entirely non-instrumental either. Our acting in concert and in openness inevitably involves birthing a purpose, a future configuration of the body politic, which is likely to impede the springing up of other potential present and future councils and town hall meetings. Moreover, with a glance towards future discussions, it should be clear that when (à la Arendt) we accept instrumentality as the *epistemological* marker of violence, it does not immediately follow that nonviolence is characterized by a *lack* of instrumentality. In other words, the instrumentality that defines violence does not necessarily refute the instrumentality of its opposite: nonviolence (see chapter 5).

Why is it that nothing "is more common than the combination of violence and power" (Arendt 1970, 46–7)? I would answer that it is because violence and nonviolence (power) arise from the same ontological grounds: *natality*. A critical reading of Arendt brings to light a new, phenomenological understanding: *the violence of life against life*. The reason, however counterintuitive, must be clear: (nonviolent) power (as acting in concert) and as founding something new (a "miracle" as Arendt would say) is interwoven with violence as instrumental that ensures that the new collective will will succeed in claiming the future and that achieves permanence by curtailing life as it appears in the existing order. *Violence and nonviolence are not pure moments.* The Greek *arché* as both humble founding and subsequent domination has an organic connection with Arendt's conceptions.

The key argument in this chapter has been to establish the *ontological* constitution of violence, a phenomenon so intimately linked to human life yet seemingly alien to it. This is why, at this point, I must elaborate on my second set of phenomenological propositions through a further exercise in conceptual phenomenology. We will attend to these propositions in Chapter 2.

2

Deworlding, Reworlding, Phenomenal Violence

Institutionalized violence is visible to all today in the catatonic state that is the gift of generalized production and administration. Measured against these, much of contemporary violence amounts instead to counterviolence. If there is a regression in denouncing thoughtlessness, it is an analytical step backward from oppressions to the economies that make them possible.

Schürmann, *Heidegger on Being and Acting* (1990, 60)

A conceptual phenomenology of the distinction between violence and nonviolence will have to proceed from the ontological character of violence, as established in the previous chapter. The proposed tripartite concept of violence paves the way for a further step towards the phenomenology of violence as well as towards reflections on the concept of "nonviolence." A phenomenology of (non)violence, foregrounded in the question of acting (chapters 3 and 4), will deconstruct *a priori* distinctions between the two concepts – distinctions that provide us with epistemological consolation.

But our conceptual excursions are still in need of vital concepts. In order to point out these absent concepts properly, we need to grasp a significant clarification: when (as in chapter 1) we theorize violence in relation to metaphysics, we may be prone to committing a *metaphysician's error* (note the irony!) *by taking metaphysics as a substance* – as an unchanging essence that has permeated Western philosophy through the ages – whose manifestation is violence in its myriad forms across different epochs. Neither Schürmann's philosophy nor that of Vattimo supports such positivistic readings. I call such a reading "positivistic" because it enables us to conceptually extract violence (effect) out of the seemingly solid substrate termed "metaphysics" (cause). In this reading, metaphysics is a catch-all term of convenience, one that supposedly designates a unitary essence, a supreme referent to which we can conveniently fasten our explanatory attempts and thereby ameliorate our epistemological anxieties. If violence is indeed connected to metaphysics, if violence is the marker of metaphysics in this specific body of thought, it is not because violence is *caused* by metaphysics, but because in perpetuating itself in myriad forms throughout the ages, violence has enabled metaphysics to reveal itself conceptually. The "essence" (*Wesen*, which for Heidegger implies "enduring" for a while) of metaphysics rests in the changing practices and logics of violence; only thus can it endure. It follows that violence cannot be understood as a representation or manifestation of metaphysics. Rather, the transmutations of violence – with its changing technologies, modes of social organization, relations of power, and religious and judicial justifications – enable metaphysics to dwell in the human world and to be grasped accordingly. Metaphysics endures by reducing the otherwise semantic diversities attached to the phenomena of violence to its own seemingly unitary term. So if it is true that, to quote Bernstein, there "is a protean quality about violence" (2013, 177), it is due to the transmutations of the modes of hubristic activities through the ages; it is also due to the changing of universalized truths that hegemonize the scene at the expense of the singulars by denying the tragic archic–anarchic strife that is endemic to every founding gesture; and it is due to the institutionalization and rationalization of life through an algorithmic language of efficiency, akin, in our day, to Weber's iron cage of bureaucracy.

The proposed tripartite phenomenology of violence – the first set of propositions in this book – offers the "transcendentally reduced" modes of violence within categorical determinants. But my phenomenology won't be worthy of the designation "radical" if I do not bring into view the fundamental condition that makes violence (and nonviolence) possible, the structure from which there emerges all violence. I therefore offer a *second set of propositions*.

Deworlding, Reworlding, Phenomenal Violence

We need to bring to the fore "structural violence," the elusive but arguably also the most commonplace form of violence, the one that is generally overlooked by the uncritical gaze. To move in that direction, I first need to clarify the term "world." *Welt* (world) must be understood in

the broadest phenomenological sense as a set of relations in their totality – for Alfred Schutz, as suggested by the original German title of his
1932 book, the "meaningful construction of the social world" (1967),
and for Martin Heidegger "what is, in its entirety" (1977, 129); insofar
as I experience the world, I am *within* a world and can never be *outside* a world. As a *structure of the being of humans*, the world in which I
live and perceive things is always mine but never mine alone. Although
this world changes constantly, I am always aware, however implicitly, of
its contours. Recall that for Schürmann the representation of natality
tends to relativize other representations of the original act(s). This is
how an otherwise humble act gains foundational proportions and how,
as such, it denies and covers up its own singular (and plural) origins.
This operation allows the archic movement to become (until its downfall) a transhistorical, supreme fantasm. In this way, a phenomenalizing
gesture, a natal act, from the point of view of a multiplicity of potentially archic moments, lends itself to violence. On an epochal scale, one
natal–archic act (among many) ends up *deworlding* the existing world,
pushing it towards *reworlding* according to its own master code. I call this
phenomenal violence, which is *structural–epochal* in character. The Spanish conquest of the Americas was a prime example of the phenomenal
violence embedded in *deworlding/reworlding*, for it clearly involved bel-
ligerent colonialism revealing itself through a civilizational clash, one
that led directly to (cultural) genocide. Not so obvious, though, was the
phenomenal violence carried out by French Jesuit missionaries as they
forged an alliance with the Huron nation in North America – colonization
through acculturation. Various colonialisms exemplify this form of
structural-epochal violence revealed in deworlding/reworlding: the
hubristic imposition of the civilizational patterns of one culture on an
Other. Colonialism maybe the clearest example, but modernity is built
upon this endless process of deworlding/reworlding. A great historian
of this type of violence is Michel Foucault, although his theoretical tendencies are different from mine. His body of work offers abundant gene-
alogies of this kind of violence, from the hospital to the mental hospital,
torture, sexuality, and governmentality. Consider the case of a certain
farmhand in 1867, the bewildered subject of shifting epochal discourses
in the course of which bucolic sexual pleasure suddenly rephenomenalized as sexual perversion, with the consequent involvement of the
law, medicine, and psychiatry. For Foucault, the most significant aspect
of this whole affair was, ironically, the "pettiness of it all" (1990, 31).
Phenomenal violence, at best, passes under our gaze without attracting

attention. This is the (often shifting) structural violence to which we are
subjected on a daily basis.

Structural violence – conditioned by *epochal constellations of truth* and
thus potentially arising from a multitude of human initiatives and the
resulting institutional determinations – pertains to the experience of
the world (*Welt*). This phenomenological approach probes the experience of having one's own world – where one "feels at home" – wrested
away from the experiencing subject, not by forceful deportation of
the subject, but on the contrary by retaining the subject within an
increasingly defamiliarized world that nonetheless stays "one's own."
The subject retains his or her place of origins, but the familiar world
embracing him or her is wrested away either shockingly or through
desensitizing reinscription: the subject's cognitive map shifts, and the
habitual contours of one's life's paths are swept away from under one's
feet, gone forever, and replaced by the principles of a new order. This
aspect of violence is particularly important for our study, for it normally
hides behind various justifications: the need for modernization and
development, the exigencies of political decisions, austerity measures,
or revolutionary transformations. Let us for the moment conceptually isolate this world as the received experience of the totality of all
that surrounds me: my lifeworld (*Lebenswelt*), which includes interpersonal relations as well as structural relations to civilizational objects
and institutions, including the symbolic order. Husserl teaches us that,
in and of itself, the lifeworld is not a purposeful structure (Husserl
1970, 382). In Schürmann's terms, though, the relations that establish my lifeworld are constituted by a certain founding order (*archê*),
its justificatory principles and norms (*principium*), and its enforceable
laws through authority (*princeps*). The world into which I am born may,
from a metatheoretical point of view, entail violence, but in order to
make such a judgment one must step outside the civilizational ambit.
Only in modern times has judging one's world from the standpoint of
another – arrogant, self-serving, and potentially imperialistic – become
a familiar discourse. Examples include Marx's critique of the so-called
pre-capitalist order (recall his 1853 letters on India, in which his historical materialism justified British imperialism; Marx 1972), as well
as Western feminists' advocacy of women's rights in Asian and African societies based on liberal-humanist discourse, which leads many
non-Western advocates of women's rights to refuse to call themselves
"feminists" (Kishwar 1990). These two positions in effect impose one
world's principles upon another, a consequence of European claims to

universality. Furthermore, both positions are based on claims to transhistorical and trans-civilizational values.

Historical cases of deworlding abound. I mentioned the Spanish mercenaries' conquest of the Americas and their swift subsequent eradication of the Inca, Aztec, and Maya worlds, after which the shrinking population of survivors were forced to serve the extractive, now globalized, economy of then nascent European plunder capitalism. Histories of colonialism are filled with such staggering deworldings. In 1552, Bartolomé de las Casas wrote a stunning eyewitness account of the fiendish, blood-soaked conquest of the Indies and the Americas by the Spanish conquistadors. The deworlding experienced by the indigenous inhabitants of the Indies and Central America was so horrifying that within a few years of the Spaniards' arrival, according to de las Casas, the inhabitants of many Native communities hanged themselves and their children on hearing that the Spanish were approaching (de las Casas 2004). Another dramatic example is the colonization of the Congo by King Leopold II of Belgium as his private enterprise, one that involved the systematic mutilation, brutalization, and mass enslavement of the population. Ten million Congolese died as a result – the greatest genocide in recorded history (Hochschild 1998). To the long historical list of hubristic deworldings one could add the Native Americans' loss of their world as the result of a massive, unstoppable wave of territory-devouring settlers, supported by the US army in the nineteenth century. The distinctive feature of European colonial conquests is in that for Europe, the absolute alterity of the Other gave birth to modernity. As Enriqué Dussel persuasively argues, European modernity would not have been possible without the radical externalization and colonization of the Other (Dussel 1993). European modernity is best understood through the Hegelian philosophy of history according to which it was Europe, rather than Africa (and America) or Asia, that served as the bearer of the development (*Entwicklung*) of Absolute Knowledge, and thus Enlightenment (*Aufklärung*): "The History of the World travels from East to West, for Europe is absolutely the end of History, Asia the beginning" (Hegel 1991, 103). As for Africa: "What we properly understand by Africa, is the Unhistorical, Undeveloped Spirit, still involved in the condition of mere nature, and which had to be presented here only as on the threshold of the World's History" (1991, 99). There is a reason for my diversion to Hegel at this point: given that Europe as the bearer of knowledge was "innocent," acting as the "invisible hand" of *Geist*, its role in world conquest was "emancipatory," however violent such imposed transformation of the Other might be (Dussel 1993, 75). The (Hegelian) claim here is that the violence of deworlding represented the moment of forcing the Other into maturity, an extension of the Enlightenment project. Precisely because of its moral and developmental character, the deworlding achieved by self-righteous European modernity was not only global in its magnitude but also "desirable," once its logic was revealed to the heretofore clouded gaze of the immature.

There have been many similar civilizational or mass deworldings, both past and contemporary. Consider the Muslim-Arab Umayad Empire's invasion of Andalusia (southern Spain) in the eighth century. And the twentieth century is hardly alien to violent reworldings. Consider the Nazis' campaign to eradicate Europe's Jews, Romani, and homosexuals; Stalin's dekulakization of Ukraine and collectivization of agriculture; Mao's Great Leap Forward; and the Khmer Rouge creation of peasant-communism in Cambodia, which led to the loss of one-quarter of that country's population. Setting aside how tragic these acts of violence were, how cruel these forceful reshapings of history, I cannot help but wonder about how, in these contexts, the individuals on the proverbial "day after" – wounded, bewildered, dazed – awoke to their new reality, and how they tried to grasp the "new" imposed, remoulded lifeworld, a world simultaneously intimate and alien to them.

Deworlding modes of violence often contain dramatic structural reshiftings that catch the keen observer's eye, and that is how they are identified: through the act that changes the world. Often, though, such deworldings are *subtle*. The aforesaid dramatic events obscure our view of the flip side of deworlding: *re*worlding. Because it is impossible for humans to ever live outside a world – or *Welt* as a set of social relations (Schutz) into which one is "thrown" (Heidegger) – every deworlding simultaneously involves a reworlding act, whether the victims survive the deworlding violence or not. A classic work about reworlding is Friedrich Engels's *The Condition of the Working Class in England* (1845). This book amounts to an "ethnography" of social calamities intrinsic to expanding industrial capitalism in nineteenth-century England, a painful tale of human abjection and daily struggles for survival, a story that continues to happen today in the sweatshops of Bangladesh, Mexico, and other corners of the world where, in the absence of workers' rights, cheap labour shoulders the harrowing burden of mass production – to be more precise, the production of massive wealth for the few in a world in which the eight richest individuals possess wealth equal to that of the poorest half of humanity (3.6 billion people in 2017) (Elliot 2017). This inequality is even more staggering when one finds that only three years earlier, in 2014, it was eighty-five individuals who held that amount of wealth (Heaven 2014). Engels offers a humanist's account of the mass displacement and dehumanization caused by a structural–civilizational shift that was deemed inevitable from the perspective of historical materialism, a shift that was violent at its core. He recounts how migrant peasants, having been uprooted from the countryside, were moulded into the emerging working-class lifeworld in polluted and alienating industrial towns and cities such as London and Manchester. Engels, like his French counterparts Henri de Saint-Simon and Auguste Comte, maintained that modernity was an epoch of violent displacement, of deworlding and reworlding, of making humans moveable and mouldable according to the requirements of capitalist modernization. Modernity, in its continuous reshaping and reshifting of the social fabric, is an age of violent deworlding and reworlding according to the requirements of technological Enframing.

From ancient times to today's world of mass migration, exiles have known this experience of deworldedness all too well and have endlessly tried to come to terms with it (see Vahabzadeh 2006; 2012a). For now, though, visualize this scenario: a middle-aged immigrant woman of colour in Toronto, having worked hard for years since arriving in her new home, making ends meet and putting herself through school, and having risen in social status and raised a family, has held for several years a top managerial position in a clothing chain's regional headquarters after working her way up from the bottom. One day while resting at home, she receives a phone call asking her to visit the office briefly to sort out an urgent issue. She visits the office, where she meets the regional superintendent, who hands her a pink slip. With one scratch of the proverbial pen, the position she has held for many years has been eliminated. She is suddenly dispossessed of her entire world and the future that has always been attached to it. She has been deworlded. Within days, her angry disbelief gives way to depression and a sudden disk problem in her lower back. Her existential horizons dim: she is confused, and given her age, she is uncertain whether she will be able to start over in a highly competitive labour sector in a comparable position. Is this scenario all too familiar? Modern society offers mechanisms for managing this systemic–procedural violence of deworldedness: in welfare states, programs such as employment insurance and social assistance are meant to keep people like her afloat until the capitalist machine can accommodate her.

Medical treatment, counselling and therapy, and government-sponsored retraining (if available) also offer avenues for reworlding her. The system is meant to provide hope for this violently deworlded subject and to resocialize her into the capitalist market and Enframed civilization. Simply by living in this age, this woman remains the subject of invisible violence. Under modernity, deworlding and reworlding create generalized socio-economic but also existential displacements. We all know that life is not (always) fair, yet we are unable to grasp the depths of displacement's violence. "It could happen to anyone ..." "Displacements are a fact of life ..." Truisms like these conceal the violent nature of systemic displacement.

One could object that such is modern society – it is a capitalist socio-economic system based on social mobility – and that casting this woman's plight as a form of violence involves essentializing or moralizing the subject matter, implying that by some eternal or universal fiat humans should not be displaced. Interestingly, this objection points precisely back to my argument, except that I intend neither to essentialize nor to moralize the subject matter: in pointing out the matter-of-factness of such displacements – deworlding and reworlding – I want to shed light on the systemic and procedural violence endemic to modern society, not from the standpoint of some presumably fundamental right (adhered to by various social justice discourses) or some essential characteristic of the subject (reminiscent of Marxist class essentialism or liberal discourses of individual pursuit of happiness), but from the standpoint of existential *Weltanschauung*, which, in awakening the subject to the shock of finding him- or herself in a displaced world and facing dimming horizons, reveals the structural–epochal constellation of our age. Humans are made "standing-reserve" (*Bestand*) in relation to the inner workings of this technological age.

So far I have spoken of the deworlding/reworlding pair through clearly oppressive examples of colonialism, totalitarianism, and capitalism. Yet deworlding/reworlding also occurs at historical moments of revolutionary social justice. The American and French revolutions as well as the Bolshevik Revolution stand out as expressions of liberation or emancipatory social change. The moral, historical, and popular justifications attached to any revolution in which the social fabric of society undergoes massive transformation to the extent that the revolution becomes the marker of a historic break in subsequent literature cannot conceal their violent deworlding/reworlding. That an entire people is liberated from violent colonial rule, or that a suppressed class emancipates itself (and other classes) by ending the conditions of its subjugation through revolutionary action, consitutes the *raison d'être* for deworlding/reworlding. But these revolutions do not alter the mechanisms of such transformations. Liberals will use my observations to rationalize abandoning revolutionary justice in favour of reformist solutions as a means to avoid deworlding/reworlding violence. In other words, they opt to continue with the existing oppressive conditions indefinitely; this position is ultimately an apology for the status quo.

Invoking the American, French, and Bolshevik revolutions, as well as anti-colonial movements, means that my argument can only proceed with an important proviso. Let us ignore the important differences between the American and French revolutions and take them both, in contrast to the Bolshevik Revolution, as archetypes – that is, as founding moments of liberal-democratic and socialist modernities, respectively. When humans are seen as endowed with natural and thus inalienable rights – this master code of political modernity – then France's oppressive monarchy was an impediment to the fulfilling of human potential. Once people's fundamental rights become the measure of humanity, monarchy and the treatment of humans as the monarch's subjects constitute an already worlded violence inherited from tradition. The "subject" is essentially "rightless" and thus not entirely "human." In light of such age-old violence in a world in which only subjects (aristocracy and royalty excluded) were born, the French Revolution's *Declaration of the Rights of Man and the Citizen* (1789) amounted to the constituting of a new world and new humanity. It released our humanity from these subjugations and thereby allowed the modern world to be born. By virtue of the notional emergence of the rights-bearing citizen, an entire epoch dropped its cloak of legitimacy and exposed itself as ruthlessly violent. We do indeed live in the world of appearances (Arendt 1970, 66), and those appearances are not our handiwork. The Bolshevik Revolution epitomized the emancipation of the exploited classes from an age in which humanity, alienated from itself as a result of value extraction from labour, reconciled with itself and overcame the systemic violence that is endemic to capitalist production. Enabled by the forces of history (through the unfettered development of universal productive forces), the Bolshevik Revolution appeared as a historical necessity, receiving its legitimation from the laws of historical development. Unlike the birth of the rights-bearing citizen, which was ultimately a constitutional revolution, the new humanity born out of the Bolshevik Revolution needed to

undergo a process of acute resocialization if it was to expel from itself
the toxin of individualist-competitive self-interest; both production and
the distribution of basic needs were also resocialized back into collective
life according to this directive: from each according to her or his ability, to each according to her or his needs (Marx). The worlded order
of capitalism, made obsolete and "burst asunder" (Marx) by history,
collapsed (was deworlded) to make room for the necessary (socialist)
reworlding. In the liberal *and* communist cases, deworlding/reworlding
violence retained its reach. And by virtue of this violence a new epoch,
and thus a new humanity, was born. The power of liberation does not
really rest in its liberation of an already existing people but in the *constitution* of a people, the "act of founding of the new body politic" (Arendt
1963, 223).

Clearly, I regard liberatory moments as violent even when partaking in a certain course of action is absolutely necessary. I argue that
human action, following Arendt, *changes the world, and thus, I add, every
form of social transformation involves deworlding and reworlding*. The
deworlding/reworlding pair points to the structural frame of transformation. Pursuing this line renders humanist readings of Arendt
obsolete: human action changes the world, but action originates with
humans who are already inserted into specific nodes of historical
and structural frames and who confront particular horizons of possibilities. These determinants and the responses to them constitute
"economies of violence."

Is it possible to conceive humanity outside of structural de-/re-
worldedness? Phenomenologically, the concept(s) of *deworlding and
reworlding capture the originary and ahistorical structure(s) of violence* and
manifest phenomenal violence. As such, deworlding/reworlding precedes the *original and historical* "structural violence" (e.g., patriarchy)
that is part of my proposed tripartite concept of violence. Deworlding/
reworlding provides the means to distinguish between, on the one hand,
archic, universalizing, isomorphic violence, and on the other, an-archic
phenomenalizations that hold together the natal power of growing and
the irreducible multiplicity of things – loosely speaking, modes of nonviolent coexistence. Deworlding/reworlding also allows us to see how
closely these two poles are connected to each other.

My phenomenological conceptual reduction has brought us to the
point where we need a shift in pace. At this point, we can understand
violence more clearly by *looking away* from it and gazing upon violence's
supposed negation: nonviolence.

What's in a Word? Reflections on "Nonviolence"

I begin by focusing on the word "nonviolence" and on my amazement about it: for a long time I have wondered why, in the various European and Asian languages I have looked into, there is no word signifying the opposite of violence. I am surprised that references to forms of action, communication, or approaches that refuse violent methods are always uttered in the negative. Latin- and German-based languages refer to *non-violence* as a *privative* term (e.g., *no violencia, nonviolenza, non-violence, Gewaltlosigkeit*). Similarly, the term coined by one of the most influential champions of nonviolence, Mahatma Gandhi, is *ahimsa*, literally meaning "to not harm," the negative form (*a-*) of *himsa*, injury or harm. The Persian adjectival form, *bikhoshunat* (non-violent), or nominal form, *khoshunatparhizi* (refraining from violence) are recent neologisms arising from translations of European and Gandhian equivalents, words that have no indigenous Persian linguistic roots. Of course, I cannot generalize this observation without a thorough study of world languages. But I think there is a subtle intimation here: if in many languages "nonviolence" can be thought about only in terms of *avoiding* violence, does this not indicate that violence, besides being pervasive and commonplace, is indeed foundational to human social life? In short, the human world seems to *phenomenalize* through violence – that is, it appears and expands through violence; and this violence is *ontological* and therefore "internally" hegemonic in that it permeates almost every form of social organization or has the potential to do so. Therefore, advocacy of nonviolence, even in the most minor contexts and cases, should logically go against a foundational and fundamental feature of human civilization. Lexically, peace is the absence of war and the two terms are contraries. What word is there in our languages to denote the condition in which violence is absent? If we think along these lines, we will be able to locate within our language – the "house of Being" (Heidegger) – the ontological and systemic constitution of the fabric of various forms of social, political, economic, and cultural organizations. So understood, violence proper precedes any of its specific manifestations and agents, although violence has never lacked for machinery for its application, or for perpetrators to partake in its operations. Alas, when universal systems of repression are in place, we are bound to find more than we need of those who will man and maintain the repressive machine.

The lineage of (re)thinking violence within twentieth-century Continental thought confirms my earlier observation that violence has an *ontological* character always already manifest to us through its concrete configurations as well as its (changing) technological or institutional tools. I therefore submit my *hypothesis of the ontological primacy of violence.* I must make two key remarks here. First, this hypothesis is consistent with my "foundational" reading of (post-)Heideggerian thought, according to which violence is connected to the history of European metaphysics. In other words, the ontological primacy of violence reveals the "essence" (*Wesen*) of metaphysics, but this "essence" is of changing character. In this book's conclusion we will see how, with the hypothesis of metaphysical closure, the hypothesis of the ontological primacy of violence yields yet another hypothesis. Second, the careful reader will note that when I make this grand claim regarding violence's ontological primacy, I inevitably end up offering this historically bound knowledge through a *metatheoretical* gesture. This is a *paradox.* In other words, I could not have made that claim from within the epochal ambit in which I am historically inserted, because as a hegemonized subject bound to this epoch, my knowledge, however critical, is inevitably anchored to the epoch's principles and to its hegemonic terms that render violence intelligible, even desirable. So my aforesaid assertion, emphatically, can only be a *hypothesis*, a guidepost, and only "testable" as such, and, of course, always changing. This hypothesis becomes an organizing tool, a phenomenologist's lantern, through which the dark, subterranean relations of the otherwise heterogeneous, even incommensurable, approaches to violence and nonviolence – the very relations these approaches often deny – are brought into view, holding these often diverging approaches under one proverbial conceptual roof. Like any hypothesis within the scientific method, the hypothesis of the ontological primacy of violence will inform my subsequent interpretations and arguments (without excluding other interpretations). Making this gesture, I remain unconvinced that the deconstruction of metaphysics (Heidegger's *Destruktion*) provides no platform for a critique of violence. On the contrary, I think it does: Vattimo, for instance, provides practical positions for critiquing metaphysics' manifestations. Admittedly, though, a deconstruction of epochs leaves me facing the abyss. In any case, as we rethink violence further and deeper, we will realize the difficulty of *thinking* today's pervasive modes of violence *back* to their systemic and thus tacit and implicit forms. After all, war, armed conflicts, and unilateral interventions; genocide and massacre; rape and abuse; exclusionary prejudices (racism, sexism, ageism, ableism, speciesism, homophobia, transphobia, xenophobia, and linguicide) are (to varying degrees) in the fabric of countless human civilizations.

The phenomenological tradition brings to our attention that normative impositions inform the "infrastructure" of manifest violence. Violence, whether it arises from institutionalized practices or from individuals and groups, always remains hubristic: it is an imposition of one mode of life, in its specific aspects, upon another. We also notice that the hegemonic sovereign, enlivened by a creative, *archic* moment (Arendt's concept of natality) rises and reigns only to enter its inevitable pull towards mortality. As the sovereign loses energy and gradually meets its own impoverishment, it becomes more aggressive, more demanding, and increasingly violent in asserting itself. Such knowledge refers us back to the "economies of violence" that are tied to the epoch's normative–legislative–predicative economies (Schürmann 1990).

Of course, the "ontological primacy" hypothesis does not negate the presence of human acts characterized as "nonviolent": unconditional care and love are as old as humanity itself. But the reader will recognize that we cannot simply fasten nonviolence to love or care at the personal or communal levels, since acts of love and care, if we refrain from idealizing them, can both be genuine and contain conceit and hubris. So I ask, what does the ontological constitution of violence imply? If anything, it hardly means we should resign ourselves to our fate. The fact that we can think and rethink violence and endeavour to surpass it, and the fact that we can devise in our acting and thinking means that are distanced from violence, allude to the steps we have already taken towards changing our collective histories by bringing violence to its impoverishment (see this book's conclusion). Nonviolence, it seems, can only be thought in privative terms, as that which we deny, we the children of this age who audaciously challenge our very own ontological constitution. To extract the "non[-]" in *non*violence due to the privative nature of "nonviolence": this is the daunting and mind-boggling challenge of our time. We know that "nonviolence" inevitably remains unthought and can only be pondered in relation to that which remains almost effortlessly thinkable and doable, which is violence. To rest my case apropos the challenges of nonviolence, let me quote Faisal Devji's observation on Gandhi: "Unlike nonviolence, which possessed only a negative meaning, violence enjoyed a positive existence and was implied in all action, including the everyday processes of living that wore down the body and eventually destroyed it. Nonviolence, therefore, was meant not to provide some alternative to violence but instead to appropriate and … to sublimate it" (Devji 2012, 7–8).

As the signifier of an absent presence, the term "nonviolence" cannot denote any "state" in which a being is experienced in concrete fashion.

Ontologically, this is precisely what makes it so challenging to rethink or enact nonviolence. Yet, as attested by our attempts over the past two centuries to figure out what exactly *is* it that constitutes *non*violence aside from refraining from violence, we have ended up grasping nonviolence by hanging this elusive and unintelligible concept to *assumed* foundations, morals, or goods. Nonviolence has unquestionably expanded in our collective horizons of the doable and thinkable, but only as riveted to these supposed grounds. In other words, most major thinkers and advocates of nonviolence – as will be seen the second part of this book – have tried to *extract positively locatable concepts* from the *ontological negativity* of nonviolence. I will argue that these thinkers of nonviolence have erred in explaining nonviolence by creating *algorithms of nonviolence* formulated by tethering nonviolence to positively ascertainable common notions such as strategic necessity, democracy, utility (and disutility), social justice, the moral good, love, or Truth. In mathematics and in computer science, an "algorithm" refers to a closed and finite problem-solving procedure for calculating a function or analysing a data set through determinate steps. Algorithms are means of producing answers – true or false – and thus belong to the realm of the absolutes, be they scientific or religious. For me, a conceptual algorithm is a closed system for calculating and thereby determining the output of an enigmatic conceptual input (I exclude randomized algorithms here). As such, an algorithm renders intelligible an otherwise enigmatic concept by subjecting it to a predetermined investigative procedure. In our case, these algorithms, these conceptual equations, are meant to compensate for the ontological elusiveness of nonviolence – that is, to compensate for nonviolence's defining yet ungraspable "lack" (of violence). Stated differently, through attribution and substitution these algorithms try to "substantiate" nonviolence. As can be expected, a phenomenology of nonviolence must bracket operative assumptions like these, which I intend to do in the second part of this book. As so often happens in phenomenology, though, exposing and bracketing these algorithms yields pleasant surprises, and I hope to show how these attempts to turn a negative concept into a positive and ascertainable one actually reveal aspects of nonviolence that have to this point remained largely concealed.

It must be added here that in rethinking (non)violence, many outstanding thinkers have reasserted the connection between nonviolence and ethics, and there is no need to deny the ethical component of nonviolence. I will suggest that nonviolence can only be "thought" through action, specifically when structurally and economically imposed violence

is transformed, through our actions, into an opening, a moment of decision in which we refuse to partake in prescribed and instituted violence
and rethink our options with heightened sobriety. This is philosophizing
with our hands, shouts, plans, communities, marching feet, and above
all, our friendships.

In short, I intend to dismantle and deconstruct violence in whatever
form it takes. That is what makes struggles for a better, nonviolent future
so challenging. And this brings us to the question of action. *From the point
of view of acting, violence and nonviolence are often distinct but are not opposites.* Acting potentially contains both violence and nonviolence. Even
plainly nonviolent modes of action can turn into their opposites: state
protection of citizens' rights and property is attached to the element of
police violence (both sanctioned and excessive). Legal procedures and
bureaucratic-rational systems always encompass systemic discrimination
against specific social groups. Even a loving relationship can contain, and
hide, exploitation and abusive behaviour.

Violence and nonviolence are intimately braided concepts. I now offer a *third
set of propositions* and explore the thesis that no human action with an
impact on another existent (human or non-human) is *purely* violent or
nonviolent.

Rethinking (Non)Violence Phenomenologically

To reiterate, violence and nonviolence reveal themselves only through
human action. Put another way, *human action is the privileged and ontic locus
of manifestation of (non)violence.* To be precise, "action" captures (a) "live
action," best manifested in hubristic violence; (b) "sedimented acts," as
in institutionalized violence (often masked by the nonviolent appearance of the law or bureaucratic proceduralism and corporate rule);
and (c) "structurally determined action" arising from epochal codes
and the human condition. I regard action as a *privileged locus* because
human action is capable of founding something new and opening new
paths (Arendt's concept of natality). Phenomenologically, *action takes
place before it can lend itself to either violence or nonviolence;* put differently,
acting happens before the act lands on the pre-existing, agreed-upon,
constructed, historically received, and epochally given categories of violence and nonviolence, even when we carry out sedimented or structurally determined acts. In a phenomenological moment of *epoché* when
we bracket our judgments – our constructed categories and representational thinking of (non)violence – we find that no act represents *purely*

violent or nonviolent modalities. In short, if we can envisage action in isolation, no act in and of itself is purely violent or nonviolent. Whether an act is violent or not is a function solely of its consequences, for those consequences are received by a community that has its own values and perceptions. This is because every act, in retrospect, always leaves a trace behind: it opens certain possibilities and forecloses others, and thus it changes the course of future actions. Provisionally, we can say that the new, arising from action, can be brought into this world through violence (and its instrumentality) as well as through nonviolence (Schürmann's anarchic acting). However, due to the hypothesis of "ontological primacy of violence," nonviolence can only appear in relation to violence's universal reach: as a privative and relational concept, nonviolence is always conditioned by violence and is a response to it. Thus nonviolence is never a stand-alone concept and no act can be identified as nonviolence in and of itself.

Now, if both violence and nonviolence arise from and reveal themselves through human action, and if action is the privileged locus of phenomenalization for both, then (to reiterate) *we need to abandon violence and nonviolence as pure moments*. But this last statement needs to be qualified. Violent and nonviolent acts often *appear* differently in concrete acts, just as they produce measurably different and even starkly contrasting consequences. This is why we need to navigate the following discussion before revisiting the concept of action in the *precategorical moment of liberation* (chapters 3 and 4).

In order to clarify my thesis properly, I first need to summarize the contributions of phenomenological approaches to (non)violence; after that I should address the rather formalistic understanding that may be extracted from the preceding excursions. At its abstract level, Schürmann's conceptualization of violence disallows immediately practical and concrete rethinking of the issue; he generally shunned philosophers like Vattimo and Derrida who engaged with the concrete manifestations of the political violence of our time. So the present book, just like my previous one (Vahabzadeh 2003), sets out to engage with the issue of violence at an analytical level that Schürmann's thinking would not accommodate. I engage with the "intermediate" analytical level (i.e., between highly abstract and concretely applied) because while structural analyses correctly attribute violence to metaphysics – an essential point for the present inquiry – such analyses can hardly accommodate those sociological analyses concerned with how the modes of violence we concretely experience *appear* to us. Here, a phenomenologically enabled sociological theory presents the ontic cases through which the ontological structure can be identified.

One last but important point regarding the ontological condition of violence: the economy of presence, identified through reductive phenomenalization, constitutes *primal violence* and is represented by *phenomenal violence*. By denying the motility of beings and the possibility of their re-emerging in myriad ways, stability begets *violence as the reduction of not only the diversity of all but also the inner plurality of one.* "In this sense, for two and a half thousand years we have lived but a single fantasmic hegemony: the one that has forced all phenomena into the isomorphic" (Schürmann 2003, 540). Thus, throughout the history of European metaphysics we find violence that has *rendered stable* otherwise motile and plural existents.

Returning to the issue at hand: I extracted three major concepts from Schürmann's philosophy – the structural conditions of evil (maximization and dispossession), hubris (as "unrestrained self-imposition"), and institutionalized or systemic violence. These three concepts must be properly understood within Schürmann's "anti-humanist" approach. The positions extracted from a phenomenology of violence cannot yield to the humanist, liberal gesture that action is a matter of intention (to which the question of responsibility is related). Obviously, hubristic self-imposition, viewed phenomenologically, is not essentially a matter of will, and as such, it does not imply a Kantian notion that views evil as arising from the subject's free will. The "conditions of evil" are not ethical or moral but "phenomenal" (2003, 621).

The proposed tripartite concept of violence is not meant to offer a taxonomy of violence, although it inevitably does that. Such taxonomy is useful for the purpose of categorizing action or applied research. My task, however, requires that we pick up the tripartite concept of violence with the intention of enabling a conceptual "fusion": this will enable us to recognize just how integrated contemporary civilizational violence actually is; it will also lead us back to the moment in which it becomes possible – theoretically – to end all violence (liberation). In my interpretive incorporation of Schürmann's concept of violence, I argue that as "denying dispossession," evil leads that which opposes evil to impose a "legitimate use of force" (Weber) of its own: the self-acclaimed good posits itself as good and thus maximizes itself through gestures of legitimacy and desirability. I have evoked this point in due detail apropos the liberal defence of state violence in response to the fear, or real acts, of terrorism. Evoking a neo-Hobbsian defence of democracy, as an unquestioned good against the threat of terrorism, this approach ultimately comes to serve as an excuse for the state's "state of exception" (Vahabzadeh 2005). When this happens, the good yields two movements: first, the good promotes itself in the manner of hubris, as "unrestrained self-imposition," however justified in the eyes of the constituents; and second, the good enacts institutional violence in the form of legal proceduralisms intended to expunge evil from public life. One upshot of this double-movement is the elimination of diversity through specific measures of repression, colonization, marginalization, assimilation, and co-optation – measures applied to different groups with different dosages. The eradication and suppression of diversity, of course, allows the good (in denial of its own denial) not only to maximize itself but also to claim history so that it stands out as a champion of progress. In this way a new historical protagonist is born. All that this hegemon commits to and carries out (however random and extralegal) now defines the "order"; all action outside of it becomes "anarchy." Examples abound. The "war on terror" is the most recent case in point. This example shows how intricately the three components in my concept of violence are related to one another on the global scale. But this example is too obvious. The model I propose can be applied to many other situations and human relations. To state the obvious, structural violence stamps today's state system; (calculative) bureaucracy clearly indicates institutional or systemic violence; and hubristic violence is evident in interpersonal relationships. Today's interventionism and unilateralism by the United States and Europe in the Middle East stands out as a fusion of the three aforementioned modalities of violence. Even better: take the IMF and the World Bank. Drawing from an important Foucauldian study (Escobar 1995), I offer a Schürmannian reading here: by articulating the (supposed) Third World subsistence economy (in contrast to First World advanced capitalism) as a manifestation of "dispossession" (by equating subsistence with poverty), and by denying that one's own (Western) economy is dispossessed (albeit in a different way, which is leading to ecological collapse on the global scale), modern capitalism has discursively emerged as the "good" and as the object of desire. The Eurocentric perceived "lack" in diverse world economies led to the invention of the concept of "poverty," and in response to this "poverty," the concept of "development" was born (Escobar 1995). I cannot resist adding the polemical point that this is one of the oldest tricks in the book: the rich create the poor by exploiting them; they then cast themselves as an object for the poor to envy, even while blaming them for their poverty. Anyhow, for the sake of pulling the subsistence economies of Africa, Asia, and Latin America into the world capitalist system, the IMF and the World Bank have been imposing "structural adjustment" programs, which entail transforming the subsistence economies of Third World countries into export economies; this in turn ruins local economies, forces broad swathes of Third World citizens into poverty, and destroys regional ecologies. The hubris of the First World in all of this is obvious; perhaps not so obvious is the concomitant institutionalized violence. The world is forced into capitalist *economic isomorphism,* its diversity is denied, and this denial is also denied. The economic and financial crises that cyclically occur in various world economies as a consequence of this hubris are addressed simply by imposing further hubristic restrictions on economies through plans that are doomed to generate further problems and hurt millions more. This scenario has been repeating itself since the 1950s and has even become part of Europe's own reality – witness the austerity measures imposed on Greece, Ireland, Italy, and other European economies by the very institutions that are responsible for the economic sufferings of these countries. It seems that the painful reworlding/deworlding of the "Third World" is now knocking on the First World's door! We are dealing, on a local *and* global scale, with a structure that is intrinsically violent and that is intent on eradicating economic, not to mention cultural and human, diversity.

This is why we should take the phenomenological "analytical step backward from oppressions to the economies that make them possible" (Schürmann 1990, 60). Examining these economies reveals how, in modernity, surveillance arises as hubristic violence – as a rampant violence, so aptly exposed by Foucault (1979), that restricts human action by means of the panoptic gaze of an omnipresent overseer. Yet the disciplinary society is not essentially punitive; it is primarily administrative. Schürmann characterizes it as a society of "generalized production and administration." Specifically, I have used the term "technological liberalism" to show how liberal-democratic states do not fall outside this measure of social control, for in such states, liberties are bestowed only on already forged subjects through "op-pressive categorization" (oppression means "pressing near" or "holding together") of irreducible human diversity into administratively manageable categories (Vahabzadeh 2003, 115–17). This isomorphic violence – so commonplace that we tend not to see it – defines our age.

The examples of the World Bank and the IMF illustrate a dominant modality of isomorphic violence akin to Heidegger's concept of technological Enframing or *Ge-stell*. Here we witness a persistent drive for civilizational deworlding/reworlding: deworlded diverse economies that have the potential for long-term sustainability are (forcefully) reworlded into imposed isomorphism, already bearing the prospect of imminent ecological catastrophe. Through the discursive articulation of economic logic and "necessity," propagated incessantly through corporate media, the inherent violence of this enframed system is normalized. In linking violence to human action, Arendt was correct to identify violence in terms of instrumentality and in relation to natality as the phenomenological potential to expand particulars into universals. However, we need to place Arendt's approach to violence in proper civilizational (historical and conceptual) context via Enframing and the phenomenological double-movement of deworlding/reworlding. This is how deworlding/reworlding reduces action to agency, and otherwise diverse, heterogeneous actors to Kafkaesque, isomorphic bureaucrats of hegemonic logic. Only a resuscitation of action is capable of challenging hegemonic agency, in which we inevitably partake in order to push ontological–structural–civilizational violence towards its possible demise. The question of "action" – in resisting hubristic or systemic violence as well as the violence embedded in the law – evokes the issue of *responsibility*, not as an ethical stance but in terms of "responding to" violence. Moreover, systemic violence reveals systemic injustices. Here, injustice is to be understood in terms of being forced into isomorphic agency and thus partaking in the very violence that victimizes its agent. It is through its critique of violence that radical phenomenology joins the struggles for social justice.

So the question would naturally be: given the economies of violence that permeate almost every aspect of life, what accounts for the rise of critical reflections on (and thus resistances to) violence? The answer to this question inevitably points towards that which remains, à la Derrida, "undeconstructable": dignity. The concept of dignity enables us to avoid essentialist arguments for one socio-historical position or another as well as substantiation of the historical agent. Like violence itself – which is "protean" in character (Bernstein 2013) – dignity arises in many different ways in different contexts. We can agree that dignity emerges from the defence of one's conditions of existence when such a defence involves *self-authentication* (individual and collective) against the forces that sweep away one's world in the complex processes of deworlding/reworlding. To be precise, *self-authentication refers to the moment in which in finding one's conditions undignified and seeing one's world disappearing violently and for the worse, one tries to act according to one's denied dignity such that one's being and acting become one according to the possible modalities of acting and being within the horizons of the epoch.*

Response to an Objection

It may be objected that my tripartite concept of violence – especially the concept of hubris therein – commits the very metaphysical fallacy it sets out to expose and dismantle. This objection proceeds that when I argue that violence *violates* and imposes (potentially) universal rules or restrictions on the actions of an entity outside of the violating agent, I assume that this entity or individual holds an original "essence" against which the violence of maximization and universalization is measured. My position assumes – the objection continues – that the violated entity has a measurable substance or a fixed identity, which the violating agent denies. Therefore – the objection concludes – my position conceals a metaphysical understanding of entities as stable presences – a position contrary to my post-metaphysical orientation. In short, it is objected, I contradict myself. Furthermore, if violence is measured against an existing "state of beings," then we basically end up having a concept of violence so generalized that it loses its meaning, let alone its applicability.

I hope this objection will be resolved convincingly in the book's conclusion. My response here is that when we apply the tripartite concept of violence, phenomenologically, we inevitably end up with the concept-pair *deworlding/reworlding* as the fundamental structure of violence. Here is where the applicability of the tripartite concept of violence merges with a phenomenologically informed sociology of knowledge. Since no human can live outside a world (*Welt*), insofar as one finds one's world taken away from him or her by forces *beyond* his or her control, and thus insofar as one finds oneself compelled to move into another set of social relations (*Welt*), one awakens to the violence to which one is subjected. Exiles and refugees experience the violence of deworlding/reworlding with their flesh and skin. In terms of existential, lifeworld knowledge, the process of deworlding/reworlding involves a complex and often painful process of defamiliarization and refamiliarization; the loss of tacit knowledge and forced acquisition of new knowledge, beginning with the know-how of the new conditions in technical terms; and, above all, permanent loss of the sacred. This is how violence *violates* primarily a lifeworld constructed around the knowledge that allows one to live one's life as a matter of course. This latter point is key because it shows that violence has no transhistorical "objective" reality, although the outcomes of violence are always concretely experienceable. All manifestations of violence are thus context-specific and epistemologically bound. It is an objectivist's error to mistake my "active" existential–epistemological approach to violence with an approach that wants its object of knowledge as pregiven, stable, and passive. In other words, all violence is received in an epistemic way, and this includes epistemic violence. Hence violence's "dependence" on the epochal codes of intelligibility within an existing economy of presence. A phenomenological approach shows that the act of violence is bound to the epochal code, just like shared knowledge about what constitutes violence. The victim of violence cannot have a stable presence in advance of the act of violence. But at the same time, the protean character of violence, too, reveals violence's lack of a stable presence. In our age, for instance, the discourse of human rights, as the contemporary articulation of our epochal code, provides the epistemic markers for identifying violence; while simultaneously, as a universal code bound and implemented by an institutional set-up, the human rights discourse often yields the epistemic modes of violence enacted through, for example, the residential schools of Canada's First Nations or the "humanitarian interventions" of present-day imperialist powers. My theory, therefore, assumes neither a "substance," nor an "essence," nor a stable presence (against whose supposedly solid and pristine entity an act is measured as violence), nor a generic and universal applicability regardless of the conditions. In the end, it is a collective, epochal awareness that calls violence into question.

Back to the Originary Moment

Our phenomenological inquiry into violence (and nonviolence) has been enabled by Schürmann's methodological guideline in the epigraph to this chapter. In this chapter and in chapter 1, I took the "analytical step[s] backward from oppressions to the economies that make them possible" (Schürmann 1990, 60). I discussed how, in the Western philosophical context, the history of violence has been grounded in metaphysical maximizations containing epochal constellations of Truth that enable economies of violence. This book is predicated upon Schürmann's "hypothesis of metaphysical closure" – that we are possibly standing at a historic juncture in which it is possible for us to have futures radically different from our pasts. From the standpoint of this hypothesis, our present-day turn to nonviolence attains civilizational proportions.

We can go back in our histories and find at remarkable historic moments principled acts of refraining from partaking in violence or counter-violence. In the cultural memory of much of the Christian world today one is quickly reminded of Jesus Christ. Jainism and Buddhism also offer profound traditions of nonviolence. It is tempting to try and locate the emergence of the political idea of nonviolence within a specific time and place in history; this has clearly been a growing idea since the late nineteenth century. But such claims would require historical-conceptual substantiations that clearly go beyond the scope of this book. Here I can only proceed with the caveat that my analysis is inevitably limited to a particular time and space – that is, from the late nineteenth century onwards and in the context of current, established political, moral, sociological, and philosophical literature on nonviolence (beginning with Thoreau, Tolstoy, and Gandhi and continuing onwards). If we focus on this period and within this now widely recognized body of nonviolence literature, we notice that this literature has vastly influenced present-day approaches to nonviolence and peace activism. Here, my argument is rather nuanced: this literature has been growing at a time when the technologies of war and repression have created staggering tragedies with which the readers are only too familiar. Now, without trying to universalize this strange experience, if we revisit this peculiar tendency – nonviolence growing even while violence has become ever more endemic – in light of the "hypothesis of metaphysical closure," we can view the growing tendency towards nonviolence in our age in a civilizational context and consider the provisional idea that *as metaphysics is losing its violent, hegemonic hold over phenomena (including humans), nonviolence provides a mode of action that may lead to a possible turn towards a post-metaphysical future.* Reading the fact of rampant violence in the twentieth century on systematic, massive scales against the spreading and compelling influence of nonviolent theory and practice is obviously a hermeneutic task informed by a phenomenology of epochs. Note that, as previously discussed, metaphysical universals become ever more violent as their hegemonic reach becomes weakened. At this historic junction, dignity and justice – the undeconstructables – will be our guiding concepts towards such a "turn." I will elaborate on these points in my conclusion.

The controversial point to be considered right now is that seldom is any single act in and of itself *ontologically* violent. Violence cannot be properly understood outside the *economies of presence* that make it possible, giving it its reach, its intelligibility, and its applicability. The quality of hubris can only be properly brought forward through structural and institutional economies of practice: hubristic violence shows itself in abuse, rape, war, murder, assault, the death sentence, imprisonment, police/military violence, exploitation of humans, and appropriation of nonhumans. Structural violence is present in patriarchy, speciesism, heterosexism, capitalism, and Euro- and ethnocentrism, among many other things, and in conjunction with hubristic violence it unleashes practices like slavery and colonial invasion. Institutional violence reduces us to compartmentalized beings, the subjects of bureaucratic management and representative governments: in becoming rights-bearing citizens we allow institutions to manage our affairs through universal rules. As students we are taught *the* knowledge that makes us ancillaries to the extractive–capitalist economy (instead of being encouraged to think and judge for ourselves); as single mothers we are entitled, in many welfare state countries, to state protection that feminizes poverty (instead of being empowered to take our affairs in our own hands); our political involvement has become increasingly meaningless, with the result that we end up politically apathetic or having to choose the lesser evil in every election without recalling that "those who choose the lesser evil forget very quickly that they chose evil" (Arendt 2003, 36). Such manifestations of violence and their economies are never mutually exclusive. Our epoch is indeed saturated with violence. But then we have to ask: War is violent, without a doubt, but what about going to war against an invading army or fighting back with mortal force against a vicious rapist? Are these acts also violent? When Yazidi women and men in Iraq and Syria took up arms against the invading Islamic State (*Da'esh*) forces that killed Yazidi men and enslaved Yazidi women and children, was their armed resistance really violent? Any answer would be at best insufficient. This is our common human condition: however we look at such situations, the outcome is always inevitably *irreversible*: an act can never be taken back because it leaves behind consequences – be they calculated or unintended – that outlive those acts. Arendt writes that action is irreversible because we can never know the consequences of our actions. So let me offer a phenomenological proposition: *irreversibility is a signature of violence*. No wonder, then, that from time immemorial violence has been epitomized by death! "Once released from the bow," the classical Persian poem avers, "the arrow will never touch the thumb again." Action is irreversible because, à la Heidegger (1996), time is the horizon of our existence. Life is also irreversible: I can only age, and I cannot un-raise the beloved son I raised. This is uncanny: *life and violence are intimate like parent and child.* Irreversibility, then, existentially links violence and action (and its institutionalizations). We might argue that the irreversibility of action can be addressed through new initiatives, thanks to natality, whereas irreversible damage caused by violence can never be undone. One can never be un-raped, un-abused, un-injured, un-tortured, and the years of her imprisonment will never return. So many advocates of nonviolence appeal to this very argument (not to hurt), as if they can recuse themselves from the human condition of irreversibility through other acts, as if any action whatsoever can be reversed. We will revisit these gestures in the second part of this book. The irreversible character of both acting and violence – which makes the two interrelated – requires from us a heightened sense of responsibility as we partake in action, but we cannot adequately begin to think of nonviolent acting insofar as we are caught up in the normative, legislative, and predicative economies and their concomitant forms of violence. To properly situate (non)violence in light of the above discussions, we should refrain from all sorts of truisms and refuse *a priori* and positivist distinctions between violence and non-violence. I contend that at a time when metaphysical solidities are being radically questioned and their violent impacts are being exposed, championing nonviolence is a sign of our epochal awareness of the rampant civilizational harm we have been inflicting on ourselves and on the earth that nourishes us since the dawn of history. But this is no great humanist discovery! It is the *hallmark* of our time, a mode of revealing the tragic conditions of our being. Given our acute awareness of the metaphysics of violence, advocacy of nonviolence may offer modes of acting and thinking our way out of our common epoch of technological–algorithmic civilization on a planetary scale. *A defence of nonviolence* (which will be offered later in this book) *must entail a phenomenological critique of the humanist critique of violence, which tends to measure* – in a rather calculating way – *the impact of violence solely in human terms.* Such a mindset is endemic to the liberal perspective and to moralistic philosophies (and badly misunderstood deconstruction!). By contrast, the positivist (under various mantles) avoids the question of acting and systemic violence altogether and relies instead on uncritically assumed, pre-existing categories that place the act within an epistemic framework of categorical references even before the act manifests itself. By reducing violence to conflictual violence, defenders of nonviolence have largely turned a blind eye on structural and institutional forms of violence (the law, reductive categorization, education systems, or the forging of rights-bearing subjects within epistemic regimes of citizenship), or the violence arising from the universalization that denies singularity (nation-state, capitalism). *Epistemologically, convenient conceptual oppositions such as violence–nonviolence hide the originary conditions in which these so-called oppositions arise.* The opposition is constructed out of the commonly held distinction between the two – remember here that every reasonable human being knows the difference, to some degree, even when it is s/he who is committing violence. A phenomenologist steps back "from the manifest to manifestation" (Schürmann 1993, 193), subjects these binaries to the phenomenological *epoché,* and seeks to push (non)violence into the precategorical moment. *This precategorical moment is the moment of acting,* a moment prior to epistemic knowledge of the measurable consequences of an act, which by definition is an open and singular moment. Recall that only when an act exceeds the existential ambits of its actor and imposes itself on another does it constitute (hubristic) violence. Since every act is enabled by natality, it has the potential to grow into archic universalization and its ensuing violence (war, retribution, imposition, abuse). Simultaneously, though, because of natality every act is potentially open, non-imposing, an-archic, and nonviolent (care, charity, rehabilitation, mutual aid, cooperation, ecological symbiosis). An act contains the seeds of both (nonviolent) life and violence (epitomized by death). Obviously, these are conceptual clarifications, since in our civilization, violent human action is largely (structurally and institutionally) predetermined, and breaking away from such determinants will be a feat of epochal proportions. If, as suggested, the hegemonic–civilizational violence of our age can be brought to an end through collective human action, the perceived moment of the civilizational demise will amount to a structural shift in almost every relation (human and non-human). Regardless of its form, this will be a moment of massive, structural *violent shift* – which may actually be "nonviolent" – since it involves an entirely new civilizational deworlding/reworlding. This shift represents "a violence to end all violence" (Wohlfarth 2009a, 23): *a Messianic break in history that we call "liberation," an originary moment* in which action emerges regardless of, and thus precedes, *a priori epistemological categories* of violence and nonviolence, when action *is* (non)violence.

A radical phenomenology of (non)violence must attend to *liberation* as the rare (epistemological) moment in which human collective action virtually suspends the distinction between violence and nonviolence – and that constitutes a moment of *epoché.* I owe the discovery of this moment to radical phenomenology and cherish it as a gift.

In the next two chapters I will attend to the question of liberation.

3

Acts of Liberation

And turning His gaze toward His disciples, He began to say, "Blessed are you who are poor, for yours is the kingdom of God. Blessed are you who hunger now, for you shall be satisfied. Blessed are you who weep now, for you shall laugh."

Luke 6:20–21

Do not suppose that I have come to bring peace to the earth. I did not come to bring peace, but a sword.

Matthew 10:34

Perhaps what the familiar, culturally propagated images and tropes of radical social change all have in common are accentuated elements of unimaginable and unrestrained violence. Since the French Revolution, modern revolutionary discourses have promoted an image of a groundswell of sacred rage that hurls destruction at the *ancien régime*, obliterating it. This brings about a top-to-bottom restructuring of the social fabric – an unrivalled undertaking that can only be carried out by the privileged agent called the modern state, characterized by Weber as having a "*monopoly of the legitimate use of physical force*" (1946, 78; emphasis in original). In revolutionary discourses, this sort of revolutionary violence is often justified using tropes similar to the Marxian metaphor of "birth pangs" (of a new society). In staging revolts against existing, oppressive systems, the revolutionaries had to justify violence by "naturalizing" or historicizing it and by casting it as not just necessary but "inevitable." In order to build a better world, revolutionary movements resigned themselves to what they viewed as foundational and creative violence; yet in practice, they were carrying out *ruthless* and *oppressive* violence. These movements disguised this latter type of violence as the former type within their populist–moralist political discourses. By all accounts, they created *new societies*, but they failed to populate these societies with *new humans*. It seems that there was no actual birth, but only lasting birth pangs.

My third set of propositions (see the previous chapter) will be fully developed here through conceptual phenomenology. I now turn to a genealogy of the concept of violence in relation to liberation.

The Conceptual Uniqueness of Liberation

Did the revolutionary leaders ever pay close heed to how their acquiescence to violence transformed their utopias into dystopias and the movements they led into tyrannies? This question is often raised and widely discussed because it is so simple to grasp. But it is misguided in its trajectory, for it deliberately avoids or bypasses a major theoretical dilemma. Conceptually, as proposed in chapter 2, the moment of *liberation* – when the new is *actually* born on a societal scale (i.e., when society is reworlded) out of existing unjust conditions – cannot be otherwise than "violent" if this term is properly understood: every world-historical event involves *phenomenal violence*, even – indeed, *especially* – when justice finally arrives (if it does) through the double-movement of deworlding/reworlding, when those "who weep now … shall laugh" later, as the Messiah declared. This position, however, cannot excuse the rise of tyrants in the aftermath of many modern revolutions. Strictly speaking, revolutionary violence has very little to do with the dystopian unfolding of post-revolutionary social reorganization, because dystopias are born out of the continuation of age-old violence at the systemic level through new means and ends. In light of this, Russell Jacoby suggests that we distinguish between "blueprint utopians [who] map out the future in inches and minutes" (2005, xiv) and "iconoclastic utopians, those who dreamt of a superior society but who declined to give its precise measurements" (2005, xv). Having as they do a messianic component (following Walter Benjamin), iconoclastic utopias are based on dialectical negation (2005, 147). I argue that we need to uphold the idea of "liberation," notwithstanding the disastrous dystopian programs carried out in the name of liberation during the twentieth century. Liberatory action simultaneously arises from and interrupts the present economies of violence.

In order to understand (non)violence properly, we need to conceptually isolate the moment of liberation as a systemic–structural shift. Liberation offers a glance into the precategorical moment, an abstract-historical moment that "precedes" the positivist categories of (opposed notions of) violence and nonviolence in various epistemic communities. In fact, *liberation is one of the rarest historical moments, one that coincides with a phenomenological suspension (epoché), when the hitherto existing opposition between violence and nonviolence is deferred due to acting as self-authenticating.* I judge this moment to be most revealing for a phenomenology that probes the (changing) *Wesen* of (non)violence. To explain why in the moment of liberation the opposition of violence and nonviolence is suspended, let us recall (from chapter 2) the concept of dignity and how in resisting imposed deworlding/reworlding, the actor partakes in self-authenticating, liberating modalities of action. *It is the moment of authentication that renders the opposition of violence and nonviolence deferred,* though not entirely nullified. Recall the example of the Spanish conquest of the Incas, which involved the violent and bewildering loss of a common, familiar world (deworldedness) and the subsequent forced residence (of the survivors) in an entirely new world (reworldedness). There is no change – certainly no revolutionary transformation – that does not entail the phenomenalizing process of deworlding/reworlding. But since liberation is distinct from other transformations in that it involves and declares itself to represent the *authentication* and self-realization of the collective – that is, *the emergence of a new people* – it offers a glimpse into the possibility of a reworlding that is not imposed. Phenomenologically and in this context, authentication refers to releasing the "collective self" from the imposed economies of presence as manifested in the anonymous masses. Precisely because of the manifestation of the messianic gateway into a liberated future, *at the moment of liberation the distinction between violence and nonviolence becomes inoperative in action and thus the two no longer stand in opposition to each other.* It is true that in our collective experience emancipation has been associated with militantism and revolutionary violence, and this has been used by advocates of nonviolence (and liberal-democratic states) as a justification for rejecting revolutionary praxis *in toto*, but we should be clear that such association is bound by the emergence of the nation-states in Europe in the nineteenth and twentieth centuries and by the post–Second World War postcolonial national liberation.

To bring to light the curious moment of liberation, this chapter and the next offer a close reading of the conceptual genealogy of the moment of liberation; this will allow us to arrive at a phenomenological understanding of (non)violence. Interestingly, the proponents of this stream of thought actually regard their work as primarily concerned with violence. Violence, it seems, is entangled with questions of liberation.

Sorel: The General Strike as an Originary Moment

I begin with a foundational treatise that set the stage for a subsequent lineage of reflections on transformative violence generated by twentieth-century theorists. *Reflections on Violence* (1908) is the decisive work by French syndicalist-socialist George Sorel (1847–1922). Before attending to his treatise, we need to understand Sorel's historical–theoretical context. In offering the genealogy of the concept of hegemony, Ernesto Laclau identifies three responses to the "logic of contingency" that permeated socialist politics in the nineteenth and twentieth centuries. The term "logic of contingency," as opposed to "logic of necessity," captures the historical–theoretical situation in which, contrary to Marx's prediction, the economic basis of capitalism and its consequences (increased polarization and class antagonism) did not produce grounds for unity of the proletariat and its revolutionary action. The first response to the "logic of contingency," Laclau states, was the advocacy of economic determinism by the "Marxist orthodoxy" of Karl Kautsky and Georgi Plekhanov. The second response, Eduard Bernstein's "revisionism," promoted political intervention (see Laclau and Mouffe 1985, 7–36). In Laclau's genealogy, Sorel provides the third response. "What Sorel found attractive in Marxism was not in fact a theory of the necessary laws of historical evolution, but rather the theory of the formation of a new agent – the proletariat – capable of operating as an agglutinative force that would reconstitute around itself a higher form of civilization and supplant declining bourgeois society" (1985, 37). For Sorel, Marxism was both science and ideology (1985, 38). So the concept of "general strike" (see below) as a "phantasmatic dimension" (Laclau 1996, 81) serves to overcome class dispersion and unites the proletariat towards social revolution. For the record, the concept of hegemony, first coined by Lenin but theorized by Gramsci, is the fourth response to contingency in the field of socialist praxis (not discussed here).

In Sorel's time, a theoretical turn towards the proletarian mass strike was emerging in Marxist literature. That turn flowed from the 1905 Revolution in Russia, which Lenin famously called the "dress rehearsal" for the 1917 Revolution. In *The Mass Strike* (1906), Rosa Luxemburg makes the case for linking expanding labour unionism – especially in Germany – to revolutionary struggle, but she realizes that the mass strike, as a specific modality of action, can arise both from anarchism ("mechanically") and from Russian Social Democracy ("objectively") (2005, 20). In other words, the mass strike stands out as a modality of action that can lend itself to diverging bases. The *ambivalence* of the strike – that it can have divergent outcomes – spurs Luxemburg to find a way, in theory and practice, to construct a *determinate* way of directing the mass strike to the service of proletarian emancipation. The proletariat expresses itself through the mass strike: "In a word, the mass strike, as shown to us in the Russian Revolution, is not a crafty method discovered by subtle reasoning for the purpose of making the proletariat struggle more effective, *but the method of motion of the proletarian mass, the outward manifestation of the proletarian struggle in the revolution*" (2005, 47; emphasis in original). In other words, the mass strike is not simply a means; it is the *only* act that captures *proletarian existence*. We can deduce that because *proletarian self-realization* (emancipation) depends on it, the mass strike acquires the status of an ontological action. A mass strike in isolation (as a union tactic) does not rise to this level of action; therefore, a mass strike will only succeed within a social movement (2005, 66). This is why, she observes, economism is a digression from Marxism: all action must lead to the emancipation of the proletariat (2005, 33). Luxemburg discerns that "when the social foundations and the walls of the class society are shaken and subjected to a constant process of disarrangement," the "worker [is] suddenly aroused to activity by the electric shock of political action" (2005, 52). On this basis, Luxemburg offers a revolutionary stagism (akin to Lenin's) to forge a "close union of economic and political struggles" (2005, 71).

There arises from Luxemburg's theoretical attempt a brilliant paradox: the mass strike, as the "ontological" act of the proletariat (which is an ontologically constituted class), is an authentic act in relation to proletarian existence, although it can be used in inauthentic ways (by labour unions). Yet, we observe, the strike *leads* to emancipation – or put differently, emancipation is an outcome of action and thus beyond the latter. This is also how a modality of action, despite its authenticity, is surprisingly reduced to instrumental activity. In Luxemburg, a specific genus of action leads to the solidification of proletarian self-realization; whereas in Sorel, proletarian self-realization rests in its action, which he identifies as violence.

Sorel understands violence, *stricto sensu*, as the genuine marker of proletarian revolutionary politics (Sorel 2004, 56). This allows him to *distinguish violence from savagery* (2004, 118) or brutality (2004, 190), since "the term *violence* should be employed only for acts of revolt" (2004, 171). For Sorel, conflict is not primarily between proletariat and bourgeoisie, but between "decadence and full realization of society" (Laclau 2014, 31).

In this context, "the object of force is to impose a certain social order in which the minority governs, while violence tends to the destruction of the old order" (Sorel 2004, 171). The violent character of the proletarian revolution, therefore, rests with the "destruction of the old order" – that is, in the radical restructuring of the social order. "Without confrontation there is no identity; social identities require conflict for their constitution" (Laclau 2014, 31). Generative social revolution, as envisaged by Marx, has a pure form. An anarcho-syndicalist, Sorel calls this pure form the "myth of general strike," noting that the general strike is not a strike (Sorel 2004, 157). There is no doubt that the "strike is a phenomenon of war" (2004, 274) – class war, to be exact:

> Proletarian acts of violence have no resemblance to these proscriptions [punitive forms of violence]; they are purely and simply acts of war; they have the value of military demonstrations, and serve to mark the separation of classes. Everything in war is carried on without hatred and without the spirit of revenge: in war the vanquished are not killed; non-combatants are not made to bear the consequences of the disappointments which the armies may have experienced on the fields of battle; force is then displayed according to its own nature, without ever professing to borrow anything from the judicial proceedings which society sets up against criminals. (2004, 115)

Clearly, in the above statement Sorel does not refer to "total war" – a hallmark of the twentieth-century wars. Violence makes it possible to prevent decadence (Laclau 2014, 32). The significance of his concept of the "myth" lies in its resolving the "epistemological dilemma" of revolutionary movements. The myth is therefore "identical with the convictions of a group, being the expression of these convictions in the language of movement" (Sorel 2004, 50). If the epoch-making proletarian revolution will indeed bring into realization the emancipation of humanity through the destruction of the old, savage order (of capitalism), then the revolution is essentially an event from the *future*, and it will inevitably remain an *epistemological obscurity* for the revolutionary agent. Stated differently, the proletariat engages in revolutionary action for the purpose of realizing the moment of liberation of which it has no experience (hence the messianic character of liberation; see below). Sorel resolves this epistemological dilemma by bringing into view *a memory from the future*, one that can only appear to us in the form of a *myth*, since this emancipatory moment always seems around the proverbial corner, within reach and achievable upon acting, yet it remains unrealized, always farther down the road, always "to come" (*a-venir*), to borrow a term from Jacques Derrida. Sorel's theoretical innovation, the myth, therefore allows revolutionary proletarians to perceive, beforehand, the moment of final confrontation with the savage bourgeois social system, a confrontation that will be revealed through supreme, structural violence, which takes the form of the general strike (which sounds nonviolent!). By allowing concrete, actable substitutions for the abstract concept, as an "empty signifier" (Laclau 2014, 33, 73), the myth allows the moment of radical social transformation to emerge as an object of knowledge, a representation of the unrepresentable. This last point invites us to explore certain affinities between Sorel's "myth" and Karl Mannheim's concept of "utopia," according to which "certain oppressed groups are intellectually so strongly interested in the destruction and transformation of a given condition of society that they unwittingly see only those elements in the situation which tend to negate it" (Mannheim 1969, 36). Mannheim's "utopia" – as opposed to "ideology" or the (universalized) worldview of the ruling class – primarily relates to the *knowledge* regarding revolutionary action, rather than to perceptions of action (Sorel), yet we can see how without the myth this knowledge cannot begin to emerge in the epistemic universe of the proletariat. The *violent character of the general strike proves to be the epistemic marker (knowledge) of the moment of emancipation.*

What is unique about the concept of the myth is that it essentially captures *revolutionary action*, a praxis that distinguishes revolutionary syndicalists from reformist, parliamentary socialists (Sorel 2004, 120), those who are contaminated with decadence and who offer only a semblance of socialism, a socialism bereft of *praxis* but engaged in (staged) political struggles. The proletariat must refuse the latter. Having lost faith in the perceived self-destruction of capitalism, Sorel intends to maintain the proletarian movement through violence anchored to the myth (Laclau 2014, 71). Action brings about "the *framing of a future, in some indeterminate time*" (Sorel 2004, 124; emphasis in original). Thus "the general strike contains everything that the Socialist doctrine expects of the revolutionary proletariat" (2004, 127). The general strike unifies action, and it measures the collective commitment to a common future beyond the structural conflict at hand. The myth provides a normative path towards a final signpost, a perceived *telos*, whose exact configuration remains undetermined owing to the *futurity* of the liberatory moment. It is through praxis that we gain the capacity to stretch our existence into the future; it is through action that the future – and the class struggle that will lead to it – will become intelligible and desirable. So the "myth of general strike" offers a *principle of intelligibility*. As a mode of action, however, the general strike is not teleological: the proletarian self-realization is not an outcome of its action; rather it "is in strikes that the proletariat assert[s] its existence" (2004, 274). *Self-realization arises from an act of liberation* that resolves the epistemological dilemma and enables the structural, and thus violent, shift. Sorel refers to this as the "ethics of violence," which he poses against the liberal moralists (2004, 180). "It is to violence that Socialism owes those high ethical values by means of which it brings *salvation* to the modern world" (2004, 249). It is through this violence – that is, (class) conflict (2004, 186) – that the proletarians can *authenticate themselves through emancipation*.

Subsequently, the foundational transformation of society that is embodied by the general strike will entail violence, properly understood (2004, 57). Social refoundation, the creation of the new, is inevitably violent, and the myth enables us to recognize this violent moment epistemologically, accept it, and prepare for the revolution. The myth now functions as an educational power (2004, 242): a normative social imaginary. The proletarian revolt enables this imaginary to grow through the proletarian action: this is how the myth nullifies the empty talk of socialist pretenders, draws a line between true and pretend socialists, and renders revolutionary praxis intelligible for the masses (2004, 42). Antonio Gramsci recognizes the power of the myth when he emphasizes the resemblance between Sorel's "myth" and Machiavelli's Prince: the myth is neither "a cold utopia nor ... learned theorising," but instead "a creation of concrete phantasy which acts on a dispersed and shattered people to arouse and organise its collective will" (Gramsci 1971, 126). The myth, in the Gramscian model, is that which enables the subaltern to escape the universal and all-embracing worldview of the hegemonic class, even while continuing to be ruled by it.

An Arendtian reading allows us to observe that Sorel's proletarian–revolutionary violence designates the moment of *birth*: natality enables a new, life-bearing force that expands into the world, a force that rephenomenalizes the world and that radically rearranges its existing phenomenal relations according to an emerging phenomenon with the potential to grow into a universal power. Dismissive of Sorel, Arendt observes, not without sarcasm, that he "ended up proposing nothing more violent than the famous myth of the general strike, a form of action which we today would think of as belonging rather to the arsenal of nonviolent politics" (Arendt 1970, 12). Paradoxically, there is an uncanny insight in

Arendt's seemingly off-hand remark and in her *erroneously* viewing the Sorelian general strike simply as a tactic, and thus ignoring the structural, epoch-making character of Sorel's concept. We know, however, that Sorel's "general strike" gives its agents focus and direction for radical transformation. Consider how Sorel compares revolutionary syndicalism to Christian Reformation: "like the Reformation, revolutionary syndicalism may prove abortive, if it loses, as did the latter, the sense of its own originality; it is this which gives such great interest to inquiries on proletarian violence" (Sorel 2004, 56). Reflecting on Arendt's observation, I think that a nimble and elusive truth slips through Arendt's sarcasm. What for Arendt is a matter of amusement for us reveals something essential about the central concern of this book: that the emancipation of the proletariat inevitably goes through violence *par excellence*, and this intelligible and desirable violence that ends the savage violence of class society goes through the "nonviolent" (Arendt) act of the general strike. The general strike materializes through nonviolent "acting in concert" (power) and *forces* a total structural shift. Without hubristic violence, the general strike imposes destruction upon the structural and institutional violence of the status quo. As an epoch-making moment of deworlding/reworlding, *Sorel's nonviolent myth of the general strike represents the transformative–violent moment in human history*. At the moment that self-authenticating action calls the general strike, the epistemic and *a priori* categories of violence and nonviolence lose their intelligibility and applicability. Stated differently, refounding rephenomenalization (deworlding/reworlding) – through which authentication and self-realization of the oppressed is achieved in acts of liberation and of dismantling the old order (which reconciles humanity with itself) – suspends the existing epistemic–moral judgments as an "ethic of violence" prevails. This is the phenomenological *epoché* embodied in the historical action. The form (general strike) maybe truly nonviolent (Arendt), but the transformation inevitably entails the "phenomenal violence" of life against life. The moment is indeed (non)violent: the conceptual opposition of violence and nonviolence loses its sway.

One last observation: as *the opposition between violence and nonviolence is suspended at the moment of emancipation and self-realization*, we retain our capacity to distinguish the epoch-making (non)violence from the systemic and structural savagery of bourgeois society. We do not slip through epochal caesuras with erased memories or vanished knowledge. We retain the ability to identify brutal or savage exploits (massacre, genocide, rape, internment camps, poverty, discrimination, racism, sexism, surveillance, or the police state) because these exploits retain the status quo and block liberation. Categorically, the "violence" of the general strike cannot belong to the arsenal of systemic or hubristic violence (Schürmann). Following Arendt, the aforesaid acts remain the instruments of violence, while the emergence of the new – due to its natality – belongs to an entirely different genus of force.

Benjamin's Critique of Violence

Sorel's theory has left an ambivalent, even contradictory, legacy, from Italian fascism to Fanon's liberation theory – evidence of his theory's broad applicability. His work has compelling epistemological affinities with millenarian or epoch-making movements from Christianity to the French Revolution. It has also influenced one the most influential essays ever written on the subject, "Critique of Violence" (1921) by Walter Benjamin (1892–1940). Benjamin's enigmatic prose aside, his key distinction between "mythic violence" and "divine violence" helps us understand not only the relationship between violence and power – specifically, state power – but also the quintessence of originary, foundational violence. In Benjamin, the term "violence" is a translation of the multifaceted German word *Gewalt*, which signifies "violence" but also "force," in addition to its original meaning, "authority" (as connected to power).

Benjamin opens his argument by invoking two "diametrically opposed" (1996, 237) concepts: "natural law" and "positive law." The law (*Recht*) is deemed to be a means to an end: justice. But then *Gewalt* (force/violence) seems to be the means in relation to the law. Regardless of the type of state under which we live, there is always "law *enforcement*" as a means of upholding the laws of the land. It is with regard to the law's instrumentality in relation to an end – which is justice – that natural laws differ from positive laws. Both natural laws and positive laws provide legitimation for the violence within the law, albeit from different sources. In natural law, violence is a "natural datum," while for positive law, violence is "a product of history" (1996, 237). Natural law "perceives in the use of violent means to just ends no greater problem than a man sees in his 'right' to move his body in the direction of a desired goal" (1996, 236). It is therefore conceptually tied to the "physicality" of human life and to the action it enables; in this way it expresses the phenomenality of violence. In natural law, humans regard it as their natural right to impose directions towards perceived goals. Justness resides in the goal, and the means attribute their justness to these just ends and thus criticize existing laws by questioning the justness of the ends they pursue (1996, 237). Positive law, by contrast, judges the existing law by criticizing its means because it intends to "guarantee" the just ends by the justness of the means (1996, 237). Benjamin observes that "if positive law is blind to the absoluteness of ends, natural law is equally so to the contingency of means" (1996, 237). Here he probes the logic of this opposition: "The question would remain open whether violence, as a principle, could be a moral means even to just ends" (1996, 236). At issue is not just the instrumentality of violence but also *its relation to the goals that justify it.*

This raises the matter of sanctioned and unsanctioned forces (1996, 237) or legitimate and illegitimate violence. Key here is Weber's definition of the state as claiming "*monopoly of the legitimate use of physical force* within a given territory" (1946, 78; emphasis in original). We are confronted by the question of legitimation, a question that rises above the principles of both natural law and positive law: "If the criterion established by positive law to assess the legality of violence can be analyzed with regard to its meaning, then the sphere of its application must be criticized with regard to its value. For this critique a standpoint outside positive legal philosophy but also outside natural law must be found" (1996, 238). Stated differently, any critique levelled against the legality of violence must be *metatheoretical*, launched from outside of both natural and positive laws. It follows that such critique requires us to abandon the "transcendental" justifications for the use of *Gewalt* within the law. The law's monopoly over *Gewalt* is intended to prohibit the individual use of force/violence at all costs. When confronting violence outside of itself, the law reveals that its intention is not to "preserv[e] legal ends" – that is, protect legal rights – but rather to "preserv[e] the law itself" (1996, 239). In other words, far beyond justifications flowing from natural law or positive law, the law's use of *Gewalt* is self-serving – or more precisely, self-*pre*serving. Violence, "when not in the hands of the law, threatens it [the law] not by the ends that it [extralegal violence] may pursue but by its mere existence outside the law" (1996, 239). By virtue of its foundation, "modern law [intends] to divest the individual, at least as a legal subject, of all violence" (1996, 241). The law must be preserved by eliminating all violence outside of the law. This is the source of the law's appeal to *Gewalt*: to eliminate all violence outside of the law, the law must apply force/violence of its own.

Benjamin calls the latter type of violence "law-preserving," evidenced through administrative violence (1996, 252). He also identifies the "law-making" violence that precedes law-preserving violence (1996, 240), pointing out that in parliamentarism, "legal decrees" have their origins in violence (1996, 244). Now if violence is merely a means to particular ends – Benjamin's example being the "primordial" and "predatory violence" of military law (1996, 240) – then all such violence *potentially* contains a lawmaking character (1996, 240): "All violence as a means is either lawmaking or law-preserving. If it lays claim to neither of these predicates, it forfeits all validity" (1996, 243). Thus, all laws oscillate between lawmaking and law-preserving violence. It is interesting here that police forces function in the middle ground between lawmaking and law-preserving violence. Indeed, there is something peculiar about police violence, in that police use force "for security reasons" (1996, 243) where no "legal" situation exists.

As such, lawmaking violence "is foundational; it is the performative violence of a new constitution or a declaration of independence. The violence here is that of inauguration, of the law's original setting-into-force. It is the violence of self-positing, the violence of an emergence *ex nihilo* of a legal/social/political system" (Abbott 2008, 82). We can see how Benjamin's concept of lawmaking violence can converge with the phenomenological concept of violence as maximization. Naturally, we cannot reconstruct Benjamin as a phenomenological precursor in relation to violence, given that the originative moment from which lawmaking violence arises remains obscure in Benjamin; even his concept of "divine violence" does not locate the source of violence in the maximized phenomenalization of an otherwise humble *arché*, in natality. Rather, he attributes the moment to God (thus mystifying that moment; see below). Thus, there is no phenomenological conceptual stepping back in Benjamin. Nevertheless, I argue, Benjamin is looking in the right direction. He points out that the law can never abandon its originative moment; it is always already bound by it, and during crises of legitimation, it has no recourse except to it foundation. This point is best exemplified by the way in which the autocratic leaders of post-revolutionary states glorify their revolution over and over in order to reinforce their legitimacy. This happens (and sometimes succeeds!) because of the twofold function of lawmaking: first, "lawmaking pursues as its end, with violence as the means, *what* is to be established as law"; and second, "at this very moment of lawmaking, it specifically establishes as law not an end unalloyed by violence but one necessarily and intimately bound to it" (Benjamin 1996, 248). This is how by virtue of its origins all law is always already permeated by violence. As can be expected, lawmaking violence generates power (1996, 249). What is important, however, is "that all law-preserving violence, in its duration, indirectly weakens the lawmaking violence it presents, by suppressing hostile counterviolence" (1996, 251). In its frequent references to lawmaking violence, law-preserving violence only brings about the former's gradual ruin. The more that law-preserving violence calls upon lawmaking violence to legitimize itself, the more the lawmaking moment runs out of steam, is emptied of its content, and becomes a caricature. What remains is a situation reminiscent of Agamben's "state of exception" (see below).

Obviously, in locating Benjamin's concept of violence within my interpretive genealogy I am pursuing specific interests. So before turning to Benjamin's famous distinction between mythic and divine violence, I need to substantiate his indebtedness to Sorel. Benjamin's interest in him rests precisely in the way in which Sorel conceptualizes violence (and thus Benjamin and I run parallel interests!). Benjamin asks whether nonviolence is possible at all. He answers in the affirmative – it is possible by way of conferences and civil agreements (1996, 244). Note that he confirms the *possibility* of nonviolence only in the context of conflict (as foundational) specifically "relating to goods" (1996, 244). He notes that "there is a sphere of human agreement that is nonviolent to the extent that it is wholly inaccessible to violence" (1996, 245). Inaccessible? What is the condition for that? It is refraining from punishment even upon one party's lying, Benjamin asserts. "For in it not only is nonviolent agreement possible, but also the exclusion of violence in principle is quite explicitly demonstrable by one significant factor: there is no sanction for lying" (1996, 244). This is when human conflict is resolved outside of the sphere of violent action even though there may be potential for the disputing parties to manipulate the outcome. This constitutes *inaccessibility* to violence. Understanding *Gewalt* is key here: no *force* makes the lying party not lie, and the cost of lying is not *violence.* Such a possibility of nonviolent conflict sets up Benjamin's approach to the "general strike" as a nonviolent choice instead of sabotage: "it is the fear of mutual disadvantages that threaten to arise from violent confrontation" (1996, 245).

In discussing the difference between the general strike and the strike (1996, 246), Benjamin draws on the state's monopoly of violence in the form of the law, in that "the violence that present-day law is seeking in all areas of activity to deny the individual appears really threatening, and arouses even in defeat the sympathy of the masses against the law" (1996, 239). But the law legitimizes itself (and, I add, conceals its violent nature) based on the threat of violence that lies outside the law. Irving Wohlfarth's interpretive elaboration of this aspect of the law (Wohlfarth

2009a; 2009b), and that which the law establishes as its "outside" (the "anarchy" that the law must repress in order to remain the law), pointedly describes this curious situation. I quote him at length:

> "Order" creates its own anarchy; anarchy liberates its own order. Haunted by a prospect that once constituted its own programme, the bourgeois order conjures up the age-old specter of Anarchy, the better to ward off its double – the spectre of a truly anarchic, finally viable management of human affairs. In short, the forces of Reaction choose to misunderstand what they understand all too well. They pass off the danger to their existence as one to civilization in general and conflate the promise of a revolutionary leap *beyond* the law with the threat of an inevitable relapse into what allegedly reigned *before* it. Such wilful misunderstanding of what anarchism is, or could be, belongs to the system of defences with which any ruling order protects and justifies its existence. (Wohlfarth 2009a, 14; emphasis in original)

It is necessary for the law to conflate liberation (which in my formulation involves structural transformation in reaction to, but also involving, deworlding/reworlding) with the constructed chaos out of which the law claims to have first arisen and with the perceived chaos against which the law must (re)assert itself, whatever the cost, by appealing to the state of exception. The law, in other words, must repress all violence outside the law (Agamben 2005, 53).

The strike has an interesting place in this relation. The "workers' guaranteed right to strike" (Benjamin 1996, 239) represents a legal accommodation of the strike by the state as a means to avoid "violence." Benjamin clearly understands Sorel's position that in the context of class struggle the strike is not an end in itself; Benjamin views the strike as "[a] form of extortion" (in that it forces the employer to meet the workers' demands) (1996, 239). "Understood in this way, the right to strike constitutes in the view of labor, which is opposed to the state, the *right to use force in attaining certain ends*" (1996, 239; emphasis added). Does this right of workers to use collective force against an employer – a right recognized by the state – guarantee nonviolence during a strike? The use of force – "extortion" – surely qualifies as violence, yet "[a]gainst this view there is certainly the objection that an omission of actions, a nonaction, which a strike really is, cannot be described as violence" (1996, 239). Recall Arendt's characterization of Sorel's "general strike" (as proletarian violence) as nonviolent. A strike, we know, cannot be deemed a non-action, for it indicates a regulation of otherwise "anarchistic" action by the state. Even so, the point is once again well taken: a *radical undecidability* permeates strike action. It remains (non)violent.

Turning to Benjamin's characterization of the general strike, we note interesting complications. He holds that a strike is anarchistic whereas "the general strike" has a "lawmaking" character (1996, 246) that qualifies it as violent. This position is obviously in alignment with Sorel's revolutionary general strike, which transcends the legal "right to strike" as it prepares the workers' consciousness for the forthcoming transformative politics – a (positive) right beyond all legal rights. In fact, my case study (Vahabzadeh 2015) shows that revolutionary action always inevitably invokes this "supreme right," which annuls the state-sanctioned rights (tied to citizenship) precisely because the right to transformative action throws privileged institutions (the state) out of their seat. Therefore, the lawmaking character of the general strike is innate to social refoundation – an idea that confirms my hypothesis of ontological primacy of violence, and thus violence's institutive character. Yet the general strike remains a nonviolent method.

Here is where, in thinking violence further, Benjamin introduces the distinction between "mythic violence" and "divine violence." Mythic violence is identical to lawmaking violence. Divine violence, by contrast, represents the moment of *coup de grâce*. "Just as in all spheres God opposes myth, mythic violence is confronted by the divine. And the latter constitutes its antithesis in all respects. If mythic violence is lawmaking, divine violence is law-destroying" (Benjamin 1996, 249). Divine violence annuls the "dialectics" of lawmaking and law-preserving violence (Agamben 2005, 53). The Sorelian general strike, then, falls within this law-destroying divine violence. Interestingly, Jacques Derrida interprets mythic violence as Greek and divine violence as Jewish (Derrida 1992, 31) and thus messianic. This is important, because divine violence constitutes a "pure violence" (*reine Gewalt*) in that it takes place outside of the law (Agamben 2005, 61). Divine violence represents the messianic moment when the destruction of the status quo becomes possible, a moment reminiscent of the Sorelian "general strike" – epoch-making and "pure means" (Wohlfarth 2008, 11) – when through the abolition of the law – and its source, the state – a new epoch may be founded (Benjamin 1996, 252).

Here a clarification is in order: that messianism permeates the thought of Benjamin or Derrida regarding the future is certainly attributable to their "Jewish" thinking, but it is not reducible to it. So it is absurd to claim, like Christopher Wise, that Derrida's "messianic structure" – essentialized (by Wise) as strictly Jewish – constitutes "the cultural hegemony of a historically specific universalism" against Christian and Muslim thought (Wise 2009, 65, 39). It is not the reduction of Islamic or Christian messianisms to that of Judaism (2009, 66) that is at issue. Messianism lies on the horizon of anticipating – an open horizon indeed in that with every step taken by the future-oriented itinerant, the horizon moves farther away – indeed a "receding signified" (Vahabzadeh 2003, 93). Messianicity – distinguished from religious messianisms – is therefore enabled by our inescapable *epistemological obscurity* as regards the future. For us, the relentless campaigners for a new world to take the place of the disastrous one we have inherited, the waiting game constitutes the universal messianic *structure*, not any religious figuration. This temporality – with its expansions and constrictions – describes our ontological constitution.

Let me digress somewhat and note here that the abolition of the law – to be exact, of mythic violence, which the law embodies – can be expected to take the form of revolutionary catharsis, the purging of the old by the new through revolutionary agency. Yet one can also identify Weber's (1946) charismatic authority – as opposed to traditional authority (the "eternal yesterday") and rational-legal authority – as a manifestation of pure violence in that the "gift of grace" (or, with a slight slippage, embodied messianism, to foreground Benjamin's argument) of the charismatic leader enables – indeed requires – the suspension of the law. The two cases (revolutionary agency and charismatic leadership) seem to diverge, but they have a common denominator, that is, the *social element* – the presence of a privileged agent (class or charismatic authority) to mobilize and lead the masses. This is how Antonio Gramsci connected the two in his thinking in terms of "hegemony" as "intellectual and moral leadership" (1971, 57), and this is how he came to perceive the Communist Party as the "Modern Prince" when reflecting in prison on the rise of Italian fascism following the Red Years (1919–1920) in northern Italy. Weber and Gramsci, I argue, show that this "pure violence" is a political moment, one that involves mobilization, organization, and commitment, despite or perhaps *because of* the messianic aura of the concept. Clearly, such "rationalization" of divine violence is incompatible with the Talmudic tendency in Benjamin's thinking, but my argument here is that pure violence can yield to such "rationalization" (or proceduralization) beyond the established reason of the law.

In one of his more cryptic observations, Benjamin writes: "Mythic violence is bloody power over mere life for its own sake; divine violence is pure power over all life for the sake of the living. The first demands sacrifice; the second accepts it" (1996, 250). For us, the keywords are "for the sake of the living," the conditions resulting from divine violence, in which the "force of law" (of law-preserving violence) is subdued to that which upholds the life of the living: justice. Mythic violence exercises force upon life (the individual) in order to preserve power, and it is only thus sustainable; while divine violence, though still accepting this sacrifice, subverts the power for the sake of the living's transformative life-activity. Wohlfarth specifies that mythic violence remains unredeemed whereas divine violence is redemptive (2009a, 21). Divine violence accepts mythic violence and its sacrifices by incorporating, cancelling, and transcending it (in the dialectical sense of *aufheben*), because divine violence enables the oppressed to finally own their history. Divine violence therefore arises in every genuine revolutionary change. Phenomenologically, *transformative* violence – inevitable as deworlding/reworlding restructures the world of the living and things alike – cannot be epistemologically perceived through long-held notions of violence associated with hitherto institutional, maximizing, or hubristic modes of violence. It is "a violence to end all violence" (Wohlfarth 2009a, 23). Wohlfarth recognizes that revolutionary violence does not grant lethal power over others (2009a, 21), for it is "violence against things" and not "violence against human beings" (Wohlfarth 2008, 12). As a messianic moment, therefore, divine violence involves *a certain, partial* erasure of memory, a suspension of knowledge. It captures, in other words, the phenomenological moment.

Messianism, Benjamin's signature concept in formulating revolutionary transformation, both unsettles and reaffirms that transformation. His concept is undoubtedly anarchistic, which is the underlying reason for his attempt to reconcile Marx's historical materialism with his own Talmudic–messianic view of the potentially imminent epoch-making transformation. Or, as Wohlfarth states it, Benjamin forges coherence between the anarcho-theological critique and historico-material "theses" in his approach to violence (2009a, 18). Benjamin pursues this theme in "Theses on the Philosophy of History" (1940). In a way reminiscent of Sorel's dismissal of parliamentary socialists who "fake" working-class agency by depriving it of its ontologically bestowed class action (the general strike), Benjamin elucidates the process whereby revolutionary action is domesticated and thus wiped out of memory. This is achieved by stripping liberatory action from the revolutionary agent:

> Not man or men but the struggling, oppressed class itself is the depository of historical knowledge. In Marx it appears as the last enslaved class, as the avenger that completes the task of liberation in the name of generations of the downtrodden. This conviction, which had a brief resurgence in the Spartacist group, has always been objectionable to Social Democrats. Within three decades they managed virtually to erase the name of Blanqui, though it had been the rallying sound that had reverberated through the preceding century. Social Democracy thought fit to assign to the working class the role of the redeemer of future generations, in this way cutting the sinews of its greatest strength. This training made the working class forget both its hatred and its spirit of sacrifice, for both are nourished by the image of enslaved ancestors rather than that of liberated grandchildren. (Benjamin 1968, 260)

The Social Democrats made compromises with the status quo in the name of the oppressed, thereby maintaining law-preserving violence over the oppressed, and their compromise therefore qualified as a form of violence (Wohlfarth 2009a, 19). This is how in the hands of the parliamentary socialists the "poetry of the future" (Marx) was wrested from the proletariat. This poetry can, of course, be brought back through liberation. It is through liberation that history is owned by the oppressed, since "only a redeemed mankind receives the fullness of its past – which is to say, only for a redeemed mankind has its past become citable in all its moments" (Benjamin 1968, 254). The Social Democrats therefore remain trapped in history. The historical materialist, by contrast, "recognizes the sign of a Messianic cessation of happening ... a revolutionary chance in the fight for the oppressed past," Benjamin adds (1968, 263). Recognition of this moment, an outcome of our method, involves blasting "a specific era out of the homogeneous course of history – blasting a specific life out of the era or a specific work out of the lifework. As a result of this method the lifework is preserved in this work and at the same time canceled [Hegel's *aufheben*: to cancel, to elevate, and to preserve]; in the lifework, the era; and in the era, the entire course of history" (1968, 263).

This brings us to the concept of liberation. For Benjamin, "our image of happiness is indissolubly bound up with the image of redemption. The same applies to our view of the past, which is the concern of history. The past carries with it a temporal index by which it is referred to redemption" (1968, 254). Liberation – redemption – is subject not to the progressive determinism of Marxian–Enlightenment historical materialism but to the messianic time, which "comprises the entire history of mankind in an enormous abridgment, coincides exactly with the stature which the history of mankind has in the universe" (1968, 263). For the messianic time is characterized by its openness to the moment of redemption: "For every second of time was the strait gate through which the Messiah might enter" (1968, 264). Liberation involves a "*weak* Messianic power, a power to which the past has a claim. That claim cannot be settled cheaply. Historical materialists are aware of that" (1968, 254; emphasis in original). Class struggle is not over the spoils of the capitalist production; it is about taking ownership of history, since only redeemed humanity can own a conclusive history. In fact, only the humanity that has taken possession of its past can be truly liberated from forces of history imposed upon humanity. "The Messiah comes not only as the redeemer," avers Benjamin, "he comes as the subduer of Antichrist" (1968, 255). The Messiah resets history by *slightly changing its tune,* and *the world re-emerges as new.* The Messiah will enter through the gate we cannot identify in advance, due to our inescapable epistemological blindness to the future. Experiencing this unique deworlding/reworlding moment, we emerge as new. All violence is now suspended.

Yet this is the moment of "pure" violence that ends all violence: the violence of structural–systemic transformation (deworlding/reworlding). Wohlfarth's eloquent words capture this moment: "'Pure' violence, which coincides with pure non-violence, is... to end the reign of 'mythic' violence and 'depose' (*entsetzen*) the state. Its highest political expression in present-day Europe is the general strike – not of the 'political' type calculated to extort improved conditions, but the 'proletarian' one directed at the 'annihilation of state violence'" (Wohlfarth 2009a, 16).

Regarding my central question, we have Benjamin's case in which the pure violence of redemptive history – class struggle of the oppressed – reveals itself in a naked fashion. We know that Benjamin rejected the opposition of violence to nonviolence (Wohlfarth 2009a, 20). The Messiah appears, with the "pure" violence of redemption, in nonviolence. In his reflections on Kafka and with reference to the folk song "The Little Hunchback," Benjamin indicates the nature of Messiah's coming: "This little man [the hunchback] is at home in distorted life; he will disappear with the coming of the Messiah, of whom a great rabbi once said that *he did not wish to change the world by force, but would only make a slight adjust-ment in it*" (Benjamin 1968, 134; emphasis added). Liberation's violence (*Gewalt*), in other words, is achieved through the "'most unobtrusive' of changes" (Wohlfarth 2009a, 15), certainly without force (*Gewalt*). The magic of the transformative nonviolence of otherwise violent liberation rests in that – as a messianic movement – it enables *justice* by removing impositions and *letting things rephenomenalize authentically*. If changing the world – which qualifies as the most violent of all transformations due to deworlding/reworlding – cannot be achieved through force, if it cannot force itself, then it can only appear through adjustments, without maxi-mization, uninstitutionalized, and in a non-hubristic way, through the gentle, natal power of (emancipated) life itself.

The conclusion is inevitable: for Benjamin, *the most violent form of epoch-making historical transformation* – in that it represents "pure" violence – *is thus nonviolent*, as the liberation of humanity, in the messianic moment, is achieved through slight (law-destroying) adjustments outside of the sphere of force (*Gewalt*). The emancipatory, violent overthrow of the status quo thus falls outside our tripartite categories of violence. Messi-anic action nullifies bifurcated categorical conceptualizations and proves itself to be (non)violent. *The supposed opposition of violence and nonviolence is thereby suspended* as the new is born, and with its birth our memories of violence are "erased." In this "phenomenological" moment of history, when the opposition of violence and nonviolence reveals itself as the fictitious construct of the powerful and the moralists alike, and when such opposition is inexorably suspended, even rendered futile and inept, liberated humanity comes to own its past through the action of the oppressed.

Derrida's Interjection

I have already raised the inescapable epistemological dilemma we encounter when facing an impending moment of epochal transforma-tion – that which appears to us, at least at the outset, within the horizon of liberation or emancipation. Because it pertains to *acting* at the (per-ceived) messianic *moment*, this dilemma is as abstract-conceptual as it is concrete-historical. How do we know, here and now, that the revolution-ary movement in which we take part is *the* revolutionary movement that will give birth, in the not-yet, to the *genuinely new*? And how do we know the historical moment is right? When these questions are raised in rela-tion to Benjamin's critique of violence, they pose demanding conceptual challenges: divine violence (an act of God) appears to us at the messianic moment, to which we (finite, mortal beings) should (re)orient our action, but if this is a pure and divine moment, then how do we know this is *the* transformative moment, the violence that ends all violence? *Emancipatory action appears in abyssal acting, groundless and an-archic, a leap of faith indeed, bereft of any hint of epistemological and historical assurances.* We have no means by which we can measure the outcome of our transformative action. The poetry of the future, to paraphrase Marx, cannot extract principles of knowledge from the past.

In his extensive analysis of the Red Army Faction (RAF) in the Federal Republic of Germany in the 1970s and RAF's invocation of Benjamin's critique of violence as one of its theoretical pillars for political violence (Veron 2004), Wohlfarth poses this epistemological dilemma accordingly:

> If men cannot know when "pure" violence has taken place, it follows that they cannot appeal to it to justify their actions. It is, on the other hand, difficult to avoid the conclusion that the violence championed by the RAF was and is "recognizable with certainty" as being not of the "expiatory" but of the "guilt-incurring' (*verschuldende*) kind which, far from breaking the ancient mythic cycle, perpetuates it. How to break this *Schuldzusammenhang* [context of guilt; by implication the RAF generation's "burden of guilt" inherited from their parents involvement with, or silence under, the Nazis] through a *pure violence that,* as Benjamin variously presents it, *is as powerful as it is powerless* [as we saw above]: this is the enigma with which the "Critique of Violence" leaves us. (Wohlfarth 2008, 12; emphasis added)

This dilemma, of course, is revealed in all genuinely transformative politics and is not exclusive to Benjamin's work. In this dilemma *at least* two major categorical responses are to be identified. One response – not aimed at Benjamin but certainly addressing our issue here – is that of Gandhi, for whom nonviolent action is a response to this epistemological shortcoming. Because of our epistemological blindness to the consequences of our actions, Gandhi precludes all actions categorically deemed as violent. Instead he relies on the existing and available categories (some of which are obviously experienced and regarded as violent universally, while others remain to be seen due to the Protean nature of violence) to exclude all actions that may lead to violence. Gandhi's approach can perhaps be called "un-phenomenological" in that it retains and reaffirms the knowledge of the past beyond the transition into the new. We will return to this discussion in chapter 8. The other response is exemplified by Derrida's interpretation of Benjamin's critique of violence, to which I attend now.

Derrida holds that the distinction between pure and impure violence can be drawn only by God, not by us; thus he invokes divine violence with reference to the Final Solution, this "extreme consequence of a logic of Nazism" (Derrida 1992, 58). Derrida's interpretation of Benjamin's critique of violence – through which Derrida declares justice to be unde-constructible – leads to a controversial and "disturbing" (Bernstein 2013, 66) "*Post-scriptum.*" Theoretically, Derrida meditates on the "possible complicity between all these discourses and the worst (here the final solu-tion)" (Derrida 1992, 63). He begins with a proviso: "I will not ask myself what Benjamin himself thought of Nazism and antisemitism" (1992, 58). In the background of Derrida's argument rests the conceptual problem I evoke in this book: "But it is, in *droit*, what suspends *droit*. It interrupts the established *droit* to found another. This moment of suspense, this *épokhè*, this founding or revolutionary moment of law is, in law, an instance of non-law" (1992, 36). From one phenomenal arrangement we slip into another, from one law (oppressive) into another (emancipatory/anarchic), and we transition through *non-law*. From a Derridean perspective, the law imposes violence as "arché-writing." In the absence of law there arises the moment of divine violence: the source of such extralegal violence is God (Wohlfarth 2009a, 20). Walking above the abyss to get from one side to another: Is this not, as I called it, a leap of faith?

Derrida interprets the Nazis' Final Solution through Benjamin. That such an interpretive decision on Derrida's part remains a *choice* should be obvious (that is why it shocked unsuspecting scholars). His decision to do so, therefore, remains *contingent*, and this lack of essential or necessary links between the concept and the case is precisely why his interjection should be taken seriously. Derrida was attacked, among other things, for mixing up historic and intellectual contexts (Bernstein 2013, 71). We do know that Benjamin's is a theory of revolutionary (proletarian) action situated, theoretically, somewhere between Marxian historical-materialism and Talmudic messianism. Yet Derrida's intervention is far from arbitrary.

Derrida questions whether mythic and divine violence should be con-trasted. He is drawn to and guided by the conditional clause in Benja-min when he writes: "But if the existence of violence outside the law, as pure immediate violence, is assured, this furnishes proof that revolution-ary violence, the highest manifestation of unalloyed violence by man, is possible, and shows by what means" (Benjamin 1996, 252; see Derrida 1992, 55; see also Bernstein 2013, 67). Benjamin "speaks in the conditional about revolutionary violence (*revolutionäre Gewalt*): 'if,' beyond *droit,* violence sees its status insured as pure and immediate violence, then this will prove that revolutionary violence is possible … But why is this statement in the conditional?" (Derrida 1992, 55). The conditional clause, the conditionality of this knowledge, for Derrida, pertains to the decision (*Entscheidung*): "the one that permits us to know or to recognize such a pure and revolutionary violence *as such,* is a *decision not accessible to man*" (1992, 55; emphasis in original). In other words, the "distinction between the *Gewalt* [force] of 'pure' actualization and the *Gewaltsamkeit* [violence] of 'impure' galvanization is intuitively compelling and theoretically indispensible. But who, short of God, is unfailingly competent to make it?" (Wohlfarth 2009a, 19). So the distinction between mythic and divine violence is permeated with a *radical undecidability*. This, Derrida writes, is how, through the Final Solution, "Nazism, as the final achievement of the logic of mythological violence" (Derrida 1992, 59), reached its limits: "Not only because there was a destruction … but also because the system of mythical violence (objectivist, representational, communicational, etc.) went all the way to its limit, in a demonic fashion, on the two sides of the limit" (1992, 60). The limit indicates that the decision where to mark off mythic from divine violence is not made by humans. As such, I think Derrida actually *confirms* the Talmudic-messianic (divine) aspect of Benjamin's thought over the Greco-rational (mythic) one. But we can achieve this confirmation only by collapsing the apparent binarism between divine and mythic violence, since divine violence cannot be submitted to rationalist-positivist benchmarks against which mythic violence is identified, surveyed, affirmed, and upheld. In this *undecidability,* there dwells evil

> from the fact that one could not distinguish between founding violence and conserving violence … On the contrary, as soon as one leaves this order, history begins – and the violence of divine justice – but here we humans cannot measure judgments, which is to say also decidable interpretations. This also means that the interpretation of the final solution, as of everything that constitutes the set and the delimitation of the two orders (the mythological and the divine) is not in the measure of man. (1992, 61)

Derrida's turn in interpreting Benjamin's polysemic and perplexing terms is a choice, as I said earlier, but one that is not taken arbitrarily or lightly. Derrida knows too well that one "is terrified at the idea of an interpretation that would make of the holocaust an expiation and an indecipherable signature of the just and violent anger of God" (1992, 62). That the Final Solution rendered a form of sheer violence that was "nihilating, expiatory and bloodless" (referencing Benjamin, Derrida invokes the gas chamber as "bloodless"), and that it bore the very characteristics of a "divine violence that would destroy current law through a bloodless process that strikes and causes to expiate" (1992, 62) raise serious concerns.

In taking this controversial position, Derrida is guided by the logic of *différance* (1992, 47, 63), that is, the difference that is always already deferred. This logic, *différance*, wrecks the hopes of positivist revolutionaries who seek decidable and predetermined distinctions, to use contrasting jargon between revolutionary and reactionary violence or between the violence that ends all violence and that which perpetuates it, possibly in new forms. This position harks back to my phenomenological probing of the "epistemological" issue pertaining to future-oriented human action (such as the general strike). Derrida is right to deny positivist readings of Benjamin. Even so, divine violence holds something in its core that conceptually eludes its total degeneration into mythic violence. It is called *justice*: that which in a Benjaminian vein *cannot be achieved through terror* (Wohlfarth 2009a, 18). Moreover, Wohlfarth maintains, "Benjamin claims that while 'justice' (*Gerechtigkeit*), in contrast to 'right' or 'law' (*Recht*), is 'generally valid,' it is not 'susceptible to generalization.' It can only be done to a specific 'situation,' never, as in the case of law, to a 'case' – unless each case be one unto itself" (Wohlfarth 2008, 8). This is how divine violence, for Benjamin, represents pure violence *for the sake of the living* (1996, 250). Since justice cannot be substitutable by the law, that which feigns to represent justice (Derrida 1992, 47; see also Vattimo 2004), the Final Solution, as the simultaneous law-destroying (literally: rights-destroying; the French word *droit* means both law and right) and law-preserving (its own peculiar foundation) violence, can *never* distinctly evoke, let alone represent, divine violence, in spite of the radical undecidability that permeates the distinction between mythic and divine violence. Past the moment of pure (non)violence – past the radical experience of deworlding/reworlding – it should not be possible to invoke mythic violence, since this messianic moment is permeated by the impulse of justice and since the categorical knowledge of that which constitutes violence is suspended. Phenomenologically, *divine violence can lead back to mythic violence* – note my expression's reversal, enabled by historical materialism – *only through the corruption of the sign* (Derrida recognized this) *in which only simulacra of justice remain to guide action.* This is when the reactionary Final Solution is mobilized as revolutionary insofar as the system of signs is constantly fed through Nazi propaganda by their renewed foraging for depleting substitutions. Derrida's undecidability, in other words, does not prevent action towards that "pure" moment of violence that ends all violence. Indeed, the awareness he gives us calls for acute attention to what action can yield. And what is the only measure of liberation or emancipation? Justice: situational and not "susceptible to generalization" (Wohlfarth 2008, 8), that which is achieved through *slight adjustments*, when the deworlded order can no longer be reproduced and humanity can no longer extract its poetry from the past.

Derrida's interjection gives us an important alertness: Derridean concepts of undecidability and *différance* rouse us to the question of the *reversibility* of revolutionary action – a question that is conceptually (and systematically) excluded from theories informed by historical materialism's (historical) progressivist–Enlightenment gestures (Sorel, Benjamin, revolutionary Marxism; with the exception of Gramsci). Ironically, this exclusion is a consequence of the messianic aspect of liberatory action, since the Messiah's coming cannot be undone! Partaking in this pure, revolutionary moment, as I have maintained, requires a leap of faith, due to our inevitable epistemological lag. But this reversibility does not just concern historical progress. Incidentally (or perhaps not incidentally!), my detour into Derridean intervention, which does not quite follow the logic of this chapter, has revealed two important points. The first is the *reversibility* of the transition from nonviolence of messianic, liberatory action to rampant violence and unimaginable evil. To complicate the issue using Derridean terms, just as the distinction between violence and nonviolence – at the seminal, epoch-making moments in history (the thesis advanced through my readings of Sorel and Benjamin) – is informed by *différance* as ontologically deferred difference, so is the *passage* from violent-institutional phenomenal arrangements to nonviolent rephenomenalization informed by justice. Once again, we can see that violence and nonviolence arise from action: in the case of the aforementioned double-reversibility, we can see how action can liberate itself from institutional and hubristic frames; or in the process of liberating itself, action can fall back into the very frames it claims to dismantle. Second and in light of the problem of reversibility, Derrida calls our attention to the issue of *responsibility* – that without our vigilance we cannot ensure the passage from violence to nonviolence. We partake in emancipatory action in order to remain authentic to ourselves, to live in dignity, and to acquire justice in the face of widespread tripartite violence (fantasmic maximization and denial of singularities, hubris, and institutional violence) to which we are subjected. So in every act of liberation we risk the reversibility of divine violence (messianic nonviolence) for the sake of living into mythic violence that demands sacrifice. Reversibility calls for responsibility, for constantly challenging the rampant "thoughtlessness" (Arendt) of partaking in existing violent structures and procedures. Or as Schürmann averred in a related context, what can lead to a collective destiny free of metaphysical, normative violence is "the thoughtfulness of present and future actors. Any other reference game would constitute pure speculation, pure dogmatic construction" (Schürmann 1990, 208). These conceptual predicaments will be resolved once we stop perceiving of violence and nonviolence as opposites. That project will be undertaken in this book's concluding chapter.

In our common experience, we have seen the staggering human and non-human cost of mistaking, misunderstanding, and/or distorting mythic and divine violence. We have seen it in the French Revolution, in Russian and Chinese revolutions, and in the Cambodian resetting of history. Slavoj Žižek points out, with reference to Stalinist Russia and Nazi Germany, that these regimes degenerated into Gulag and Auschwitz when the movements they arose from were not pushed to their radical potentials – the creation of a new humanity (Žižek 2008, 195). (What the Nazi "new humanity" would have looked like remains disturbing!) It is not simply the failure to radicalize that which leads to degeneration and ensuing atrocities: the failure arises from resorting to some "natural law" or "law of history" as the substitute for justice. Faced with this human condition, this epistemological risk, which has shown itself time and again in the horrendous consequences of our leaps of faith, we can either resign to the security of the existing technological-liberal order, with its systemic–institutional violence, or continue searching. That which we collectively choose will decide our common future.

Derrida shows the dilemma of liberation in a conceptual way. Two decades or so before his engagement, though, a psychiatrist and theoretician from the Caribbean island of Martinique had anticipated this radical undecidability and pondered the possibility that revolutionary action is *reversible*. That is why, to get the full picture of liberation, we need to turn to Frantz Fanon, who joined the war of liberation in Algeria, Derrida's birthplace.

4

On Liberation's Magical Moment

Yes we are professionals. But our profession is hope. We decided one good day to become soldiers so that a day would come when there would be no need for soldiers.

...

P.S.: Here we live worse than dogs. We had to choose: to live like animals or to die like dignified men. Dignity ... is the only thing that must never be lost ... ever.

Subcomandante Marcos,
Shadows of Tender Fury (1995, 167, 169)

The era after the Second World War saw the rise of national liberation movements in Africa, Asia, and Latin America that gave the question of liberation new magnitude. These simultaneously pan-continental and nationalist movements, unlike the previous emancipatory movements of the working class, did not claim any historically privileged agency. It was with these movements' decolonization that national liberation led to the birth of a new nation. Or so it seemed.

Fanon and the African Liberation

Frantz Fanon (1925–1961) offers a rare glimpse into the Algerian war of liberation, and not simply as what it actually was – a protracted civil war that resulted in unimaginable atrocities: confirmed casualties of over 250,000 (roughly 90 per cent of them Algerians); estimated war casualties as high as 2 million. Fanon was intent on showing what a war of liberation could bring about – that is, a new world – notwithstanding its enormous human cost, or perhaps precisely because of that cost.

Fanon's arguments – which would later inspire postcolonial studies – were complex and at times ambivalent; he continuously situated his treatises between the concrete-historical and the abstract-conceptual. As is well-known, Fanon did more than theorize the Algerian liberation; he was also a high-ranking activist with the FLN (Front de Libération Nationale). We will see that there is a certain "family resemblance" between Sorel's proletarian emancipation and Fanon's anticolonial war of liberation. The European "general strike" aligned roughly with the liberation of Africa: both provided the conditions for epistemological break. To grasp this, we need to unpack four pillars of Fanon's thought.

(a) *Africa is a European invention*. Colonialism was a historical process over the course of which the European powers occupied huge swathes of territories in Africa and Asia for the purpose of extracting the raw materials Europe needed in order to come out of its prolonged medieval stagnation, launch its rapid industrialization, and develop global markets for its goods. Fanon observes that through colonialism, Europe constructed its *absolute Other* – absolute in the sense that this Other was unassimilable and thus could only be the subject of domination. Through the process of colonization in Africa, black Africans were created and rendered "biological" beings (Fanon 1967, 161). A colonial Manichaeanism thus developed in which the colonized subject was "reduced to the state of an animal. And consequently, when the colonist speaks of the colonized he uses zoological terms" (Fanon 2004, 7). Colonized people were not simply dominated people: the colony was identified with nature and thus needed to be tamed:

> A hostile, ungovernable, and fundamentally rebellious Nature is in fact synonymous in the colonies with the bush, the mosquitoes, the natives, and disease. Colonization has succeeded once this untamed Nature has been brought under control. Cutting railroads through the bush, draining swamps, and ignoring the political and economic existence of the native population are in fact one and the same thing. (2004, 182)

As such, a mutual exclusivity defines the colonial reality. The colonist looks down with disgust on the colonized, while the colonized identifies the colonist in terms of domination, wealth, and colour – indeed, as the object of envy. "This compartmentalized world, this world divided in two, is inhabited by different species" (2004, 5). The colonial sector is "a sector of niggers, a sector of towelheads. The gaze that the colonized subject casts at the colonist's sector is a look of lust, a look of envy. Dreams of possession. Every type of possession: of sitting at the colonist's table and sleeping in his bed, preferably with his wife" (2004, 5). Under colonialism, one's humanity is determined by one's skin colour, and thus the African is robbed of humanity. "I begin to suffer from not being a white man to the degree that the white man imposes discrimination on me, makes me a colonized native, robs me of all worth, all individuality, tells me that I am a parasite on the world, that I must bring myself as quickly as possible into step with the white world" (Fanon 1967, 98). In search of his or her "humanity," the African tries to assimilate to European ways: "Then I will quite simply try to make myself white: that is, I will compel the white man to acknowledge that I am human" (1967, 98). But this effort only brings him face to face with the vicious cycle of blackness. The colonized black who wishes to assimilate to the white European reality cannot overcome colonial compartmentalization. To want to be white, as a black, is to further subjugate oneself (see 1967, 63). Thus, without "turning to the idea of collective catharsis, it would be easy for me to show that, without thinking, the Negro selects himself as an object capable of carrying the burden of original sin. The white man chooses the black man for this function, and the black man who is white also chooses the black man" (1967, 192). This relationship complicates Marxist class analysis of colonialism, for the extractive economics in play do not lend themselves to the colonial–racial context: "In the colonies the economic infrastructure is also a superstructure," and "the cause is effect: You are rich because you are white, you are white because you are rich. This is why a Marxist analysis should always be slightly stretched when it comes to addressing the colonial issue" (Fanon 2004, 5). This is how Africa, so rich in human diversity before colonial times, becomes a unified object of the colonizer's project – one continent – as a consequence of the Europeans' mindset of racial otherness: "For colonialism, this vast continent was a den of savages, infested with superstitions and fanaticism, destined to be despised, cursed by God, a land of cannibals, a land of 'niggers'" (2004, 150). Colonialism eradicates difference and robs the colonized of individual expression, for it lumps all Africans "together under the designation of 'Negro people'" (Fanon 1994, 17). Africa becomes a fixed object of otherness.

The impact of all this on the colonized is curious. The African is now "Negro," not black. The internalization of one's skin colour, which under colonialism condemned one within a system of distribution of cultural and material elements to an unchangeable, condescending position, constitutes the psyche of negritude. A psychiatrist, Fanon was especially interested in understanding the psychology of negritude. He found negritude's outcome pathological: "A normal Negro child, having grown up within a normal family, will become abnormal on the slightest contact with the white world" (Fanon 1967, 143). Colonialism obviously needs to restructure the fabric of the society it controls in order to bring it in tandem with the European Enlightenment project. Colonial efficiency depends on such restructuring, and sectors of the colonized therefore have to be repositioned through apparatuses of administration. Situated in this inescapable context, the colonized is reshaped into new functionaries of colonial institutions – modernized, Europeanized, and given the opportunity for upward mobility – even while the unalterable lines of segregation are maintained. "The singularity of the colonial context lies in the fact that economic reality, inequality, and enormous disparities in lifestyles never manage to mask the human reality. Looking at the immediacies of the colonial context, it is clear that what divides this world is first and foremost what species, what race one belongs to. In the colonies the economic infrastructure is also a superstructure" (Fanon 2004, 5). Among these newly created social groups were intellectuals, administrators, and workers. This point is important because it draws Fanon towards the question of *agency*.

Because of his function in the institutionalized colonial project, the Westernized intellectual of the colony suffers from the illusion of belonging to Europe. The European values advocated by the colonized academic are now deemed universal (2004, 11). This particular position in the colonial administration of the colonized assigns these intellectuals and functionaries the role of agent of conciliation between the two worlds. "The intellectual who, for his part, has adopted the abstract, universal values of the colonizer is prepared to fight so that colonist and colonized can live in peace in a new world" (2004, 9). At best and at moments of reflection, Fanon avers, the colonized intellectual romanticizes the past (2004, 148). The colonized working class, for Fanon, is not too far behind. Fanon deprives the colonial working class of the historic agency conceptualized by Marx. For him, the colonial proletariat is a privileged class (2004, 64). Fanon is also suspicious of labour unions since their mandate is to improve the conditions of labour under colonial rule and because they sound like metropolitan institutions (2004, 74). "The workers are in fact pampered by the regime. They represent the most well-to-do fraction of the people" (2004, 75). Likewise, the nationalist, reformist parties of the colonized are ineffectual in dealing with colonialism. They merely seek concessions. This means that the now popular argument (often used to promote unprincipled nonviolence) in favour of *inclusion in citizenship – and becoming rights-bearing subjects – do not equal emancipation.* Sovereign-granted rights-bearing subjectivity in fact impedes authenticating action.

So the searching for anti-colonial agency brings Fanon to the peasantry class. The peasants, for him, represents an authentic people. The nationalist parties pejoratively view the rural masses with suspicion as "being mired in inertia and sterility," but Fanon argues that "colonialism has often strengthened or established its domination by an organized petrification of the peasantry. Regimented by *marabouts* [North African Muslim hermits], witch doctors and traditional chiefs, the rural masses still live in a feudal state whose overbearingly medieval structure is nurtured by the colonial administrators and army" (2004, 65). For Fanon, on the contrary, "in colonial countries only the peasantry is revolutionary. It has nothing to lose and everything to gain. The underprivileged and starving peasant is the exploited who very soon discovers that only violence pays. For him there is no compromise, no possibility of concession" (2004, 23). For Fanon, it seems, the peasantry represents the least contaminated body of colonized people, a group of colonized almost untouched by colonialism, and this feature bestows upon them an authentic agency; it indeed transforms them into agents of rebellion. Interestingly, this "authentication" (which in my judgment represents Fanon's unjustified *essentializing* of a group) is concomitant with his rigid distinction between town and country: the first is the domain of colonial contamination, which destroys the potential agency of workers and intellectuals, while the second remains fairly untouched, preserving the seeds of authentic anti-colonial war. "This is not the traditional opposition between town and country," writes Fanon. "It is the opposition between the colonized excluded from the benefits of colonialism and their counterparts who manage to turn the colonial system to their advantage" (2004, 67). In this regard, he points out the crippling effects of migration from country to town:

> The peasants distrust the town dweller. Dressed like a European, speaking his language, working alongside him, sometimes living in his neighborhood, he is considered by the peasant to be a renegade who has given up everything which constitutes the national heritage. The town dweller is a "traitor, a mercenary" who apparently gets along very well with the occupier and strives to succeed in the context of the colonial system. (2004, 67)

In Fanon's thinking, then, agency is granted to the rural masses without history. The militants of the liberation war discovered in the petrified state of the rural masses "a generous people, prepared to make sacrifices, willing to give all they have, impatient, with an indestructible pride ... The men from the towns let themselves be guided by the people and at the same time give them military and political training ... The armed struggle is triggered" (2004, 79). So the peasants are not simply the agents of anti-colonial liberation; they are also catalysts of armed struggle. Fanon's claim here, while it is clearly based on his actual experiences in Algeria, remains theoretically essentialist. The peasants, in his thinking, remained unchanged in their revolutionary potential – a potential that, in his conceptual framework, other classes lacked. Therefore, he argues, the workers and their unions could only emerge as authentic by linking their efforts to the agency of the colonized peasants (2004, 76). Curiously, this represents authentication through contraction! A reversal of Marxism.

The colonial context, imposed on the African, needed a specific response. The colonized could not be indifferent to it. Africa had been changed by the colonial powers, which, from the comfort of their capitals, heralded the values of humanity and progress. "For centuries Europe has brought the progress of other men to a halt and enslaved them for its own purposes and glory," Fanon reflects on this double-faced enemy. And he demands: "Let us leave this Europe which never stops talking of man yet massacres him at every one of its street corners, at every corner of the world." The reality of the colonized dictates to them a different destiny: "The new day which is dawning must find us determined, enlightened and resolute" (2004, 235). So the war of liberation is an example of the Hegelian concept of struggle for recognition (Hegel 1977; Honneth 1996). "The struggle of the inferiorized is situated on a markedly more human level," writes Fanon. "The perspectives are radically new. The opposition is the henceforth classical one of the struggles of conquest and of liberation" (Fanon 1994, 43). Referring to Hegel's master–slave dialectics, Fanon asserts that the mutual recognition of the antagonists can only be achieved when one imposes his existence on another in order to be recognized. In the context of decolonization, it is the colonized (the slave) who demands recognition, and only a mutual recognition thus achieved can end the cycle of violence. The African is not free when *given* freedom (Fanon 1967, 216–17). The colonist's politics of recognition is therefore an extension of colonialism (Coulthard 2014). To become another Europe is no option for Africa, for Africa needs to be innovative in order to become the pioneer of humanity. "For Europe, for ourselves and for humanity, comrades, we must make a new start, develop a new way of thinking, and endeavor to create a new man" (Fanon 2004, 239). This is how the exploited colonized peoples embark on a historic and novel journey.

(b) *As praxis, liberatory violence marks the birth of a nation.* Fanon's concept of violence needs to be properly situated and grasped. For him, liberatory violence represents a particular praxis and a new modality of acting, one that is proper for the *imposed,* Manichaean reality of colonialism. This violence is neither voluntary nor arbitrary. Nor is it brutal or barbaric, and though it is imposed, it is *not* reactive (see below). It is a necessary response to the colonial violence, which being bereft of reason, it "is naked violence and only gives in when confronted with greater violence" (2004, 23). In Fanon's view, the *apolitical* violence of the colonist is met by the *political* counter-violence of liberation. Since the colonized has been reduced to the state of an animal, the colonizer's violence against Africans constitutes violence against nature and enjoys impunity. The anti-colonial praxis is necessary because through its inevitable violence it allows the suppressed humanity of the colonized to emerge. Liberation alone signifies the reassertion of one's humanity. Writes Fanon: "As soon as you and your fellow men are cut down like dogs there is no other solution but to use every means available to reestablish your weight as a human being. You must therefore weigh as heavily as possible on your torturer's body so that his wits, which have wandered off somewhere, can at last be restored to their human dimension" (2004, 221). In the colonial context, freedom cannot be achieved through the expansion of citizenship. Fanon explicitly positioned himself against France's extension of citizenship – and its concomitant rights – to Algeria; for him, citizenship without liberation was absurd (Fanon 1994, 158), for it impeded the colonized's emergence as a people. France's ploy involved citizenship without emancipation: legalized colonization. It prevented Algerians from acquiring national consciousness and collectively pondering their future as a postcolonial nation. Just as Sorel dismissed the socialists in parliament because they lacked emancipatory drive, so Fanon rejected the reformist nature of the nationalist parties within colonial Algeria. Those parties were substituting the authentic praxis of the colonized with a semblance of movement and thus in effect demobilizing Algerian liberation (Fanon 1991, 100). Reformism did, however, prove that liberation was a necessity. "For a long time," Fanon argued, "political action in a colonized country is a legal action that is carried on within the parliamentary framework. After a certain period, when official and peaceful channels are exhausted, the militant hardens his position" (1991, 101). Freedom needs to be fought for, and "rights are *taken*, not given away" (*haqq gereftanist, na dadani*), as we say in Persian, evidencing a radical distrust of the self-appointed grantors of rights. The slave who has been freed by the master is not free; he is assimilated (Fanon 1967, 219), and the assimilated colonized will be incapable of emerging as free and self-conscious. In more recent times, the two Palestinian uprisings known as *intifada* (1988–93 and 2000–5), against Israeli occupation represent the liberatory movement of the colonized and their resistance against assimilation. The *intifada* – a widespread social protest movement comprised mainly of young Palestinians – was clearly confrontational but essentially nonviolent (despite the armed clashes). Fighting for one's freedom presents the proof that life is not mere bare existence and that life has an essence: self-realization. "Thus human reality in-itself-for-itself can be achieved only through conflict and through the risk that conflict implies" (1967, 218). Observing the other side of the conflict, Fanon stated that the war of liberation had confused French colonists regarding the nature of the Algerian struggle (Fanon 1994, 58), just as it had puzzled French leftists (1994, 79–80, 88–9).

The anti-colonial violence, therefore, represents a new political direction, Fanon asserts, one that "is national, revolutionary, and collective. This new reality, which the colonized are now exposed to, exists by action alone" (Fanon 2004, 96). Liberation is therefore inseparable from violence, which also means that it is through anti-colonial violence that the naked reality of colonialism will be received fully by the colonized. "Violence alone," Fanon submits, "perpetrated by the people, violence organized and guided by the leadership, provides the key for the masses to decipher social reality. Without this struggle, without this praxis there is nothing but a carnival parade and a lot of hot air" (2004, 96). So here violence does not just have an instrumental character, although, as Arendt would say, it always serves to achieve a purpose: violence bears the essence of politics such that to "wage war and to engage in politics are one and the same thing" (2004, 83).

Moreover, Fanon argues that liberatory praxis of violence is *totalizing* (2004, 44), just as it also divides the society (he declared that after launching the war of liberation, every Algerian had to decide) (Fanon 1991, 102). Speaking of liberatory praxis as both totalizing and dividing may sound contradictory but this is not true. One always inevitably takes a side in a war of liberation; staying neutral is simply impractical in a binary situation. While it is possible to refrain from judging or from making a decision (if one has such a privilege), no decision will remain neutral in bifurcated colonial society, and any apparently "third option" will eventually boil down to choosing one course of action over another (e.g., reformism justifies colonialism). Indeed, colonialism produces self-division (Fanon 1967, 17). As people choose one side over another, the numbers on both sides grow, dialectically, from the few to the many – that is, the situation totalizes and fractures simultaneously. Liberatory violence, as the colonized's praxis, remains irreversible. "For the colonized, this violence represents the absolute praxis. The militant therefore is one who works ... The group requires each individual to have performed an irreversible act" (Fanon 2004, 44). From this, we can see how in its dividing, totalizing, and irreversibility, liberatory violence – as anti-colonial praxis – constitutes a new people and marks the birth of a new nation (2004, 44).

We must make two qualifications when considering Fanon's concept of praxis and violence. First, we need to remember that violence is imposed but this does not mean it is reactive. This is because of the *educational* character of liberatory praxis. As Fanon argues: "Man's behavior is not only reactional. And there is always resentment in a *reaction*. Nietzsche had already pointed that out in *The Will to Power*." He adds: "To educate man to be *actional*, preserving in all his relations his respect for the basic values that constitute a human world, is the prime task of him who, having taken thought, prepares to act" (1967, 222; emphasis in original). So anti-colonial violence is not merely counter-violence (reactive); liberatory violence is fecund because (and herein lies Fanon's philosophical anthropology) humans are life-oriented and thus will not tolerate the loss of their dignity – in short, humans entail both aggression and love (1967, 41). "*Yes* to life. *Yes* to love. *Yes* to generosity," declares Fanon. "But man is also a *no*. *No* to scorn of man. *No* to degradation of man. *No* to exploitation of man. *No* to the butchery of what is most human in man: freedom" (1967, 222; emphasis in original).

The second point of clarification pertains to Fanon's concept of anti-colonial violence as a war of liberation, which (referring to the FLN) was a principled, measured war. Fanon assertes that unlike the French colonial army that massacred Algerian civilians, the FLN targeted military posts, units, and personnel. The FLN bombing of civilian establishments in the French districts of Algiers and other cities towards the end of the war, which resulted in civilian casualties on the French side, while certainly disturbing, had primarily symbolic significance (to show that the French army was unable to protect French nationals); it was not intended to eradicate the French population in Algeria, nor was it a racially motivated assault. The many French nationals in Algeria who had joined the FLN ranks or had helped the movement attested to the racial neutrality of the war of liberation as well as political divisions among the French over that war. Fanon seems to be suggesting that if the war of liberation is not conducted in a principled manner, it would erode into pointless brutalism that will defeat its very purpose. "In a war of liberation, the colonized people must win, but they must do so *cleanly, without 'barbarity.'* The European nation that practices torture is a blighted nation, unfaithful to its history," while the "underdeveloped nation is obliged to practice fair play" (Fanon 1991, 24; emphasis added). A colonizer's war might amount to a "total war" (involving civilian casualties and the destruction of villages and means of livelihood in order to eradicate the guerrillas' infrastructure and social support network, as was indeed the case in the way the French fought against the FLN). *A war of liberation can never be a total war.* As I said, liberatory praxis is *generative*: it is meant to produce a new society. That is why revolutionary violence should be distinguished from barbarity or brutality: "Because we want a democratic and a renovated Algeria, because we believe one cannot rise and liberate oneself in one area and sink in another, we condemn, with pain in our hearts, those brothers who have flung themselves into revolutionary action with the almost physiological brutality that centuries of oppression give rise to and feed" (Fanon 1991, 25). If a war of liberation is not principled, a new people with democratic and dignified aspirations cannot arise from it. Fanon developed these ideas in his many essays, especially the ones published in the FLN's *El Mudjahid* (compiled in A *Dying Colonialism* [1991], originally *L'an V de la Révolution Algérienne* [1959]), in which he insisted that existing forms of (colonial) violence be disavowed and disowned. But this is half the story. We will return to the other half below, when we discuss his shift in attention and show (sociologically) the generative power of revolutionary violence, a thesis related to the theme of this chapter.

Fanon was not naive about the possible outcomes of national liberation. He wished for Africa to emerge united and free, but he also witnessed corrupt postcolonial regimes and the arrival of neocolonialism in the aftermath of African liberation.

(c) *War of liberation can have three possible outcomes.* Independence rolls out three possibilities before the victorious postcolonial nation. The ideal scenario would be liberation of the colonized and the unification of Africa, Fanon's African version of the Bolivarian revolution. Postcolonial pan-Africanism was an inevitable outcome of the colonial binarism that situated Africa against Europe. Fanon holds Europe responsible for racializing the colonized: "Colonialism did not think it worth its while denying one national culture after the other. Consequently the colonized's response was immediately continental in scope." This continental tendency manifested itself in the literature of colonized Africa, which in his time (the 1950s and early 1960s) "has not been a national literature but a 'Negro' literature. The concept of negritude for example was the affective if not logical antithesis of that insult which the white man had leveled at the rest of humanity" (Fanon 2004, 150). The postcolonial situation has the potential to create a model participatory political framework in which, unlike in colonial times, people are no longer considered a "hindrance" to government and instead are now its "driving force." This was how the Algerians became "political people" through the war of liberation (2004, 131). This is how liberation leads to political development. Postcolonial politics, argues Fanon, cannot replicate the past: traditional authority has to go before this new political formation can emerge: "The elimination of the *kaids* and the chiefs is a prerequisite to the unification of the people" (2004, 51). Although liberation necessarily transforms the traditional structure into a modern one, the dismantling of traditional authority is not simply of a developmental character. It is enabled by revolutionary violence:

> At the individual level, violence is a cleansing force. It rids the colonized of their inferiority complex, of their passive and despairing attitude. It emboldens them, and restores their self-confidence. Even if the armed struggle has been symbolic, and even if they have been demobilized by rapid decolonization, the people have time to realize that liberation was the achievement of each and every one and no special merit should go to the leader. Violence hoists the people up to the level of the leader. (2004, 51)

In Fanon's vision, liberated people do not need leaders: "*Leader* comes from the English verb 'to lead,' meaning 'to drive' in French. The driver of people no longer exists today ... The nation should not be an affair run by a big boss" (2004, 127; emphasis in original). We will see shortly that Fanon views this tendency to "drive" people as leading to postcolonial corruption. In his vision, only democratic, participatory, postcolonial governance is compatible with the liberatory struggle for recognition. Stated contrariwise, the form of postcolonial governance reveals whether the people are truly liberated. Furthermore, previously held oppositions would lose their importance in the postcolonial era. Although it is clear to Fanon that capitalism will impede the postcolonial "national and universal project" (2004, 55), he argues that the Third World must refuse to choose between socialism and capitalism: liberation movements have used the "savage competition between the two systems in order to win their national liberation," but the liberated nations "must ... refuse to get involved in such rivalry" (2004, 55). In the end, what matters is the redistribution of wealth: this is the horizon of humanity (2004, 55).

Liberation's promises, however, have sometimes produced the opposite results. Having travelled to several postcolonial countries as an FLN emissary, Fanon had found that in the aftermath of wars of liberation in Africa, dictatorships had arisen in the place of colonial subjugation. A new comprador bourgeois class had risen among the anticolonial leaders, mimicking (like the colonized reformists before liberation) the Western bourgeoisie (2004, 101). National landowners had replaced the colonial landowners (2004, 102). Fanon recognized that the corruption of postcolonial leaders had arisen from the lack of institutionalized participation of the masses in the context of underdevelopment in a resource-based postcolonial economy (2004, 112), and he sketched accurately the process of transposition: "The party becomes ... an intelligence service. The militant becomes an informer. He is put in charge of punitive missions against the villages." This was followed by a situation in which "a single party and the government candidate receives 99 percent of the votes. We have to acknowledge that a certain number of governments in Africa operate along these lines" (2004, 125). The dictatorship of the postcolonial "bourgeois caste" aimed to lead "the underdeveloped country, at first with the support of the people but very soon against them" (2004, 125). At that point, the masses and observers alike realized that the anticolonial revolution had brought about no significant change.

The postcolonial dictatorships, of course, could not have arisen without neocolonialism. In Fanon's view, it was the striking of new economic pacts with the former colony that bred the new dictatorships: "Every new sovereign state finds itself practically under the obligation of maintaining definite and preferential relations with the former oppressor" (1994, 120). This was how independence failed to bring about a new historic direction. The colonial extract-and-export economy continued in postcolonial nations (2004, 100). Dictatorships and neocolonialism were signs that the revolution had not been radical *enough*. For the real Africa "that we had to guide, mobilize, launch on the offensive" – for this "Africa to come" (*avenir*) (1994, 179) – to be realized, no return to the past, no revivalism or traditionalism, could be allowed. "I will not make myself the man of any past," Fanon asserts. "I do not want to exalt the past at the expense of my present and of my future" (1967, 226). This unity of the new Africa is a legacy of European colonialism (an indication of Fanon's dialectical thinking) (2004, 106). As the promise of the Third World (2004, 238), Africa is destined to offer something new; it cannot offer a "grotesque and generally obscene emulation" (2004, 239) of Europe.

The aforesaid discussion is not meant to simply enumerate the possible outcomes of national liberation. Rather, it must be properly situated within Fanon's dialectical framework. "The upheaval reached the Negroes from without," avers Fanon. "The black man was acted upon ... The upheaval did not make a difference in the Negro. *He went from one way of life to another, but not from one life to another*" (1967, 220; emphasis added). The new life should be the outcome of liberation. Colonial Manichaeanism has been maintained during the years of decolonization; liberation can lead to postcolonial rephenomenalization and reworlding only if, in emerging as a *new* people, a nation incorporates and lays claim as *its own* the terror, pain, subjugation, resistance, and sacrifices of its colonial past, nurse its colonial scars, turn colonists into compatriots, and overcome violence and bitterness, so that it can heal. In this way, truth will clear the way for a new nation to emerge (2004, 14). Much like Benjamin, Fanon contends that healing will come only when the redeemed postcolonial nation is able to own its history with all its ashes and diamonds.

(d) *Violent liberation is simultaneously nonviolent rephenomenalization.* Among Fanon's unique perspectives on the war of liberation was his meticulous sociological view of the *rephenomenalization* of life as Algerian people participated in, and Algerian society underwent, this process. Without his dialectical understanding of the liberation process, he could not have developed this perspective. For national liberation to take place, the individual has to have begun her or his liberation already (1994, 103). "The Revolution in depth, the true one, precisely because it changes man and renews society, has reached an advanced stage. This oxygen which creates and shapes a new humanity – this, too, is the Algerian Revolution" (1991, 181). In my reading, "revolution in depth" relates to *phenomenal reworlding*, which is nowhere more evident than in the violence that enabled a new Algeria to emerge even before liberation was won. Let us be careful here: it is not violence that begets this "depth"; yet "revolution in depth" cannot be thought outside of violence, properly speaking. Reflecting on the collective experience of educated Algerians, he mentions the three phases of development of colonized intellectuals through the war of liberation: in the first phase, the colonized functionary "proves he has assimilated the colonizer's culture." Then, in the second stage, he has "his convictions shaken," while in the last, "he turns into a galvanizer of the people. Combat literature, revolutionary literature, national literature emerges" (2004, 158–9). If Fanon had only documented the process of colonized intellectuals' acquisition of self-consciousness he would not have said anything new. But in his (rather phenomenological) book, *A Dying Colonialism*, he succeeded in documenting a fascinating process of *reworlding* in sociological terms: the birth of a new society through new social relations. Of course, given that he was a non-Algerian who did not speak Arabic and who was rather alien to the Algerian culture, his observations were at times controversial, even faulty. I am not fact-checking here, though: his observations reveal a method that is important for this study. *A Dying Colonialism* contains Fanon's psychological and sociological diagnoses of how, through a war of liberation, prominent aspects of Algerian social life reappeared differently: there was a break both from tradition and from the colonial past. This reappearance, though, pointed at structural shifts that were not yet institutionalized. The war of liberation enabled the *reworlding* of the existing colonial aspects of society so that they emerged as institutions of liberation. The veil, the radio (and the voice!), the family, medicine, and Algeria's European modernity – all of these were transformed so as to fit the requirements of liberatory action, even while the colonial system slowly died. This is indeed an account of deworlding/reworlding – of a violent shift, taking place within a war of independence – that brings about, by all measures, *transformative nonviolence*. Reading through Fanon's "phenomenology," one cannot but be reminded of Benjamin's "slight adjustment" of the Messiah that changes the world.

In arguably the most controversial part of *A Dying Colonialism*, which reveals Fanon's foreignness to Algerian society despite his dedication to its liberation, he maintains that the Algerian woman's veil revealed the European colonial complex regarding coloured women and simultaneously the locus of colonial destrcturing of Algerian society (1991, 46). European notions of westernizing women through unveiling amounted to disarming them (1991, 65). As such, the veil re-emerged during the war of liberation as a centre of contention (1991, 36). "It is the white man who creates the Negro. But it is the Negro who creates negritude. To the colonialist offensive against the veil, the colonized opposes the cult of the veil" (1991, 47). The colonizer had fanaticized the unveiling of the Algerian woman and tried to win "the battle of the veil" at all costs in order to crush the natives' resistance (1991, 48). As a result of the colonized women's participation in revolution, the veil no longer symbolized the tradition; instead the veil was rephenomenalized as revolutionary means. Furthermore, Fanon observes, Algerian women's participation in that revolution gradually enabled the liberation of women from traditional roles (in this regard, he recorded the gradual process of recruiting women). The liberation of women was well under way as Algerian society tried to delink itself from colonial rule (1991, 51). As a consequence, the existing rules governing marriage also changed in that the Algerian woman gained a say in choosing her life partner (1991, 59). It was not that male revolutionaries "liberated" women; rather, both men and women moved down the path of mutual liberation from traditional role demands. In this way the veil took on an entirely different function during the revolutionary war (1991, 63). According to Hamid Dabashi, "by insisting on *veiling* as a sign of resisting colonialism, Fanon marked the moment when the body was no longer a mere biological proposition and had radically metamorphosed into a site of colonial contestation between the colonizer and the colonized" (2012, 13; emphasis in original).

The Algerian family underwent a similar process of rephenomenalization: liberation caused a generational rift and shift (1991, 103). The relationship between traditional father and *maquis* son reoriented the family towards the cause (1991, 103). And since in "the Algerian family, the girl is always one notch behind the boy" (1991, 105), the relationship between father and daughter changed as well. By virtue of her participation in the revolution, the young woman could no longer be treated as a "minor" protected by male family members (1991, 106). Thus the young men and women's partaking in revolutionary action changed the dynamics of Algerian family and society. "The unveiled Algerian woman, who assumed an increasingly important place in revolutionary action, developed her personality, discovered the exalting realm of responsibility. The freedom of the Algerian people from then on became identified with woman's liberation, with her entry into history" (1991, 107). The FLN also deeply affected relations between brothers and within couples, as well as the norms of divorce and marriage (1991, 114). These were sweeping social changes: Fanon paid close attention, for example, to how medical science (which came with colonialism and was viewed with suspicion by non-urbanite Algerians) was gradually accepted by average Algerians as a result of the revolutionary process (1991, 121). The liberation war turned the doctor–patient relationship into one of egalitarian trust even while colonialism revealed its violence in its medical war against the FLN (1991, 139).

The FLN also changed the "voice" of the nation. It is well-known that in the modern world, consciousness-raising is tightly linked to the media, be it print, electronic, or digital. In his theory of mediology, French philosopher Régis Debray refers to the "technical means of intellectualizing the proletariat and proletarianizing the intellectual" as a "double movement" (Debray 2007, 6). Fanon was an editor of the FLN organ *El Mudjahid*, for which he wrote extensively. He was therefore a media man of Algerian liberation as well. In his fascinating discussion of Radio-Alger, he reflected on the use of radio broadcasting in liberation: as Radio-Alger (est. 1954) emerged as a counter-voice to colonial radio, warfare by broadcast became a factor in the war of independence (Fanon 1991, 85). So much so that in a colonized nation whose broadcast soundscape was dominated by the French colonists, by 1956 to purchase a radio was to express sympathy for the revolution (1991, 83). FLN's radio programming decolonized the French language and changed its colonial essence so that it became "an instrument of liberation" (1991, 89). Arabic remained the language of society, but French was suitable for "operational concepts of a modern revolutionary war" (1991, 91). The disassociation of the language from the colonizer allowed for the integration of the French language into the war of liberation. But the appropriation of French by Algerian revolutionaries was not merely instrumental: Fanon's originality rested in offering a psychopathology of the "radio voice" and the use of French. The colonized people claimed and successfully appropriated that which was essential (second to military and administrative rule) to the demarcation of the colonizer from the colonized: the colonizer's language. The imposing colonial voice of the radio changed accordingly: "the radio voices became protective, friendly. Insults and accusations disappeared and gave way to words of encouragement" (1991, 89). Having been appropriated, French rephenomenalized as the language not just of liberatory war but also of a new people.

Lastly, in the process of rephenomenalization, Fanon attended to the status of Algerian minorities. Recall that for Fanon, properly understood, liberation always involves the liberation of all. No one is to be left behind. The war of liberation in Algeria, he observes, integrated the minorities into the Algerian nation. In that sense, the Algerian war of liberation truly was a process of national birth. *"For the F.L.N., in the new society that is being built, there are only Algerians. From the outset, therefore, every individual living in Algeria is an Algerian. In tomorrow's independent Algeria it will be up to every Algerian to assume Algerian citizenship or to reject it in favor of another* (1991, 152; emphasis in original). Algeria's minorities were at first reluctant to accept revolutionary violence (1991, 165) but gradually found themselves taking the FLN's side. The (postcolonial) Algerian nation-to-come would embrace *all* of its children – including the Jews. Most Jews supported national liberation (1991, 155). Finally, liberation even changed Europe (1991, 160), including the French in Algeria. Fanon claims that not "a single Frenchman has revealed to the colonialist police information vital to the Revolution. On the contrary, the arrested Europeans have resisted long enough to enable the other members of the network to disappear. The tortured European has behaved like an authentic militant in the national fight for independence" (1991, 151).

Fanon is indeed the chronicler of a rephenomenalization of a colonized people into a liberated nation, or a postcolonial hybridity, as he envisioned it (2004, 155), since a liberated people cannot uphold racial prejudices (Fanon 1994, 43). His acknowledgment of the need for anti-colonial violence should not overshadow the nonviolent process of actual decolonization through the *birth of a new people*. We will fully appreciate Fanon's nuanced understanding of violence when we focus on the nonviolent path through which a new, liberated nation is born. Once again, *the violence–nonviolence opposition is suspended.*

Fanon did not shy away from defending the position that the destructive violence of colonialism must be challenged by the generative violence of liberation. The former is destructive because it subjugates and alienates; the latter is generative since it involves emancipatory self-authentication. The latter, one can observe, is necessary in order to "reset" the imposed, colonial social relations. Anti-colonial liberation, therefore, qualifies as Benjaminian "divine violence" in that, as lawmaking, it is cathartic of colonial "mythic violence." Recall from Benjamin (on Kafka) that Messianic pure violence will change the world only through "slight adjustment." Having read Fanon's "moment of liberation" in terms of Benjamin, I am inclined to suggest that "pure violence" cannot exist because there can be no pure action: *phenomenologically, action simultaneously contains both destructive and generative violence, as well as violence and nonviolence.* This complex web of action emerges when the possibility of a new world emerges on our collective horizon, when we can "see that another solution is possible. It implies a restructuring of the world" (Fanon 1967, 82).

Yet as Derrida recognizes, the "pure violence" of liberation can indeed be reversed. Fanon found such reversals in postcolonial dictatorships and neocolonialism. To continue with Derrida's logic in the context of Fanon's disappointments with certain outcomes of African national liberation movements, I suggest that *liberation is indeed an irreversible mode of action,* due to its refoundational power (when the new is founded upon the old), but that *its outcome can involve a sharp reversal of liberation itself* (when the old returns, penetrates, and corrupts the new). An act's outcome can therefore contain that act's undoing. This possibility arises because, as a messianic moment, emancipation and liberation suspend all knowledge and leave us with no universal yardstick with which we can measure freedom as the collective horizon of liberatory politics. Fanon seems to recognize this *epistemological obscurity* with regard to the future when he declares: "Because decolonization comes in many shapes, reason wavers and abstains from declaring what is a true decolonization and what is not" (2004, 21). We remain suspended in the phenomenological *epoché.*

Fanon shows in his "phenomenology" of relational–structural shifts in Algerian society that however violent a nation's liberation war, change will inevitably arise from the nonviolent transformation of the collective Self, of liberated humanity. "It is a liberated individual," Fanon avers, "who undertakes to build the new society" (1994, 102). To the undialectial ear, Fanon sounds like a great justifier of violence. The question he poses *seems* like this: either violent liberation or nonviolent nonliberation. That binary is false. What Fanon teaches us is that liberation will be "violent" even when it is in fact nonviolent. This logic undermines his own advocacy for the destruction of Algeria's traditional social structure as necessary for liberation. He clearly adheres to the European language of progress in this respect (2004, 123). The structural shift to post-traditional society – with its voluntarism and negotiations sketched in *A Dying Colonialism* – seems nonviolent. Yet, I argue, the destruction of tradition qualifies as structural violence – a deworlding/reworlding. From a liberatory standpoint, traditions may be "violent" in their social organization and cultural practices, and colonial violence may overshadow the age-old violence of tradition. And while it is true that postcolonials cannot return to precolonial times (which renders tradition unsustainable), this cannot dissipate the violence of structurally shifting a social organization that, for better or worse, has sustained a people for a long time. So even the nonviolent shifting of social relations inevitably has violent aspects.

One last observation: Fanon's distinction between violence and barbarity is not a rhetorical justification for violence; rather, its purpose is to show the nonviolent nature of anti-colonial emancipation. Jean-Paul Sartre's famous preface to *The Wretched of the Earth* (September 1961) worked against the spirit of Fanon's understanding of liberatory violence, and unfortunately, it generated serious misgivings about the merits of Fanon's non-binary thinking in the binary situation of colonialism. Sartre, a prominent European thinker who was ashamed of Europeans' criminal endeavours in the Third World, glorified violence and produced bombastic statements like this one: "A fighter's weapon is his humanity. For in the first phase of the revolt killing is a necessity: killing a European is killing two birds with one stone, eliminating in one go oppressor and oppressed: leaving one man dead and the other man free; for the first time the survivor feels a *national* soil under his feet." Similarly, he declared that as soon as the war of liberation "begins it is merciless" (Sartre in Fanon 2004, lv; emphasis in original). Sartre recognized the extent of the violence in Algeria but blamed the French for it, referring to the anti-colonial war of liberation as French violence "on the rebound, that grows and tears ... [the colonized] apart" (Sartre in Fanon 2004, lii). Sartre was right to point out the colonial source of the violence, but his view lacked the depth of reflection one finds in Fanon's creative application of dialectics in the colonial context. In my view, Sartre framed Fanon's complex thought in an unwarranted way – so much so that when Arendt reflected on violence in the late 1960s, she missed the point as well. Homi Bhabha's reflections on Arendt's take on Fanon (and Sartre) – despite his own liberal reading of Fanon – are accurate when he points out that Arendt's attack on Fanon "was an attempt at staunching the wildfire it spread across university campuses, while she readily acknowledged that it was really Sartre's preface that glorified violence beyond Fanon's words or wishes. Sartre fanned the flames ... while arguing that despite the doctrine of liberatory violence, Fanon, 'the man, deep down hated it'" (Bhabha in Fanon 2004, xxi). Arendt, then, ended up missing the unlikely overlap between her thought and Fanon's as well as the emancipatory tradition of thought with which Fanon identified. Above all, she did not see that liberation, for Fanon, was the condition under which colonized people, unifying as diverse equals and by (nonviolent) acting in concert, emerged as political beings entitled to rights and thus yearning for freedom. Incidentally, this last point leads us to Arendt to find out whether her thought is also permeated with the *undecidability* of violence and nonviolence.

Arendt's Predicament: On Liberation's Excesses

Arendt is possibly the unlikeliest candidate for a conceptual excursion such as this. She explicitly rejects any notion of liberation that is not related to individual liberty, just as she expressly refutes that rights can be conferred upon a "people" rather than the individual. In its innermost, her theory remains essentially Aristotelian (and non-Weberian), and thus she has no "elective affinity" (using Weber's term, who borrowed it from Goethe) with the emancipatory theories of Sorel, Benjamin, and Fanon. Nonetheless, I will point out the liberatory kernel of her thinking and how her thinking is permeated with a predicament reminiscent of the collapse of the positively ascertainable distinction between violence and nonviolence. In fact, I argue, she actually offers great insights into liberation and (non)violence that are fairly, though not entirely perhaps, congruous with the thesis of this book.

In order to glean from Arendt's thinking insights into liberatory moment in which the distinction between violence and nonviolence is suspended, let us first return to her concepts of action and power. For Arendt, *natality enables the human action of founding a new body politic.* One cannot properly situate this without probing her ontology of politics in *The Human Condition.* I argued in chapter 1 that Arendt's concept of power captures the sociological concept of "collective action," but with a key proviso: power – as acting in concert – allows a "people" to emerge, to rise above mere existence; power marks the formative political moment that has its roots in the human capacity of natality, of beginning a project and bringing something new into this world (Arendt 1958a, 9). Let us also recall that because her concept of "labour" concerns human subsistence (it sustains biological life and is thus *animal* activity), it has no *telos*: "It is indeed the mark of all labouring that it leaves nothing behind" (1958a, 87). Labour gives life, and because it does not endure and remains cyclical, it is not, properly speaking, a *human* activity. By contrast, "work," which pertains to the ability to fabricate, will *endure* through its product, which renders fabrication essentially violent as an activity (Villa 1996, 26–7). Work gives the human world (of things). In short, work is destructive; labour is not (Arendt, 1958a, 100). In work, *violence's creative and generative capacity* is revealed. Arendt's concept of work, I argue, captures a phenomenological understanding of violence.

The common aspect of work and action lies in their leaving something behind, and thus, they are distinctly human feats in that both endure, except that, *stricto sensu, action allows the violence that is inherent in fabrication to be "overcome."* Action gives plurality and thus human relations. It is due to action that the emerging of a "people" becomes possible, whence there also emerges a new "body politic," a *political association of diverse equals* in which the founding *individuals* are both equal and free (thus retaining their differences while belonging to a community). Although together they forge a new body politic that transcends each, these individuals are not reducible to a people. Politics is therefore understood in the manner of the Greeks as based on *persuasion* (*peithein*, relating to Peithô, goddess of persuasion) (Arendt 1990, 73), which means that politics involves speech plus rules; in other words, politics takes place "where speech rules supreme" (Arendt 1963, 35). Arendt explains this on the basis that humans live in the "world of appearances" (Arendt 1970, 66) in which we rely on words to reveal public matters (*res publica*). We have already seen why action and power are so closely related to each other. "The grammar of action: that action is the only human faculty that demands a plurality of men; and the syntax of power: that power is the only human attribute which applies solely to the worldly in-between space by which men are mutually related, combine in the act of foundation by virtue of the making and the keeping of promises, which, in the realm of politics, may well be the highest human faculty" (Arendt 1963, 175). The space thus conceived – this in-between plurality of actors – is the space that has the potential to develop into political space. "Only the political life, the life of action and speech, is free: only the political life is human" (Villa, 1996, 28). Hence the importance of public debate and discourse. Because action is about diverse equals persuading one another in public, *action remains nonviolent.* It is precisely by abolishing this space that totalitarian regimes destroy politics altogether and render man superfluous (Arendt 1958b, 457). In so doing, by eliminating (political) differences, totalitarian states abolish society and constitute a "society" epitomized by the labour camp. Worst of all, Arendt warns, we have no safeguard against totalitarianism (1958b, 437).

Back to our discussion: it is well-known that Arendt held power (acting in concert) and violence as antithetical yet never regarded these as pure moments (Arendt 1970, 52, 56). Accordingly, the conceptual distinctness of power and violence primarily reports the theorist's normative gesture, an imagined moment at best. We cannot, for that matter, take power to be purely synonymous with nonviolence without violating the integrity of Arendt's thought: "it is not correct to think of the opposite of violence as nonviolence; to speak of nonviolent power is actually redundant" (1970, 56). Indeed, "nothing ... is more common than the combination of violence and power, nothing less frequent than to find them in their pure and therefore extreme form," she declares. "From this, it does not follow that authority, power, and violence are all the same" (1970, 46–7). Yet acting, and persuading in the founding moment, enable the experience closest to pure nonviolence.

Arendt expands on her thoughts on the human ability of founding in *On Revolution* (1963), a book that focuses on the French and American revolutions. In a revolution, she argues, it becomes clear that the origin of power resides with the people (1963, 179); furthermore, "revolutions are the only political events which confront us directly and inevitably with the problem of beginning" (1963, 21). With a revolution "the course of history suddenly begins anew" (1963, 28). Revolutions signify a founding that is directly but not exclusively related to decline of power: "Where power has disintegrated, revolutions are possible but not necessary" (Arendt 1970, 49). The term revolution is derived from Copernican astronomy, which originally signified restoration and a return to the original order. This is evidenced in the first modern revolution – the English Revolution – which was intended to restore monarchy. When restoration becomes impossible, revolutions beget something new. It was during the French Revolution that the term "revolution" was used politically for the first time (Arendt 1963, 37, 42–3, 45, 47).

The study of the French and American revolutions brings Arendt to a controversial aspect of her theory: the "social question," which she persistently excludes from the body politic (Villa 1996, 29). She unambiguously rejects the concept of *social* revolution; in fact, an entire chapter in *On Revolution* is dedicated to the social question and the French Revolution, which she calls a revolution of "want" in contrast to the American Revolution, which epitomized power (acting in concert). A critical examination of this aspect of her work requires an independent study. One can begin by stating that her observation – that the French Revolution devolved into tyranny and failed to institute the rights of man – does not necessarily mean that the social question is *incapable* of founding politics. We do know that, in her view, the social question (the "want") represents the pre-political since the "want" relates to *labour* as unenduring means of sustenance, and therefore it cannot be brought into, and represented in, the body politic. Naturally, we need to incorporate this aspect into our reading of her theory of revolution. We must be clear that the body politic for Arendt is conditioned not on the *natural* equality of men but on their *political* equality: "We are not born equal; we become equal as members of a group on the strength of our decision to guarantee ourselves mutually equal rights" (Arendt 1958b, 301). Equality of individuals is achieved, not given (which reminds us of Rousseau's paradox of foundation). She positions herself against the confusion of the "rights of man" (signified by the American Revolution) with the "rights of a people" (à la the French Revolution), which she identifies with the Third World liberation movements. The so-called "rights of people" fail to create a body politic based on the association of individuals who seek liberty in their converging on that which they collectively bring to this world. This position unmistakably sets Arendt apart from emancipatory politics and is thus important to closely investigate here. With her zeal to dismiss postcolonial liberation movements in one slate, Arendt famously declares: "The Third World is not a reality but an ideology" (1970, 21). Already in her exilic political essays of the 1940s, some twenty years before the publication of *On Revolution*, she had rejected the idea of a "people" as the object of love in the political context in which loving one's own people is supposed to motivate one to take action against their misery. "I have never in my life 'loved' any people or collective," she proclaims, "neither the German people, nor the French, nor the American, nor the working class or anything of that sort" (2007, 466–67). One can only love one's friends; only an individual can be the object of love.

The confusion of the "rights of man" with the "right of people" stems from the very act of founding that enables humans to claim *the right to have rights* – this is the birth of political modernity, which in its founding gave rise to the association of individuals as diverse equals. Historically, in the process of nation-state building, and thus national liberation, the rights of man was confused with the rights of people, and that is how the very concept of rights disappeared altogether in the French Revolution's "reign of terror" and in garden-variety postcolonial dictatorships. Arendt's argument is that when the "rights of man" are held as "inalienable," then man himself becomes the source and the goal of the laws.

"Man appeared as the only sovereign in matters of law as the people was proclaimed the only sovereign in matters of government," Arendt argues. "The people's sovereignty ... was not proclaimed by the grace of God but in the name of Man, so that it seemed only natural that the 'inalienable' rights of man would find their guarantee and become an inalienable part of the right of the people to sovereign self-government" (1958b, 291). In short, the concept of "right of people" is not compatible with that of "rights of man": the latter provides "the new fundament for civilized societies" (Arendt 1958b, 293). What happened, though, was that the issue of having rights merged with emancipation and popular sovereignty. Paradoxically, therefore, as soon as individual humans emerge as the bearers of rights, they disappear into a "people." Man becomes as abstract as the rights to which he is entitled, losing individuality in the process. Arendt continues:

> The full implication of this identification of the rights of man with the rights of peoples in the European nation-state system came to light only when a growing number of people and peoples suddenly appeared whose elementary rights were as little safeguarded by the ordinary functioning of nation-states in the middle of Europe as they would have been in the heart of Africa. The Rights of Man, after all, had been defined as "inalienable" because they were supposed to be independent of all governments. (1958b, 291)

Let us ignore the tint of Eurocentrism in her statement. Since inalienable rights of humans are not safeguarded by the state, two possible outcomes emerge. In the passage above, she discusses one: that of national liberation and self-determination and the rise of a rights-bearing "people" at the expense of the individual. In Arendt's view, this outcome represents a perversion of real solutions. For her, liberation leads to liberty, not to the emergence of a people as the defining figure of political life. But there is also the second outcome she overlooks: by virtue of Arendt's own logic, this perversion is enabled by the ability of a people to act in concert and to found something new. That Arendt does not wish to accept that the liberated individual – the bearer of inalienable rights – always inevitably emerges from the formation of a "people" remains baffling though not unexpected. Here is where I suggest that we read Arendt against Arendt, and to prove my point, I refer to her reflections on the Jewish army and the Jews as a political people – a position she seems to

have drawn back from later in her career, although not entirely and
never clearly.

When violence defines political life and humans are rendered rightless (the status of the Jews and other minorities under Nazi rule), then
rights must be earned, and this requires *imposing one's existence as a group*
on the totalitarian state. This is how a group – the Jews in Arendt's case –
emerged as a political community. Arendt consistently refuses to endorse
reformist or compromise (conceptual) solutions to the Jewish question,
and she clearly positions herself against the *realpolitik* of businessmen
(2007, 242). The distinction between pariah and parvenu is key here. As
pariah people, the Jews must assert themselves *as* Jews – a political people –
and not as individual achievers (parvenus) waiting to be included in
political community. What Arendt seeks is "an admission of Jews as *Jews*
to the ranks of humanity, rather than a permit to ape the gentiles or an
opportunity to play the parvenu" (2007, 275; emphasis in original). The
"exceptional Jew," the parvenu, forced on Jews an image that made it
more difficult for the Jews to imagine themselves as a people (2007, 141).
While in France and on the escape route from the Nazis that eventually
landed her in America, Arendt worked with the World Zionist Organization, helping transport Jewish refugees to Palestine. The idea of a Jewish
army dawned on Arendt at this time. It is known that her relationship
to Zionism changed after she moved to the United States. "In exile in
Paris she was active with the [World] Zionist Organization," writes Edna
Brocke. "She understood Zionism as a concrete way of combating rising
National Socialism." In the United States, "she came in contact with a
large and diverse Jewish community whose Zionist organizations were
structured differently from the Zionist groups she had encountered in
Germany and France" (Brocke 2007, 517). What remained, though, was
her assertion that the Jews needed to establish themselves as political
people in the face of Nazism, which treated them as rightless *homo sacer.*
Let us recall Arendt's position that only the "rights of man" can prevent
the reduction of humanity to naked life (1958b, 300–2). From 1941 to
1944, she worked for *Aufbau,* the only German-speaking Jewish weekly
newspaper in America (Brocke 2007, 516). It was on the pages of *Aufbau*
that she promoted the idea of a Jewish Army.

For the purposes of our conceptual excursion here, we need to
leave aside the historic significance of Arendt's position. Once we
capture the logical gist of her argument we will be able to see with
relative clarity why in Arendt's thinking nonviolent power as acting
in concert cannot be separated from the inevitably violent act of

founding a new people. And it has to do with the recognition of the Jews as a pariah people:

> The storm that will be unleashed in our own ranks by the formation of a Jewish army with volunteers from around the world will make clear to those in honest despair that we're no different from anyone else, that we too engage in politics, even if you usually have to extract it painfully from the murky code of the petitions of Jewish notables and charitable organizations, and despite the fact that our politics has been especially adept at alienating itself from the Jewish people. We are, however, hardly the only people who have been led to the rim of the abyss of destruction by a plutocratic regime. War is too serious a matter ... to be left to the generals. Well, *the existence of a people is definitely too serious a matter to be left to the rich.* (Arendt 2007, 138; emphasis in original)

Arendt was demanding a Jewish army to defend Palestine, which at the time of her reflections was a British protectorate. But this was not to be merely a defensive brigade; instead, it would take up the cause of liberating the Jews from the Nazis. Arendt was asserting here that the Jewish people would only emerge if they fought *as* Jews, from Palestine *and* the diaspora, presenting a "unifying bond of world Jewry" (2007, 146). So the idea of such an army "must tomorrow become the living will of a majority of the Jewish people to join the battle against Hitler as Jews, in Jewish battle formations under a Jewish flag. *The defense of Palestine is part of the struggle for the freedom of the Jewish people.* Only if the Jewish people are prepared to give their all for this struggle will they also be able to defend Palestine" (2007, 137; emphasis in original). Arendt rejected the idea of Jews joining the British army to fight Nazism (2007, 138). What was needed was a Jewish army under a Jewish flag that would enter into an alliance with the British army in the battle against fascism. "Above all there is the fact that they fight under their own flag – and that means that they intend to battle *as Jews* for the freedom of Jews" (2007, 200; emphasis in original). This is a significant observation: "One truth that is unfamiliar to the Jewish people, though they are beginning to learn it, is that *you can only defend yourself as the person you are attacked as.* A person attacked as a Jew cannot defend himself as an Englishman or Frenchman" (2007, 137; emphasis in original). One's inclusion in political life cannot be a result of another's allowance: *one must constitute herself as a political being through an unambiguous act of liberation.* Partaking in a war is clearly not an easy matter. "War demands not only a horrible readiness to kill, but also the readiness to die. But you can be ready to die only when you know for certain why you are fighting, and only when you are a full-fledged citizen of the community that embodies that 'why'" (2007, 145). In April 1944, Arendt celebrated the anniversary of the Warsaw Ghetto Uprising (19 April 1943) and the formation of Jewish partisan bands in Eastern Europe. "And in doing so they ended the pariah existence of the Jewish people in Europe and, by claiming equal rights, joined the ranks of other European peoples in the struggle for freedom" (2007, 199). This is how "[h]onor and glory ... [have become] new words in the political vocabulary of our people" (2007, 199). It was not enough, in her thinking, for migrant Jews to live in security under British protection; what was needed was for world Jewry to rise to the ranks of other nations as a people with equal rights. Fighting as Jews was the only way the Jewish people could end anti-Semitism in Europe (and elsewhere) (2007, 200).

When the Jewish army did not materialize despite five years of negotiations with the British, Arendt woefully reflected in a letter (dated 6 October 1944): "A Jewish army at that point [1942] would have helped deter the 'conspiracy of silence' that accompanied years of Jewish extermination and would never have let it come to the unbearable humiliation of the Jewish people, who felt that the whole world had damned them to the degrading role of victimhood. It is too late for all that now" (2007, 228). The Jewish army never came, but regardless of whether Arendt the scholar in the 1960s would have endorsed Arendt the refugee of the early 1940s, the idea remains more or less intact: in order to achieve liberty, to emerge as rights-bearing individuals in a body politic, and more importantly, to emerge through the *nonviolent* acting and founding subsequent to the consensus of diverse equals, one must be ready to go through the *trial of liberation*, however violent the force of circumstance dictates it be. *The opposition between violence and nonviolence is once again suspended.*

Personal responsibility under dictatorships is a well-known theme in Arendt, who never ceased to believe that acting is always possible because humans have the ability to judge (2003, 18–19). Reflecting on the plight of the Jews under the Nazis and on how Germans (and others) should have reacted, she endorsed the possibility of non-participation as the first step towards judgment. In a "clarification" letter (24 July 1963), she averred: "I said that there was no possibility of resistance, but there existed the possibility of *doing nothing*. And in order to do nothing, one did not need to be a saint, one needed only to say: 'I am just a simple Jew, and I have no desire to play any other role'" (2007, 468; emphasis in original). Yet because politics is carried out by individuals (a point to which I will return), one judges but is also judged through his or her actions or with-drawal from participation. "Since we are dealing in politics with men, and not with heroes or saints, it is this possibility of '*nonparticipation*'... that is decisive if we begin to judge, not the system, but the individual, his choices, and his arguments" (2007, 469; emphasis in original). So in reflecting on what one could do under the Nazis, Arendt did not shy away from making judgments of her own: "Instead I had to limit myself to the resistance fighters, whose behavior, as I said, was the more admirable because it occurred under circumstances in which resistance had really ceased to be possible" (2007, 469). A resistance fighter does not dwell on the possibility of acting but acts under impossible conditions. She or he makes acting possible and thus opens a path. Back to my hypothetical question above, it seems clear that the mature, world-historical Arendt endorsed the position taken by the young Arendt.

To reiterate, the Jews could not emerge as the "political people" by fighting in the name of universal human rights, by marching in British brigades and under the British flag, or by waiting to be granted rights by European nation-states. Let us not forget that it was Europe that let down its Jews in the first place. Arendt's warning in *The Origins of Totali-tarianism* (which resonates with our reality six decades later) showcases the argument that insofar as citizens rely on the nation-state to uphold their rights, they remain vulnerable to the perilous suspension of those rights for one reason or another. As noted earlier, rights are *taken*, not given. In wake of the Holocaust in Europe, for Jews to found a new body politic of their own (in Palestine) in which their individual dignity and *liberty* would be respected, they would have to launch themselves as *liber-ated* people. Note that Arendt was against Jewish incursions and illegal settlements in Palestine and advised a Jewish–Palestinian federative state (2007, 146, 235, 466)

To downplay Arendt's antipathy towards liberation movements would violate her thought. So my argument here cannot take that easy road. The longer road to her thought must involve making propositional interpretations based on her own conceptualizations of how her tripar-tite concept of the human condition – labour, work, action – related to the concepts of liberation and liberty. As mentioned, Arendt excluded the "social question" from her analysis, since the movement of "want" is related to labour as cyclical and is thus incapable of founding an endur-ing body politic. In Arendt's Aristotelian political thought, insofar as lib-eration does not lead to liberty it remains trapped within the cyclical activity of labour. That is why proletarian emancipation cannot lead to liberty. Liberation must therefore be excluded from political theory. I argue that just as cyclical labour is the condition of enduring work as building and adding something to this world, so is "unenduring" liberation (through which a political people emerges) the condition for the emergence of an enduring body politic based on liberty. If liberation does not lead to liberty, it remains trapped within its cyclicality and thus will not on its own produce a durable human community. Arendt finds the "hopeless confusion and dangerous ambiguity of almost all modern national liberation movements" (2007, 169) alarming because, conceptually, the liberation movement does not view itself as a means to an end but rather as an end in itself. As Fanon pointed out, that liberation movements fell slowly into dictatorships in Asia and Africa was a consequence of their being trapped in the cyclicality of want, which precluded acting in concert to achieve power.

Now the story should get even more exciting. Work and action both have the capacity to initiate and endure. Given that it extracts, implements, makes, and adds something of relative permanence to the world, work is *necessarily* violent. Action, by contrast, begets power and thus remains by definition nonviolent. Phenomenologically these two propositions are sound: note that in Arendt's conceptual system, without the creative capacity of work, action would not be possible. Politically, therefore, we are dealing with a simultaneously violent *and* nonviolent moment of political endurance. Of course, one may object that Arendt's concept of "work" is not meant to enter politics. I argue that it does. Both work and action dwell in the unique human ability of natality, of bringing something new to this world. In Arendt's words, "the act of foundation inevitably develops its own stability and permanence, and authority in this context is nothing more or less than a kind of necessary 'augmentation' by virtue of which all innovations and changes remain tied back to the foundation which, at the same time, they augment and increase" (Arendt 1963, 202). Stability and permanence result from a foundational act that is meant to expand: Are these not the signs of phenomenological deworlding/ reworlding and the violence of life against life that arises from natality? Arendt recognizes that acting – which is nonviolent by definition – will inevitably perpetuate itself through instrumental violence. This inevitability arises from the fact that humans never create anything entirely new (1963, 28). She argues that the act of founding remains concerned with durability and that it is the vista of stability that makes the republic appealing to the people (1963, 223–4). So she suggests two meanings of "constitution" as an act of natality: constitution simultaneously signifies an act and the result of an act (1963, 203). Arendt is acutely aware of this dilemma of constituting, and she makes efforts to isolate the moment when action, in the form of power as the congregation of diverse equals, stands out as a purely nonviolent beginning. Her cases include the town hall meetings during the American Revolution as well as the workers' soviets during the 1905 and 1917 revolutions in Russia. During the February Revolution of 1917, Russian "workers in the factories organized themselves into councils, *soviets*, for the purpose of representative self-government" (1963, 262; emphasis in original). What is significant about this experiment is that the soviets created a body politic specific to a specific task. Arendt, too, pauses on this unique feature of the councils: "It would be tempting to spin out further the potentialities of the councils, but it certainly is wiser to say with Jefferson, 'Begin them only for a single purpose; they will soon show for what others they are the best instruments'" (1963, 279). The council system was a genuine experiment in that the council was not an ideological construct or an instrument for the politically ambitious. "For the remarkable thing about the councils was of course not only that they crossed all party lines, that members of various parties sat in them together, but that such party membership played no role whatsoever. They were in fact the only political organs for people who belonged to no party" (1963, 263). Referring to the role played by the soviets in the 1917 Russian and 1956 Hungarian revolutions, Arendt avers: "In both instances councils or *soviets* had sprung up everywhere, completely independent of one another, workers', soldiers', and peasants' councils in the case of Russia, and most disparate kinds of councils in the case of Hungary: neighbourhood councils ... so-called revolutionary councils ... councils of writers and artists ... students' and youths'... [and] workers' councils, ... councils in the army, among civil servants, and so on" (1963, 266–7; emphasis in original). Here let us note that in relation to Arendt's ignoring the "social question," the quest for freedom that epitomized (for Arendt) the Hungarian Revolution as a genuine attempt to build a body politic took place in the *aftermath* of the social reforms and equality of conditions brought about by socialism. So in Arendt's view, this genuine body politic, shaped from below, qualified as politics as such. No wonder then that she contrasted the council system with today's mass democracy. In the councils she saw the possibility of political revival, revitalized liberty, and the emergence of nonviolent acting in concert. Referring to

Jefferson's reflection on American town halls (quoted above), Arendt did not hesitate to substantiate what instrumental value the councils might have: "the best instruments, for example, for breaking up the modern mass society, with its dangerous tendency toward the formation of pseudo-political mass movements, or rather, the best, the most natural way for interspersing it at the grass roots with an 'élite' that is chosen by no one but constitutes itself" (1963, 279). She could not have been clearer. The councils – these embodiments of acting in concert in which a plurality of individuals converge as "emergent publics" (Angus 2001) attending to *res publica* and thereby creating the "public realm" – are the only means through which a genuine body politic can transform fabricated parliamentary democracy. No wonder, then, that her political ideal was a confederation of autonomous republics (Bernstein 2013, 100). In other words, "the polity she comes to imagine, however briefly, is something other than the nation-state: a federation that diffuses both claims of national sovereignty and the ontology of individualism" (Butler 2007).

Yet Arendt's endorsement of the councils does not stop her from taking issue with those whose ideas seem close to hers: the anarchists. She blames Proudhon and Bakunin – nineteenth-century anarchists who advocated the council system – for not fully understanding the conceptual limitations of their thought and thus remaining in the dark as to why "successful" revolutions led not to the dissolution of the state but rather to the forging of new forms of government (1963, 261). In fairness, Proudhon and Bakunin could not have applied the wisdom of hindsight enjoyed by Arendt. But the point is taken. From medieval Swiss cantons to modern-day councils, examples of genuine self-regulating, autonomous bodies politic emerging out of individual liberty and thus protecting it abound. But "the point of the matter is that none of them, with the possible exception of the medieval town, had ever the slightest influence on the minds of the people who in the course of a revolution spontaneously organized themselves in councils" (Arendt 1963, 261). Arendt underscores the *spontaneity* of councils and bitterly laments revolution's failure – unaccounted for by the anarchists – to dissolve the state, which returns (with a vengeance) in the post-revolutionary period. Conceptually, this failure stems from the intersection of work and action. Because we do not create a new body politic in a vacuum (as mentioned in chapter 1), force and violence are needed to ensure that what is founded will endure. We encounter a genuine dilemma: "when the moment of revolution had come, it turned out that there was no power left to seize, so that the revolutionists found themselves before the rather uncomfortable alternative of either putting their own pre-revolutionary 'power', that is, the organization of the party apparatus, into the vacated power centre of the defunct government, or simply joining the new revolutionary power centres which had sprung up without their help" (1963, 257). We do know the choice made by modern revolutionaries. This dilemma stems from the fact that it is *natality* – the ability to bring about something new – that *politically links human work and action to both nonviolence and violence.* In one of her best phenomenological moments, Arendt clarifies the commonplace yet avoidable *formative violence* (through the example of the English Revolution) as follows:

> [Cromwell] introduces ... the means of violence which indeed are ordinary and necessary for all purposes of fabrication *precisely because something is created, not out of nothing, but out of given material which must be violated in order to yield itself to the formative processes out of which a thing, a fabricated object, will arise* ... What happened was that together with the new beginning the aboriginal, legendary crime of Western mankind reappeared in the scene of European politics, as though once again fratricide was to be the origin of fraternity and bestiality the fountainhead of humanity, only that now, in conspicuous opposition to man's age-old dreams as well as to his later concepts, violence by no means gave birth to something new and stable but, on the contrary, drowned in a "revolutionary torrent" the beginning as well as the beginners. (1963, 208; emphasis added)

Although a compelling historical reality with more cases than any one person can remember, the degeneration of power into violence – endemic to the founding moment – is *not* inevitable. Every beginning involves deworlding/reworlding, and thus it is never nonviolent, strictly speaking, and the violence of fabrication devours both founders and founding by conjuring up the forces of "aboriginal, legendary crime." In this nuanced understanding of founding (non)violence rests Arendt's critique of Sorel and Fanon. She does not refute that liberation necessitates violence, for natality is linked to both fabrication and individual liberty. Rather, she objects to the *rationalization of violence* by whatever name. She finds Sorel's concept of "violence" as instrumental and rational activity objectionable (Arendt 1970, 79), even though it matches her definition entirely. In Arendt's words:

> Violence, being instrumental by nature, is rational to the extent that it is effective in reaching the end that must justify it. And since when we act we never know with any certainty the eventual consequences of what we are doing, violence can remain rational only if it pursues short-term goals. Violence does not promote causes, neither history nor revolution, neither progress nor reaction; but it can serve to dramatize grievances and bring them to public attention. (1970, 79).

I interpret this point as such: although a "given material ... must be violated in order to yield itself to the formative processes" (Arendt 1963, 208), and although due to the force of circumstance (for Arendt "force" denotes inevitability) I may end up engaging in the violence that comes with the act of founding and enduring, I must never accept violence. The acceptance and thus naturalization and rationalization of violence guarantee the demise of action. The conclusion, then, cannot be clearer:

> To sum up: politically speaking, it is insufficient to say that power and violence are not the same. Power and violence are opposites; where the one rules absolutely, the other is absent. *Violence appears where power is in jeopardy, but left to its own course it ends in power's disappearance.* This implies that *it is not correct to think of the opposite of violence as nonviolence;* to speak of nonviolent power is actually redundant. Violence can destroy power; it is utterly incapable of creating it. (Arendt 1970, 56; emphasis added)

Humans are instruments of the beginnings (Arendt 1963, 211). The act of beginning inevitably brings with it its own *principium*, which renders the principle and the founding "coeval" (1963, 212–13). With the beginning perceived as self-contained, a marker of its authenticity and a historic shift in temporality (1963, 206), a course of action begins, and I remain simultaneously its author and its object, the actor and acted-on. There is nothing to fall back on, neither eschatological inevitability nor dialectical history. Just as Benjamin saw it, God is needed when there are no foundations on which to rely when bringing something new to this world (Villa 1996, 59). "Thinking without banisters," I rely on my judgment alone. And thus the dilemma persists.

A passing note regarding the permanence of councils: in recent history, except for the short-lived Spanish Revolution (1936) – short-lived because it was overthrown by fascism – we have witnessed the enduring but besieged experiments of the Zapatistas of Chiapas, Mexico (1994). The initial armed uprising of Mayan indigenous peoples led by the Zapatista Army of National Liberation (EZLN) broke out in several municipalities in the southern state of Chiapas on 1 January 1994, the very same day the North American Free Trade Agreement (NAFTA) came into effect – an agreement that resulted in further disenfranchising and impoverishing Mexican peasants. After several days of armed clashes, the Zapatistas entered a long period of negotiations with the Mexican government. An international solidarity movement – a powerful one, thanks to the Internet – impeded the Mexican state's efforts to crush the Zapatistas. The EZLN failed to create a nationwide movement for participatory democracy based on justice and dignity; even so, in rebel-controlled territory (which is still under siege by the Mexican army), with international support, the EZLN has succeeded in creating a participatory, non-hierarchical system of autonomous self-governance that has significantly raised the standard of living of the rebel communities compared to that of rural Mexico in general (Debray 1996; Holloway 1998; Subcommandante Marcos 2001; Mentinis 2006).

Similarly, since 2012 when I began writing this book, the world has been witnessing a unique experiment: the democratic confederalism of Rojava (or Western Kurdistan) in northern Syria, a haven for two and a half million people of various ethnicities (Kurdish, Yazidi, Arab, Assyrian, Turkmen, Alawite Kurd, and Armenian), who have been fighting amidst a multi-sided civil war (aided and abetted by two superpowers – the United States and Russia) and who were caught between the pincers of the brutal Islamic State (*Da'esh*) and the Turkish state, both of which were/are intent on suppressing the Kurdish struggle for self-determination, until the dynamics of the civil war changed against Rojava with the Syrian government gaining control over major sections of the country and Turkey invading the Kurdish regions in northern Syria by 2018. In one of the most hostile regions in the world, in a country torn apart by a protracted civil war, four autonomous cantons (Efrin, Kobanî, and Jizîrê, and the more recent canton of Gire Sipi, which joined Rojava in late 2015 after the liberation of Tel Abyad) enabled grassroots, participatory, gender-egalitarian decision-making through an elaborate non-hierarchical system of local councils based on radical pluralism, libertarian municipalism, and social ecology. Rojava had set itself the task of ending the state and of ruling not *with* power but *against* power.

It is important to remember that in Rojava the lower councils are not required to carry out the decisions of the higher councils, in part or in whole, if they find these decisions contrary to their own visions and decisions (Strangers in a Tangled Wilderness 2015). With the changing geopolitics of the region, and the intensification of the civil war in Syria (where NATO, Russia, Iran, Turkey, and Saudi Arabia, through their shadow militias, are fighting a proxy war), the future of Rojava is seriously imperilled, in particular after Turkish invasion. Nonetheless, Rojava provides a shining example of how the people, when left to themselves, are capable of creating a body politic and public realm in participatory, democratic, and egalitarian ways, without caring much about a state hanging above their heads.

In all likelihood, given her clear positions against Black Power and the student movement in the 1960s (in *On Violence*), Arendt would probably not have endorsed the Rojava experiment due to the element of "want" in the Kurdish movement, even though Rojava encompasses the two "principles" of Arendtian "liberation" theory: first, it is resisting its antagonists (the Islamic State and Turkey), even violently, so that the Kurds would emerge as a "political people," as people who have won the right to have rights; and second, Rojava has created councils as a genuine power formation for acting in concert. Reminiscent of Fanon, but also akin to Arendt's "Jewish liberation," the Rojava armed revolution has created nonviolent acting in concert – the emergence of a new political people. Arendt affirmed the need for a Jewish army for Jewish liberation (even endorsing Jewish terrorist attacks against Nazi personnel [Losurdo 2015, 136]), but because of her assimilationist, universal-citizenship approach, she denied the African American movement precisely the same. She called African American student unions "interest groups" and called the "Negro demands" "clearly silly and outrageous" (Arendt 1970, 19). She argued that the Jews had fought against a regime that denied them their very existence, while it was possible for African Americans to thrive within the framework of the United States Constitution without particularistic rights (hence her rejection of affirmative action). While her rationale was clear, it was and still is unjustifiable: she was denying agency to African Americans and their inalienable right to define their rights! The same, I suppose, would go for the Kurdish movement, even though, to paraphrase her, "when you are attacked as a Kurd, you defend as a Kurd." The African American movement, she declared, did not "transform ... 'races' ... into peoples" (2007, 171), since African Americans were already rights-bearing citizens of the United States. She also denied Third World liberation movements (the Kurdish movement at present) the empathy she had granted the Jews. Instead of sticking to her "rights-based" political philosophy, she should have adopted Fanon's point that "Nazism transformed the whole of Europe into a genuine colony" (2004, 57), and she should have seen the connection between the Jewish anti-colonial liberation and Third World national liberation movements. That said, her conflicted position (Losurdo 2015, 136) blocks our view of what is at issue here and throughout this book – that ultimately, violence and nonviolence cannot be clearly distinguished, and when it comes to liberation, the distinction becomes ever more impossible to uphold, however noble our intentions and efforts.

Are all revolutions condemned to replace one strong state with another? Are grassroots councils inevitably ephemeral? If, despite the menacing forces, the above experiments endure and grow into models for future action and community organization, what will be their theoretical ramifications for Arendtian analysis?

Referring to Arendt's advocacy for a Jewish army, Bernstein rightly argues that her endorsement exemplifies the concept of "power" (2013, 95–6) as opposed to violence (Arendt 1970, 56). Bernstein further observes: "Although Arendt draws a sharp distinction between violence and power, and claims that power is nonviolent, she was not a pacifist. She certainly thought that there were times when violence is justified for political purposes" (2013, 95). Here is where Arendt is misunderstood. Bernstein does not see that liberation from oppression, insofar as it involves acting in concert (power) and founding a new body politic, is by definition nonviolent, regardless of the necessity or inevitability (a human condition) of (Jewish) violent, armed uprising. To state that "violence is justified for political purposes" (Bernstein) is to express an instrumental understanding of political action that is foreign to Arendt's thinking. In the moment of liberation, the very distinction between violence and nonviolence is suspended. So one cannot essentialize violence as a timeless mode of action. The tripartite concept of violence that is central to this book enables us to step back from forms of action to the conditions under which they emerge as violent and are epistemologically recognized as such. Here, for Arendt and for me, the key term is the "human condition," in which the "force of circumstance" imposes certain economies of acting. Arendt recognizes the contextuality of human action when she observes: "In a head-on clash between violence and power, the outcome is hardly in doubt. If Gandhi's enormously powerful and successful strategy of nonviolent resistance had met with a different enemy – Stalin's Russia, Hitler's Germany, even prewar Japan, instead of England – the outcome would not have been decolonization, but massacre and submission" (1970, 53). Here, Arendt errs analytically. Well, yes, if Gandhi had failed or had been killed in an earlier stage of his political career, we would not have had a successful tradition of Gandhian nonviolence to fall back on, and this book would have been much shorter! Yet Arendt errs in her causation argument by attaching India's independence – a successful outcome – to the type of colonial adversary the Indians faced (in her view, England seemed like a "gentle," almost benign, Enlightenment-style colonizer), not to postwar international circumstances that made it impossible for colonialism to continue. In other words, the "force of circumstance" is to be sought in the international economic context that led to disintegration of the colonial system and that gave birth to the national liberation movements in Asia, Africa, and Latin America. I will return to this observation in chapter 8.

The point is, Arendt would not subscribe to the *binary* opposition of violence and nonviolence – a commonplace assumption and presupposition that this study probes and problematizes. She is much closer to the phenomenological gaze of this study than first appears. She encourages us to think of violence and nonviolence (power) as conceptually distinct moments while analytically showing that these theoretically conceptualized pure moments, except for transitory historic turns, do not exist and cannot endure. She refuses the comfort of relying on fundamental assumptions or foundational gestures. She is too original for that. For her, the only condition under which nonviolent founding does not lead to violent constituting is where Jefferson's insight leads us to: a convergence of diverse equals – be it in town hall meetings, councils, or any other egalitarian-participatory bodies politic in which individuals can exercise their liberty outside of the law and engage in persuading one another towards shared goals for the purpose of reaching a common accord on a specific issue. Such a body politic can only remain genuine through its *transience*: as soon as the nonviolent constitutive act establishes permanence and "fabricates" a system of ruling and authority, it yields to a violent onslaught justified through the institutions it has founded. If it turns out to be fit for other purposes, such a body politic may serve as a useful experience and a lesson in politics, but it cannot institutionalize itself. Arendt is somewhat in sync with the original thesis of this book, I believe, regarding its tripartite phenomenology of violence; this shows the extent of Schürmann's intellectual indebtedness to Arendt. Power, when it means acting in concert, does not impose, institute, or structure in any permanent way. In the pure moment of its formation, it does not yield to hubristic, institutional, or structural violence. Power, therefore, does not foreclose on possibilities, and it leaves the future open. It is through acting in concert that a people is liberated from the tripartite modalities of violence and that it gains the ability to exercise liberty.

Arendt shows the problem of deworlding/reworlding and the collapse of the binary between violence and nonviolence that is inevitably involved in every act of constituting. Clearly, she is an advocate of nonviolence, but she also stays honest regarding the limitations of nonviolence, limitations that stem from the human condition and that make it a challenge to craft something new that will endure. I have suggested already that it is only through action that (non)violence reveals itself. At times, acting may appear to be nonviolent, but the mere *possibility* of acting – which in facing an open and contingent future tends to ensure that the action's results will endure – also becomes the source of violence in acting. What safeguards nonviolence against violence may well be our ability to deliberate, reflect, and judge (to which I will return). And this is precisely why thinking is the most perilous of all endeavours in life.

Now, we need to critically revisit one last theoretical engagement with the issue of violence – an approach that follows the intellectual legacy of Benjamin and Arendt. In reading Georgio Agamben's theory of the rightless bare life, we will return to some of the issues of Arendt's philosophy as well.

Agamben: *Homo Sacer*'s Actless Existence

The modern state's monopoly over the legitimate use of force (Weber) means that the sovereign within the state stands as the sole agent to bestow rights upon citizens. To the extent that postwar states prided themselves on granting rights to citizens, for a few decades in the West (but not exclusively there) the hegemonic construction of citizenship under liberal democracies rendered the state the agent that retained the exclusive monopoly over the legitimate distribution of rights (Vahabzadeh 2003, 122). A quick glance at the world, however, makes it clear that today the rights associated with citizenship are sharply under attack by states. The "state of exception" arising as the norm in politics today (both international and domestic) involves the *suspension of the rights* that were long bestowed upon citizens by the original social contract (constitution). Thus, *suspending the laws* that protect citizens from naked violence has also become the exclusive privilege of the sovereign. This is where the genealogy of conceptualizing the impact of violence on individuals within the sovereign's legal system becomes significant. From the "sacred man" (Benjamin), to the "end of rights of man" (Arendt), to "*homo sacer*" and the "state of exception" (Agamben), we can trace the gradual dehumanization of the subject of citizenship – a process through which the individual, deprived of the basic human rights, is reduced to mere, corporeal, animal existence. The suspension of *habeas corpus* in the aftermath of 9/11 under President George W. Bush and the infamous Guantanamo Bay prison are examples of the reduction of humans to "bare life." Note that *citizenship is the only means of communication between human individuals and the modern state*, and therefore once citizenship is suspended, the connection between the two is severed: the citizen becomes ungovernable, so to speak, and the state becomes redundant and unnecessary, for it has lost its constitutional *raison d'être*. The state now hangs above the citizenry. We will see how Agamben's approach to the "state of exception" and *homo sacer* is connected to the organizing concept of this chapter: liberation.

In "The Decline of the Nation States and the End of the Rights of Man," Arendt discusses the historical process through which the "state of exception" was achieved in Europe when the Nazis rose to power. To oust the *indésirables* from the laws connecting the citizen to the state, first a process of denationalization was implemented. In a "state of emergency," the rule of law is replaced by "rule by decree" under which there "are no general principles which simple reason can understand" (Arendt 1958b, 244). In Germany, the national element that forms a nation-state had come to be identified with claims to national – indeed racial – identity. Hence minorities – Romani or Jewish – no longer automatically qualified for citizenship and rights. This led to "the transformation of the state from an instrument of the law into an instrument of the nation" (1958b, 275). One cannot do anything about one's (perceived) origins when the origins of the individual are racialized and thus "naturalized." The point is rather tangible for us: recall the "racial profiling" in many Western states in the aftermath of 9/11. Arendt found parallels between "rule by decree" and the suspension of rights and thus the "humanity" of certain groups, on the one hand, and the demonic practice of slavery, on the other. One group deprives another from freedom, and the crime is attributed to nature. According to Arendt,

> slavery's fundamental offence against human rights was not that it took liberty away ... but that it excluded a certain category of people even from the possibility of fighting for freedom – a fight possible under tyranny, and even under the desperate conditions of modern terror ... Slavery's crime against humanity did not begin when one people defeated and enslaved its enemies ... but when slavery became an institution in which some men were "born" free and others slave, when it was forgotten that it was man who had deprived his fellow-men of freedom, and when the sanction for the crime was attributed to nature. (1958b, 297)

Here is when a human, expelled from political existence, is reduced to "bare naked life." "If a human being loses his political status, he should, according to the implications of the inborn and inalienable rights of man, come under exactly the situation for which the declarations of such general rights provided. Actually the opposite is the case. It seems that a man who is nothing but a man has lost the very qualities which make it possible for other people to treat him as a fellow-man" (1958b, 300).

In dealing precisely with the consequences of all this, in a series of influential works, Georgio Agamben elaborated on the "state of exception" in which the separation of powers has collapsed and the executive has absorbed the legislative power (Agamben 2005, 18). This is a paradoxical situation, for "the state of exception appears as the legal form of what cannot have legal form," and as such, the state of exception "binds and, at the same time, abandons the living being to law" (2005, 1). "The State ... is not founded on a social bond, of which it would be the expression, but rather on the dissolution, the unbinding it prohibits" (2007, 85). But the state of exception indeed reveals the paradox of sovereignty in that "the sovereign is, at the same time, outside and inside the juridical order" (Agamben 1998, 15). Thus, the exception is in fact the origin of the law and the sovereign (1998, 26–8). The state of exception is evoked in order for the order, the law, or *nomos* to demarcate its field of applicability. "[T]he state of exception separates the norm from its application in order to make its application possible. It introduces a zone of anomie into the law in order to make the effective regulation ... of the real possible" (Agamben 2005, 36). Since there is no divine intervention, nor are there preordained

rules of separation, the law must enact the state of exception in order
to remain applicable. Thus the "juridico-political machine" determines
the "threshold of undecidability between anomie and *nomos*" through
an "essential fiction" (2005, 86). The fiction enables the sovereign's
mode of communication, in the state of exception, with the uncommu-
nicable anomic subject that defies and thus stands outside the law. "For
the State," Agamben observes, "what is important is never the singularity as such, but only its inclusion in some identity, whatever identity"
(Agamben 2007, 85). What follows is that a "being radically devoid of
any representable identity would be absolutely irrelevant to the State"
(2007, 85). The state of exception's revealing mark is the sacrifice of
homo sacer, the sacred and thus sacrificial human, whose killing calls for
no punishment (Agamben 1998, 71, 102).

In an Arendtian vein, Agamben makes a distinction between *bios* –
the human life, the political human, the citizen – and *zoé* – the animal
life, the "natural" man, the sacrificial figure. Thus *zoé* is the pre-political
figure, but it is brought into political life, as "bare life," for the sake of
punishment and sacrifice. The natural man is thus *banned* from the political. His or her sacrifice is an expression of sovereign violence (Agamben 1998, 107). Modern democracy does not abolish the sacred life but
rather "disseminates it into every individual body, making it into what
is at stake in political conflicts" (1998, 124). Being the *outcome* of the
biopolitical machine, bare life proves the non-relationality of law and
life (Agamben 2005, 87–8). The concentration or labour *camp* is the
milieu where bare life is produced (Agamben 1998, 175); it epitomizes
the state of exception and the sovereign's executive performance on the
sacrificial life. "The state of exception, which was essentially a temporary
suspension of the juridico-political order, now becomes a new and stable
spatial arrangement inhabited by the bare life that more and more can
no longer be inscribed in that order" (1998, 175).

The singularized individual is therefore the locus of the state's exercise of violence and sovereignty. Benjamin's "sacred man" (1996, 251)
and Arendt's "the end of the rights of man" (1958b) both allude to "a
theory of the state of exception [which] is the preliminary condition for
any definition of the relation that binds, and, at the same time, abandons the living being to law" (Agamben 2005, 1). *Homo sacer* shows that
in the state of exception, the law can no longer deal with the human in
the citizen. Therefore, the citizen has to be deprived of citizenship and
become, simply, animal, so that the human, hitherto guarded by citizenship, is exposed to the sovereign's punitive decisions. The camp is the

venue in which political violence reveals itself *par excellence*. For Agamben, the camp is not just any political phenomenon; it epitomizes his *political ontology*: "the birth of the camp in our time appears as an event that decisively signals the political space of modernity itself" (Agamben 1998, 174). I will return to this point shortly.

Jacques Derrida's engagement with this tradition in "Force of Law: The 'Mystical Foundation of Authority'" (1992) relies on the accentuation of the points of *undecidability* between force and violence in *Gewalt*, on the one hand, and legitimate power and justified authority, on the other. He echoes Benjamin's point that violence is not simply a means (Derrida 1992, 31). He points out the difference between the "force of law" as legitimate and violence that is deemed unjust (1992, 6). This difference, as one might expect when reading the founder of deconstruction, is a *deferred difference* – or *différance* (1992, 39). We obey the laws not because they are just but because they imply force and authority (1992, 12). The law "is always an authorized force, a force that justifies itself or is justified in applying itself, even if this justification may be judged from elsewhere to be unjust or unjustifiable" (1992, 5). Enforceability is by necessity included in every law. And this is the source of the *aporias* Derrida discusses in his essay: the law is intended to embody justice (as *avenir*, always "to-come"), and it can only be present through force. This is because "the operation that amounts to founding, inaugurating, justifying law (*droit*), making law, would consist of a *coup de force*, of a performative and therefore interpretive violence that in itself is neither just nor unjust" (1992, 13). Derrida recognizes that in its founding moment, the origin of authority is neither legal nor illegal (1992, 14). This observation, of course, dates back to the founders of political modernity. Jean-Jacques Rousseau's writings, for instance, prefigure many of the aforementioned discussions on foundational violence, albeit within a very different discourse. In *The Social Contract*, Rousseau (1968) recognizes that the lawgiver is outside of the law, just as he points out the abyssal foundation of the state that gives humans security and preserves their lives even while demanding from them sacrifice for the sake of preserving the state. Probing the relationship between the law, on the one hand, and either justice or enforceability, on the other, enables Derrida to arrive at the radical *undecidablity that permeates every law*.

Back to Agamben, if the camp epitomizes the politically determined space in which humans are deprived of political rights (*bios*), rendered *homo sacer*, and thereby reduced to animal life (*zoë*), then the concentration camp detainee is incapable of political action. This is akin to

Arendt's observation that slavery "excluded a certain category of people even from the possibility of fighting for freedom" (Arendt 1958b, 297). Agamben's Hobbsian concept of the sovereign shows that the sovereign hangs above the very people it emerges to protect and thus has no "organic" relations with the people – in other words, "sovereign power cannot have a contractual origin" (Laclau 2014, 209; see also Agamben 2007, 86). But just like Hobbes, Agamben misses the point entirely: that the people are capable of fighting back. The problem arising from Arendt and Agamben rests with their *conceptual abandonment* of the depoliticized, and thus rightless, human as she or he who can only be killed, injured, robbed, or interned with impunity. A certain binary permeates their thinking: you are either the rights-bearing citizen or you are the rightless sacrificial man. Arendt, at least, has the idea of the "right to have rights" (1958b, 296, 298). Agamben allows the *homo sacer*, the bandit, the exile, the public enemy, or the interned, to appear, conceptually, only as a helpless victim. And this last point needs qualification and a double-critique of Agamben. That is why we should first turn to Ernesto Laclau's critique of Agamben.

According to Laclau, Agamben's "genealogy is not sensitive enough to structural diversity and, in the end, risks ending in sheer teleology" (2014, 207). He points out that Agamben treats the ban – the imposition of closure regarding who can participate in the political and who cannot and should therefore be interned – as an absolute and thereby ignores the other possible responses of the sovereign to the political crisis, of which the ban is only one. The ban excludes the individual from political community – by taking away his or her fundamental rights – in order to punish him or her outside of the law. For Laclau, Agamben's argument is based on two assumptions: he assumes, first, that the banned person, the sacrificial, natural man, is "dispossessed of any kind of collective identity," and second, that "the situation of the outsider is one of radical defencelessness" (2014, 210). Yet the exclusion, exteriority, or negativity of the banned person provides the condition of possibility of collective identity (2014, 211) beyond the positivity of the sovereign. As such, Laclau shows that Agamben completely misses this point: that collective identity and thus *particularistic* social movements are the products of radical exteriority, political exclusion, and the ban (2014, 213). The bandit and the banished (Agamben 1998, 183) therefore are not outside of the law, Laclau asserts. More radical than the exile or the banished, I argue, is the figure of the bandit as radical, incommensurable alterity. The exile fits Agamben's model, for she has been, supposedly, at some point in her previous life a rights-bearing citizen, and now deprived of those rights, she has been expelled from her city as an exile sent into Outlandia (Vahabzadeh 2006, 172; 2012a).

Bandits act according to their own laws, the laws outside of those of the sovereign. The bandit is the trope of the radically inassimilable singular, the one no sovereign can ever govern, for the bandit is the "being radically devoid of any representable identity" (Agamben 2007, 85). An equally curious case is that of the "public enemy": distinct from the foreign enemy, he is protected by the "laws of people" and must therefore be deprived of that protection (Agamben, 2005, 80). He stands as the figuration of the outside threat inside. It is precisely because of his incommensurablity that the bandit's condition of permanent anomie and sacrificiality grants him the subject position endowed with radical subversion, an *originary* political act. The implications of this critique for Agamben's theory are fatal: the binary – *bios* and *zoé* – collapses (Laclau 2014, 214). This harks back to Agamben's political ontology: contrary to his assertion, modernity is not an age in which politics is characterized by the camp (Laclau 2014, 218). Agamben acknowledges that to "show law in its nonrelation to life and life in its nonrelation to law means to open a space between them for human action, which once claimed for itself the name of 'politics'" (Agamben 2005, 88). Yet the legalist framework of Agamben's analysis is incapable of retrieving the agent of politics, and the glimmer of hope is dimmed by the shadow of the biopolitical machine. That a homogeneous and fully reconciled society can be achieved – although in a camp, through the ban, and by virtue of the sovereign's state of exception and utter exercise of force – is simply the philosopher's fancy.

I would like to dwell on Laclau's critique, in particular his collapsing of the *bios–zoé* binary, but I would also extend his critical assessment to more fundamental issues pertaining not only to Agamben but also to Arendt, from whom Agamben draws, at least in part, his political theory. I mentioned, with Laclau, that Agamben could see the banned person only as a victim, as a life reduced to animality, to sheer existence. The claim that, properly understood, *human* life can only be political reveals a certain prejudice. Arendt's notion of pre-political life, as we saw, is connected to labour's cyclical activity, and as such, she finds labour animalistic and incapable of founding something new and enduring. Hence her exclusion of the "social question." Unlike in Arendt, in Agamben pre-political life remains unexamined and simply assumed.

I wish to say that the camp, as the epitome of banned existence, has existed in various civilizational memories. From legendary slave uprisings, in particular the one led by Spartacus that led to the Third Servile War in the first century BCE, to the more recent examples of the Warsaw Ghetto Uprising of 19 April 1943 (which surprisingly lasted about a month) and various uprisings in Nazi concentration camps, to the two organized hunger strikes (2005 and 2013) by prisoners taken as "enemy combatants" at the Guantanamo Bay extra-judicial and extra-territorial internment camp – examples abound. In snatching the individual from her or his world and stripping her or him of rights, the camp represents sudden and sheer *deworldedness*; what Agamben attributes to the ban, though, is *zoé* or animal, non-political, mere existence rendered to the banned human. As such, he does not entertain, let alone theorize, the idea that merely by virtue of their existence humans are capable of fighting back, liberating themselves, reasserting their *bios*, and (re-)emerging not only as political individuals but also potentially as the founding figures of a new political order. *It is precisely when I do not have rights that I fight for rights.* Agamben misses the point that nothing can take away the possibility of *reworlding* even in the context of the banned person in the camp. Reworlding is the structural workings of phenomenalization, and it takes place simply because we exist, act, and communicate. Period.

Now, if the reduction of the rights-bearing human to sheer existence – animal life and *homo sacer* – cannot be theoretically sustained, then the very distinction between *zoé* and *bios* collapses, as mentioned. This last point should be traced back to Arendt's distinction between unenduring–cyclical (and biological) labour and enduring work and action. The conclusion seems inevitable: Arendt is wrong in viewing labour as *apolitical.* I am a banned person, and that being so, the mere sustenance of my physical body – that I live, breath, eat, and thus am able to stand before the other, cry my voice, move objects at will, reshape my surroundings and the world, that I visibly occupy space and am capable of allocating my time to resistance and plan for the *avenir* justice – is my greatest power of all, although this body is constantly imperilled in the camp. The potential for my political life resides in my sheer existence within the economies of presence that enable me to rise above my conditions. The biological life I occupy inevitably contains within it political life; seeing biological life outside political life is deeply rooted in the philosophical prejudice going back to the slave society of the classical Greeks and it was resurrected centuries later through the Cartesian supremacy of mind over body. In fact, reading Agamben backwards, we can argue that the camp is not simply the means of depriving me of my *bios*; it is, rather, primarily a "political" space built on the systematic repression, even eradication, of my *zoé* as the fundamental material–biological ground for my actions regardless of my rights. Put differently, the camp is the political space through which the sovereign denies that which denies it: the untamable life of imaginative humans who are not bound to the sovereign's laws. What radically distinguishes Arendt from Agamben is the absence of natality in his theory, that is, the creative act of founding, which is always a political act. Thus he reduces politics to the realm of sovereign's exercise of force and granting of rights. He ignores the *radical unfixity* that informs politics: that it is by virtue of exclusion that we fight for inclusion, and – in the case of expansion of rights – that the average citizen intentionally excludes him- or herself as the "radical other" so that he or she acquires the particular rights attached to his or her identity. Political life, therefore, is born outside the realm of politics; in losing what they represent, *bios* and *zoé* lose their polarity.

The camp is the epitome of sheer force and unrelenting violence. Yet the banned person, the sacrificial life, through collective action can emerge –indeed, *has* emerged in innumerable historic examples – out of this sheer existence and has taken part in creating power by acting collaboratively – the most nonviolent act. *The space of the violent camp and the violated body of the banned person become the context that gives rise to nonviolent founding through resistance and uprising:* this signifies liberation *par excellence.* In other words, it is true that the camp reduces the rights-bearing citizen to the sacrificial human, to naked life, to an object of indefinite detention, extralegal treatment, torture, and execution. This is precisely when the prisoner in the camp discovers the power of Refusal. This is not even the "right" to refusal; here, Refusal precedes and produces rights: for the one who simply exists and can thus make decisions, it is the fundamental principle of rising up. Humans rebel when they have nothing to lose but their chains, and precisely because the banned person has nothing but his or her physical, corporeal existence to fall back to – an existence supposedly outside politics – claiming one's existence as Refusal emerges as the fundamental trait of the human subject. The pre-political, banned person who is reduced to naked life is *already political.* Arendt does not see this, nor does Agamben.

Phenomenologically, *violent deworldedness,* as epitomized by the camp, retains within itself the very potential of *nonviolent reworlding.* Again, *neither violence in its most extreme exercise nor nonviolence can be found as pure and distinct moments.* I rise up, liberate, and create because despite all adversity, despite the violent denial of my humanity, I simply exist.

The Excess of Violence: Nonviolence

The trajectory of my conceptual phenomenology in this chapter reveals an important theoretical contribution – indeed, my *fourth set of propositions.* The camp is one of the most violent places in the human world, yet, following Laclau's insightful interjection, the camp is the source of emergence of collective action, the convergence of diverse equals (Arendt), and thus a founding power, which for Arendt represents nonviolence proper. If despite its hubristic and institutionalized, totalizing reach the camp remains ultimately incapable of preventing the emergence of resistance – as nonviolent acting in concert – against its systemic violence, then violence and nonviolence, as suggested, cannot be conceived in *oppositional* terms. To reiterate, camp violence is totalizing, institutional, and systemic; from the point of view of its prisoners, camp violence is *unsurpassable:* although the prisoners are able to "act in concert" and stage an uprising in the camp by putting their lives on the line, they are unable to pose counter-violence against their jailers that is potentially greater than camp violence in size or reach. In its totalizing reach, camp violence has achieved a monopoly over the means of force. Yet the sheer and ruthless violence of the camp is the condition of possibility of prisoners' nonviolent emergence as potentially liberated humanity. If camp violence is indeed understood by its totalizing reach from which no human activity can escape, then how can nonviolent liberation emerge within the camp? Here is the answer: *by virtue of its totalizing exercise, violence produces its own excess,* a field of action inadvertently opened up by violence's attempt at closure and through its totalizing effort, a field that slips through violence's domain of intelligibility, implementation, and management. Let me justify my recourse to the term "excess," as often applied (and appropriately for our discussion) in terms of "excessive force": an *over*-implementation of instrumental force that goes beyond the limits of its intended purposive rationality and thus becomes not only uncontrollable but also "unproductive" when measured against the specific logic of its application. Just as excessive nutrition causes illness and excessive exercise leads to an athlete's fatigue, excessive force produces results *contrary* to the original, institutional intent. In other words, the *excess* – the by-product – slips through the force's logic and acquires demonic and arbitrary proportions that can potentially produce the conditions for the collapse of the (rationally conceived) force. Thus, as "excessive," the force in question ends up working against its own institutional logic. Excessive force undermines the very legitimacy in the "legitimate use" of *Gewalt* (Weber). I want to push this "logic of excess" to its inevitable conclusion and propose that in its excess, violence in fact produces its own *reversal*. In other words, nonviolence is *inevitably* produced – as a *by-product* – through the excessive exercise of violence. That said, violence is far from blind to its own *excess*. When confronted with nonviolence, violence has no other means at its disposal except to increase its *intensity*, which is ultimately incapable of preventing a collective action of banned individuals from rising up. The camp's failure to prevent uprisings stems from the nonviolent response to violence in that the nonviolent response falls outside of the economy of violence. The only responses that violent force can make against nonviolent resistance are either to increase the intensity of *Gewalt* (violence and force) – that is, crush the nonviolent opposition (and eradicate the conditions under which such opposition can arise) or make concessions to the opposition, thereby keeping the structure of violence more or less intact.

This way of understanding (non)violence is consistent with my original hypothesis apropos the ontological primacy of violence. When violence works within certain rational limits – as with the institutional forms of violence that we have internalized as legitimate and necessary (the state, the police, military, or biopolitics) – it becomes a matter of course. Violence may still be challenged through legal or other "reformist" means, but the challenges fall more or less within the logic of violence. This represents the situation in which challenging violence is detached from liberation. Viewing nonviolence as the excess of violence allows our gaze to focus on a certain fact that bears epochal significance: as the *alternative* (not the opposite) to, and the *excess* of, violence, nonviolence emerges as a mode of *revealing* the possibility of new economies of action and presence. "Excess" provides a *non-exclusionary* concept of nonviolence, *consistent with the radical negativity of* non*violence*, and leads us to the following *tripartite concept of (non)violence* (in tandem but distinct from the tripartite concept of violence). The designation "non-exclusionary" is meant to capture the proposition that when we refute the common proposition that violence and nonviolence are binary opposites and thus pure moments and mutually exclusive, we inevitably open our gaze to understanding (a) *nonviolence as the mode of action that arises from violence* (the origin of nonviolence is always already violence), (b) which *exceeds the limits of exercise of violence* (nonviolent action is the by-product of violent modalities of action), and (c) and *always contains violence within it* (non-violence overcomes violence by incorporating it). The attentive reader will notice that the proposed relationship between violence and nonviolence is dialectical without *Aufhebung* – à la Vattimo's phenomenology of history (Vattimo 1991, 171–2).

For the suggested conceptualization of (non)violence to be properly situated within my theory, the three propositions above need elaboration and discussion.

(a) The *raison d'être* of the first proposition – that nonviolence as the mode of action arises from violence – should be fairly clear. Fanon, Sorel, and Benjamin see violence as internal to the system from within which resistance arises. As submitted in chapter 2, both violence and nonviolence arise from (individual or collective) human action. This statement will be further qualified in subsequent chapters. The tripartite theory of violence (structural, hubristic, and institutional) indicates the conditions under which deworlding and reworlding, as the primal markers of violence, are forced through certain modalities of (institutionalized) action. It is always inevitably in response to such deworldedness that nonviolent resistance arises, when in the face of violent deworldedness, I turn to that which always remains inalienably mine – that is, my dignity – and *challenge* violence ultimately with nothing but my sheer physical existence. Phenomenologically, *nonviolence appears where violence has already defined the terms of phenomenalization.* Nonviolence as a privative term relates to such phenomenalization.

(b) The second proposition – that nonviolence exceeds the limits of the exercise of violence – grasps this: in imposing its specific terms of deworlding–reworlding, violence defines the ambit of its exercise as well as that which falls outside its sphere of implementation. The term "excess" is meant to elucidate the point that when violence reaches its limits, when violence cannot go any further owing to its specific institutional–structural setup, violence nevertheless continues to make claims on that which falls outside of the predefined boundaries of its implementation. In short, this "surplus" of violence refers to the possibilities of action – a by-product of violence itself – that would not have existed without the terms of violent governance (as in Laclau's critique of Agamben). An excellent example of this is the (failed) Nazi camp uprisings (to which Arendt refers): the very terms of the concentration camp determined, first, a distinctly Jewish identity attached to the uprising, and second, the form of uprising, which was dictated by the camp. Violence defines the terms of nonviolent resistance. That is why, as noted, nonviolence cannot be properly understood as mutually exclusive in relation to violence. That is also why I have suggested that the very possibility of nonviolence is given by violence as the latter's excess. Thus, interestingly, *the possibility of nonviolence* – the specific modalities of nonviolent action – *resides within violence*. This idea is already present in the works of Sorel and Fanon: against the structural–institutional violence of capitalism and colonialism, the proletarian "ethics of violence" boil down to the rather nonviolent (says Arendt) general strike, just as the war of liberation against the structural–hubristic–institutional violence of colonialism can only succeed through the nonviolent transformation of both traditional and colonial institutions. In both cases, nonviolent transformation is only possible by virtue of an imposed and already present violent deworlding, which inadvertently begets the emergence of a new people, which through liberation *authenticates* itself and releases itself from the tentacles of violence. Therefore, nonviolence can only be properly studied in relation to violence and never as a separate "entity" connected to ethics, peace, or Truth. Attributing nonviolence to terms such as peace (see chapter 5) is rather arbitrary, though comforting. Nonviolence, to borrow from Judith Butler, always involves a non-peaceful conflict (2009, 182).

(c) Regarding my third proposition – that nonviolence always contains violence within it: the aforementioned formulation of the excess can also be articulated as follows. If the excess of violence is the condition of possibility of nonviolence, then *nonviolence exceeds violence by transcending the original terms of violence*. Hubristic violence best clarifies this: it involves exceeding one's measure, one's regional constitution, one's (existential) locality. Thus violence's excess refers to violence exceeding its instrumental mandate through the conceit that will potentially exhaust it. This conceptual "discovery" sheds light on the significance of the phenomenological approach to (non)violence. *First*, following Arendt, we understand violence through its instrumentality – a characterization compatible with the tripartite phenomenology of violence: structural, hubristic, and institutional forms of violence all tend to reduce life (human or non-human) and social organization to resources. So if violence is a tool crafted specifically to serve a certain purpose, then every form of violence contains limitations in terms of its utility. Viewed as such, resistance to, and rising up against, violence takes the form of a nonviolent collective action that falls outside what violence can control and utilize. This is how nonviolence, as mentioned, *exceeds* violence. Confronted with resistance, violence must morph into another form, implement other or new methods, and reach out and conquer new domains of life activity. This is also how, applying Bernstein's observation, violence gains its *protean* character. It perpetuates itself by metastasizing into the realms of collective action hitherto beyond its reach, and in the process, it transforms itself for optimum deployment. *Second*, the foregoing indicates that violence and nonviolence meet each other over a conflict (Laclau's argument). As such, neither violence nor nonviolence is intelligible outside a perceived locus of conflict, that is, outside the articulatory practices that transform existing relations of subordination into sites of antagonism (Laclau and Mouffe 1985). Therefore, the modalities of both exercised violence and nonviolent resistance are determined by the specific terms of the antagonism at hand. This proposition is crucial because it conceptually links the genus of European thought studied in this chapter to the thought and political strategies of Gandhi (chapter 8). This is why the identification of nonviolence with peace (which denotes the absence of war or conflict) is conceptually unviable. *Third*, since collective action and the possibility for resistance always arise regardless of the extent and intensity of violence, and since in response to resistance violence extends ever more into farther realms, then violence needs to mobilize high amounts of energy and resources to sustain itself. Borrowing a term from thermodynamics, I view violence as a *high-entropy system*. Entropy refers to the level of disorder in the closed thermodynamic system; it also refers to the rate of the degradation of energy and matter in the universe. Being high in entropy, violence works best when exercised within a closed, controlled system. This is why in cases of "excessive force," when legalized ("legitimate") violence goes beyond its institutional objectives and mandates, the excess causes the system to expend itself, through increased disorder, at exponential rates owing to its high entropy; it thereby loses its instrumental (and thus orderly) character that had been part and parcel of the objectives it had been deployed to achieve. But there is a proviso: the social system can never be fully totalized because it is not a closed system, so in expending its energy and resources, violence produces the nonviolent excess (its by-product) that constitutes the violent system's "disorder." Therefore, in order to maintain itself, violence needs to exceed its own limits, transform and shape-shift into a field either for which it was not originally intended or within which it loses its instrumentality. In other words, although a social system is never fully totalized, violence totalizes through expanding (as in colonialism) due to its search for non-renewable resources and energy. This is how violence ends up as a high-entropy activity: in order to maintain itself it needs to constantly and increasingly expend itself. Furthermore, as it expands and totalizes, violence perpetuates its hubristic impositions and institutional configurations. Nonviolence, by contrast, is a *low-entropy system* with minimal means of survival and marginal communication input. Mind you: because unlike isolated systems, the social system can never be fully closed, never fully totalized, we cannot speak of high entropy and low entropy as binary opposites (or as highly active and relatively passive, respectively). In actual cases, a social system is a melange of both. In other words, the conditions of possibility of both violence and nonviolence are within the social.

To begin, as suggested, collective action needs my mere physical human presence, and as nonviolent at the moment of its emergence, collective action's low entropy allows it to endure even beyond unimaginably brutal and oppressive conditions. There always resides within me the power of founding something new (natality). Nonviolence is characterized by low entropy because, strictly speaking, it is not hubristic; moreover, in founding something new, again *stricto sensu*, nonviolence does not necessarily try to institutionalize and dominate. This is how I am able to resist, even with minimal resources available to me. This is how in reducing me to bare life, violence produces me as its own excess so that I emerge as the resisting subject. Let us not forget, however, that my singular act is also potentially (although not necessarily) the source of possible future violence, should my founding act evolve so as to bring about institutional maximization and its subsequent laws (Schürmann).

Now we have a workable conception that captures the multiple propositions relating to (non)violence. I must add here that we need to further examine the various concepts of nonviolence before I can offer, in this book's conclusion, my final conceptualizations of the relationship between violence and nonviolence.

Liberation: (Non)Violence as *Différance*

Liberation refers to the movement intended to *liberate* the subject from oppression and injustice. Liberation is therefore a *negative* concept, and that is why it is consistent with nonviolence, also a *radically negative* concept. The two are linked through intended freedom from hubristic, institutional, and structural phenomenalizations of violence that perpetuate injustice.

To reiterate, the moment of liberation is the rare phenomenological moment of suspension of knowledge about that which constitutes violence or nonviolence. The messianic moment of liberation suspends all knowledge, so that the acts of liberation disallow any *a priori* binary of violence and nonviolence. While the notional distinction between violence and nonviolence always remains within my grasp, and while such distinction is always deeply connected to the context in which the "force of circumstance" (Arendt) reveals actual potentialities for me, the distinction remains inevitably time-bound and thus valid "until further notice." My readings of Sorel, Benjamin, Fanon, Arendt, and Agamben all attest to the *deferred difference* between violence and nonviolence. So does conceptually locating nonviolence in the excess of violence in light of my hypothesis about the ontological primacy of violence. What constitutes "excess" is never knowable beforehand, and it cannot be located positively within a certain practice. The violent act that becomes excessive can only be known when it produces that which falls outside its constitutive terms – nonviolence. Therefore, my proposed term "(non) violence" already captures, and is enabled by, the spirit of Jacques Derrida's *différance* (1982). *Différance* refers to the *radical undecidability* that permeates the much-coveted distinction. The concept does not allow an *arché* to assert the distinction beforehand (and thus subverts the archic–hegemonic): a hidden desire for divine knowledge that would console trembling souls accustomed to endless self-reassurances. Understanding the distinction between violence and nonviolence as *différance* will prevent us from turning the distinction into a binary opposition. Here is where, thanks to the phenomenological gaze, *the distinction between violence and nonviolence is transformed into the distinction within (non)violence.* The privative in "*non*-violence" stops being a negation *of* violence, its *a priori* exclusion; instead it now connotes "something other than violence," a difference that is bound to that from which it differs and is thus indeed a delayed difference (see the conclusion to this book).

And this brings us to one last point. We made the conceptual connection between violence and metaphysics, specifically through Vattimo's philosophy. My proposed connection between violence and nonviolence corresponds to Vattimo's Heideggerian contribution that a possible post-metaphysical destiny in which violence fades away cannot be achieved through an overcoming or *Überwindung* of metaphysics except through *Verwindung* – a process of distortion of, and healing from, violence. In *Verwindung*, instead of disavowing violence (the moralists are good at this!), we "accept" violence as a part our history and destiny so that we recover from it – as I recover from a wound whose scar will stay with me until I die, or from an infection that leaves the microscopic agent behind in my body. As Vattimo has sharply shown us (2004), *nonviolence is a part of our [in his case, European] destiny*. We advocate nonviolence because the possibility of a civilizational shift beyond metaphysical violence is potentially within our reach. That is why we cannot disavow violence by occupying the moral high ground. The rare historic moments of liberation – when the distinction between violence and nonviolence is suspended, when we, laypeople and scholars alike, think phenomenologically in our "stepping back" from the *a priori* epistemological distinctions and common notions – provide us with the possibility of thinking beyond the existing binary of nonviolence and violence to which our gazes are falsely accustomed. Nonviolence beams its modest light on the deep shadow of rampant violence because every act of nonviolent resistance alludes to a potential opening in our civilization, a possible future unlike the past. By viewing nonviolence as an epochal possibility and as our potential, common destiny, we take ownership of our violent history, and instead of shunning it, we call forth, go through, and absorb violence in all its manifestations so that we can lay it to rest. In short, *we embrace violence and carry it safely to its fate, and in so doing we discover a new, transformed, and liberated collective self*. This position situates me against the surprising observation that views refraining from violence – and thus inclining towards nonviolence – has been a disappointment, a component of imperialist hegemony and conspiracy (Losurdo 2015, 203, 221). Given the liberatory possibilities of nonviolence, Losurdo's argument remains unsustainable, although many of his case studies of nonviolent movements indicate indeed how nonviolence has been manipulated by the powers that be.

I submitted that nonviolence – acting in concert, collective action, social movements, liberation, or in short, *dignity, the undeconstructable* – always inevitably arises from violence (epitomized in its most extreme case in the concentration camp), and I suggested that we understand nonviolence in terms of a possible epochal economy of presence. If these two propositions are acceptable, at least *provisionally*, then we should begin to entertain, conceptually, the mind-boggling idea of nonviolence as central to our action. The question, then, will be this: Given Arendt's warning that the consequences of our actions remain obscure to us, that our liberating action can potentially transmute into oppressive institutionalizations, how can we act with relative certainty about the nonviolent consequence of our actions? I will return to this fundamental question in the concluding chapter.

Our immediate task, though, is to continue with our conceptual excursions. I have so far offered a (radical) conceptual phenomenology of violence as well as the condition (liberation) under which the phantom opposition of violence and nonviolence loses sway. Now we need to turn to key treatises dedicated to, and propagating, nonviolence in order to investigate the inadvertent contributions of those works to our phenomenological interpretation of (non)violence.

Interregnum

Categories of violence and nonviolence are constructed attributes of human action intended to determine not only the possible modalities of action but also the outcome(s) of specific acts. Our categorical understanding of the two – as mutually exclusive – is guided by epistemic truisms, worldviews (*Weltanschauung*) of communities, legal principles pertaining to governance, highly coveted common and societal goods, or moral values – all of these are rendered intelligible through the master codes, *koiné*, of an age. We are socialized into these epistemic truisms, which constitute important pillars of our collective worldviews and cultural determinations. (Non)violent attributes always pertain to the experiential, lifeworld understandings of *outcomes* of action – which are not the same as the *goals* of action – in relation to culturally sanctioned values. Once these understandings grow into shared knowledge through the long institutional processes of socialization, they rise to be *practical a priori qualifiers* that establish whether an act is hubristic–violent or not. They become a part of our "prejudice" – our "deep common accord," as Hans-Georg Gadamer defines it. Then, growing hegemonic, these internalized master codes operatively define our (hegemonized) experiences. In enabling us to make judgments, abstract qualifiers of nonviolence consign to oblivion the *historic and cultural conditions* under which an act becomes possible, intelligible, and actable in the first place, the conditions to which an act is a *response*. Confronted with our world's violence, philosophical approaches to nonviolence appeal to the existing categorical understandings of (non)violence. That most of these categorical approaches by and large neglect institutional violence (Schürmann) or the violence of the law (Vattimo) is rather troubling: such neglect underscores the epistemological thirst for the determinations of action

before the act is born and often without regard for the condition under
which an act becomes possible and intelligible.

In this book I critique the widely held violence–nonviolence binaries
of different schools, primarily in contemporary Western theoretical and
philosophical thought, as they have grown hegemonic in our age. These
binaries have been enabled through categorical syllogisms and their
universal–particular affirmatives and negatives. For the task of deconstruct-
ing such binaries, which is at the heart of this book, we need not necessarily abandon the often shared epistemological *distinction(s)* between
violence and nonviolence – facts of knowledge. But we do need to expose
that theorizing violence and nonviolence in binary terms can only succeed
by reifying them both, and I hope I have established, through a phenomenological "stepping back" (chapter 1), the fundamental (or in phenomenological terms, "transcendental") contours of violence, thus showing its
ontological primacy. Once it is clear what is meant, *stricto sensu*, by
"violence" – through my proposed tripartite concept – it becomes possible
to examine the concept of liberatory violence in a specific genus of contemporary European thought (chapters 3 and 4). In the preceding part of
this book I proposed that (non)violence can only arise from human action
and that the concept of liberation represents the historic (and phenomenological) moment when *a priori*, epistemological distinctions between
violence and nonviolence are suspended (however momentarily). This suspension occurs because liberation is the moment of breaking away from
an existing violent deworldedness/reworldedness through the authentic
self-realization and self-assertion that requires the suspension of knowledge hitherto gained, at the very least at the moment of emancipatory
action. It is precisely in *acts of liberation* that *homo natalis* responds to the
structural–institutional–hubristic forms of violence in an attempt to have a
fresh start, authenticate the Self, and bring something new into this world
after its existential self-reflection. Key to this inquiry is that we come to
view nonviolence not as external to violence or as its opposite but rather
as its outcome manifested through the "excess" of violence. The widely
held mutual exclusivity of violence and nonviolence is thereby conceptually abandoned.

The first part of the book, particularly chapters 3 and 4, showed how
in validating or exposing "violence," the thinkers who theorized revolutionary violence unexpectedly encountered conceptions of nonviolence
within their own theorizations, and furthermore, how the critics of (state,
colonial, or sovereign) violence inadvertently revealed the nonviolence
it begets. Theory and practice are never quite distinct: while the first

part of this book focused largely on the works of *theorists* and scholars of (non)violence (Sorel and Fanon were also activists; Arendt and Derrida were politically engaged), the second part will encompass primarily the works of *practitioners* of nonviolence who then theorized it. I will argue that, despite their mostly noble intentions, European and non-European advocates and practitioners of nonviolence did not succeed in exorcising *in toto* the various vicissitudes of violence embedded in their nonviolent approaches. From this point on, I offer close readings of key works of celebrated advocates of nonviolence and discuss their attempts to overcome the deferred difference (*différance*) in (non)violence. Each author represents a certain strand of nonviolence thinking. Linked to the moment of self-authentication that defers the opposition between violence and nonviolence, the *différance* that permeates (non)violence turns out to be so disquieting that many theorists and advocates of nonviolence shun or ignore it for the sake of advancing their approaches and gesturing towards "pure" nonviolence, instead of exploring this menacing *différance* and bringing it into the open. My proposed understanding of (non)violence in terms of *différance* cancels out the gestures of the puritan advocates of nonviolent change. I do not pretend to offer an exhaustive reading of the literature of nonviolence. For one thing, I have intentionally excluded spiritual approaches. The literature on nonviolence is vast and imposing, and huge amounts of it involve surveys and narratives of actual nonviolent experiences and movements, often registering their triumphs, and are largely unreflective and uncritical about their own assumptions. My intention with the literature I have selected for the second part of this study is to show, through critical phenomenology, the common thread that strings together diverse thinkers and advocates of nonviolence: precisely because the distinction between violence and nonviolence is never given and ascertainable in advance – because such a presumed distinction embodies a *différance* – these thinkers end up *positively asserting nonviolence by anchoring nonviolence to some ascertainable universal good that functions as a ground: democracy, peace, social justice, love, the common good, or Truth.* Their tireless efforts to anchor nonviolence to (seemingly) solid, unshakeable grounds reveal above all that, in and of itself, *nonviolence has no essence.* I have already shown that the "non-" in "nonviolence," in its radical negativity, escapes conceptual substantiations; so in the works of its advocates, nonviolence must be constructed in relation to a common notion, something (supposedly) tangible and intelligible "out there" that we are all supposed to relate to and grasp immediately (i.e., without [*im*] mediation). With regard to one of our guiding concepts in the rest of this book, and added to the foregoing, my *fifth set of propositions* holds that the proponents of nonviolence who dwell in binary categories inevitably construct *algorithmic equivalences* that enable them to identify nonviolence with seemingly fundamental and irrefutable *concepts* that are simultaneously common *notions*: freedom, moral principles, ethics, love, peace, or Truth. The notional vagueness of these terms allows them to remain operative at the cultural–exoteric *and* conceptual–esoteric levels. Stated differently, these notions succeed because they make nonviolence "make sense" (the English "sense," German *Sinn*, French *sens*, Italian *sensa*, and Latin *sensus* – all allude to "direction"). The aforesaid notions give *direction* to a certain meaning of nonviolence in common understanding. Without these common notions, an elusive concept like nonviolence will remain obscure and thus inoperative in practice. These algorithms are also a part of the hegemonic regimes of knowledge that dominate our thinking and acting. The irony of these approaches is that, for the most part, their lack of analytical–conceptual precision – which allows them to *render nonviolence intelligible* – is precisely what enables them to reify and exclude violence. The reader hopefully recalls my objective, which is to resuscitate a theoretically sustainable concept of nonviolence. Since phenomenology is the study of "appearances" (from Greek *pheinein*, "to show"; *phainomenon*, "things appearing to view"), I am intuitively interested in the ways through which nonviolence *appears* to me, and as a critical and radical phenomenologist, I need to push these appearances back to the hegemonic–epochal practical and epistemological structures (their Gestalt) that render them possible, and then I should step back from them (*epoché*) to reveal the conditions under which they appear in one specific fashion or another. I am therefore interested in all sorts of algorithms: they reveal a phenomenon in a particular light while at the same time concealing and overshadowing it. As regards our inquiry, these algorithms contain nonviolence as a radical negativity and as the *excess of violence* within an epistemological framework that renders nonviolence intelligible by ascribing to it positive and measurable attributes. Stated differently, by mooring nonviolence to a common notion or a shared value, these positive algorithms allow advocates of nonviolence to compensate for the very negativity of nonviolence that renders it ungraspable. Therefore, my aim in the following hermeneutical exercises, in the second part of this book, is obviously to critically engage with the four subsequent approaches, but I also intend to steer their insights towards possible means of nonviolence as a mode of thinking, acting, and living. Ultimately, as mentioned, my objective is to rethink nonviolence in terms of *transformative nonviolence* in light of the proposed phenomenology of violence and in relation to the existing arguments in favour of nonviolence. The term "transformative nonviolence," with its Gandhian connotations, is already in wide use with nonviolent literature, but I will try to show the potential of that transformative aspect in epochal dimensions.

To set up my advocacy of a *new* concept of nonviolence in the concluding chapter, the next four chapters offer engagements with four (overlapping) algorithms of nonviolence. These are (a) nonviolence used owing to the logistical necessities faced by citizens confronting unresponsive and repressive states; (b) nonviolence advocated for its social utility, reduction of harm, and construction of peace; (c) nonviolence measured according to the moral good and ethical responsibility; and, finally, (d) nonviolence brought about politically when politics aims not at power but at Truth. Obviously, these four categories are employed here for *analytical purposes*; in reality, the works of the proponents of these ideas – and the varied and rich nonviolent modalities of acting – cannot be reduced to one component or another. In fact, as the reader will recognize, there are analytically significant co-articulations among these algorithms. Yet I will show how these algorithms render nonviolence conceptually intelligible as well as viable in practice through substitutions and chains of equivalences aimed at substantiating nonviolence. It is not my intention to offer a comprehensive overview of each thinker or "school"; nor am I interested in contradicting the principles or assumptions of each; instead, what is important for my argument in this book is a clear summary of the main conceptualizations (and related materials) pertaining to each argument in favour of nonviolence. I will be working within the contours and according to the principles upon which these approaches are based; in this way I will be able to show how the approaches in question produce unintended theoretical consequences that take us closer to the manifestations of (non)violence. As part of my hermeneutic approach, I will closely read the works that represent a certain tendency in understanding nonviolence.

The second part of this book will therefore re-examine journeys into *quests for the pure moment of nonviolence*. The phenomenological gaze will allow us to engage with these efforts critically; it will also reveal how in these quests we may find sustainable ways to reformulate the elusive distinctions between violence and nonviolence.

5

Logistical Necessity and Pragmatic Nonviolence

Nonviolent action is a means of combat, as is war. It involves the matching of forces and the waging of "battles," requires wise strategy and tactics, and demands of its "soldiers" courage, discipline and sacrifice. This view of nonviolent action as a technique of active combat is diametrically opposed to the popular assumption that, at its strongest, nonviolent action relies on rational persuasion of the opponent, and that more commonly it consists simply of passive submission.

Sharp, *The Politics of Nonviolent Action* (1973a,: 67)

The Swaraj (home rule) movement led by Mahatma Gandhi that after decades of struggle against the British led to Indian independence (and the partition of Pakistan) in 1947, the Civil Rights Movement in the United States led by Martin Luther King Jr. in the 1950s and 1960s, and the successful transition to a post-apartheid South Africa in 1994 led by Nelson Mandela and the African National Congress (ANC) are often celebrated as significant victories of nonviolence on a world scale and as practical and historic proofs that nonviolence is a viable mode of action distinct from violent methods.

Important studies have showcased and provided details about nonviolent movements in a variety of regional, political, and social contexts. One of these works offers the historical context for nonviolent movements around the world, examining the popular movement in Hungary, that of the Indian minority in South Africa, workers' uprisings in India, anti-Nazi collective action in Denmark and Norway, and the Civil Rights Movement in the United States, among others (Gregg 1984). Another study sets out to reveal the powerful role that nonviolent movements played in the twentieth century and how they resisted terror and advocated for rights while rejecting violent means. From Russia, India, Denmark, and Poland to the Netherlands, the United States, El Salvador, South Africa, the Philippines, and Palestine (the *intifada*), examples attest to a shifting field of human collective action in the face of increased "surgical" violence (Ackerman and Duvall 2000). Yet another book offers case studies of nonviolence from the United States, Albania, Georgia, Italy, Africa, Norway, and Czechoslovakia (Bruyn and Rayman 1979); still another documents nonviolent political struggles in the Arab world (long before the Arab Spring) (Crow, Grant, and Ibrahim 1990). The literature on nonviolent movements, methods, and histories is so vast that it is impractical to attempt an exhaustive overview.

As attested by the studies cited above, the idea that carefully crafted nonviolent strategies and tactics provide a basis for democratic transition has been around for many decades. The more recent protest movements against unresponsive rulers in former communist states exemplify the effectiveness of nonviolent methods of struggle. The postcommunist Eastern European democratizing movements, also known as the "colour revolutions" – Serbia in 2000 led by OTPOR! ("Resistance!"), Georgia in 2003 led by KMARA ("Enough!"), and Ukraine in 2004 led by PORA ("It's Time!") – mobilized the masses against corrupt governments that had seized power following the collapse of the ruling Communist parties and that had stayed in power by manipulating the electoral process. The Eastern European experiences in organizing and mobilizing nonviolent resistance are captured in Tania Rakhmanova's documentary *The Democratic Revolution Handbook* (2006) (with a DVD price tag of $348, it is clear the film is not intended for the activist market!). The success of these revolutions in toppling authoritarian states (which happened to be anti-Western in their foreign policy) encouraged the propagation of literature on nonviolent methods to achieve political ends, nowadays crystallized in handbooks and training courses on nonviolent mobilization. A key example is the manual written by the OTPOR! activists who launched a nonviolent movement that brought down the authoritarian regime of Slobodan Milošević in 2000 in Serbia. In Belgrade, key figures in OTPOR! founded the Centre for Applied Nonviolent Action and Strategies (CANVAS), a not-for-profit organization, to train activists for nonviolent revolutions (Popović, Milivojević, and Djinović 2006). Recently, CANVAS had trained Egyptian activists, and it "might come then as little surprise that in 2011 a principal author of *Nonviolent Struggle*, Srdja Popović, consulted with opposition activists in Tunisia and Egypt" (Seigneurie 2012, 484). These trainings turned out to be fruitful: these activisms and their associated events helped launch the Arab Spring of 2011.

Nonviolence can be theorized as a set of carefully conceived activities distinct from violent means. To understand this, we need to investigate how these activities are constructed in relation to a political goal widely viewed as a much-coveted universal good: democracy. I intend to unpack how algorithms and conceptual substitutions enable a cost–benefit approach to rational–calculative activities capable of animating nonviolent political actions. To that end, I focus in this chapter on a key figure in, and one of the originators of, this specific approach to nonviolent action, one whose works have been demonstrably influential in nonviolent movements around the world, including in some of the more recent aforementioned struggles.

A Logistical Necessity for Citizens

Gene Sharp (1928–2018) had for decades contributed numerous books and manuals on strategic and pragmatic nonviolence, and many of his works have been dedicated specifically to effective nonviolent methods (1973b; 1973c; 2002, 79–86). Sharp was an American Professor Emeritus of Political Science who during the Korean War (1950–53) spent nine months in prison as a conscientious objector to conscription in the United States. Many of his books and pamphlets, translated into several languages, are available on the website of the Albert Einstein Foundation, a not-for-profit organization Sharp founded in 1983. Most of these volumes document successful nonviolent struggles in East Germany, Eastern Europe, Latin America, Latvia, and Lithuania, offering proof that Sharp's prescribed methods have universal applicability. While dwelling on approaches informed by political theory and sociology, Sharp cuts across various disciplinary fields in order to extract explanatory frameworks that serve his argument in favour of nonviolent methods. The corpus of his theory is organized according to conceptual justifications for nonviolent action. One cannot help but find his works repetitive, as sizeable portions of his ideas (arguments, exemplars, anecdotes) appear in more than one text. That said, all of his subsequent writings originate in, and often reference, his original tripartite treatise, *The Politics of Nonviolent Action* (1973a; 1973b; 1973c), the volumes that launched him as an architect of nonviolent movements. *From Dictatorship to Democracy* (2002), possibly his most influential book, has been translated into twenty-four languages. He chooses its arguments and cases carefully for the purpose of supporting his methods; he rarely gives serious analytic consideration to cases where his methods failed, except for the occasional broad statements against violent modes of action – for instance, when he describes (without qualification) the consequences of violent resistance as most likely "disastrous" (2009, 4). Of course, this tendency towards precluding "violence" without examining the concept (and its contexts or means) is common to the literature pertaining to nonviolence: most writers in the field simply present nonviolence as a received idea without due conceptual clarity (Ackerman and Duvall 2000; Bruyn and Rayman 1979; Jahanbegloo 2014; Popović, Milivojević, and Djinović 2006). It goes without saying that such avoidance remains contrary to the spirit of Gandhi (chapter 8), whom all aforementioned authors credit as a founder of the field. In any case, the core of Sharp's ideas has remained unchanged after half a century of research and writing about nonviolent methods.

Sharp's name was evoked after Iran's historic, nonviolent Green Movement in 2009, when through the "confessions" of the accused (leading reformists, secular intellectuals, youth activists) during show trials, Iranian intelligence framed the movement as an attempt by the United States to destabilize Iran through a "velvet revolution" or "soft subversion" – an attempt allegedly led by John McCain, funded by George Soros (Open Society Foundation), and developed through Sharp's ideas (Arrow 2011; Aljazeera 2011; Mackay 2012; Peterson 2009). In the year preceding the Green Movement, Iranian state television aired a cheap but amusing animated propaganda video about nonviolent movements (Iranian Intelligence Ministry 2008) – an indication of the significance of Sharp's approach in the eyes of that country's security apparatus. The Green Movement was eventually crushed through surgical state repression; even so, this story points to the subversive edge of Sharp's work.

I will forgo examining Sharp's prescribed methods as well as stories about nonviolent methods that succeeded – stories he loves to recount repeatedly – for attending to those would distract us from the conceptual focus of this book. Instead I will probe the three key conceptual components of his approach to nonviolence: a sociological understanding of sources of power, the universal desirability of democracy, and, lastly, the formation of a nonviolent action system for the purposes of "self-liberation."

(a) *Sociological analysis of sources of power.* In discussing the logistical need for nonviolence under repressive states, Sharp lists the ways in which citizens are denied the means to transit to democracy: free and fair elections are out of the question; violent revolutions, their human costs aside, would result only in another dictatorship; a *coup d'état* would install a new oligarchy; and lastly, gradual change would take decades and entail stoppages and reversals (Sharp 2009, 3). This leaves the citizenry with only one realistic strategic plan (Sharp 2002, 39–44), which includes guidelines (Sharp 2002, 47–9; 2003, 17–23) for "nonviolent action" (hereafter NVA). He launches NVA from the sociological observation that politics in every society hinges on the field of conflict and that most conflicts do not resolve themselves through compromise. These include conflicts over principles, which need to be resolved through power struggles (Sharp 1973a, 3) – a Gandhian point, Sharp argues (1959, 58). "In conflicts with basic issues at stake it is naïve to think and act as though the offer of negotiation or dialogue is an adequate response. Hostile opponents are most unlikely to abandon their goals or means without a struggle. It is unreasonable to aim for a 'win-win' resolution. Brutal dictators and perpetrators of genocide do not deserve to win anything" (Sharp 2003, 2–3). This observation unmistakably qualifies Sharp as a conflict theorist. When the field of conflict is deemed to be the political terrain on which rival agents are engaging in a zero sum game, what is needed is a nonviolent approach that will have the least adverse effects and the greatest promise in terms of delivering long-term results.

This view of society enables Sharp to observe that the ruling elite in a dictatorship comes from a *part* of society that rules over the *whole* (Sharp 1973a, 24). When confronting a tyrannical and non-responsive regime, the citizens are logistically weak and vulnerable in relation to government institutions. But the citizens *are* endowed with the *social power* that feeds their rulers. *Contra* the top-down assessment of political power that views people as relying on their government for security and support (more or less the classical concept in political philosophy), Sharp argues that in fact every government relies on the resources provided by the people (Sharp 1973a, 8, 10). This "social power" model allows him to challenge, on the one hand, the "monolith theory" of power according to which state power is independent and autarkic, and on the other hand, the "violent action" models (military or guerrilla warfare) that set out to end state power altogether (1973a, 8–9).

Sharp defines power as "the totality of all influences and pressures, including sanctions, available to a group or society for use in maintaining itself, implementing its policies, and conducting internal and external conflicts" (Sharp 1990, 2). Power is therefore not the same as *state* power. In fact, political power is measured not just by the ability to wield institutions and manage the populace but also – indeed *equally* – by the ability to "achieve a goal; to implement or change policies; to induce others to behave as the wielders of power wish; to oppose or to maintain the established system, policies, and relationships; to alter, destroy, or replace the prior power distribution or institutions; or to accomplish a combination of these" (Sharp 1990, 3). One can correctly infer from this structural analysis that no aspect of human public life falls outside power relations. These relations are concentrated largely within institutions of power such as the government, the military, and the courts, for it is these institutions that reveal power to the average citizen through the clear exercise of force. Sharp offers six primary sources of power: authority (of rulers and their legitimacy); human resources (the organized cooperation of citizens with the rulers); skills and knowledge (supplied to the rulers by the population); intangible factors (psychological or ideological); material resources (property, labour, finance), and sanctions (the ruler's means to punish and to apply pressure) (Sharp 1973a, 11–12; 1990, 4; 2002, 18–19; 2003, 11–12). Clearly, then, while institutions have been established to distribute and exert political power, social power is always present outside of those institutions, and potentially, this enables the populace to wield their own power. Social power constantly lends itself out to political power; without it, political institutions cannot endure or even survive. In short, "the political power that they wield as rulers comes from the society which they govern" (Sharp 1990, 3); in other words, rulers always rely heavily on the cooperation of the ruled (1990, 4).

The fruitful distinction between social power and political power enables Sharp to identify various weaknesses of dictatorships (Sharp 2002, 26–8); it also allows him to propose that the former can be used to challenge the latter, since the power of the rulers, to reiterate, "comes from the society which they govern" (Sharp 1973a, 10; 1990, 3). Thus, at moments of political confrontation, the power of the many who are deprived of voluntary and meaningful political participation can challenge and isolate the power of the few who wield the institutions of control. In Sharp's analysis, political power has a structural basis in that it relies on the loci of power in the institutions (Sharp 1990, 7). This is an important component of his analysis because here we find the distinction between democracy or "freedom" (he uses the terms interchangeably) and dictatorship:

> When power is effectively diffused throughout the society among such loci, the rulers' power is most likely subjected to controls and limits because such bodies provide the capacity for resistance to governmental control.

This condition is associated with political "freedom." When, on the other hand, such loci have been seriously weakened, effectively undermined, or have had their independent existence and autonomy of action destroyed by some type of superimposed controls, the rulers' power is most likely to be uncontrolled. (Sharp 1990, 7–8)

Thus the outcome of a nonviolent movement will be the diffusion of power throughout society. In Sharp's words, "power is an integral part of nonviolent struggles" (1990, 2). The thesis that political power has a social basis naturally invites us to consider the concept of civil society associations – for example, the family, cultural associations, religious organizations, trade unions, student groups, political parties, and human rights organizations (Sharp 2002, 22). Power relies on obedience (Sharp 1973a, 12–13), so these civil society associations hold "political significance": although generally "nonpolitical" in orientation, these associations are "loci of power" whose influence may cover a wide range from education to non-cooperation or even ending an oppressive regime (Sharp 2009, 29). "If the society has these *loci* of power in significant numbers and strengths, they can be bases for empowerment of the population in the democratization struggle," Sharp concludes. "These *loci* can greatly help the resisting population to conduct noncooperation that is intended to restrict or sever the regime's sources of power. By providing solidarity and support such bodies can also help the population to withstand extremely brutal repression" (2009, 29–30; emphasis in original).

Social power exerted through nonviolent action can enable citizens to challenge oppressive systems. Sharp recognizes that oppression is not reducible to dictatorships; there are oppressive social and economic systems as well. When people choose "to end oppression and achieve greater freedoms and more justice," nonviolent action provides a lasting means to accomplish these "realistically, effectively, [and] self-reliantly" (2009, 1). He spent his entire career answering the "how question" since the lack of knowledge of the right methods has only contributed to the continuation of oppression in a multitude of societies (Sharp 1973a, 47). This is how the method of nonviolence is conceptually linked to the collective desires of various populations for democracy and freedom.

(b) *Universal appeal of democracy.* The theoretical discovery of the social basis of political power requires that we elucidate the "motivational factor" behind movements against repression. Sharp calls this factor "freedom" – a term loosely applied as an equivalent of democracy in parliamentary systems. Democracy functions as the epistemological standard-bearer against which oppressive systems or policies are identified and gauged. In his approach to NVA, Sharp's conceptual arrangement contrasts freedom and democracy with repression and dictatorship. Thus, as we will see soon, NVA for Sharp is a rational–instrumental activity leading from repression to freedom.

Sharp observes: "Many people live in countries with governments that can be identified as dictatorships, or less harshly, authoritarian regimes. Usually, most of the people in those countries would like their oppressive regime to be replaced by a more democratic and free political system. But, how can this be achieved?" (Sharp 2009, 1). A population that is aware of its oppressive conditions has a choice: "whether they wish simply to condemn the oppression and protest against the system" or "wish actually to end the oppression, and replace it with a system of greater freedom, democracy, and justice" (2009, 1–2). Logically, when such a dichotomy is offered as a choice, the (presumably) rational answer would be the latter. The first "choice," obviously a straw man, is only meant to showcase the second. Sharp's rationale for NVA not only links NVA to democracy as an object of political desire but also contains within it the implicit promise of success. Naturally, though, it needs to be substantiated that oppression and democracy are political opposites. To identify a global trend towards democratization, Sharp turns to the "yearly international survey of the status of political rights and civil liberties" provided by Freedom House (funded partly by the US State Department and other "democratic" countries [Freedom House 2016]). According to Freedom House statistics, the number of "Free" and "Partly Free" countries in the world significantly increased between 1983 and 2009, while the "Not Free" countries experienced a decline in numbers (Sharp 2002, 2). "As of 2008, 34% of the world's 6.68 billion population lived in countries designated as 'Not Free,' that is, areas with extremely restricted political rights and civil liberties" (2002, 2). The cases include "military dictatorships (as in Burma [Myanmar]), traditional repressive monarchies (as in Saudi Arabia and Bhutan), dominant political parties (as in China and North Korea), foreign occupiers (as in Tibet and Western Sahara)" (2002, 2). Interestingly, none of these cases fall within the civilizational–imperial domain of the West! For Sharp, NVA is universally applicable; it has worked "in widely differing cultures, periods of history, and political conditions" (Sharp 2003, 4), and he provides proofs for this claim (2003, 5–7). Given the universal applicability of NVA towards which he consistently gestures, Sharp nevertheless clearly has a target audience in mind.

Aware of the social source of their political power, repressive regimes tend to control or weaken civil society associations or populate them with the regime's followers. People are atomized under dictatorships and lose trust and confidence and become frightened. As a result, Sharp observes, the population yields to suffering under repression (Sharp 2002, 3). NVA, used systematically, provides citizens with the capacity to reverse this imposed social dispersion and overcome a dictatorship. Over time, an expansion of "democratic spaces" through the development of an increasingly solid civil society will incrementally diminish repressive control. "If and when the dictatorship intervenes to halt this 'escalating freedom,' nonviolent struggle can be applied in defence of this newly won space and the dictatorship will be faced with yet another 'front' in the struggle" (2002, 69). Once the social source of political power has been positively identified, and once the *telos* of collective NVA is affirmatively located in democracy, "freedom" emerges as a normative "universal good." It is not just the application of NVA towards achieving freedom that makes it relevant; NVA for Sharp is *intrinsically* geared towards democracy, unlike violent resistance methods such as guerrilla warfare (2002, 4).

(c) *Nonviolent action and "self-liberation."* To address the "widespread confusion" over "non-violence" – because of its conceptual overlaps with pacifism, "non-violent resistance," and "passive resistance" (Sharp 1959, 41) – Sharp clarifies that NVA is neither pacifism nor a moral principle (1973a, 68). Pacifism refers mainly to protest against war (1959, 41). In an early paper (based on his MA thesis in sociology), Sharp offers a typology of generic nonviolence that includes "non-resistance, active reconciliation, moral resistance, selective non-violence, passive resistance, peaceful resistance, non-violent direct action, *Satyagraha*, and non-violent revolution" (1959, 46). Explaining each type (1959, 46–59) allowed Sharp to develop, over the following decade, his particular concept of NVA, which had a wide range of applications for targeting "limited issues, a broad policy, or [it] may even repudiate the whole regime" (1990, 2).

NVA taps into the social source of power in order to challenge political repression. Thus, NVA is a form of combat, not negotiation (Sharp 1973a, 67). Here is the difference between NVA combat and violent combat: unlike "utopians [I imagine this means the "revolutionaries" who disavow Sharp's prescriptive NVA], advocates of nonviolent action do not seek to 'control' power by rejecting it or abolishing it. Instead, they recognize that power is inherent in practically all social and political relationships" (1973a, 7). As a conflict-based approach and contrary to popular misconception, NVA does not necessarily take longer to triumph compared to other forms of struggle (1973a, 70); furthermore, it is not less efficient than violent methods (Sharp 2002, 15), nor is it powerless (Sharp 1990, 1). If people "do this in sufficient numbers and long enough," they are bound to succeed (Sharp 1973a, 64). NVA, first and foremost, requires dedication and organization. Though it carries out conflict without violence, it should never imply inaction (1973a, 64).

Sharp's objective is to develop a "new model to assist persons and groups that wish to examine the possible potential of nonviolent struggle for liberation from oppression" (2009, 15). Relying on his study of NVA in a number of contexts and encouraged by the application of NVA in "colour revolutions," Sharp declares that in the vast majority of cases, nonviolent "actionists" did not have a charismatic leader (such as Gandhi) (2009, 5; 12–14), so it is indeed possible to launch NVA in any situation. He reminds his readers that this approach is "pragmatic and strategic. It is based on reality, and not on beliefs, although the two can be compatible" (2009, 6). Although it can be implemented in a number of ways, NVA is basically a technique for matching the forces of violent repression (Sharp 1990, 1–2). He calls his proposed combative NVA "political *jiu-jitsu*" (1990, 50–1) by which he means that NVA is oriented towards allowing rebound from the opponent's repression, towards pushing back against the oppressor with increased resistance until finally the oppressor is thrown off balance. What NVA lacks in terms of access to the political power of the state apparatus, it makes up in social power (1990, 2). That power can be achieved only through the disciplined application of NVA principles. "Nonviolent action is designed to operate against opponents who are able and willing to use violent sanctions" (Sharp 1973b, 109). Sharp does not assume that those in power will simply relinquish their violent means when confronted by nonviolent opponents (1973b, 109). That said, nonviolent "discipline ... facilitates the process of 'political *jiu-jitsu*' which can shift power relationships significantly" (Sharp 1990, 13; see also 2003, 10–11; 1973b, 109–10). NVA mobilizes its supporters to undermine and strike the opponent "indirectly" (compared to violence) (Sharp 1990, 11). It works based on four mechanisms of change: conversion (which occurs occasionally), accommodation (making concessions), disintegration (dissolution of power), and nonviolent coercion (1990, 15). It is the last of these, nonviolent coercion – that is, forcing political power nonviolently to submit to the will of the oppressed – that is at the heart of NVA (1990, 16; 2002, 35–7; 2003, 13–14).

Nonviolent "actionists" (Sharp's term for activists) challenge violent rulers on the turf that is unfamiliar to the latter, a turf created and sustained by the social resources of the oppressed and on which the oppressive group cannot fully function. Sharp contends that this situation will exhaust the oppressor: "*Gandhi has compared this situation with that of a man violently striking water with a sword: it was the man's arm which was dislocated*" (1973b, 113; emphasis in original). What is significant here is that Sharp's NVA is not just another method for confronting repression and dictatorship. NVA, he maintains, is applicable in a variety of contexts: "This insight into political power, and the *cross-cultural use of nonviolent* sanctions based upon it, demonstrate that *nonviolent struggle is not restricted by cultural or national boundaries*. It is, therefore, potentially relevant to the problems of liberation, international aggression, and internal usurpation in all parts of the world" (Sharp 1990, 18; emphasis added). The attentive reader will detect a certain philosophical anthropology between these lines, one that sees in every actionist a rational–calculative and freedom-loving agent. Without these *assumed* "rational" predispositions of NVA actionists, his theory would fall apart.

Sharp tells us that nonviolent action is far more complex than violent repression (Sharp 2002, 30). As such, it requires a tripartite corpus of knowledge: "(1) Knowledge of the conflict situation, the opponents, and the society and its needs." "(2) In-depth knowledge of the nature and operation of the technique of nonviolent action." "(3) The knowledge and ability required to analyze, think, and plan strategically" (Sharp 2009, 16–17). This knowledge enables the creation of methods based on the (aforementioned) general principles of nonviolent action as well as the intelligent application of those methods according to the specific modes of conflict and struggle and the available social resources. All of these converge to maximize the effectiveness of NVA methods (Sharp 1973b, 109). As a "means of combat," NVA relies on its own "weapons system," above all "wise strategy and tactics," and it "demands of its 'soldiers' courage, discipline, and sacrifice" (Sharp 1990, 9). There are three classes of NVA on which strategies can be constructed and from which specific tactics are derived: (1) nonviolent protest and persuasion (largely symbolic); (2) social, political, and/or economic non-cooperation (the most effective); and (3) intervention (including staging strikes, setting up a parallel government, and building alternatives) (1990, 10). When people feel apprehensive and find themselves vulnerable, NVA should begin with small campaigns involving "low-risk, confidence building actions," advisably over carefully selected issues of broad concern

(Sharp 2002, 59). Beginning with small steps, a long-term struggle gradually gains momentum; the conflict gradually grows in scale in the face of increased repression, which imposes measurable costs on the oppressors (Sharp 2009, 38–9). By drawing on the social power of civil society, carefully crafted and determined NVA can sow confusion among oppressive rulers. It displaces combat, wresting it away from the opponent's initiatives and making it increasingly harder for the regime to fight back as its resources are progressively dispersed. NVA exacerbates the weakness within the existing system and causes the dictator to err. In the process, nascent democratic institutions emerge (Sharp 2002, 29–30). NVA by its very nature allows the actionists to win support "for their cause among third parties and even among the opponents' population and aides" (Sharp 1990, 14). "If the withdrawal of acceptance, cooperation, and obedience can be maintained in the face of the rulers' punishments, then the end of the regime is in sight" (1990, 6). Sharp cautions against making concessions with the embattled opponent, for this can result in the "negotiated surrender" of the movement (2002, 10–13). He reminds us: "Resistance, not negotiations, is essential for change in conflicts where fundamental issues are at stake. In nearly all cases, resistance must continue to drive dictators out of power" (2002, 13). In this context, let me point out that Sharp expressly rejects seeking assistance from outside sources, financial or otherwise (Sharp 2009, 22). As oppression nears its end, the "democrats should calculate how the transition from the dictatorship to the interim government shall be handled at the end of the struggle," he tells us. "It is desirable at that time to establish quickly a new functioning government" (Sharp 2002, 71). At this time, the actionists must remain vigilant about the dictatorship's possible return and take precautions to prevent this (Sharp 2009, 40).

Negating the Negative in *Non*violence

Sharp's prescriptive NVA is by all accounts a distilled repackaging of innumerable experiences and lessons drawn from a century of nonviolent movements around the world. The "militant" discourse of Sharp's prescriptive NVA resonates, with a certain cachet, with the young activists who have been at the forefronts of recent nonviolent movements. When combined with a specific rationalistic political philosophy (Sharp's approach is sometimes called "Machiavellian"), these nonviolent experiences (experience means having gone through peril and trial; from Latin "*ex-*," previous, and obsolete verb "*periri*," "to go through"; hence the English word "peril") allow Sharp to conceptually reconfigure specific modes of activity – carried out by certain rational–calculative types of global "actionists" – intended for the highest rate of success. Reminiscent of the universal vanguard of the twentieth-century Marxist-inspired revolutionary *agent*, NVA actionists are expected to carry out the universal task of deposing dictators through the "creative application" of NVA guidebooks to their particular conditions. Not surprisingly, Sharp's approach has generated numerous NVA manuals, which he has produced over the span of his career as a political science professor at Harvard and an advocate of nonviolence. His specific political ontology and his rationalist approach to the actionists should not be surprising, given that he belongs to a postwar generation of American social scientists whose works are deeply informed by "rational choice theory." Sharp's work also has affinities with the American social movement theory known as "resource mobilization theory."

I do not include Sharp in my phenomenological, conceptual excursions for the purpose of dismissing his work – an impression I might have left when referring to the movements he considers his legacy. Being dismissive would not be theoretical. As attested by existing success stories, his methods do indeed work. If the people in a given region choose one political imaginary over another and are willing to fight for it in a particular manner, who am I to judge them? What is important for this study is that Sharp's approach to nonviolence indeed offers a specific mode of phenomenalization of nonviolent action for our age – one that is fitting for this age of digital technology, ruled as it is through administrative machines and structured, regulative politics.

Nonviolent social and political action – in fact, *any* collective action – dialectically emerges to negate certain conditions judged to be oppressive. That being so, NVA (like many social movements) is framed in relation to the dichotomy between dictators and democrats (Sharp 2002, 14). As such, and as one might expect, NVA is identified with a number of key directive terms, which Sharp uses interchangeably: democracy, freedom, and "self-liberation." These terms are meant to invoke a common notion – freedom from imposed rule – but beyond that, Sharp is not concerned about substantiating what democracy, freedom, and "self-liberation" actually signify. He relies instead on a more or less universal common notion that identifies freedom with living in a democracy styled after the Western models found in advanced capitalist societies. Likewise, liberation for Sharp refers to setting up a "new political order" that will "allow progressive improvements to grow and succeed" – that is, to efforts at "building a durable, free, democratic, and participatory system" (Sharp 2009, 41). Because self-liberation simply denotes deliverance from imposed and oppressive rules or rulers through the institutionalization of democratic processes, the concept is cut off from collective self-authentication, and thus, once again, the concept falls back into this common notion: liberty denotes the absence of tyranny and imposed rule. These observations allow us to identify three implicit interwoven elements in Sharp's thinking: (a) his cultural prejudice, which holds and propagates American-style "managed democracy" as a supreme and universal value, (b) his universalization of configured methods of action through which this value is realized, and (c) his presupposing the existence of a certain genus of rational actionists who adhere to the first element and who choose to partake in the second. Intertwined with prescribed–instrumental activity, this universal value tends to reorient action, out of *logistical necessity* (i.e., the weakness and vulnerability of the citizenry under repressive conditions), towards "managed democracy," as evidenced by the outcomes in Eastern European countries and the former Soviet republics. Naturally, then, violence is conceptually reduced to, and thus *algorithmically* understood in terms of, certain manifestations of power such as state repression, certain policies, or the institutionally distributed hubris of a plutocracy or a *nomenklatura*. This should not surprise us: as an algorithmic model, Sharp's NVA strategy works within a closed system established to address only such problems as it can solve. Once the universal good (democracy) and the will of oppressed masses are present, the magical "know-how" (provided by Sharp) becomes relevant and necessary. As Sharp reflects: "If this theory of power [confronting political power with social power] is to be implemented, the question is *how*. Lack of knowledge of how to act has also been one reason why people have not, long since, abolished tyranny and oppression" (1973a, 47; emphasis in original). Knowledge frees and enables activism in times when activists cannot otherwise proceed.

I have no intention of comparing apples and oranges. But I would like to draw the reader's attention to an analysis enabled by my proposed phenomenology of (non)violence. If, as submitted in chapter 1, due to the ontological primacy of violence, nonviolence can only emerge in its *radical negativity*, and if both violence and nonviolence only arise from action (as action's consequence), then algorithmic attempts at substantiating nonviolence in *positive* terms and *prior to the advent of action* can only succeed by fastening nonviolence to some ultimate, universal good. Accordingly, Sharp must limit collective action to NVA by steadfastly excluding violent modes of activity: if nonviolence is linked to democracy through a conceptual equation in a formulaic fashion, then by simply inverting the terms, armed movements (and other "violent" methods) can only be identified with domination instead of democracy. In short, NVA and violent action are measured against the preset goal of democracy as the universally coveted political objective. Only when NVA is anchored to democracy can nonviolence re-emerge as *positivity* and become *intelligible, graspable,* and *predictably actable* through the prescriptive contours of NVA theory and manuals.

In this process of algorithmic establishment of an otherwise elusive concept, one should ask: What then happens to human action? As the *actor* is transformed into the manual-steered *actionist,* human collective action is *reduced* to the implementation of applicable methods and thereby stripped of creativity and context. Let us remember that when Sorel spoke of the "general strike" as the quintessential proletarian mode of action, he was articulating a new discovery in terms of the collective power of a newly emerging and "ontologically privileged" (Laclau and Mouffe 1985, 4) social force: the organized proletariat. Around the turn of the nineteenth and twentieth centuries, as this new social force emerged on the political scene in the shape of organized labour, it both provided hope for socialist revolutionaries – namely Sorel and Luxemburg – and alarmed traditionalists – above all Gustave Le Bon (2002). In this social class, these two diverging tendencies (traditionalists and socialists) discovered opposing political potentials. For Le Bon the emerging proletariat, with its enormous power, signified the loss of old Europe. The challenge for socialists, on the other hand, was to decipher how the emerging power of the working class would really act and then figure out and measure the possible outcomes of its actions. Similarly, by the time Fanon began advocating war of liberation, he had discovered that the very weapon the colonists had used to subjugate the colonized could be turned around and used against the colonizers, but with one colossal difference: an anti-colonial war of liberation was intended to liberate and reinstate a people, not to subjugate and subject them, and as such, a war of liberation could not be characterized as "violent." National liberation was therefore a new, genuine self-assertion, not to mention a great discovery. In both Sorel and Fanon, the discovery of a new mode of action pointed towards the possibility of a new world. Nonviolence, too, was a great discovery of the twentieth-century politics, a vast and diverse experience from which Sharp would extract his distilled methods. Nonviolence has emerged, and continues to emerge, experimentally and genuinely, through the creative resistance of actors from diverse walks of life, and it may in fact be energized by a certain political imaginary (democracy), but certainly it is not limited to that imaginary. A thorough study of the New Left in the 1960s by George Katsiaficas (1987) shows, among other important things, how actors creatively used nonviolent methods of action (without manuals!) in search of new civilizational imaginaries beyond the options offered by the status quo. By and large, the New Left was not intent on capturing the state; rather, its objective was to change the structural violence and injustices embedded in the system of the state and capitalism on the global scale. It is in this global context that Sharp provides a method, laid out in minute detail, for a specific genus of rational–calculative activists. But is that not what we should expect? In this technological age, democracy has been reduced to the institutionalized activity of citizens in relation to the political machine – this is "managed democracy," in which citizens, from time to time when called on, participate in choosing among institutionally determined and enacted choices that technologically embody political freedom. Because in Sharp *nonviolence*, as a mode of task-oriented and predefined activity, *is divorced from action* as such – and separated from liberation and self-authentication – the outcome is not in any way the emergence of a new body politic (Arendt) or the constitution of a new people (Fanon). In the end, though, Sharp's theory can ideally lead to what it set out to achieve. His nonviolent model ends up exemplifying "liberty without liberation" (Arendt) – liberty that can only lead to the construction of the institutional façade of democracy. It is important to point out that Sharp is able to maintain the conceptual distinction between violence and nonviolence (as positivity) only because his proposed nonviolent "self-liberation" is not intended to lead to emancipation (Sorel), liberation (Fanon), or the founding of a new body politic (Arendt). Clearly, closed algorithmic systems have their advantages!

This argument brings us to the distinction between violence and nonviolence. Nonviolence, in Sharp's theory, is not *ontologically* distinct from violence (as it is, for example, in Tolstoy and Gandhi). In other words, violence and nonviolence both belong to the arsenal of war and to techniques of political *jiu-jitsu*, and both rely on cost–benefit arithmetic. Their differences relate, quite simply, to the human costs of conflict and the clean delivery of the objective of the political struggle. The underlying reason for this is very important: the essence of modern politics – as Machiavelli showed half a millennium ago – boils down to the quest for power over others and for expansion of that power through all available

means. As such, *if we suspend the positivity of nonviolence, the opposition
between violence and nonviolence loses its grounds.* This becomes obvious precisely where Sharp opposes violence to nonviolence.

Sharp consistently rejects armed resistance because of its adverse consequences, based on two arguments. First, he measures "violent rebellion" against the desired objective of *his* NVA: democracy. He submits
that "guerrilla warfare rarely, if ever, benefits the oppressed population
or ushers in a democracy" (Sharp 2002, 4). "Violent rebellion, including
guerrilla warfare and terrorism, usually produces crushing repression,
massive casualties, defeat, and, even if 'successful,' a stronger dictatorship" (Sharp 2009, 3). Because his terms of collective action are already
set, he ends up in every instance measuring human action in relation to
the universal value of democracy. This analysis is unable to connect NVA
to democracy in cases such as the 1979 Iranian Revolution, in which a
nationwide nonviolent protest movement, eventually and despite significant resistances, brought about an authoritative regime. This indicates
that contrary to Sharp's constant reassurances, NVA offers no safeguard
against the nonviolent movement giving birth to a new repressive regime
(with democratic institutions!). Second, he blames "violent rebellion"
for intensifying repression and thereby exacerbating the existing situation, while asserting that NVA disarms repression by displacing its field of
action: "Violent rebellions can trigger brutal repression that frequently
leaves the populace more helpless than before," he observes. "*By placing
confidence in violent means, one has chosen the very type of struggle with which the
oppressors nearly always have superiority*" (Sharp 2002, 4; original emphasis).
Clearly, Sharp's conceptual preclusion of violence arises from the apparently universal objective of parliamentary democracy. This is no surprise,
given that in his adherence to a Machiavellian ontological constitution
of power, both violence and nonviolence become *instrumental.* Let us
recall that Arendt regarded violence as instrumental and therefore rational due to its fabricating property: "violence … is more the weapon of
reform than of revolution" (Arendt 1970, 79). In Sharp, both nonviolence and violence belong to the same arsenal of rational–instrumental
activity that hammers and delivers. The "added value" of nonviolent
(social) force launched against one's adversary cannot really erase this
predicament. If violence is hubristic – for it imposes a certain rationality and thus restricts the miracle of bringing something new into this
world (natality) to that which only conforms to the structure of hubris –
then with Sharp we encounter a baffling, mutant cyborg: *hubristic nonviolence.* In this way, notwithstanding Sharp's considerable efforts and

unmistakable gestures to the contrary, the opposition between violence and nonviolence is thereby suspended, if not collapsed.

In social and political theory, algorithms allow us to avoid the unsettling and perplexing conceptual inflows that would otherwise impede us from positively asserting a clear theoretical position. In the case of *non*violence, the concept's *radical negativity* can only lead to *abyssal thinking*, or "thinking without banisters" (Arendt). Many of us are unwilling to embark on such a perilous journey. The gift of radical phenomenology resides in how it exposes the non-founding in foundational gestures. Sharp offers an algorithmic theory of NVA, by adhering to a reified concept of nonviolence, but we need to further pursue this trajectory to uncover how the negativity of nonviolence is rendered meaningful with respect to the structural conditions that beget violence. A shift of terrain is therefore in order.

6

On the Utility of Nonviolence:
Peace and the Question of Justice

The important point here is that if people are starving when this is objectively avoidable, then violence is committed regardless of whether there is a clear subject-action-object relation, as during a siege yesterday, or no such clear relation, as in the way world economic relations are organized today. We have baptized the distinction [between the two kinds of violence] in two different ways, using the word-pairs personal-structural and direct-indirect respectively.

Galtung, "Violence, Peace, and Peace Research" (1969, 171)

Phenomenologically, what violence has in common with acting as such is *irreversibility*, but in its aftermath, generally speaking, the irreversibility of violence is far more damning in human terms than other modalities of action. It is particularly painful, even regardless of the injuries, to supersede violence through new initiatives. It is true that every act changes the world in ways of which, despite our intentions and plans, we are not fully aware due to our finitude. The point is, having gone through violence leaves me with scars that will remain with me, on my back or on the back of my memory – individually or collectively.

Advocates of nonviolence propose a rationalistic argument based precisely on this ontological and existential character of violence: that the impact of violence is ultimately unpredictable and incalculable and thus possibly irremediable. However, in terms of its philosophical foundations, this argument is based on analytical philosophy, and its point of departure is the idea of the social-structural "utility" of nonviolence, measured mainly in terms of human cost. The central component of this argument is that violence is damaging both to the present society and to its future. Violent conflicts have serious and irreversible consequences in terms of both lost lives and social costs. Moreover, violence often instigates counter-violence, which in most cases produces a cycle of violence in which the lives of more than one generation are caught, and economic and social resources are wasted on destruction instead of going to public infrastructure, social institutions, and universal education, and health care. In cases of conflict between two adversaries over a disputed object, NVA is preferable for its "controlled" future impact. In other words, compared to violence, NVA allows us a clearer roadmap into a collective future. In this sense, NVA will likely reduce harm in pursuit of collective objectives and political action, for it leaves behind measurably fewer irreversible consequences. So *action* – pertaining to both violence and nonviolence – is measured largely in terms of the extent to which the future impact of an act can be predicted. In contrast to Sharp's prescriptive and purposive approach, in this school NVA is advocated in terms of its present and future utility as well as the reduction of harm and human and social costs. Once the *utility* of nonviolence is established, the theory expands into the fields of peace and conflict resolution.

This is a significant approach, particularly due to its influence on policy-makers and international conflict resolution bodies and training. This chapter offers a phenomenological reading of the arguments favouring nonviolence based on its "utility" in order to pursue the basic argument of this book: that the presumed mutual exclusivity of violence and nonviolence is only sustainable through epistemological exclusions, and that both violence and nonviolence are revealed only through human action.

From Nonviolence to Peace

Norwegian sociologist Johan Galtung offers a notable conceptual approach to nonviolence through the lens of analytical philosophy. He regards his approach as the "sociological instead of usual ethical point of view" (Galtung 1959, 83). Galtung, to whom we owe in part "peace and conflict studies" as a discipline that has been influencing international NGOs and peace research, was the founding director of the Peace Research Institute in Oslo, Norway (est. 1959) and the founding editor of *Journal for Peace Research* (est. 1964), in which he published his principal articles on peace-building and nonviolence. Unwavering in his advocacy of nonviolence and peace, Galtung nonetheless admits that due to certain conditions and realities in this world "the traditional dichotomy violent/nonviolent does not give us much of an analytical cutting edge" (Galtung 1989, 61). A close reading of his key concepts on nonviolence and peace will therefore contribute to our conceptual excursions into the distinction between violence and nonviolence. Consistent with our interpretive approach, the intention here is to offer not a comprehensive overview of Galtung's works but rather a deep reading of select works that capture his key ideas.

In his original and influential contribution, "On the Meaning of Nonviolence" (1965), Galtung offers an important clarification of the concept of "nonviolence" in the face of "extensional definition," "diffusion of certain semantic habits," "anti-militarism," and the psychological approach (Galtung 1965, 228–9). His "action theory" involves an Ego, an Alter, and the action that inevitably takes place between them, for which four conditions are to be met: "1. the action has to be biologically possible, 2. the action has to be physically possible, 3. the action has to be perceived or cognized, 4. the action has to be 'worth while'" (1965, 230). "Action system" refers to acts "involving more than one person," and he "restrict[s] the analysis to *social conflict*" (Galtung 1959, 67; emphasis in original). Given this proviso, a specific action between Ego and Alter depends on several calculable factors pointing at "the *utility and disutility* of the consequences" (Galtung 1965, 231; emphasis in original). In fact, Galtung suggests that the calculation of the costs of violence invites research into peace (Galtung 1969, 182). In terms of *utility*, an "action-set" may prove to be positive (+), neutral (0), or negative (–). "Thus, a simple measure [M] of the degree of satisfaction Ego obtains from Alter's actions after a sequence of N [number of actions] emitted actions would be": $M = (N+) - (N-)/N$ (Galtung 1965, 232). Regarding conflict, Galtung avers: "For our purpose it is useful to conceive of 'conflict' as a property of an action system, viz., when two or more incompatible or mutually exclusive values are pursued. *Conflict is value disagreement*" (Galtung 1959, 67; emphasis in original). Since Alter and Ego need to coexist on the same turf – or, sociologically speaking, because the conflict between the two parties is over common resources that lend themselves to the realm of politics – the relations between Alter and Ego essentially boil down to two kinds of influence: "*the negative approach*: increase the probability that Alter refrains from actions negative to Ego," or "*the positive approach*: increase the probability that Alter performs actions positive to Ego" (Galtung 1965, 232; emphasis in original). Galtung asserts that Alter and Ego conclude that they build their interaction around a *shared axis* (1965, 232), and they learn this through "socialization" (1965, 234). What is important is the utilitarian point that such an agreement (tacit or explicit) ensures *coexistence*, but more importantly, this agreement makes

the conflict *political*. To explain the political-conflictual aspect of Galtung's argument, perhaps we need a concrete example of the Ego–Alter
relations in terms of the utility of their acts, as in the most vivid instance
of a war situation in which the utility of Ego's war effort is calculated in
relation to the disutility imposed on Alter (Galtung 1965, 231). This is
consistent with the concept of violence as *restriction* imposed on "action-
spaces." The concept of "action-space" is key to Galtung's theory of violence. Also, it enables him to make a crucial distinction between personal
and structural violence (1969).

Galtung acknowledges that the border between violence and NVA
remains problematic and unclear. Thus he lists three conceptualizations
of violence: (a) a *narrow* concept, which takes violence as bodily incapacitation in various forms, the negation of which will constitute NVA;
(b) a *middle* concept, which understands violence as the reduction of the
possibility of performing, such that NVA would naturally be a negation
of that reduction; and lastly, (c) a *broad* concept of violence, which posits
that "*violent influence is the use of negative approaches, nonviolent influence is
the use of positive approaches*" (Galtung 1965, 236; emphasis in original).
Note that in (a) and (b), nonviolence appears only as a "negation" of violence, in fact as a "reactive" concept, whereas in (c), nonviolence osten-
sibly takes on its own measurable characteristics. Galtung thus defines
violence as "any activity that aims at reducing human action-spaces by
excluding actions" and non-violence "as any activity that aims at enlarg-
ing action-spaces by including actions or making them more attractive"
(1965, 236). These definitions reflect a more *systematic* understanding
of violence and nonviolence compared to his earlier conceptualization
of violence as "an act ... intended to hurt the person(s) against whom it
is *directed*. The ambiguity in the word 'hurt' is useful because it gives us
the useful dichotomy between physical and psychological violence – violence with the 'body' as its aim and violence with the 'mind' as its aim"
(Galtung 1959, 68; emphasis in original). Clearly, his concepts problema-
tize approaches to NVA as mere political strategies and tactics (chapter 3). Interestingly, Galtung makes praising reference to Sharp, but he
also mentions that in the West, NVA is based on negative nonviolence –
a significant observation that, from his perspective (1965, 234), shows
the *overlap* of violent and nonviolent approaches when they both aim
at reducing action-space. That approach is also a departure from the
Gandhian concept of Satyagraha-based non-cooperation (Gandhi 2011,
496), which I will discuss later. Stated differently, for Galtung there are
nonviolent techniques that are violent in that they reduce action-space

(1965, 237). Nevertheless, a key difference remains between violence and nonviolence, a difference that is captured through the concept of *reversibility* exemplified in Galtung's contrast between lethal and non-lethal action (1965, 235). Lethal and many non-lethal actions that bring bodily harm to the actor are irreversible. Nonviolence, which can avoid such *irreversibility* (and thus retain its utility), involves the challenge of cognitive "delearning" (1965, 237).

Societies, Galtung observes, tend towards violence (1965, 239). He acknowledges that violence is positively sanctioned in many cultures wherein "physical power is interpreted as an indicator of being morally right and defeat in a violent conflict as an indicator of being morally wrong, [thus] violence may very well lead to accepted solutions" (Galtung 1959, 68). When physical prowess and the overwhelming of an adversary or an Other is received as a signifier of moral justness and historic righteousness, Galtung observes, then violence becomes an accepted solution. "However, even in such a culture, it may be true that non-violent actions can also lead to accepted solutions; this may be the result only when, in addition, there is an equally internalized ideology against the use of non-violent means" (1959, 68). He asks: "Why do so many societies have a large and elaborate establishment for the detection of negative deviance and its proper punishment, and a minute establishment (the institutions of orders, awards and citations) for the detection and reward of positive deviance?" (Galtung 1965, 239–40) He sees a "basic asymmetry between negative and positive values" (1965, 240). Yet surprisingly, he notes that meritocracy and positive sanction in society exaggerate negative sanction (1965, 240). To address the issue of increased violence, Galtung engages with and rejects the common claims that secularism and democracy are more normative and less coercive (1965, 241) and that contractual relations increase nonviolence. For him, the distinctions among coercive, normative, and contractual relations are "not relevant to our basic problem" and simply miss the point (1965, 241). These critiques and engagements allow Galtung to offer five approaches to nonviolence: (a) the action-space approach, which holds NVA as a dramatic show involving "positive role playing" and a "repertoire of nonviolent actions" (1965, 244) – in this case, NVA is taken as a mode of communication; (b) the physical approach (e.g., sabotage); (c) the sanction approach based on the similarity of action–reaction, in which positive sanction presupposes that the classification of action is agreeable to both Alter and Ego; (d) the amplification of action, which entails using one's own suffering (Gandhi); and lastly, (e) the role-playing approach, in which Alter uses action to get a response from Ego (1965, 244–8). The role-playing approach in Galtung opens up three different options: cooperation, refusal, and resistance (1965, 249).

So far, violence and nonviolence have been viewed in terms of a reduction or enhancement of action-spaces within the physically and intelligibly possible modalities of action available to us and in terms of the conflict between Self and Other. It would be an error to understand Galtung's theory in binary terms. To understand violence/reduction of action-space and nonviolence/expansion of action-space as binary would be to misapprehend his theory, as these four terms criss-cross more often than not. Galtung remains realistic about the limitations and measurable outcomes of NVA, referring to examples of NVA under conditions he describes as "extreme oppression." Acknowledging that "nonviolence works, but not unconditionally" (1989, 19), he expands on his theory of nonviolence by factoring in, through his "great chain of nonviolence hypothesis," a third agent. We saw how he developed a theory of violence and nonviolence that hinges on the concept of "action-space" (and its reduction or expansion) in relation to the two antagonists, Ego and Alter, trying to influence the outcome of their conflict, depending on the social forces and political power they can mobilize. Under extreme oppression, where the oppressed are almost completely deprived of agency, it becomes possible for a third party, an in-between agent, to advocate the cause of the oppressed on their behalf. This agent enjoys a unique social situation: it is close to the oppressor and shares privileges identified with the ruling group or class but is socially connected with and thus concerned about the oppressed. This intermediary agent has the potential to bridge the social gap between polarized antagonists (Galtung 1989, 13–33). As can be expected, this view has implications for the concept of agency. In Galtung's words, "it is not obvious that nonviolence against an oppressor is primarily the task of those who are oppressed" (1989, 20). Here, he is referring to the "in-between" agent (see below). As an example, Galtung points to the nonviolent protest of German women married to Jewish men, who had been rounded up during a targeted Gestapo raid for transport to Auschwitz. On 27 February 1943, these German women protested in Berlin against the deportation of their husbands, and to everyone's surprise, they were successful: their Jewish husbands were released on 6 March. Of course, as we know, the Gestapo later arrested these men without a round-up; gradually and silently, one by one, the security forces nabbed these Jewish men and deported them, in this way avoiding another mass protest (1989, 4–6). Galtung offers this example and others – such as teachers' non-cooperation in Nazi-occupied Norway and the Solidarity Movement in Poland (1989, 1–4, 6–10) – to indicate, first, that NVA is possible under extreme oppression despite its (possibly) limited success, and second, that NVA taps a third agent to bridge the social distance between the oppressor and the oppressed. From the above case, we can see how the *in-between* agent, German women, was connected to the German ruling racial group while simultaneously having a social connection (through marriage) with the racially oppressed Jews. "The 'Aryan' wives bridged the gap, being the Self in the Other to the Nazis and the Other in the Self to their husbands. Without that bridge it would not have worked" (1989, 23). Galtung also offers seven cases that attest to the particularity of the intermediary agent (1989, 26–32). The relationship between the socially intermediary agent and the oppressor may do little to improve the conditions of the oppressed (see 1989, 16–21). This is because of the third party's links with the ruling group – the problem of "collusion," as he calls it. According to his collusion hypothesis, the oppressed remain dehumanized and distanced, while the ties and interests of the intermediary agent become more closely aligned with those of the oppressor (1989, 28–31). Thus, while barriers of race or gender can be overcome to connect the oppressed to the in-between population, the social distance (class difference) between the oppressor and the in-between population and the oppressed remains constant (1989, 28–31). Obviously, there are lessons here for a broader concept of nonviolence that lend themselves to conflict resolution and peace. Consider, for instance, Colombia's peace process in the aftermath of five decades of civil war between the government and assorted paramilitaries on one side and the Revolutionary Armed Forces of Colombia (FARC), the National Liberation Army (ELN), and smaller guerrilla groups on the other. One particular study has documented the features and outcomes of decades of arduous civilian grassroots initiatives, both regional and national, to broker a peace between the warring sides. That study reveals grassroots peace initiatives and documents the peace initiatives between 1997 and 2003 as well as a political process for achieving peace that was enabled through civil society (García-Durán 2004, 24–7, 18, 34–7). A similar study attributes the momentum behind the peace process in part to the initiatives of "peace communities" – grassroots movements within communities that refrained from taking sides in the conflict, often by risking their lives and sustenance in a situation in which the warring factions recognized no protagonists for change (Alther 2006). These were the "unacknowledged actors" who enabled reluctant but necessary collaborations between the antagonists and important players in Colombian civil society (Bouvier 2006). The Colombian example, a peace process still moving towards its conclusion (despite the 2016 referendum that defeated the government's initiative), shows the practicality of Galtung's "chain of nonviolence hypothesis." Perhaps because the Colombian experience does not entirely adhere to Galtung's envisaged "privileged agent," it reveals that the social distance between the conflicting parties can be bridged without the presence of a privileged intermediary. Civil society, when supported by international pressure, can indeed play an intermediary role, theoretically speaking, without an essential connection to the ruling group.

. We must note how Galtung's analysis views solutions to conflicts: he reserves the term "conflict solution" to denote "the absence of conflict," but this absence could actually mean the presence of no competing value, or in other words,

> the state of the action-system under consideration where only one of the competing values is pursued or enjoyed. This is the case when one of the parties to the conflict is exterminated or subjugated to the point where he can no longer voice his view or is segregated and downgraded so much that he may present his values but will have no impact on the actions of the total system. All these examples have one thing in common: they refer to non-accepted solutions only. (Galtung 1959, 67)

It goes without saying that "conflict solutions" do not contribute to *peace,* which for Galtung represents, in its positive modality, *the highest state of nonviolence.* Appropriately, his example of "conflict solution" through the elimination of a competing social agent relates not to a dictatorship but rather to our very own majoritarian democracies in which the decision-making process tends, in effect, to disenfranchise minorities (1959, 67). Obviously, such democracies do not represent an acceptable approach for Galtung, who invokes the "Quaker technique" of mandating a consensus rather than a vote in such situations (1959, 68; see also American Friends Service Committee 1955). We should note that "conflict solution" – the elimination of conflict through unilateralism – is different from "conflict resolution" and peace, which involves the conflicting parties partaking in striking a solution, based ideally on the expansion of action-spaces. To this end, Galtung devises several possible strategies for the resolution of conflict (Galtung 1959, 79–82), which for brevity's sake I will not discuss here.

The above elements constitute Galtung's original contribution to understanding violence and nonviolence. The implications of these propositions are forthcoming. Galtung also appropriately explores the semantics pertaining to NVA, pacifism, and peace, describing their inter-connectedness, dimensions, and typologies. In this regard, in a later important paper (Galtung 1969) he rethinks the concept of nonviolence in terms of "peace" and an earlier term, "pacifism" (Galtung 1959), in terms of "nonviolence" (see below). But the original distinction between pacifism and nonviolence is important.

> A distinction is ... often made between pacifism or non-violence by *expedi-ency* or by *conviction* ("non-violence of the weak" and "non-violence of the strong" in Gandhi's terminology). By the former is meant a non-violence which would have been replaced by violence if the means for violent action had been present, by the latter a non-violence which would be preferred to violence even if the violent means were present. Pacifism proper is concerned only with this latter kind, which means that the internalization of the ideology to such an extent that the norms are perceived as valid under a large variety of circumstances is an important, if not an absolute, condition of non-violent action. (1959, 73; emphasis in original)

Thus, by "pacifism," à la Gandhi, Galtung means "active" nonviolence. We will see that these are not merely "semantic" moves, but conceptual ones, and for theoretically significant reasons. His propositions allow for critical engagement with rather naive concepts of peace, which he offers in another paper, "Violence, Peace, and Peace Research" (1969). Here is where Galtung's acumen leads him to assert the need to pursue *social justice* by ameliorating personal *and* structural violence through research and in practice (1969, 185). The notion of "peace" is "so often used and abused," Galtung observes, because the term "peace" functions "as a means of obtaining verbal consensus" (1969, 167). In trying to explain the conceptual connection between violence and peace, he also simultaneously advances a workable concept of "peace." He begins with the most common notion of peace: "The statement *peace is absence of violence* shall be retained as valid" – a definition that obscures more than it clarifies (1969, 167; emphasis in original). Using the common understandings of violence and peace as mutually exclusive, he probes what constitutes violence in such a way that he would later re-examine the concept of peace as negation. What does constitute violence? Galtung rejects the "narrow concept of violence" that defines it as "*somatic* incapacitation, or deprivation of health ... at the hands of an *actor* who *intends* this to be the consequence" (1969, 168; emphasis in original). He notes: "Highly unacceptable social orders would still be compatible with peace. Hence, *an extended concept of violence is indispensable* but that concept should be a logical extension, not merely a list of undesirables" (1969, 168; emphasis in original). This enables him to offer the following definition: "*Violence is here defined as the cause of the difference between the potential and the actual,* between what could have been and what is. Violence is that which increases the distance between the potential and the actual, and that which impedes the decrease of this distance" (1969, 168; emphasis in original). If one dies of a treatable disease in our age of advanced medical science, it constitutes violence, whereas dying of natural causes does not. In other words, the outcome of a circumstance in which an unavoidable natural disaster impacts me negatively and irreversibly is not violent because I am forced into an actual from which I cannot escape. When the actual falls below the potential, there is violence (1969, 168–9). This approach allows Galtung to further expand the concept of violence and to introduce two more variations of violence: "direct violence" (killing pushes a person's actual somatic realization below his potential somatic realization, or simply, prevents the slain from exploring his or her future potentials), and "indirect violence" (deprivation of resources, as in poverty, which divests the individual of his or her potential) (1969, 169). The distinction between direct and indirect forms of violence is also present in Galtung's earlier definition of violence in terms of "harm" (Galtung 1959, 68): physical violence can involve bodily injury or the use of force (direct) as well as economic boycott or exploitation (indirect), while psychological violence can include verbal violence or "systematic distortion of the adversary's opinion" (direct) as well as cultural violence such as the "destruction of cultural symbols dear to adversary" (indirect) (1959, 69). These variations indicate that Galtung is trying to extract an *a priori* and measurable definition of violence – in terms of *one's actual falling short in relation to one's potential.* Obviously, the definition allows for an epistemic assurance needed to proceed from this point onward. Yet his definition of violence is sufficiently flexible to pave the way for his compelling contribution: the concepts of personal and structural violence.

Galtung makes six distinctions with respect to violence: (1) between physical and psychological violence; (2) between negative and positive approaches to violence; (3) whether or not an object has been hurt through violence; (4) whether there is a subject who delivers violence through action; (5) between intended and unintended violence; and

(6) between manifest and latent violence (Galtung 1969, 169–72). Let us recall that (inter)personal violence involves subject–action–object relations (1969, 169). Here we should expect complications. The above distinctions enable Galtung to further probe the concept of violence. For one thing, if violence is about influencing, then "negative violence" impedes one from a course of action whereas "positive violence" persuades one to partake in a course of action required by violence. Objectless violence (objectless in the sense that the object of violence is not an actor), such as the destruction of *things*, can still amount to violence, for it imposes a threat – of psychological violence or of deprivation of means of survival. Subjectless violence enables a view into *structural or indirect violence* (1969, 170). "Structural violence" factors in the uneven distribution of resources and of the power to distribute those resources (1969, 171); violence becomes structural (as opposed to personal) when it does not involve a "subject–action–object" relation (1969, 171), which leads to the question of the intended or unintended consequences of violence (1969, 171–2), which in turn brings us to the distinction between personal and structural forms of violence, just as *manifest* and *latent* forms of violence do (1969, 172). Now we arrive at the interaction between personal and structural violence (1969, 180), given that the two forms of violence are not logically or empirically connected (1969, 182). In other words, we cannot judge in abstraction which type of violence is worse in terms of its cost (1969, 183), although the short-term costs of personal violence seem small compared to the long-term costs of structural violence (1969, 184).

Only after this meticulous exposition of aspects of violence does the statement "peace is absence of violence" reveal its fruitful theoretical consequences. Now peace, as absence of violence, points sharply at both personal and structural modalities of violence. The bar is now set higher. Taking steps to reduce personal violence – through measures such as education or the legal code – seems fairly intelligible and doable. A structure entails a "set of ... systems of interaction" (1969, 175); thus structural or "silent" violence enjoys stability (1969, 173), which makes it a complicated challenge to abolish, since *silent violence* also involves physical and psychological forms of violence (1969, 177).

Personal violence is known for its characteristic use of *tools* and *organization*: tools beginning with "the human body itself ... proceeding towards all kinds of arms culminating, so far, with ABC weapons," and organization "starting with the lone individual, proceeding via mobs and crowds ending up with the organizations of modern guerrilla or army warfare" (1969, 174, emphasis in original). Here one is reminded of Arendt's concept of violence as instrumentality, an approach obviously different from that of Galtung, who views instrumentality as including the human body or the individual. Now that I have invoked Arendt, let me point out that Galtung's view of structural violence goes against Arendt's persistent exclusion of the "social question" in her analysis of violence and the political. Precisely this is what makes Galtung's theory compelling:

> If we accept that the general formula behind structural violence is inequality, above all in the distribution of power, then this can be measured; and inequality seems to have a high survival capacity despite tremendous changes elsewhere. But if inequality persists, then we may ask: which factors, apart from personal violence and the threat of personal violence, tend to uphold inequality? Obviously, just as military science and related subjects would be indispensable for the understanding of personal violence, so is the science of social structure, and particularly of stratification, indispensable for the understanding of structural violence. (1969, 175)

Yes, structural violence and therefore the structures of inequality are indeed perpetuated through personal violence or the threat of personal violence, but the former in fact exceeds the latter. There are six factors (not discussed here) pertaining to inequality and thus structural violence (1969, 176). However, we need to conceptually establish that *inequality is violent* because it is through inequality, regardless of its content, that the "lowest-ranking actors" face an actuality that systemically impedes them from reaching their potential; they are often even deprived of access to the means of subsistence or survival. These actors "are deprived because the structure deprives them of chances to organize and bring their power to bear against the topdogs, as voting power, bargaining power, striking power, violent power – partly because they are atomized and disintegrated, partly because they are overawed by all the authority the topdogs present" (1969, 177).

It is possible to have personal and structural violence in pure forms when the former is "structure-invariant" (bullies) and the latter "person-invariant" (feudalism) (1969, 178). But generally these forms can only exist in the "prehistory" of violence, at its point(s) of origin. As Galtung observes, "one may argue that all cases of structural violence can, by closer scrutiny, be traced back to personal violence in their *pre-history*" (1969, 178; emphasis in original). This idea, cautiously speaking, has some affinity with the concept of institutional violence as the institutionalization of an archic act (chapter 1), although phenomenologically, no act is ever "personal." In any case we know that violence breeds, but it also cross-breeds (1969, 178), producing "structures yet unknown to us" (1969, 180). Richard Bernstein, as mentioned earlier, captures the shifting shapes of violence, describing it as having a "protean" character (Bernstein 2013, 177). Structural forms of violence are maintained through the use of "mercenaries": "the police, the army, the thugs" (Galtung 1969, 179), in the course of which, say, police apply personal violence to defend structural violence (1969, 179–80, 181). Conversely, revolts represent moments in which personal violence is applied to repress structural violence (1969, 181). The bottom line is that violence is repressed by violence (1969, 181). This is how we are caught in cycles of violence, and this is precisely why the concept of *peace* should denote the "transcendence" of existing forms of violence.

Returning to the common notion of "peace as the absence of violence," we can see how Galtung's assertion that an *"extended concept of violence leads to an extended concept of peace"* allows him to propose the term "negative peace" to designate simply the absence of violence and "positive peace" to refer to social justice (1969, 183; emphasis in original). Negative peace is the absence of violence without meaningful changes in the conditions that breed violence. This is how peace is maintained under oppressive conditions. Positive peace aims at transforming these conditions and therefore summons a theory of "vertical development" in that it takes into account the conditions under which one's actual leads to one's potential (1969, 183). Properly understood, peace brings out conflicts rather than eliminating them, and this is a requirement for an egalitarian structure: the conflicts on which violence hinges must be brought into the open (1969, 179). Peace is not the norm but the exception: "structural violence seems to be more 'natural' than structural peace," avers Galtung, and "[p]ersonal violence is perhaps more 'natural' than personal peace" (1969, 179). Because doing nothing perpetuates violence, Galtung endorses a theory of conflict (1969, 184), and he holds, in his discussion of pacifism, that conflict is not negative (1959, 74).

Galtung asks, "if our choice of means in the fight against structural violence is so limited by the non-use of personal violence that we are left without anything to do in highly repressive societies, whether the repression is latent or manifest, then how valuable is this recipe for peace?" (1969, 184). He registers four possible outcomes: (1) we relinquish the structural definition of peace because retaining both social justice and the absence of personal violence is utopian, because social justice is "not seen as an adornment to peace as absence of personal violence, nor is absence of personal violence seen as an adornment to peace as social justice" (1969, 185). (2) We "give up the word 'peace' and simply state our interest in one or both of the two values and then try to do our best along both dimensions" (1969, 185). (3) We combine the first two approaches and think of social order as "a choice between two evils, direct violence or social injustice, using what [is] seen as the lesser evil to drive out the greater evil (possibly ending up with both)" (1969, 185). Lastly, (4) we keep both values (absence of personal violence and presence of social justice). There are many forms of social action that combine the two:

> We are thinking of the tremendously rapid growth in the field of nonviolent action, both in dissociative nonviolence that serves to keep parties apart so that the weaker part can establish autonomy and identity of its own, and associative nonviolence that can serve to bring them together when a basis for equal nonexploitative partnership exists. We are thinking of all that is known about the theories of symmetric, egalitarian organization in general. We are thinking of the expanding theory of vertical development, of participation, decentralization, codecision. (1969, 186)

So peace as the absence of violence should involve both dissociative and associative nonviolence. This will ensure proper conflict resolution involving vertical development so that the oppressed group can expand its action-space and find its potential. Galtung remains resolute in linking nonviolence to social justice and to *the right of the oppressed to revolt* – here he is borrowing from Gandhi. He stays steadfast in supporting the Palestinian cause, a position of theoretical importance for our study of (non)violence. Above all, Galtung's approach to the Palestinian issue shows that *he refutes the commonly held (moral) contrariness of violence and nonviolence.* With respect to the Israeli–Palestinian conflict, the issue is how to instigate NVA in a situation in which there is "a conflict not between right and wrong, nor between wrong and wrong, but between right and right – both Jews and Arabs in the core area having a right to settle – which makes it even more intractable" (Galtung 1989, 37, 52). As a result of Israeli unilateralism and encroachments, the Palestinians have been rendered "second-class citizen[s]," which is a "travesty of any idea of peace" (1989, 38). This is why locating the potential intermediary agent to enact the "great chain of nonviolence" on behalf of the Palestinian people remains an insurmountable difficulty. The difficulty of finding such an agent is further exacerbated by the European cultural bias in favour of the Jews (1989, 50), which translates into support for the State of Israel. Polarization tends to replace conflict with aggression and blocks the channels of communication between the two parties (Galtung, 1959, 76–77). Galtung proposes replacing the one-state and two-states solutions with the "confederate solution," which is based on the rights of people instead of the rights of states (Galtung 1989, 43). The confederate solution is "inherently" nonviolent because it governs based on reconciliation (1989, 49).

Given the unbearable conditions to which the Palestinians have been subjected for so long, Galtung endorses the Palestinian *intifada* or "uprising" – or in his rendition, "shaking off" (1989, 61) (he is writing during the first *intifada*, 1987–91). He wishes that the *intifada* had been more nonviolent, in a Gandhian fashion (1989, 72), but he is not willing to measure the uprising against abstract expectations. Here is where Galtung boldly declares: "I must admit that the traditional dichotomy violent/nonviolent does not give us much of an analytical cutting edge" (1989, 61). Palestinian youth stage protests, and in the worst clashes they throw stones at Israeli soldiers. But a stone is hardly a weapon at all; if anything, it is a weapon of humiliation: "This is what you deserve, you are not worthy of the gun, the real stuff" (1989, 62). There is an unmistakable nonviolent "shaming" aspect to the *intifadah* in that the Palestinians are willing to "absorb the violent revenge" so as to bring their plight to the view of the world (1989, 72). The Palestinian *intifada* makes this clear message: "we are limiting the violence in this confrontation" (1989, 62). The clash, however, highlights the *inequality* that is essential to violence: "on the one hand, one of the most famous armies in the modern world; on the other ... a third-grade class, with a first-grade political weapon [stones]" (1989, 62). The *intifada* contains both the right of a people to revolt and their control of nonviolent action under military repression:

> What about the nonviolent aspects of the *intifadah?* They have been there: general strike, boycott of Israeli goods, civil disobedience in general and not necessarily accompanied by violent words. However, the *intifadah* does not communicate to the world nonviolence in a positive sense. It becomes one additional strategy in a wide spectrum of approaches. The point has been made several times that the efficacy of the nonviolent end of the spectrum might be higher than the violent end. Harm has been caused to the Israeli economy. Tourism is down as a result of the *intifadah*, and Palestinian cheap labour is less available at the same time as Palestinians do their very best to do without Israeli goods ...

On the other hand, the other aspect of strikes and boycotts in a nonviolent perspective also looms high. The purpose is not only strikes as means
to embarrass, to hurt, and to some extent paralyze the other side. Much
more important is the use of strikes and boycotts to build Palestinian self-
reliance ... The Gandhian formula of parallel government seems already to
be operative. (1989, 64)

As Gandhian strategy of "parallel government" (Galtung 1959, 82),
nonviolent means (general strikes and boycotts) also entail the element
of harm to the other side, and not just to the adversary's military machine.
The harm may not be "directly personal," but since the economic outcomes of strikes and boycotts involve "direct structural violence," they
inevitably produce "indirect personal violence" (without personal injury)
that affects average Israelis, however legitimate the Palestinian struggle.
This reminds us of Gandhi's apology to Manchester textile mill workers
for the personal and economic harm the Indian boycott of British woven
goods had caused them, although as is known, the workers actually
cheered Gandhi (at the Greenfield Mill, Spring Vale, Darwen, outside of
Manchester, on 27 September 1931) and supported his boycott initiative.
Galtung has already warned us that the personal and the structural are
inseparable and that NVA in most cases affects both. The opposition of
violence and nonviolence thus loses its assumed credence. Once again,
we remain *dispossessed of the pure moment.*

Revisiting (Non)violence

Galtung's theory is wide-ranging, far-reaching, and compellingly analytical. His work cannot be reduced to one or another principal component.
My focus on some important junctions in Galtung's theory of nonviolence affords me an interpretation that accords with the indisputable
contours and identifiable trajectories of his thought; simultaneously, as
a hermeneutic turn, it allows me to highlight certain algorithms of nonviolence within his theory. Those algorithms, which include pacifism,
utility, peace, and social justice, render a negative concept (nonviolence)
affirmatively graspable. Stated differently, these algorithms provide conceptual paths through nonviolence (and also violence) that make these
elusive concepts concretely measurable and intellectually graspable.
Concepts such as pacifism (the "active" refusal to participate in violence;
a mode of action) and utility (a measurable outcome of action) prepare us for a conceptual turn towards the structural conditions known as

peace and social justice. All of this confirms my thesis that as a negative concept, nonviolence has no "substance" of its own, and that nonviolence's abyssal phenomenalization, its *absent presence*, can only be comprehended through its substantiations in normative – albeit honourable – gestures towards peace and social justice. These are significant aspects of Galtung's theory, and his proposed algorithmic equivalences – defining violence and nonviolence in terms of, respectively, the reduction and expansion of action-spaces – in the end enable him to link nonviolence (pacifism as a mode of action) to utility such that this proposition, in turn, allows for a definitive move towards a certain idea of *transformative nonviolence*: the concept of nonviolence is reconfigured to produce a concept of peace, and the latter can only be achieved through social justice.

Here the concepts of social justice and peace acquire conceptual significance (in addition to their practical attractions!). "Peace" achieves two theoretical outcomes. First, contrary to public perceptions, our present cultural obsession with, and moral inclinations towards, nonviolence as a one-size-fits-all solution to various complex conflicts (besides launching many academic and consultancy careers!), indicates that nonviolence, while a useful and humane normative orientation of action, cannot impact the fundamental seedbed out of which violence grows: injustice. So "peace," conceptualized as the structural diminishment or absence of violence accomplished through social justice, allows Galtung to eschew the conceptual "dependency" of nonviolence on violence. Second, recall Galtung's declaration: "Nonviolence works, but not unconditionally" (1989, 19). In switching from nonviolence to peace, Galtung highlights *conceptually* the differentiation so often ignored in the interest of upholding and cherishing nonviolence unconditionally. The distinction between nonviolence and peace allows us to see the former as a strategy to achieve the concrete conditions of social justice. Thus the algorithmic relationship between nonviolence and peace enables the latter to supersede the former. In this way Galtung's theory serves as an invitation to structural changes as the required social conditions for a concrete and practical nonviolent future. In fact his theory appropriately conditions nonviolence on the realization of peace not simply as the absence of violence but as something that arises from social justice. This is a "structural" peace.

To conclude this chapter, let us quickly reorganize and revisit the key concepts in Galtung's theory. Galtung's multiple definitions of violence and nonviolence – indeed, his conceptual triangulations – reveal the paradoxes and complexities that we need to bring to the fore and discuss.

With his unwavering advocacy of nonviolence and as a consequence of his structural-functional analysis, Galtung boldly shows that violence and nonviolence are not pure moments. If, in the end, the two concepts are mutually permeating, then the highest justification for nonviolence basically boils down to one simple notion: *utility*, or in my terms, *the avoidance of irreversible modes of action*. Here I *interpret* utility as a *tendency towards a low-entropy* (nonviolent) system that, unlike high-entropy (violent) systems (see chapter 4), veers away from excessive resource consumption (leaving behind waste or heat) and high-volume communication (filling the system with noise) over a conflict. Disutility, then, denotes allocating resources to solving a conflict that exceed the disputed resource at stake, rendering conflict resolution "uneconomic." Disutility thus exhausts the system in the long run. In this sense, we can observe, "utility" is no longer exclusively a utilitarian concept; nor is it simply a shared value: while retaining both aspects within itself, utility re-emerges as the signifier of social justice, a standard-bearer of nonviolence, and a measure of the long-term survival of our collectives through our inescapable and even necessary conflicts.

Galtung (1965) defines violence and nonviolence in terms of the reduction and expansion of action-spaces respectively. For Galtung, action is key to nonviolence (and to violence, for that matter): "Nonviolence is built around the basic hypothesis that persuasion is more effective if it is expressed in action terms, rather than in words" (1965, 252). The concept of action-space – and of its constriction and expansion – should be connected to his understanding of violence as an increased (read: imposed) impediment to one's potential compared to one's actual (Galtung 1969). Note that we are dealing with the issue of violence at two levels: in the first, violence is revealed in the field of human (individual or collective) action, and in the second, violence manifests itself through structural impediments to human (individual or collective) development. Let us forgo the European cultural prejudice that governs Galtung's theory in that it views violence and nonviolence in terms of freedom (action-space) and development (actual-potential) – his implicit philosophical anthropology that views human essence according to (presumed) expanded domains of action. I must note, however, that Galtung's advocacy of the right of the oppressed to revolt (which resonates with my proposed concept of "liberation") is detached from self-authentication. For an action-oriented theory, this is somewhat strange.

In this regard, Galtung's Gandhian concept of pacifism – as an active and deliberate choice of nonviolence – is important especially where his advocacy of nonviolence is linked to his defence of the Palestinian cause. The *intifada* exemplifies a people attempting to use nonviolent means (protests, boycotts, general strikes, art) to expand their action-spaces under imposed structural impediments in order to achieve their potential. We saw that certain nonviolent actions (boycotts and general strikes) emerge as the Palestinians' enactment of action-space under extreme conditions. While nonviolent by nature, the Palestinians' boycotts and general strikes hurt many average Israelis by restricting their action-spaces and sapping their potential. Recall that for Galtung, both of these situations unequivocally indicate violence. This is a sensitive issue, for it could be misunderstood as a wholesale and undiscriminating notion of violence that discounts the measurable distinctions between economic hardship (Palestinian boycotts hurting average Israelis) and homicide (Israeli soldiers shooting Palestinian protesters) in the case of the *intifada*. The two cases are distinguished by the latter case's irreversibility; nevertheless, both consequences are violent. Based on these observations, we can say that there are *nonviolent techniques with violent consequences* because these techniques reduce the Alter's action-space (Galtung 1965, 237). Turning for a moment to Galtung's binary, we notice that the utility–disutility pair (in terms of irreversibility of the consequences of action) no longer lends itself to the nonviolence–violence pair, at least not without vivid paradoxes. This is the moment when our analytical sociologist *accidentally* commits phenomenology and takes us back to the ambivalent moment in Sorel, Galtung's seemingly polar opposite. Phenomenologically, the constructed conceptual equivalences initially grant us an intelligible view into the phenomenon, but on further and persistent gazing, as the conclusion to this book will show, those same equivalences reveal movements opposite to the original observation. In their multifaceted appearances, *violence and nonviolence criss-cross the field of conflict*, leaving us with no choice but to acknowledge that *while epistemologically distinct, violence and nonviolence lose their oppositional purity at the moment of confrontation.*

Algorithms and conceptual substitutions – action, pacifism, peace, social justice, development – provide us with an opportunity to experience that which is scarcely experienceable in its own terms, owing to the *radical negativity* of *non*-violence. Common, received notions rescue an abstract and ungraspable idea from obscurity and unexperienceability. My hypothesis

of the "ontological primacy of violence" is affirmed. In my reading, Gultang stands close to Vattimo in seeing social justice as the condition for
reducing violence. In light of what we discovered in this chapter and specifically with respect to the irreversibility of human action, we need to ask
the dreaded question: Is it existentially possible to walk away from a conflict unscathed? Can I ever leave my experience of violence unaffected
by it? Can I be un-raped, un-abused, un-injured? Does even entertaining
this idea not indicate a form of (religious) puritan thinking involving
deliverance and atonement? We must deal with these questions through
ethical and moral approaches to nonviolence.

7
Ethics of Nonviolence

The Christian may be subjected to external violence, he may be deprived of bodily freedom, he may be in bondage to his passions ... but he cannot be in bondage in the sense of being forced by any danger or by any threat of external harm to perform an act which is against his conscience.

Tolstoy, *The Kingdom of God Is Within You* (1951 [1894], 117)

All men [and women] recognize the right of revolution.

Thoreau, "Civil Disobedience" (1993, 3)

Hubris breeds violence. It is the *quintessence* of violence in the *primordial* as well as the historical manifestations of that which *violates*. Hubris reveals itself in the act of one against another; in due course, it mobilizes the normative imposition of institutional–maximizing practices on the populace; and it is enabled by the structural configurations that make such imposing (and imposed) practices possible, intelligible, even desirable. While the modalities through which violence manifests itself belong to different levels of practice and thus vary in extent and reach, they all pertain to acting insofar as one actual mode of practice restricts other possible modes of action. As radical maximization, *violence always reveals itself through an act that restricts not only the actions of others but also acting as such.* These observations are gifts of phenomenology. Although unconceptualized in the works of advocates of nonviolence, these aspects of violence resonate (albeit differently) with different treatises on nonviolence. We observed that in his specific rationalist way, Sharp recognizes that violence is inherently restrictive, and thus he conceptually devises NVA as a counter-imposition on violent rulers or imposed policies. As for Galtung, he acknowledges, through his analytical theory, how nonviolent struggles should initiate expansion of the "action-spaces" restricted by violence. Every time we think about (non)violence, our gaze is inevitably directed towards acting. Acting is the common denominator of (non)violence, and both Sharp and Galtung acknowledge the conflictual nature of non-violence. They establish the conceptual relationship between nonvio-lence (and violence) and acting as mediated through certain algorithms.

When violence is measured in terms of the human costs of specific acts – death, injury, destruction, impoverishment, repression – one possibility for advocating nonviolence reveals itself through the view of the *other* not as an Other, an Alter always confronting the Ego, but as an exten-sion of the autonomous Self. This relationship enables two interwoven approaches to nonviolence understood in terms of love as well as ethical or moral terms. The theme of love as a passageway leading to nonvio-lence has been the subject of popular works (see Rosenberg 2003). Every time nonviolence is advocated – regardless of the specific algorithmic rationality used to render nonviolence intelligible – an ethical principle is inexorably evoked: ethics presents itself as the high ground. As Gal-tung states and wonders: "The whole theory of nonviolence is based on the idea of *Self recognizing the human being in the Other*, appealing to that human being not only for compassion with one's own plight, but also for self-interest in a better future, to be enjoyed together. But what if a pro-cess of dehumanization has taken place, already beforehand ruling out the Other as a human partner?" (1989, 14, emphasis added).

One can conveniently claim that the most straightforward approach to nonviolence arises from moral approaches contextualized in terms of received cultural and religious values. It is often argued that non-violence has its roots in Christianity in the West and in Jainism and Buddhism in the East (Jahanbegloo 2014, 27–40, 11–26). Religious values can indeed be evoked within the social and political fields to support present-day advocacy of nonviolence. But by anchoring non-violence to moral principles we risk losing sight of the conceptual rootedness of nonviolence in human collective or individual action. Friedrich Nietzsche once observed that action is separated from the actor by morality (1967, 45). An inescapable insight informs his obser-vation, and the phenomenology of (non)violence enables us to bring Nietzsche's observation to light.

The literature on nonviolence and ethics/morals is vast and diverse. Ethical approaches often significantly overlap with other approaches to nonviolence – in particular the advocacy of nonviolence from the point of view of its utility. We thus need to isolate the ethical–moral components by offering deep readings of the key proponents of this approach.

Tolstoy: The Law of Love

As a founding figure of nonviolent discourse, Leo Tolstoy expressly rejected violence by relying on *moral* imperatives. His thought trails the nineteenth-century traditions of Christian-inspired pacifism and Abolitionism in England and the United States and their contradictory legacies (Losurdo 2015, 7–19). The concept of nonviolence, and reworked conceptions of violence, are indeed products of late-nineteenth- and early-twentieth-century social thought in the works of Tolstoy, Thoreau, and Ruskin. Showing how the concept of non-violence emerged at this time would require a thorough conceptual history – an independent study indeed – although I will be making allusions to it here. Tolstoy's writings on violence, love, and Christian anarchism reveal him to be an originator of the *concept* of nonviolence, even though the term "nonviolence" does not appear in his writings. Nonetheless, the great twentieth-century champion of nonviolence, Mahatma Gandhi, acknowledged Tolstoy's *The Kingdom of God Is Within You* (along with Ruskin's work) as the main inspiration for his ideas (Gandhi 2011, 98), declaring himself "a humble follower of that great teacher" (Gandhi, in Tolstoy 1909, 1).

Tolstoy's refutation of violence arises from his adherence to a particular reading of the teachings of Christ. Tolstoy writes about the "necessity for religion" (2010, 11), but religion understood not in terms of the doctrinal or organized religion one is born into or that to which one (tacitly) conforms. Instead, religion for him involves active and conscious devotion to a faith that ties one to a community. Adhering to a certain pastoral romanticism, Tolstoy blames the loss of harmony in society on man's beastly progress (2010, 9, 15); that progress keeps humans away from "a spiritual, moral principle that would unite them in a society of peace and concord" (2010, 15). Faith is the natural condition of life (2010, 88); faith is what connects one to a community. The false Christianity of the Church (i.e., the Russian Orthodox Church's endorsement of the tsar's brutal rule) and thus the loss of faith have contributed to the malaise of the modern age (2010, 10). Modern, individualistic society, in other words, has lost the moral component – the Law of Love – that holds the community together. All "social conceptions of life" are prone to this essential defect (Tolstoy 1951). Under these conditions, misery leads to "the oppression of part by the rest" (Tolstoy 2010, 17), that is, the imposition of societal expectations on those who reject proscribed practices. By nature, Tolstoy argues, humans do not wish to live under oppression; they are nonetheless held (captive) "in society by the aid of violence" (2010, 18). These conditions render men irrational. "It is because the long duration of the lie has caused them to lose all notion of the bond that exists between their servitude and their participation in violence" (Tolstoy 2010, 45). Habitual and rampant modes of violence render humans insensitive not only to the perpetual violence to which they are subjected but also to the extent of violence in which they partake. Being desensitized to violence: this is a symptom of the progressivist mentality that has rationalized submission to violence in its myriad manifestations. Even the emancipatory model of socialism is not immune to such desensitization. Tolstoy calls socialism slavery: "One of the most striking phenomena of our times is precisely this advocacy of slavery, which is promulgated among the masses, not by government, in whom it is inevitable, but by men who, in advocating socialistic theories, regard themselves as champions of freedom" (Tolstoy 1951, 119). The key argument here is that, for Tolstoy, improving material conditions will not liberate humans (1951, 120). Modern humanity needs *moral* liberation.

In exposing and criticizing the violence of his time, while citing economic injustices that allow "a handful of idlers" to control and oppress "a majority of working people" (Tolstoy 1909, 2), Tolstoy specifically names *the state* as the source of violence because of its exclusive "armed force" (2010, 59). The authority of government, situated within modern, impersonal, utilitarian society, is morally corrupt in its essence. The state is the embodiment of violence *par excellence*. Lacking a moral component, the state increasingly relies on sheer force. In fact, the fusion of religion with the state (as in Russia) has fostered the "means of persecutions and punishments sought to compel men to accept religious laws authorized by the rulers and conflicting with the truth" (Tolstoy 1909, 4). "The obsolete religious justification of violence consisted in the recognition of the supernatural personality of the God-ordained ruler ... This has been superseded by the 'scientific' justification" (1909, 6). According to Tolstoy, "scientific justifications" inform "the principle of coercion" in modern society (1909, 6). Thus, all governments are based on violence or fear (Tolstoy 1951, 159). Speaking to the realities of his time, Tolstoy sees military service as ancillary to state violence (1951, 99). This is particularly important, because military service reveals that which is defective about the "social conception of life":

> In the social conception of life it is supposed that since the aim of life is found in groups of individuals, individuals will voluntarily sacrifice their own interest for the interests of the group. And so it has been, and still is, in fact, in certain groups, the distinctions being that they are the most primitive forms of association in the family or tribe or race, or even in the patriarchal state. Through tradition handed down by education and supported by religious sentiment, individuals without compulsion merged their interests in the interest of the group and sacrificed their own good for the general welfare. (1951, 93)

Tolstoy's critique of individualistic self-interest could not be clearer. In his time, Tolstoy raised his voice against conscription, which he equated with military murder in a manner reminiscent of Thoreau. In his writings, he perceives the "social conception of life" as the context of state violence. He refers to the "state of stupefaction" (1951, 50) – implicitly, the ideological justification for state violence in the modern age – as a collective and cultural justification for accepting this violence. And he vehemently rejects utilitarian justifications for sacrifice and violence, such as the government's need to maintain security. These justifications ultimately rationalize violence and render it acceptable. Tolstoy even rejects punishment for criminals (1951, 25–26), since it affirms state violence. In fact, all authorities have become violent, and all forms of installing an authority, whether by heredity or through elections, have proved "ineffectual" (1951, 94). "[P]articipation in election, government, or law business is participating in government by force" (1951, 15). All persons who participate in ruling in whatever capacity become evil (1951, 164). Yet men are unaware of the evil they commit, for authority has lifted the burden of responsibility from the shoulders of individuals (1951, 173). Authority defines itself as good and defines evil in terms of opposition to authority. Thus the commonly held good-versus-evil binary is ultimately defined by power (1951, 106).

Tolstoy affirms that even revolts against this system lead to tyranny (1951, 109): in most cases the people's rising against oppression only perpetuates a cycle of violence (Tolstoy 2010, 19). We do not clearly see the horrors of our time, and this is partly why Tolstoy explicitly rejects counter-violence (2010, 95). He argues that "*recognizing the necessity of opposing evil by violence is only the justification of our habitual vices: vengeance, cupidity, envy, ambition, pride, cowardice, and spite*" (Tolstoy 2010, 106; emphasis in original). He believes that human life is linked to community and that humans live *outside* of the "static [civilizational states'] organization"; as a consequence, "Christian communities deny public authority" (2010, 92). This is how Christianity has come to hold an anti-authority essence that enables Christians to act against all manifestations of violence by invoking their faith in Christianity's highest teaching: love. Faith-based refusal to participate in violence can be found in many religious communities around the world (2010, 68–9, 70). He cites those religious communities that refuse to become the state's subjects based on their unwavering adherence to a faith that excludes evil from human action. Among these communities are the Doukhobors in Russia (whom Tolstoy financially assisted to relocate in Canada) and the Bábis in Iran (a mid-nineteenth-century millenarian sect; the Baha'i Faith is its offshoot) (2010, 68–9, 70). As mentioned, Tolstoy's refusal to participate in state-sanctioned violence originates in the teachings of Christ, in particular the "commandment of non-resistance to evil by force" (Tolstoy 1951, i).

I credited Tolstoy earlier as an originator of nonviolence, although he did not coin the term and in fact never used it. The teachings of Christ offered him the essence of nonviolence that guided his moral–political discourse. According to Tolstoy, Christianity allows for a *language of love* – one that has been forgotten for eighteen hundred years – in the face of modern-age violence. Tolstoy extracts from Christianity, as a religion of love, a moral approach towards the *Other*, a religion that bars one from inflicting harm on the Other. Love is the highest law, Tolstoy submits (Tolstoy 2010, 32–3). This position enables him to counterpose love to violence, arguing that each term in this binary follows its own logic; as such, he views love and violence as incommensurable. As the *essence* of Christianity, love reveals itself in "humanitarian doctrines" that may have nothing to do with Christianity but that are in fact "partial manifestations of the Christian conscience." Interestingly, these include "the socialist, communist and anarchist doctrines" (2010, 30). He regards the law of love as universal conscience and "as the *supreme law of life* ... Then will come to pass everything dreamed of and promised to-day by socialist and anarchist builders of future worlds" (2010, 89; emphasis in original). He calls love the "universal principle of life" (2010, 128).

Contrary to popular assumptions, the love Tolstoy advocates does not resemble the humanists' concept of it. The aim of life, holds Tolstoy, is to fulfil God's Law of Love (Tolstoy 1951, 117). "The doctrine of love for humanity alone is based on the social conception of life" (1951, 61), a position he rejects. Love for oneself or one's loved ones is natural, but at the same time, the social conception of life creates a chain of extension – the "aim of the individual life" – to family, clan, tribe, and the state. Such extension may be possible in relation to the family, but it will be "more difficult and requires social training" in relation to the state (1951, 61). Here is where the social conception of life reveals its problem: love cannot be extended to the state or to any corporate-like and thus artificial (human) *Gesellschaft*, to use Ferdinand Tönnies's concept, because "love must have an object, and that humanity is not an object. It is nothing but a fiction" (1951, 62). "The fallacy of the argument [of the social conception of life] lies in the fact that the social conception of life, on which love for family and nation is founded, rests itself on love of self, and that love grows weaker and weaker as it is extended from self to family, tribe, nationality, and state; and in the state we reach the furthest limit beyond which it cannot go" (1951, 62–3). Insofar as love arises from the Self, it remains tied to the interests of the human person, and thus love weakens as it expands towards unfitting objects. Due to its humanism, this social conception produces a limited conception of love. Tolstoy's argument here is rather nuanced: he agrees that love must be expanded to all, but he also notes that it cannot be expanded through an extended chain of potential objects related to the Self. In Tolstoy's words, "the necessity of extending the sphere of love is beyond dispute. But in reality the possibility of this love is destroyed by the necessity of extending its object indefinitely. And thus the insufficiency of personal human love is made manifest" (1951, 63). Christianity offers a "new and higher conception of life" (1951, 103). Genuine love originates with the love of God alone. All other expressions of love are only semblances of God's love. Therefore, "here the advocates of Positivist, Communistic, Socialistic fraternity propose to draw upon Christian love to make up the default of this bankrupt human love; but Christian love only in its results, not in its foundations. They propose love for humanity alone, apart from love for God" (1951, 63). With love steadfastly anchored to God and only thus understood, the love for humans will only emerge as a by-product. The humanist's love may be tried, but without secure foundations in the love for God it will diminish into the social conception of life. Love is the essence of God: "For God so loved the world that he gave his one and only Son, that whoever believes in him shall not perish but have eternal life" (John 3:16). "The Christian doctrine brings a man to the elementary consciousness of self, *only not of the animal* [human corporeal] *self, but of the divine self*, the divine spark, the self as the Son of God, as much God as the Father himself, though confined in an animal husk," writes Tolstoy. "With the Christian conception of life, love is not a necessity and is confined to no object; it is the essential faculty of the human soul. Man loves not because it is his interest to love this or that, but because love is the essence of his soul, because he cannot but love" (1951, 63, emphasis added).

As a moral–social thinker, Tolstoy explores the outcome of this divine concept of love for human action. Love calls on us to render evil obsolete and ineffectual while refusing to partake in challenges to evil. Tolstoy draws on the principle of "nonresistance to evil by violence" (2010, 124). The word "non-resistance" comes from the Sermon on the Mount or from the Creed (Matthew 5:38–42) in which Christ averred the command, "Resist not evil" (Tolstoy 1951, 47, 14). The modern age has corrupted Christianity, for the Church has abandoned the most fundamental and exclusive teaching of Christ: non-resistance to evil by force because of love (1951, 104). Consistent with my phenomenological observation, albeit discursively distinct from it, Tolstoy observes that evil always resides, and thus manifests itself, in an act measured against its hubristic outcome. Furthermore, and more importantly, evil has rendered us numb about partaking in hubristic evildoing. "All the evil of our life seems to exist only because it has been so for so long; those who do the evil have not had time yet to learn how to act otherwise, though they do not want to act as they do," Tolstoy observes. "All the evil seems to exist through some cause independent of the conscience of men" (1951, 111). People genuinely detest manifest forms of evil, "oppression, inequality, [and] class distinction" but are unaware of how to fight these injustices (1951, 111). Counter-violence or rebellion of men against oppression can only perpetuate violence. That is why, following Christ's Sermon, Tolstoy regards adherence to nonviolence (non-resistance to evil) as the duty of all (1951, 105) and therefore as a universal condition for acting. Since in Christianity evil has no form, this universal imperative requires from us unending vigilance. Two consequences follow. First, this is why religion acquires new significance: "the essence of religion lies in the faculty of men of foreseeing and point out the path of life along which humanity must move in the discovery of a new theory of life [as opposed to the social theory of life], as a result of which the whole future conduct of humanity is changed and different from all that has been before" (1951, 53). In other words, after centuries of corruption and obliviousness to the true teachings of Christ, the age of Christianity is approaching. This is when the "Christian principles of equality and fraternity, community of property, non-resistance of evil by force" will embrace humanity (1951, 67). Thus, second, each of us is now required to reorganize his or her own life, *but not the lives of others*, according to Christ's teachings: "Let each one understand that he has not the right, or even the possibility, to organize the lives of others, but that he, in his own life, should act in conformity with the supreme religious law that has been revealed to him" (Tolstoy 2010, 113). Humans cannot be led to a new society like a flock of sheep. "A new conception of life cannot be imposed on men; it can only be freely assimilated" (Tolstoy 1951, 103). The outcome will be the disappearance of oppressive societies based on *social* conceptions of life. The future society, driven by a Godly concept of life, will then be based on the "requirements of the Christian doctrine – of universal brotherhood, suppression of national distinctions, abolition of private property, and the strange injunction of non-resistance to evil by force" (1951, 66). Because it is prohibited for any true Christian to lend allegiance to any government (1951, 118), Tolstoy's envisioned Christian communism certainly has an anarchistic character.

As Tolstoy pioneers thinking about the domains of action that may possibly exist outside the dominant modern and rational-purposive violence that embraces us all, he ventures into an undiscovered realm. Passive resignation, and thereby involuntary participation, in this epistemic regime constitutes servitude (Tolstoy's word), and servitude manifests itself in violence. One must first acknowledge that Tolstoy has indeed succeeded in decoding and thereby exposing the violence that is innate to modern society. Therefore, before being an advocate of nonviolence, Tolstoy must be regarded as a thinker of violence. Given his belief, naturally his exposing of violence and his advocacy of the law of love – nonviolence – must be understood as an outcome of the discovery of Christ's Law of Love and the principle of non-resistance to evil. This is the "master code" that allows Tolstoy to rise as the social thinker of (non)violence. Here it seems that Tolstoy's moral advocacy of nonviolence – the product of his steadfast subscription and internationalization of the norm of highest perceived value – restricts the realm of human action ("non-resistance to evil"). This will preclude violence because violence does not accord with the essence of the Christian conception of life. Such a reading of Tolstoy is not incorrect, but there is more here than meets the eye. Just as with the thread running through this book, Tolstoy simultaneously offers a theory of violence *and* nonviolence. The Christian moral principle of love and non-resistance allows him to measure both violence and nonviolence against an *a priori* epistemological pillar that ensures unwavering attachment to that which will deliver humans from oppression: love, or nonviolence. As such, I argue, a subtler *epistemic challenge* underpins Tolstoy's seemingly dichotomous conception of love versus violence.

Key here is that the principles of love and non-resistance cannot be imposed as normative dictates though they do in fact provide normative epistemic guideposts. This is obvious where Tolstoy (as quoted above) declares that congregations of believers cannot be driven towards love or non-resistance. On the contrary, one must assimilate oneself to Christian love. The true Christian needs to develop a conscience that has internalized those two principles; in doing so, she or he finds a new domain in which to resist. Tolstoy asserts that *one has dominion only over oneself* – a theme (to be discussed) that appears in many of his fables (1962, 74–80, 82–8). When one has dominion only over oneself, the political outcome cannot be anything but an *autonomous anarchistic community*. It seems at first that his advocacy of anarchism is hardly a cause for alarm: he seems to be advocating a return to the pre-political life of a community gathered together around a universal moral principle – the Law of Love – whatever the outward manifestations of that community (Christian, socialist, communist, anarchist). Here a clarification is in order: Tolstoy's resort to the Christian Law of Love often masks his anarchistic discourse. He does indeed associate faith (and thus love) with community, but the key point is that for Tolstoy, the concept of community is not based on faith despite appearances to the contrary. Tolstoy's rejection of authority has its roots in the fundamental "lack of right" – that is, no one has the right to organize other humans according to a certain, imposed rule. Which brings us back to the point that we all have dominion solely over our individual selves. Moral principles preclude actions that are contrary to the principle of non-resistance to evil. Once one voluntarily embraces nonviolence, one seems to lose the freedom to partake in all (violent and nonviolent) available modalities of acting. Yet the avoidance of violence shatters this superficial notion of freedom: in rejecting servitude – that is, violence – and in refusing to impose one's will on others (hubris), one finds freedom, which is the quintessence of nonviolence. Evil consumes us by imbuing us with the urge to violate others out of our individual or collective self-interest. This is how the cycle of violence perpetuates itself. This is also how "non-resistance" arises as the doctrine of withdrawal from violence. Because I am aware of what amounts to evil as soon as I engage in hubristically violating another's life, *it is impossible for me to measure my*

act of love without reference to evil. Thus, one withdraws from the predefined
fields of violent action precisely because, epistemologically, one can only
arrive at nonviolence through the experience of violence. *Violence and
nonviolence, distinct in terms of the hitherto known domains of action, now lose
their oppositionality.* The epistemological marker that separates violence
from nonviolence is thus suspended, despite Tolstoy's emphasis on it.

I called Tolstoy's utopian community "pre-political," and this description holds accurate insofar as we understand politics – via a long Western
tradition – as a field of conflict among the many aggregates in which the
question of political power reigns supreme. In the context of this tradition, Tolstoy's understanding of "pre-political" community defies our
common understanding. If I recognize that I have no right to impose
my will or social organization on others because I have dominion only
over myself and only in the moment at hand, I can only be oriented
towards the *others* with whom I will participate in forming a community
through a prior epistemic but perhaps tacit agreement. Since in this
community imposition is unthinkable, my relationship with the others
will have to be based on love – and not love of community (an abstract
notion rejected by both Tolstoy and Arendt) but love of my fellow flesh-
and-blood communitarians. This is a highly unconventional understanding of community. Such an understanding of love, of one's "dominion"
over oneself, and of one's ephemeral temporality (due to my mortality)
can only lead to self-sacrifice and thus to losing the fear of suffering and
death in face of violence (a central theme in Gandhi and Tolstoy). This
community's non-resistance to evil, which puts an end to the cycle of violence by precluding all hitherto known violent acts, emerges through an
intentional, praxiological exodus. Ideally, pacifist, communist, Christian
communities such as the Doukhobors, the Mennonites, and the Amish
embody this thought. The exodus from the reach of violence produces a
curious generation of exiles: the practitioners of nonviolence emerge as
self-exiled from the universal (ontological) reach of human acting and
thinking – deemed to be violent – that has informed our civilizations
throughout recorded history. These practitioners consciously defamiliarize the violent world in which they tacitly partake and the violent ways
that are in the air they breath. As such, *the nonviolent exodus involves the
volitional process of invoking deworlding/reworlding;* but since this process
of abandoning the realms of violent action through self-exile and self-
extraction is not imposed but voluntary, the deworlding/reworlding is
bound to bring about liberation and is thus detached from its violent
ontology. I shall return to this point.

We can see how the "moral" ink of Tolstoy's vision loses its opacity: granted that he borrows the language of moral absolutes and communities of faith, it turns out that we are gently tethered to a vision of "mutual love" as the building blocks of community. We see that the Law of Love and non-resistance to evil together serve as the moral *axiom* that renders nonviolence intelligible, desirable, righteous, and practical. I wonder: If my interpretation of Tolstoy (beyond the Count's intentions!) is correct, how else could he have rendered this complex process – the conjuring of the spectre of living nonviolently in an inherently violent world – intelligible outside the parameters of Christian-moral axioms? Once we isolate this axiom-algorithm, we find that owing to the dominion of the conscientious one over oneself alone, the moral principle *potentially* yields to the practical nonviolence that permeates all flourishing life. In the absence of imposed social relations (epitomized by the state or the social conception of life), violence fades away, since it arises from the imposition of order on life's unending and surprising vicissitudes. *Violence dies out while the ones it has been violating survive.*

Thoreau: Twisted Emergence of Nonviolence

The ethical considerations in advocating nonviolence are hugely diverse, in terms of both their conceptual foundations and their advocacy of ethical action in situations of conflict. In the broad literature of nonviolence, Henry David Thoreau (1817–1862) stands as a pioneer. Although he wrote little about nonviolence compared to key contemporary advocates of it, his thought represents a key moment in the American libertarian tradition. His libertarian anarchism is fundamentally suspicious of government in particular and political power in general, and he urges his fellow citizens to critically examine government-imposed laws – in his case, the poll tax (he was jailed for one night for refusing to pay that tax and was bailed out by his aunt; Arendt 1972, 59–60). Government, for him, is an imposition on the rational individual's free will and faculty of judgment. He bases this view on the principle of individual freedom; in fact, he regards such freedom as higher than the state (Thoreau 1993, 18). We are human beings with conscience first; only then are we citizens. As such the laws of the land may well clash with my rights as an individual. "The only obligation which I have a right to assume is to do at any time what I think right" (1993, 2). The social contract as expressed by the Constitution determines the rights and duties of citizens; however, that contract can become corrupted by corrupt politicians; when that happens, the government can devolve into an institution that allows rulers to take advantage of citizens (1993, 1). More importantly, the rights and duties that a constitution defines often end up mobilizing citizens to support the wrong (i.e., that which arises from the interests of the rulers).

A conscientious human has a *duty* not to support what is wrong (e.g., slavery in Thoreau's pre-Abolition times). One's guiding (moral) principles are therefore more fundamental than any social contract. "Unjust laws exist" (1993, 7). "It is not a man's duty, as a matter of course, to devote himself to the eradication of any, even the most enormous wrong; he may still properly have other concerns to engage him; but it is his duty, at least, to wash his hands of it, and, if he gives it no thought longer, not to give it practically his support" (1993, 6). Thoreau calls on us to confront those situations where, to use contemporary terms, civic rights and duties are in conflict with human freedom and moral–ethical responsibilities. Civil liberties are limitations imposed on human freedom and human potential; but we accept them in return for security – a point argued in various ways by the social contract thinkers of the European Enlightenment. Liberty remains a limitation, but what are we to do if this limitation expresses itself as duplicity – for example, as tacit agreement to slavery by virtue of citizenship? This is Thoreau's point: we are dragged into the state's hubristic (and self-serving) actions as a consequence of our citizenship. In the settler-colonial state of Canada, as a case in point, population growth boosted by steady immigration, especially in urban areas, has been an effective means for the state to dispossess Aboriginal peoples from their ancestral lands. That process has been so stealthy, so hegemonized by the public discourse hinging on "development" and "prosperity," that average Canadians barely notice. Thoreau's notable insight is that we fight the "paper" of the law, not the men who defend it. "My civil neighbor, the tax-gatherer, is the very man I have to deal with, ... and he has voluntarily chosen to be an agent of the government" (1993, 8). We confront each other, and the unjust law slips by. This means that to change an unjust law (or, borrowing from Vattimo, to reassert justice from out of the law), we need to engage with the defenders of unjust laws. In sociological language, we need a *social movement*. This is what Thoreau calls "[a]ction from principle – the perception and the performance of right – [which] changes things and relations; it is essentially revolutionary" (1993, 7).

Thoreau suggests that commitment to human dignity as the fundamental springboard for rights links his "acting from principle" to justice, in that he rejects any allegiance to a state that does not provide welfare

(1993, 15), since only laws that are "human" (read: just) are worthy of respect (1993, 26). The revolutionary undercurrent of this approach is quite inspiring. He rejects the "lesser evil" argument that accepts civic life as it is bestowed by the state. Instead he argues: "They think that, if they should resist, the remedy would be worse than the evil. But it is the fault of the government itself that the remedy *is* worse than the evil" (1993, 7, emphasis in original). Thus we see a refreshingly classical conjunction of civil disobedience with revolutionary spirit, a theme in the air in much of the contemporary world, in social movements and in the "movement of the movements" (Mertes 2004). These affinities aside, one must not conflate Thoreau's position, strictly speaking, with defiant collective actions. In Thoreau, the question of civil disobedience and acting from out of one's conscience takes on an *ethical* dimension in that one is responsible for oneself: one must remain true to one's conscience and act against what one finds unjust, unacceptable, and undignified. It is by remaining true to one's conscience against the unjust decisions of the government and the people who meekly submit to it that one can object to unconscionable acts – for instance, slavery.

Between Tolstoy and Thoreau we see the emergence of the politics of Refusal, of withdrawal from participating in the matter-of-course processes that render one (the unwitting) ancillary to violence and injustice arising from the state (but not exclusively). Here is where we see the distinction between the *moral* (extracted from principles) and the *ethical* (oriented towards the *Other*) as they produce a similar nonviolent effect: while for Tolstoy Refusal is extracted from religious dictum (the Law of Love and non-resistance to evil) and has thus a vivid moral component, in Thoreau Refusal arises from his "ethics," which rely on the individual's judgment regarding the treatment of the conscientious Self (and thereby of the Other) with dignity in the face of the state's laws as they are forced upon the individual. While there is no doubt that Thoreau was immensely influenced by the American religious movement known as Transcendentalism, his ethics rely primarily on the enlightened individual's judgment – that is, on one's verdict concerning the manifestations of hubristic violence from the perspective of one's free will and ability to judge. As such, I suggest, Thoreau's "rationalistic" ethics are not extracted from pregiven moral principles.

For both Tolstoy and Thoreau, in confronting rampant violence the conscientious individual is led to Refusal, withdrawal, and self-exile. Thoreau's two-year experiment in "living deliberately" in a cabin on the edge of Walden Pond brings to light the libertarian, "anarchistic" tendency

of his thought. While for Tolstoy the politics of extracting oneself from
the violence that contains us all inevitably finds a communitarian aspect
owing to his moral–Christian principles, for Thoreau civil disobedience
and the politics of Refusal always arise from the individual's spirit of freedom. By opening a path, an individual's act can indeed leave a lasting
impact. "For it matters not how small the beginning may seem to be: what
is once well done is done for ever" (Thoreau 1993, 9). This is how one
leaves an enduring legacy.

Thoreau's civil disobedience and Tolstoy's non-resistance to evil represent the original moments of the emergence of the *concept* of nonviolence. Neither of them, of course, coined or used the term. *The notion,
idea, or intuition always precedes the concept.* Each in his own way, Tolstoy and
Thoreau clearly see the various modalities of violence. Tolstoy's nonviolence leads to a politics of withdrawal without submission but nonetheless a *non-confrontational* politics; Thoreau's civil disobedience ultimately
registers a politics of confrontation. With Thoreau, the communitarian utopia of Tolstoy is given up for a vivid political stance. This is why,
although Thoreau's historic moment is prior to Tolstoy's, the former is
"ahead" of the latter in exploring what one can actually and collectively
achieve through Refusal. Civil disobedience marks off the "right of revolution" (1993, 3) in action. In so doing, it exposes violence and therefore has an educational component. It wakes the citizens to the repressive system to which they tacitly lend allegiance. Civil disobedience, as
a mode of action, carves politicized citizens out of indifferent apolitical
compatriots. Gandhi's confrontational nonviolence (chapter 8) is markedly influenced by this turn.

For our conceptual excursion, though, what is significant is to observe
the emergence of this elusive concept. With the *idea* of nonviolence growing into a shared notion, and later a concept, resistance against rampant
and omnipresent violence finally becomes *intelligible*, and that is made
possible by tethering nonviolence to religious–moral or rational–ethical
algorithms. For example, as early as the first half of the nineteenth-
century Christian non-resistance movements in the United States, non-
resistance advocates equated this concept with peace – hence pacifism
(see Losurdo 2015, 7–10), thus enabling an algorithmic understanding
of the otherwise ungraspable concept. Religious–moral or rational–ethical
algorithms therefore afford essential epistemic tools: by referring to
some abstract (moral or ethical) principles or timeless axioms (e.g., it is
preferable to be harmed than to cause harm), these algorithms enable
thinkers of nonviolence to identify the modes of violence that contain

us, the hegemonic and matter-of-course violence of which the majority of the populace remains unaware or towards which it stands indifferent. *Civil disobedience intends to defy violence from within its purview with the intention of exhausting it.* In constituting nonviolence in terms of civil disobedience, nonviolence exercises a curious form of irrepressible action: to defy power from out of power's reach while standing within the purview of power. Facing violence without resorting to violence requires *self-sacrifice,* it requires imperilling the very body that stands up to power not with the intent of overwhelming it but for the purpose of exhausting and annulling it. The body that stands up to forces numerous times stronger *shall be violated;* it may even perish. If there is any "essence" to nonviolence it is *non*compliance – ironically, another negative term! Violence may repress actors, movements, uprisings. But here is where something magical shines forth: *the actor dies yet the act remains as an open horizon,* always already within our grasp. Violence cannot eradicate action. What the actor leaves behind is an act that is irrepressible. *Irrepressibility is therefore the marker of all acts of nonviolence.* Curiously, as soon as I try to extract myself from the known fields of violence (hubristic, institutional, or structural), I find myself having to go through the experience of violence. My nonviolent act subjects me to violence. Once again, the long-held *binary between violence and nonviolence thus collapses.* Love, refusal to commit evil, or disobeying the unjust by reasserting my true self: these cannot shine forth except against the silhouette of violence.

Arendt's Interjection

Thoreau's conception of individual responsibility – with its ethical component in keeping the integrity of the Self in the face of injustice – defines a critical concept of citizenship that involves speaking truth to power. Tolstoy's acting in good conscience, regardless of the Christian shade of his moral arguments, is not far from Thoreau's concept of the autonomous, libertarian citizen, although it carries a markedly different social outcome: Tolstoy advises withdrawal from participating in injustice rather than confronting it, although, it must be noted, the young Russians escaping conscription were tried and shot after arrest. This suggests that withdrawal may amount to confrontation, depending on the context. In any case, both men recognize, as does Vattimo, that justice is different from the law, that the law (*droit*) is not necessarily right – morally or ethically – and that the law always posits itself as (supreme) *good.* By the same token, that which lies outside activities sanctioned by

law is deemed to be *evil*. To register this discord in terms of personal
responsibility, which has always informed the human condition in times
of revolt, a further step must be taken.

So once again we visit Arendt, who recognizes personal responsibility
while reflecting on a different context. One's faculty of *judgment* is inten-
sified under a dictatorship, during which the cost of acting according
to one's conscience is particularly and measurably high (Arendt 2003,
17–48). Since legality is not the same as morality, the conscientious individual under these conditions is torn between ethical/moral judgment,
on the one hand, and being a citizen of the repressive and non-responsive
state, on the other. The concept of judgment, which is key to Arendt's
later work, dislocates the moral/ethical argument for nonviolence, but I
regard it as a necessary interpolation, although it requires us to be alert
to the *conceptual slide* from violence to evil. So let us proceed with the
caveat that it is not my intention to extract an ethical theory from Arendt
in the following discussion.

As is well-known, the traditional concept of evil is associated with
the Abrahamic religions (although it originated in the ancient Manichaean religions) in which the realms of good and evil pre-exist
human experience and action by virtue of existing scriptural fiats that
categorize and bifurcate deeds and thoughts across the two opposing
and incommensurable fields. For brevity's sake, let us fast-forward to
the modern interpretation – in particular, to Kant, who invoked the
term "radical evil" philosophically and located the source of good and
evil in free will, thereby holding humans accountable (owing to the
Subject's volition) for the "choice" of one or another course of action.
Obviously, this is an Enlightenment-era understanding of human
agency. In the context of Kant's (Christian) morality, failure to respect
the (moral) laws leads to self-conceit and corruption, which is the
source of all evil and thus "radical" (Bernstein 2002, ch. 1). Through
personal and intellectual excursions, Arendt becomes critical of the
Kantian notion in that freedom of choice (which is at the heart of
Kant's Enlightenment moral philosophy) includes the choice of evil,
but this means that because of my entitlement to freedom of choice, I
am infinitely *responsible* for my actions. This idea develops into Arendt's
famous thesis on the "banality of evil," as opposed to Kantian "radical evil" (which Arendt had accepted earlier on in her thinking), a
significant contribution shaped profoundly by Arendt's presence during the trial, in Jerusalem in 1961–62, of Adolf Eichmann, the high-
ranking Nazi who did so much to administer the Holocaust. The trial

presented to Arendt "the lesson of the fearsome, word-and-thought-defying *banality of evil*" (1965, 252, emphasis in original). In her report of the trial, she points out that Eichmann's work involved the logistical organization of the Holocaust and that he was fully aware of the goal of his administrative work. It was a job that practically any average man could have done, Arendt points out, and she shows that Eichmann was indeed an average man. Those who committed such horrendous crimes, she avers, were "terribly and terrifyingly normal" (1965, 276). Naturally, Eichmann's excuse, and that of almost all Nazis tried during the Nuremberg Trials (1945–46), was that they were "following the rules" as they had sworn to do in a Germany ruled by the *Führerprinzip* (1965, 148). According to Arendt, every human is capable of such evil, but the source of the committed evil is not self-conceit and thus not an infringement of the moral laws; rather, it is *thoughtlessness* – the inability to correctly see and understand the consequences of one's actions. The "strange interdependence of thoughtlessness and evil" (1965, 288; Arendt 2003, 166) shifts the question of administered, systematic, and sweeping violence to the field of judging – that is, a course of action *always in formation* based on experience – instead of attributing violence to failure to extract the right action (good) from *a priori* moral principles. The question is, "[C]ould the activity of thinking as such, the habit of examining and reflecting upon whatever happens to come to pass, regardless of specific content and quite independent of results, could this activity be of such a nature that it 'conditions' men against evildoing?" (2003, 160). Arendt refers to Socrates, the prototypical civil disobedient who was widely held by fellow Athenians as a "gadfly" (one who disturbs the comfortable slumber of others), a "midwife" (one who helps deliver opinions to the world), and an "electric ray" (one who paralyses, on contact, the normal course of life) (2003, 174–5). For Arendt, these three unsavoury designations characterize thinking. The very performance of thinking, she advocates, may condition one "in such a way that he is incapable of evil" (2003, 180). Two Socratic hubris-resisting propositions, Arendt reports, are: "It is better to be wronged than to do wrong"; and "It would be better for me that my lyre or a chorus I directed should be out of tune and loud with discord, and that multitudes of men should disagree with me rather than that I, *being one*, should be out of harmony with myself and contradict *me*" (2003, 181, emphasis in original). Here, to repeat our earlier discussion on thinking, let us recall Arendt's distinction: "Thinking deals with invisibles, with representations of things that are absent; judging

always concerns particulars and things close at hand" (2003, 189). The
bottom line is this:

> Politically speaking, it is that under conditions of terror most people will
> comply but *some people will not,* just as the lesson of the countries to which
> the Final Solution was proposed is that "it could happen" in most places
> but *it did not happen everywhere.* Humanly speaking, no more is required, and
> no more can reasonably be asked, for this planet to remain a place fit for
> human habitation. (Arendt 1965, 233;, emphasis in original)

Arendt's observations enable an ethics that leans towards judging and
thinking without reference to the luxury of moral fundaments or even
the humanity of the Other. Interestingly, with Arendt, even though she
was no wholesale advocate of nonviolence, the "ethical argument" is
shifted onto a political argument: our ethical responsibility towards a
thinking and judging *Self* – and only thereby towards the *Other* – becomes
a condition for political participation.

Arendt's thesis works insofar as we take thinking in her specifically
Socratic manner – that is, it works by virtue of *constricting* the concept of
thinking. If we agree on her basic – but contestable – concept of thinking, then we notice that our ethical action always arises from somewhere
between thinking (things through their appearances) and judging
(things close at hand), or, to invert the terms, it is through one's act that
thinking and judging *may* meet. I agree with Arendt that thoughtlessness
(the inability to think) almost certainly guarantees evil, besides rendering it banal and commonplace. But this does not mean that thinking
can categorically lead us away from evil. Thinking may be our best bet in
avoiding evildoing, and it certainly elevates the thinker from that which
is banal; but "thinking," even when taken in the Arendtian fashion, cannot provide any assurances against evil or violence. Arendt's appeal to
thinking, besides revealing her humanism and ultimate faith in human
judgment, simply *assumes* that thinking's critical reflection will categorically evade violence. Certainly, as "coming-into-the-nearness of distance"
(Heidegger 1966, 68), thinking allows me to reflect on my wrongdoings
and helps me regret and correct my past decisions, become aware of my
responsibilities, and issue a harsher verdict when it comes to judging
myself. Yet when Arendt argues that there are no safeguards against evil
other than thinking, I respond that thinking (being "without banisters,"
by definition) is itself *ontologically unstable,* for it is tied to the epochal
modes of intelligibility. Let us not forget Heidegger (as if reflecting on

his Nazi past): "He who thinks greatly must err greatly" (Heidegger 1971, 9). If for the moment we take violence as being equivalent to evil (in its hubris), then we realize that the otherwise soothing and reassuring division of violence and nonviolence remains as precarious as ever, and that we may still decide, as one of our better options, to hang our hopes on thinking's gentle power to cut through matter-of-fact evildoings through critical judgment; yet that has never safeguarded us against violence. Thinking about, reflecting on, and judging that I may be committing violence in my act will not prevent me from partaking in violence. We can see how the quest for safeguards against violence lures a brilliant thinker like Arendt to algorithm by factoring in thinking and judging (or the lack thereof) when reflecting on resistance to evil, even while thinking by definition eludes all algorithms. Arendt's "thinker" *assumes* a moral–rational subject. Thinking cannot positively maintain violence and nonviolence as opposites. In the end, what remains in appealing to thinking is a beautiful attempt at "consoling of the soul" (Schürmann 2003, 296).

Butler and the Injurability of the Other

Let us now focus on an important interjection made by the contemporary American philosopher Judith Butler, who is known for her compelling "performative" approach to subjectivity and identity. Cautioning against nonviolence as a "principle" or a virtue, Butler refutes the widely acclaimed mutual exclusivity of violence and nonviolence – a proposition that resonates with the thesis of this book but that arises from an entirely different argument. Violence "is not foreign to the tone to whom the address of non-violence is directed," Butler proposes. "Violence is not, at the start, presumptively 'outside.' Violence and non-violence are not only strategies or tactics, but form the subject and become its constitutive possibilities and, so, an ongoing struggle" (Butler 2009, 165). We are partly formed by violence within a "matrix of power," and we become the *subject* through our unsolicited violent constitution. Violence exploits our bodily presence through which we exist in a "primary way … as bodies, outside ourselves and for one another" (Butler 2004, 27). "Indeed, it may be that precisely because one is formed through violence, the responsibility not to repeat the violence of one's formation is all the more pressing and important" (Butler 2009, 167). We can observe that my "responsibility" not to perpetuate the (violent) system of subjection that has unfortunately, but

perhaps also unavoidably, produced and shaped me in the first place
will reintroduce my act as an ethical one. Stated differently, the ethics
of nonviolence come from violence, which of course takes us back to
the lack of a clear distinction between violence and nonviolence (2009,
170). I would add that the distinction – or better, the lack thereof –
is both conceptual and practical. This ethical instance constitutes the
agency of nonviolent actor, and with this agency, due to the subject's
injury, a choice is born: either "(a) … injured and rageful subject …
gives moral legitimacy to rageful and injurious conduct, thus transmut-
ing aggression into virtue," or "(b) … injured and rageful subject …
nevertheless seeks to limit the injury that she or he causes, and can do
so only through an active struggle with and against aggression" (2009,
172). "Moral sadism" involves the kind of persecution that poses itself
as a virtue, while responsibility takes possession of aggression with an
"ethical mandate" to eradicate it through nonviolence. Note here that
aggression is not necessarily violence, in that aggression may be used
in a protective manner (2009, 176–7). What is important for us to
recognize, however, is the *injurability* of the Other, although in cases
such as the sovereign's violence, the violent act "produces the appearance that the subject who enacts violence is impermeable to violence"
(2009, 178). The perception of invincibility is indeed an *effect* of violence. Now, the recognition of the sovereign's injurability, or generally
the injurability of the violent party, is expected to morally impede the
victim of violence from partaking in counter-violence. Butler fittingly
rejects this position: the recognition of the injurability of the Other
cannot produce the ground for nonviolence. Quite the contrary, she
observes – injury can produce the ground for violence. Yet the acknowledgment that in a conflict – in fact, in *any* human relationship involving
diversity and variance – there is a possibility of the injurability of every
party, reflects upon me that I too am capable of committing violence
against others. As the reader observes, Butler's distinction is nuanced
and subtle. Nonviolence therefore arises from the possibility of my own
violence. To complicate the matter, the condition for using nonviolence is inevitably defined, in that there are those upon whom violence
ought not be applied and those regarding whom the question of nonviolence (or violence) simply remains irrelevant. Recognizing that lives
are grievable provides us with an *egalitarianism* that becomes the condition of nonviolence (2009, 179–81). "I'm not sure non-violence saves
the purity of anyone's soul," avers Butler, "but it does avow a social
bond, even when it is violently assaulted from elsewhere" (2009, 178).

That I have become conscious of, and reflect on, my violent constitution, that I have emerged in my world by virtue of having been *violated*, does not necessarily make me responsible for initiating nonviolence. Consistent with her performative approach, Butler invokes the concept of "iterability" to declare that "even if norms originated in violence it would not follow that their fate is only and always to reiterate the violence at their origin" (2009, 168–9). In other words, the existing norms, having originated in a violent constitution, need not necessarily remain violent. Stated differently, it is possible for the original violence to be reiterated in terms other than their original iteration. That is how Butler accounts for the openings that follow the original violence, openings out of which arise the possibility of nonviolence. While Butler's observation is correct, a phenomenologist's response would involve the reminder that her approach remains *ex post facto*: I have no experience nor possibly even a memory of my original constitution *as* violent. If I am aware that I have been produced through violence while being aware of the violence I am undergoing – as a sweatshop labourer or a conscript solider – then this violence will shape me but will not constitute me. My constitutive violence – the violence I endured as a child, in family, in school, or from my peers – will always inevitably come to light as *constitutive through reflections* after I have already passed through the formative stages. Thus the memory of the original violence, *stricto sensu*, is not performative but constructed, and there always remains the possibility – for me, the hegemonized subject – of the hegemonic experience of violence as something other than violence itself. Violence's protean character renders our experiential knowledge of violence as always after the fact. And in the production of our collective knowledge of violence Butler also inevitably participates in our intersubjective construction.

Butler's position, although not entirely new or unique, dwells in the *undecidability* of a course of action in the immediate future, and in response to a situation, based on the "choice" of violence or nonviolence. As she judiciously asserts, the fact that I have been subjected to violence does not necessarily makes me refrain from subjecting my adversary or anyone else to violence. As an ethical choice, nonviolence cannot automatically or even exclusively be deduced (or expected) from the victim of violence and the experience of victimhood. Butler challenges the present-day "hierarchy of grief" in favour of a *universal mourning* that connects us to one another through our universal vulnerability (Butler 2004, 17–49). The recognition of universal grievability, to which we are all equally prone and entitled by virtue of our mortality and sociality, allows her to find a "ground" for nonviolence – one that allows for a community (of nonviolent subjects) to come, a norm without normative hubris.

Butler's thought enjoys a vast trail of secondary scholarship. It is not my intention to engage with this scholarship, nor with Butler's thought *in toto*. Just as with the conceptual excursions throughout this book, I am interested in showing the various conceptual efforts in trying to locate (non)violence, whether practically, sociologically, politically, or morally. Phenomenologically, grief is tied to the loss of entities within my horizon of existence. Grief always indicates a partial deworlding. I will therefore only mourn those to whom I am related and connected in my *Welt* and with whom I live. *Mourning is indeed discriminatory*. I cannot mourn every loss I witness, only those that are meaningful within my existential horizons. I am indeed deeply saddened and outraged by the loss of hundreds and thousands of humans and millions of non-humans that I witness on digital screens losing their lives owing to avoidable causes and human atrocities, conceit, and avarice. But I am too finite to mourn them all. To reiterate, mourning, grief, and sorrow are fundamentally discriminatory, not egalitarian. This is because through mourning I identify with my community, or through mourning my community embraces me. Universal grievability remains an abstract idea. Like love, grief cannot exist outside of concrete relationships. Grieving for every loss is as inconceivable as loving one's country.

Still, my criticism of Butler, despite the fact that I personally relate to her position, lies elsewhere. I contend that because egalitarian grievability and injurability cannot *in essence* open up a specific course of action (nonviolence) while closing down another (violence), they leave us, once again, with the spectre of an *undecidable* nightmare, one that reduces our choices to individual choices, the ones that are informed by egalitarian injurability but that cannot sufficiently rely on this universal condition of injurablity or universal mourning to justify choosing one course of action over another. Challenging the "hierarchy of grief" in favour of universal mourning and acknowledging egalitarian injurability will only bring us to the old humanist adage that lies at the substrate of every universal ethics: "Do not do unto others what you do not want others to do unto you" (Confucius). Or as Galtung declares (quoted earlier), the entire idea of nonviolence is based on the recognition of the human in the other, thus the Self's treating "the Other as a human partner" (1989, 14). Once we bracket, for the moment, the deconstructive language of Butler, we find that her position is essentially not much different from the humanist–sociological position of Galtung and of many other advocates of nonviolence, for that matter. They all *assume* that our shared humanity somehow constitutes a binding power that enables us not to objectify and thus not to violate, punish, or abuse one another. The idea behind them is that once I recognize the *Other* – who is facing me (as an *alterity*, possibly even as a potential *threat*) – as the likeness of myself, then by virtue of the knowledge of the universal human tendency to avoid injury and loss that is within me and also within my Other, I recognize that I share my fate with my Other. In this way a community is born out of these minimal, "negative" conditions of egalitarian injurability and relational mourning. The problem is that the recognition of these morbid universals does not necessarily lead to empathy. It is completely possible to recognize and acknowledge the other's injurability, and that the death of the Other is mourned by his or her kinspeople with profound grief, and still inflict pain, harm, and death upon the Other with a clean conscience. Universal injurability – the vivid phenomenalization of our violent ontological constitution – provides no grounds for universal grievability. Shared humanity is a fable, a vestige of abstract humanism of the Enlightenment that paradoxically fed off European colonialism. But as humans, we do indeed share something. In Joseph Boyden's words, "humans, in all their many forms, are an unruly bunch, prone to fits of great generosity and even greater meting out of pain" (Boyden 2013, 153).

There are simply no moral or ethical – let alone social, cultural, or political – substrates whatsoever to foreground my future (re-)action (vengeance or forgiveness) once I re-turn to life after having survived the diabolical and injurious experience of hubris. Neither injurability nor mourning can sustain the opposition between violence and nonviolence.

Tolstoy Reloaded

It is safe to claim that Leo Tolstoy's fables and fairy tales reflect his particular Christian morals of compassion and love, pacifism, and denial of materialism. It can also be said that his stories and fables – rather insignificant compared to his literary accomplishments like *Anna Karenina* and *War and Peace* – also signify a poetic return to the simple origins of fiction in his childhood. I will return to these two observations – his advocacy of *certain* ethics and his poetic return to the original experience of fiction narrative. Here I offer some phenomenological reflections on the conditions of evil through an interpretation of two of Tolstoy's short stories.

The first story of interest to us, written in 1903, is called "Esarhaddon, King of Assyria." The reference to the Biblical narrative of King Esarhaddon is clear, although the story departs from the biblical version in favour of a fictionalized epitome of Tolstoy's *ethics of alterity*. Historically, Esarhaddon succeeded his father, who was slain by Esarhaddon's two brothers in 681 BCE. He restored Babylon, received tribute from King Manasseh of Judah, and conquered Egypt. Esarhaddon died in 668 BCE while campaigning to suppress an Egyptian uprising. He was succeeded by his son Ashurbanipal, whom he had promoted to power just before his death. Of King Lailie we know very little except that he was the trusted viceroy of the Bazu region in Esarhaddon's kingdom. In Tolstoy's narrative, King Esarhaddon has conquered the renegade King Lailie's region, captured him and his family, and subjected Lailie's family and warriors to unimaginable atrocities. The story opens at night as the victorious Esarhaddon, while resting from the day's exploits, contemplates about to which prolonged manner of killing he would subject Lailie. A strange old man abruptly appears before him, asking him whether he has been pondering how to slay Lailie. Taken aback by the unwavering mannerism of the unsummoned old man, he confirms that he has, only to hear the sage tell him, "But you are Lailie." With a hubristic gesture of denial, Esarhaddon alludes to the unfortunate fate that awaits Lailie at daybreak, when he will watch him slowly die. "You and Lailie are one," insists the old man. "It only seems to you that you are not Lailie and that Lailie is not you." And he reminds Esarhaddon that he cannot destroy Lailie's life (Tolstoy 1962, 74–80). On further inquiry, the perplexed king agrees to hold his head under the water the old man pours slowly from his jug in order to see the truth for himself. In this process, he finds himself as Lailie, not Esarhaddon.

As Esarhaddon (re)lives Lailie's life, he comes to realize that he is essentially no different from the once mighty king he has vanquished. He also grasps that the power that has enabled him to crush and impose today will one day inevitably diminish, as it did in Lailie's case. Esarhaddon experiences the life of Lailie through and through, including his downfall. He also experiences Lailie's painful decision to declare war on Esarhaddon after he has received back the emissaries whom he had sent, along with tributes, to Esarhaddon with their noses and ears cut off. In the end, Esarhaddon finds Lailie's life identical to his own: the lives of the two men, one at the apogee of his power and the other facing his doom, are essentially the same. The prospect of oblivion when he finds himself as Lailie being taken by thugs to his "gory execution site" horrifies Esarhaddon so much that he pulls his head from the sage's truth-revealing water. Stunned speechless, he listens to the sage, who, before vanishing, reminds him:

> *You thought life dwelt in you alone,* but I have drawn aside the veil of delusion, and you have seen that in doing evil to others you have done it to yourself as well. *Life is one in everything,* and within yourself you manifest but a portion of this one life. And only in that portion that is within you can you make life better or worse, magnify or diminish it. You can make life better within yourself only by destroying the barriers that divide your life from that of other beings, and by regarding others as yourself and loving them. To destroy the life that dwells in others is not within your power. The life that was in those you have slain has not been destroyed: it has merely vanished from before your eyes. You thought to prolong your own life and to shorten the lives of others, but you cannot do this. *For life there is neither time nor space. The life of a moment and the life of thousands of years, your life and the lives of all creatures seen and unseen, is one.* (1962, 80, emphasis added)

The next day, Esarhaddon orders the release of Lailie and all prisoners and appoints his son, Ashurbanipal, as his successor. "He himself withdrew into the wilderness to meditate on all that he had learned. Later he went as a pilgrim through the towns and villages, preaching to the people that all life is one, and that men do evil only to themselves in desiring to do evil to others" (1962, 80).

This captivating tale departs from the moral dictum and extractive logic of the earlier Tolstoy. It also carries within it the "universal principle of life" (as opposed to the social principle, which he rejects) that stems from *The Kingdom of God Is Within You* (orig. 1894) and that grows into an ethical principle in this story (1903). Tolstoy, it seems, has turned increasingly to metaphors as the "principle of life" takes on a life of its own, one that leaves behind the expressions of Christian moral discourse. Notable in this story is the allegorical presence of wisdom in lieu of – and obviously to represent the essence of – the God in *The Kingdom of God* and *The Law of Love.* This wisdom, embodied by the mysterious sage in this story, now becomes the source of ethics – a literary move that attests to Tolstoy's Christianity. Hence, in lieu of God and moral imperatives, Tolstoy advances his call for nonviolence through the key distinction between "life" and the "living." Life, existence as such, is never exhausted by the perishing of the living.

The unity of all life offers us the wisdom that "in doing evil to others you have done it to yourself." Tolstoy issues a warning that we can interpret as a normative ground for refusing hubristic violence. It seems, after all, that in Tolstoy a normatively monistic notion of life fills the now empty place of God. This observation indicates that Tolstoy's ethics of alterity has already undergone secularization. However, the adage that in "doing evil to others you have done it to yourself" can also be interpreted as testimony that both the actor and the acted-upon within the relations of violence are caught in the inescapable normative imposition governed by a practical selfsameness of action and reaction. To be clear, the adage is telling us that having committed an act of violence, the perpetrator is forever connected to the victim, which in turn creates the *conditions* from which this hubristic relation cannot be separated. Through this relation certain conditions arise in which violence (and counter-violence, for that matter) are normalized, rationalized, and naturalized. What always hides violence is its matter-of-course character. The condition that thereby arises reminds us of what Schürmann called the "conditions of evil": it is a condition determined by the law (read: legitimations and justifications) inasmuch as the law appears to attempt to stabilize it, a condition always already in denial of its violence. Both Schürmann (2003, 625) and Tolstoy (1951, 106) recognize how the supreme good monopolizes the privilege of defining the Self as good and the Other as evil – a monopoly over hegemonic knowledge production – thereby projecting onto the Other that which is deemed to be evil and in this way legitimizing the use of violence to suppress the Other.

Accordingly, evil is never separable from the *conditions* (not *the* condition as singular) that give rise to it. A phenomenology of the conditions of evil allows us to see the good as not the opposite of evil, and not negation of negation, but rather as a preordained measure that denies the possibility of the conditions that give rise to the normative dictates we consider evil. The good cannot overcome the cycle of violence we saw in the case of King Esarhaddon; the good would only deny violence by appealing to the laws that only perpetuate the denial of the Other. In Tolstoy the possibility of overcoming the conditions of evil arises from an acknowledgment of violence and subsequently from a transgressive Refusal. As such, hubristic self-imposition – in denying life its myriad manifestations – takes the form of systemic violence. In the absence of higher moral principles, whose comfort Tolstoy denies himself in the story, the self-appointed good as the law proves to be without merit in removing the conditions of evil. Transgressive Refusal, an act that expresses a gentle power, puts an end to such violence, and that is why the king, as the embodiment of power and the locus of force, must relinquish the position of the sovereign altogether. For a phenomenology of the conditions of evil, then, the questions are these: how is self-positing possible without denying the Other? And under what conditions will self-constitution *not* lead to a hubristic act against an Other?

We can infer from the fable's striking line – "You thought life dwelt in you alone" – that the condition for hubristic violence is the Self's perception of existential and phenomenal autarky. Not attending to the fact that it is *the Self's dependence on the Other that provides the Self with the possibility of hubris* as "unrestrained self-imposition" (Schürmann) results in the mode of self-positing that gives one the illusion of being the permanent actor in the face of the permanent acted-upon. The sociological term for this ultimate relation of alterity is "objectification." By objectifying the Other, one removes the latter from potentially reciprocal relations: a safeguard against one's angst in the face of one's inevitable demise.

This is where we need to make a few observations with respect to the implicit concept of *empathy* in Tolstoy. Some remarkable things happen in the story: King Esarhaddon's violent suppression of Lailie is disrupted by a *mystical experience of alterity*, when he is offered the possibility of living his Other's life; this allows Esarhaddon to *reflect* on his part in inflicting violence on Lailie. Tolstoy seems to be suggesting that a Self that has gone through the experience of his or her Other in a given situation is bound to act based on that experience, but that he or she is bound to act in a *transgressive* way by breaking free of the conditioning norms that breed hubristic violence. In this story the transgressive act will halt the cycle of violence that has normatively perpetuated itself through the structure of oppressive ruling and punitive warfare, which, in Esarhaddon's case of genuine reflection, involves *relinquishing power* altogether and beginning a simple man's life, but not an attempt at changing that structure. This can be interpreted as an indication of the sway of violence's civilizational "reason" over the structure of kingship. *Once the Other's suffering is experienced as one's own, an ethics of alterity – a respect for the Other's life through selfsameness with the Self – is born.* So Tolstoy shows us. *Instead of grounding nonviolence on moral dictum issued from an unshakeable authority* (as in earlier Tolstoy), *we have a structure of empathy* that *may* lead to nonviolence, respect for life, and thereby respect for the living. This position is close to Butler's. Is empathy essential to nonviolence proper? No! Recall Sharp's strategic or Galtung's structural–sociological advocacies of nonviolence. The question is, in excluding the realm of violence from human action, will empathy constitute a solid normative ground that will lead us to non-violence (here withdrawal from the kingship structure) as the expression of life? Phenomenologically, (cosmic) *life as such* (which includes human life) is alien to violence (this may sound contradictory to the violence of life against life, proposed earlier, but the reader must note that the latter's context is human life), and that which we call suffering (say, from illness) is only a sign of our mortality. Expressions like the "violence of nature" are therefore absurd. Nonetheless, empathy is an expression not of life but of a certain relationship. Let me elaborate.

It is true that with this turn in Tolstoy, empathy conceptually dislocates the Law of Love and the principle of non-resistance to evil because *empathy disturbs the algorithm that operates within the derivatives of moral principles*, while *paradoxically*, empathy remains consistent with love and non-resistance. Yet the *experience* of one's suffering through the experiencing of an Other's plight *replaces* the *moral axioms*. Accordingly, as the Self's sharing and participating in the Other's world (*Welt*) and horizons of meanings, empathy is primarily existential–structural rather than moral–ethical. In other words, beneath the ethics arising from empathy there is always a structural–horizonal substrate that enables my *relating* to the Other, my experiencing by conceptual proximity my Other's plight. Empathy, consequently, does away with algorithms that anchor nonviolence to moral discourses. Instead, empathy shifts the intelligibility and desirability of nonviolence onto a field of relations with no blueprints. Common sense understands empathy as a relationship between Self and Other; this understanding, however, reveals one of the deepest prejudices of modernity, one that hinges on the *autonomous subject*, that *obsolete vestige* of European Enlightenment. Radical phenomenology (which exposes the hegemonic codes of epochs that have permeated us through our tacit agreement to partake in matter-of-course processes of political life and common knowledge) has no interest in resuscitating or reinstating the subject. Such phenomenology inevitably leads to the *dissolution of the philosophically privileged subject*. If empathy in Tolstoy's story arises from the experience of the Other's suffering – in this story, through the selfsameness of the two kings – then empathy arises from the *dissolution* of relations of alterity and the erosion of the distance between Self and Other. Since both Self and Other have gone through the structural reshifting that displaces them both (Esarhaddon relinquishing power, Lailie regaining freedom), there remains no place for enacting subjectivity. The truth revealed to King Esarhaddon is inescapable and leaves him with no choice. This reading, I submit, is consistent with Tolstoy's narrative in that such dissolution in fact verifies the "life principle" that he advocates. But there remains a key aspect: empathy cannot be fully grasped outside of *Verstehen*. Such an understanding arises from a certain history, is bound by historical context, takes shape through intersubjective and tacit agreements, and becomes meaningful within a certain world (*Welt*, set of social relations). Empathy curiously works only in one direction: it emanates from the subject positions of the unsuffering, the privileged, even the oppressor towards the suffering, the underprivileged, and the oppressed. Stated differently, *at the moment of empathizing* (regardless of the subject's actual status, which may actually involve suffering), *the agent occupies a socially privileged position*. Empathic relations are relations initiated by an actor or observer towards an acted-upon; they are constituted by a certain *structural asymmetry*, and thus *empathic relations are not egalitarian*. Through Tolstoy's lens we can surmise that the one who suffers (Lailie) cannot empathize with the tormentor (Esarhaddon), since he or she is unable to erase the distance and thereby transcend the asymmetrical relations between the two agents through a trembling, haunting, and novel experience. In a curious way, it is the privileged Esarhaddon who gains a new experience by reliving the suffering of Lailie, thus experiencing his own mortality. At the same time, I imagine that the victim's "options" are fairly clear: (a) develop Nietzschean *resentiment* while enduring suffering, in the manner of master–slave relations, which for Nietzsche inform Christianity's otherworldly salvation or socialism's averageness; (b) rebel and/or wreak vengeance, as epitomized by the French Revolution; or (c) forgive – an "option" that always inevitably appears to us through revolt and that is subsequent to liberating oneself from certain relations of domination that hitherto constituted and shaped one, in the manner that Fanon anticipated from the postcolonial wars of liberation. (We must note that one can only forgive when one has liberated oneself from oppression, since forgiveness cannot arise from abjection.) The attentive reader will notice that from the first option to the third, there is a process of *transformative nonviolence*. This process, of course, does not preclude the possibility of the oppressed empathizing with the oppressor, however strange this may sound. Such empathy, it seems, may contain elements of spiritual nonviolence. But this kind of empathy alone will not open a path to an alternative course of action or to the structural transformation that leads to the liberation of the oppressed. If one learns anything from Tolstoy's fable of King Esarhaddon, it is that empathic identification with the victim will, at the very least, bring about a withdrawal from the structures of oppression and violence.

That said, unless the empathic actor holds a privileged position (the king in Tolstoy's story) that gives him or her the power to rectify an injustice by incorporating and supplanting it, empathy's act of encompassing the Other may not lead to mutual recognition or reconciliation, let alone justice. In and of itself, empathy does not involve egalitarian relations. The connection between empathy and reconciliation remains conceptually precarious. Tolstoy's attempt to link empathy to reconciliation and the rectification of injustice works precisely because the two antagonistic characters in his story are socially and politically unequal. While clear, the structural asymmetry of empathy strikes us as counter-intuitive. This is why I submit that *empathy cannot be algorithmic*: empathy arises from the experience, and experience alone, of the Other's suffering, and as such, in leading to the inevitable collapse of Self/Other distinctness, it can lead neither to extractive–moral logic, nor to rational calculation, nor to normative expectations, nor, above all, to universal fiats. Since it is a matter of individual conscience, I can develop empathy towards others, but I cannot expect from others *genuine empathy*. And in fact, since mutuality in recognition is precarious in empathic relations, the outcome of empathy always inevitably remains obscure. An ethics that relies on empathy's inescapable precariousness rests its foundation on shifting sands, and this is precisely the ethics of our times, which we must be prepared to embrace.

Tolstoy's story is not exhausted by my phenomenological interpretation. The hubris of imposing the Self on an Other constitutes violence and evil. If it is true that "in doing evil to others you have done it to yourself," then for the perpetrator of hubristic violence to be protected against his or her self-inflicted eventual demise, he or she must resort to increased use of force. Force will compensate for the vital energy that is withering away within the perpetrator, and there will be an *inverse association* between instrumental use of force to subjugate and repress, on the one hand, and life energy, on the other. At its zenith, domination needs little repression, thanks to hegemonic constellations of life-horizons that make the existing relations of domination matters of fact. As hegemonies lose momentum, force grows, and its high-entropy growth brings demise to both victim and perpetrator. Yet while operative, these are simply conceptualizations. That "in doing evil to others you have done it to yourself" remains intuitively relatable and intelligible, although why one relates to it remains a mystery.

The other story, "The Three Questions," also written in 1903, represents continuity but also a certain departure from the first, and as such it can be interpreted as a radicalization. Tolstoy narrates the story of a king who, in order to ensure that "he would never fail in anything," searches for answers to three questions: "*how to know the proper moment for every deed, how to know which were the most essential people, and how not to err in deciding which pursuits were of the greatest importance*" (Tolstoy 1962, 82–8; emphasis in original). Dissatisfied with the answers he receives from his advisers and courtiers, he embarks on a journey to anonymously pay a visit to a hermit, renowned for his wisdom, who lives simply in a forest. Faced with the hermit's refusal to provide express answers to his three questions, the king stays with him, helping him with tasks that challenge the hermit's frail build. A while later, the two notice a man, wounded and soaked with blood, running out of the woods. Under the hermit's guidance, the king attends to the now unconscious stranger's wounds, stopping the bleeding and saving his life. On regaining consciousness, the wounded stranger professes to the king that he had intended to assassinate him to avenge his brother's murder and the seizure of his property on the king's orders. His plan failed when his ambush was discovered by the royal guards stationed on the edge of the forest. Wounded, he narrowly escaped capture. Touched by the king's compassion, the assassin appeals for forgiveness, which fills the king with the delight of reconciliation with his mortal enemy. The king promises to rectify his injustices. Upon departure, the king puts the three questions to the hermit one last time, only to be reminded by the sage that he has answered his own questions already: "Remember then," avers the hermit,

> there is only one important time – *Now*. And it is important because it is the only time we have dominion over ourselves; and the most important man is *he with whom you are*, for no one can know whether or not he will ever have dealings with any other man; and the most important pursuit is *to do good to him*, since it is for that purpose alone that man was sent into this life. (1962, 87–8, emphasis in original)

The purpose of life, which harks back to Tolstoy's "universal principle of life" (that all life is One), provides a ground for Tolstoy's ethics, and although we may contest this particular belief, we do not conceptually need to examine Tolstoy's ethical philosophy according to such a grounding gesture. Viewed as such, Tolstoy's emerges as an ethics involving three essential vectors: *temporality*, *alterity*, and *responsibility*. Since "now" is "the only time we have dominion over ourselves," I am granted the *possibility of acting in a genuine way*, and given Tolstoy's resistance to the pervasive violence that contains us all, we can infer that the *present* is the time when I can emerge as acting without any regard for the normative (not to mention possibly violent) modalities of action already prescribed for me. Since the most important person is the one whom I am facing in the moment, I have only this present time to deal with my interlocutor, and since in dealing with my *Other* in this moment the possibility of genuine action is given to me – when I can actually emerge as a genuine actor and not as the agent of normative–legislative–predicative frames – then I have only one option: "to do good to" my Other, not in the sense that I am mandated to "do good" in a predetermined way, but because, having released myself from imposed norms of action at this "now" that is mine, I am *able not to bring harm* to my interlocutor. Thus, by responding to that which constitutes my alterity, I emerge as a genuine actor. The genuine actor in me becomes the alter of the normative subject in me. There emerges the possibility of being responsible for my Other in ways that do not conform to the normative dictates that I had tacitly internalized due to my "thrownness." Here temporality is important: I cannot change my past, but I can change the future, and I am granted this privileged position by my Other: it is she who provides me with the possibility of carving a future unlike my past, and as such I am indebted to, and thus responsible for, my *Other*. Tolstoy's suggested triangular ethics – *temporality, alterity, and responsibility* – speak the final word in constructing an ethics that makes foundational gestures but works just fine without such grounding morals. It also provides us with a structural configuration and the conditions of possibility of ethics and politics of alterity, which removes ethics from the realm of individual choice, transcendental subjectivity, or acting out of moral dictates. Accordingly, Tolstoy's thought comes close to the philosophies of Derrida and Emmanuel Levinas, in particular Derrida's ethics of hospitality and "cities of refuge" (2001), and my modest contribution to the "politics of transcendence" (Vahabzadeh 2007; 2012b).

What is more, if this "present time" presents me with the possibility of a nonviolent future unlike my violent past, Tolstoy's ethics of nonviolence essentially hinges on forgiveness. The story raises a crucial question: under what conditions can evil be rectified? Note that both the king and the assailant – caught, until the moment of their face-to-face encounter, in the cycle of violence – are bound by evil insofar as their actions are informed by a denial of the Other and by systemic violence, which each man, in accordance with his own capacity, wishes to turn in his own favour to the detriment of the other. The king is not automatically or arbitrarily granted the position of the good in the story, and if it were not for his quest and his humbling experience at the hermit's service, he might not have forgiven the assassin, and we would return to the cycle of violence. Yet due to his power, the king remains the exclusive agent to initiate reconciliation. Here we can clearly see that reconciliation – and by implication, nonviolence – arises from confrontation, from an attempt to rectify a wrong, that which calls for justice, although this attempt may crystalize in (the assailant's) vengeance. The inevitable conclusion seems counter-intuitive: *the victim (subject) of violence re-emerges simultaneously as the agent of both vendetta and forgiveness*, with the tasks associated with either already at the agent's disposal, as they both depend on confrontation. From this observation we can extract what Gandhi concluded later: that the possibility of nonviolence resides in confronting violence (and its agents).

Of the two men forgiving each other, it is the assailant whose forgiveness has the greatest impact on reconciliation, because he forgives the unforgivable, the death of his brother, although as Derrida would say, the abyss remains and the assailant does not receive justice despite his forgiveness (Derrida 2001, 54). Confiscated property can be restored to its original owner; one can be compensated for material losses; death is irreversible and cannot be rectified. But in the story, a death becomes the ground – a *groundless ground* or an abyss indeed – for the surpassing of the cycle of violence, a pathway towards supplanting evil through reconciliation or an act of mutual recognition. *The condition of possibility of forgiveness is violence*, and forgiveness appears on our horizon in the face of that which is unforgivable (Derrida 2001). *Forgiveness is the only act that can transcend evil and violence not by subduing or supplanting it but by incorporating it generously, taking possession of the history of violence that is always my own history as well, and thus putting violence out of operation.* It must now be clearer why I called nonviolence the *excess* of violence (chapter 4): as with the term "excessive force," in violence's unending attempts to violate and dominate by reaching out into ever more domains of action, it generates ever expanding circumferential domains in which it exhausts itself. Structurally, forgiveness exists within these circumferential domains. Forgiving always occurs as a result of experiences of violence. Thus understood, forgiveness does not constitute the binary opposite of violence. Hence, to reiterate nonviolence's ontological dependence on violence, nonviolence emerges from the outward excess of violence and exceeds it from violence's expanding circumferences inward. Thus, nonviolence encloses violence within it.

We must still probe this question: under what conditions can evil be rectified? We are confronted, *categorically*, with two options (and other options, I presume, eventually boil down to these two). The choice between these courses of action is never clear from the outset when we experience violation or displacement. Phenomenologically, taking either course cannot be extracted from some *a priori* universal or an ultimate Truth. When facing evil, we have the option of overwhelming and nullifying it, eliminating the perpetrators (vengeance) or punishing them (through criminal codes). The law embeds codified vengeance in its proclaimed aim to restore justice, since it intends to maintain the very order it is deployed to protect. Therefore, revenge and punishment show that the human ability to act through infinite possibilities cannot be erased, and it is precisely due to the *irreversibility* of an act that the culprit must be excluded (through vengeance or punishment) from the domain of action that makes us human.

Alternatively, we can put violence out of operation by eliminating the conditions of possibility of evil, by "removing" the victim of evil from its reach, even though this option may require self-sacrifice (Gandhi's nonresistance to evil). This choice requires forgiveness, not as a one-time act for seeking "closure" and "moving on" (those common clichés and illusions of our age), but as a perpetual refusal to punish, avenge, sanction, or exclude. It is only through forgiveness, in this strict sense, that I can incorporate evil, absorb it, and thereby nullify it and render it inoperative. Forgiveness acknowledges that the pain inflicted on me will stay with me but also allows me to rise above my condition. Forgiveness enables me to take ownership of my pain, embrace it, care for it, and remember the evil that gave me my pain without being hurt by it.

Note that there is no pure victim in either story. All of the characters are actually or potentially culpable and responsible for violence. Those who are not violent – the mysterious sage and the hermit – do not live in human society. Tolstoy seems to be suggesting that without the experience of violence, advocacy of nonviolence – as life – is not possible. Thus the road from violence to nonviolence is paved with the forgiveness that renders obsolete the effects, utility, and necessity of violence. As such, forgiveness turns violence around; in so doing, it repositions both the aggressor and the victim, transforming them. This is precisely the "transformative" aspect of nonviolence. This is how nonviolence is manifested in the *excess* of violence, as a course of action that moves beyond the ambit of violence. Nonviolence arises as the unhindered and untameable vigour that emerges from and expands beyond violence. Nonviolence encircles violence, absorbs it, puts it out of operation, and leads it to its final resting place in fables, memories, and lessons for the young. Just as in Tolstoy's fables. In light of my readings of these stories, it seems implausible that the mutually exclusive Law of Violence and Law of Love precede – as ontological conditions of possibility of – violent and nonviolent action in Tolstoy. The *mutual exclusivity thus collapses*, as one cannot conceive one without the other.

Ethics and *Verwindung*

As is well-known, it was not until the twentieth century that the *concept* of nonviolence gained *political* currency in the West and became widely shared as strategy and tactic and as a way of life. But it was in the late nineteenth century that the *idea* of nonviolence emerged. Among its precursors were concepts such as the Christian "non-resistance to evil" and, later (in its secular form), civil disobedience, empathy, and compassion. This new concept could not have been born without *referential* attachment to preexisting (moral) principles, good conscience, universal conditions, and so on – in short, *axiomatic algorithms*. Historically, then, the elusive concept of nonviolence must have been understood in terms other than its own.

There is a more vivid tendency towards, and a more vehement search for, robust algorithms within moral and ethical arguments in order to anchor the need for and possibility of nonviolence to some timeless moral principles, universal conditions, or value axioms. Yet compared to the arguments that build on the logistical necessity of freedom, or on utilitarian–sociological conditions, appeals to morals and ethics as immovable principles are shaky, though they may *seem* steadfast. I imagine that in our epoch of instrumental reason and atomistic, self-interested individualism, one can be persuaded towards nonviolence when it is rationalized in terms of measurable and desirable individual and collective outcomes. It seems that the non-utilitarian and altruistic ideas of moral and ethical nonviolence that inevitably accompany the values of compassion, empathy, generosity, and forgiveness have become increasingly besieged by calculative rationality.

The guiding thinker of this chapter, Tolstoy, shows us how appeals to universal moral axioms can and in fact do give way to ethical approaches that are informed by such axioms but are not bound by them. Of course, it would be contrary to his understanding to position the moral Tolstoy against the ethical Tolstoy or to claim that he abandoned the first in favour of the second. The two are not mutually exclusive, and there is indeed consistency in the way he moves between the two positions. But my interpretation intends to mark a conceptual difference that is important for this study: I submit that while the moral principles – the Law of Love and non-resistance to evil – initially render nonviolence intelligible, nonviolence takes on a life of its own in later Tolstoy, and soon in the twentieth century, the concept of nonviolence multiplies and flourishes. Significant to my conceptual hair-splitting is that moral principles involve the *preclusion* of certain categories of action whereas the ethical approach must always remain *open* to the possible modalities of action. Moral principles require loyal agents. With ethics, by contrast, genuine action is born. And Tolstoy's triangular ethics (temporality, alterity, and responsibility) turns the past tense of violence into a future tense of nonviolence and thus involves transformative nonviolence.

Phenomenology treats ethics the way it treats any other subject of its inquiry: by suspending the common and received knowledge attached to it and thereby pushing it against its *Gestalt* and contexts – in radical phenomenology, epochal contexts – in which ethics becomes meaningful. The erudite reader will be aware of Werner Marx's contribution to non-metaphysical ethics (1987), a magnificent book that my humble contribution cannot even begin to match. Enabled by Heidegger's thought, Marx argues that such concepts as "letting-be" and *Gelassenheit* (release-ment) in later Heidegger provide a course of "responsible action" that appears "ethical" but that lacks foundations. Responsibility in this sense pertains to "responding" through the Event of Appropriation (*Ereignis*) to the epochal mode of unconcealment (*alétheia*) of phenomena. The scope of this study does not invite delving deeply into the implications of Marx's work for an ethics of nonviolence, although the relevance remains self-evident.

I stated earlier in this chapter that the practitioners of nonviolence endeavour to defamiliarize our violent world by withdrawing from the matter-of-course violence that permeates every aspect of our lives (self-extraction from a world that is inherently violent amounts to self-exile, but to where?). This transformative effort will inevitably lead to deworlding/reworlding. The act of withdrawing seems volitional, but is it really? At this historic juncture, I believe, we have an opportunity to act in ways that, unlike in past epochs governed by metaphysical ultimate referents and their normative–legislative–predicative frames of violence, may lead to a different future, to the "other or new beginning" (Heidegger). Such deworlding/reworlding *potentially* involves liberation, the extent of which will be far-reaching and epochal. As such, the "ethics of nonviolence" should not be understood in ethical (or moral) terms at all. Phenomenologically, what we regard as *ethical* in our advocacy of nonviolence is in fact simply a mode of *attunement* to the future openings in our possible epochal destiny – an opening of whose contours we only have a glimpse. Our Refusal to partake in violence in its various manifestations therefore goes against the proposed "ontological primacy of violence," since such Refusal gains epochal proportions and possibly goes against history itself in that the mode of deworlding/reworlding to be experienced will be of a liberatory quality that humanity has not yet experienced. Naturally, history remains open, and to achieve this destiny (see the conclusion to this book) "we will have to rely on the thoughtfulness of present and future actors" (Schürmann 1990, 208). It is eerie and uncanny (*unheimlich*) to declare that it is thanks to our violent history that we are given the possibility of overcoming (*Überwindung*) our epoch by distorting violence, incorporating it, and healing from it (*Verwindung*). *The oppositionality of violence and nonviolence, once again, proves unsustainable, indeed imaginary.*

Back to a point I raised earlier: it seems that the retrieval of a new ethics towards the end of his life, an ethics justified not *directly* by Christian axioms but by celebrating life as such (not just human life), was coincidental with Tolstoy's poetic return to his original – juvenile – experience of fiction narrative in children's fables and fairy tales. Does this mean that a decisive response to the genuine experience of our crisis remains inevitably poetic and that with each transgressive act based on such experience – which involves the unlearning of normative principles – we return to our childhood, that is, our existential inception – even as we prepare ourselves for our decisive departure?

8

The Conflictual
Politics of Nonviolence

I do believe that where there is a choice only between cowardice and violence, I would advise violence.

Gandhi, *The Essential Gandhi* (1983, 137)

To speak of the "politics of nonviolence" is a redundancy; at best, it is stating the obvious. Of course, the *concept* of nonviolence goes beyond politics (in moral and personal practices or in diverse cosmologies and life-philosophies). This is because the prevailing structures of our dominant civilizations – which hinge on the system of sovereign states, the vicious plundering and abuse of nature, extensive capitalist exploitation, punitive legal systems, normative education, rape culture, and systematized brutality against non-humans on a mass scale – are based on violence. In this context, adopting nonviolence as the guiding principle of acting and living inevitably leads to political resistance against powers that be – interestingly, even when a commitment to nonviolence takes the form of pacifist withdrawal. The tripartite concept of violence – structural, institutional, hubristic – leaves little if any room for conceptions of a pure and autarkic nonviolent life in the present-day world order we have regrettably inherited.

In the common notion, as previously discussed, nonviolence is perhaps best understood as a moral and ethical approach, as an axiomatic truism. Any politics that identifies with nonviolence will therefore appeal, at least in part, to some (acclaimed) moral superiority and the values attached to it. This moral superiority arises from, and shines forth through, various binary constructions and the notional

associations thereby produced. For instance, the constructed binarism of good versus evil is associated with, respectively, the violence–
nonviolence binary. Tolstoy's thought largely represents this tendency.
Even the strategic–pragmatist approach of Sharp and the sociological–
structural approach of Galtung invoke refusal to injure the Other as a
moral principle. So it comes as no surprise to understand nonviolence
as a form of politics, one that has been expanding since the late nineteenth century, a mode of politics whose development and outcomes
are yet to be witnessed.

We saw in previous chapters how nonviolent politics may arise from
a number of theoretical approaches that otherwise offer no vivid conceptualization of political nonviolence. A case in point is Arendt's conception of politics as a public realm involving perpetual contestation of
power by free and equal citizens over current issues. In the public realm,
the plurality of ideas and the diversity of actors – the two are indivisible –
define the condition of possibility of political life as such. The elimination of the contesting actors, the repression of dissent, and restrictions on
freedoms (in the name of security, in our time) will therefore lead to the
erosion of politics. In this respect, Ian Angus argues quite appropriately
in favour of nonviolence. In drawing a key connection between social
movements and public debate, which constitutes the essence of democracy, Angus advocates a conflictual model of politics. "While publics do
come into conflict, the role of public discussion is to bring such conflict
into the realm of debate where more inclusive solutions can be proposed"
(Angus 2001, 68). He draws on Chantal Mouffe, who proposes the radical democratic model of "agonistic pluralism" in which the "enemy" is
turned into an "adversary": instead of eliminating an antagonistic party,
we will include it in the democratic debate (Mouffe, 1993; 2000; 2005).
Angus rightly dissociates violence from conflict, a rather common but
mistaken notion. "Violence does not stem from conflict," he avers, "but
from *attempt to suppress conflict*. Social movements give us the opportunity
to search for solutions" (Angus 2001, 68, emphasis added). Politically
speaking, violence arises from the elimination of an antagonist, be it
the defiant, the anarchist, or the exile. As we saw, this understanding of
politics, and thus violence, harks back to Arendt's theory of politics as
ongoing public debate among diverse equals and power viewed as acting
in concert. That which tends to reduce diversity amounts to violence.
Returning to the Arendtian public realm, nonviolence arises from the
denial of that which constitutes political life, properly speaking.

But for the most part, Western theorists of nonviolence remain bound to their Occidental philosophical traditions, which inevitably contextualize and contain their thoughts within received intellectual territories that anchor these thinkers to certain fundamental Greco-Christian assumptions such as individuality, freedom, free will, sovereignty, and/or structure and agency (the list is vast). Yet it is perhaps universally agreed that no other thinker reflected on a politics of nonviolence more deeply than Mohandas K. Gandhi, the Mahatma, who developed and enacted a theory that largely does away with the aforementioned assumptions. So it seems only logical for us to attend in this chapter to his works, for he was the incontestable architect of modern politics of nonviolence, whose legacy utterly transformed the world of political action. Consistent with this book's hermeneutic approach, I do not intend to provide a comprehensive account or a summary of his philosophy. But we will be exploring how violence and nonviolence are given a bold new configuration in his philosophy – a point missed by the multitude, who have turned his profound thought into soulless guides to nonviolent practice or "cookbooks" for (middle-class) personal happiness. By this I am referring to the readers of Gandhi (especially in the West) who try to extract breeze from the hurricane!

Gandhi: Searching for Violence

In my judgment as a reader of Gandhi, his thought is far more radical, multifaceted, and complex than that of the great majority of his contemporary interpreters or the propagators of nonviolence inspired by him. In fact, the understanding of social and political change, and the requirements for a *fundamental* transformation, among sizeable groups of contemporary advocates of nonviolence rarely match the depth of Gandhi's engagement with the question of *ahimsa* and nonviolent collective action. Much of the popular literature of nonviolence nowadays is full of sanitized and sterile notions, touched up with identifiable "urban middle-class," "self-help," and "pro-democracy" tints, none of which reflect the spirit of the enormous challenges the Mahatma undertook. Many readers of Gandhi are oblivious to his "militant" concept of action, which views the adversary as an inherently valuable life instead of reducing the "enemy" to some inferior entity deserving abuse, repression, or eradication. Some readings of Gandhi nowadays embrace the second Gandhian component but not the first. Others neglect the Gandhian streak of social justice that is intimately linked to nonviolence. What most advocates of Gandhi neglect is that Gandhian politics should be sought in a philosophy that is fundamentally alien to Enlightenment and post-Enlightenment political thought, which is obsessed with sovereignty and security and the desired rational, calculative connection between the two – thought that is deeply informed by the seemingly incurable Hobbesian politics of fear or the Schmittian justification for a state of permanent exclusion and violation of the Other (both of which have increasingly dominated global politics since 9/11). Gandhi rejects the mutual externality of violence and nonviolence that informs Western philosophy. Contrary to the many approaches that tend to retain the liberal tradition of formal equality based on self-interest and the social contract, Gandhi's politics are not about power but Truth, indeed life (*ahimsa* refers to the unity of all life). Different means lead to different ends. As such, *nonviolence is not a means to an end but an end in itself*, and the outcome of nonviolence can take any political form (see Devji 2012, 4, 5, 93–4). Clearly, then, approaches like Sharp's do not qualify as Gandhian *stricto sensu*. In fact, Sharp's methods are hardly "nonviolent" in the Gandhian sense. Gandhi would have abhorred the suggestion that NVA can be used to overwhelm a political establishment and replace it with a new one without radically transforming both the actors and the (former) rulers and abusers. Galtung's structural–sociological approach seems closer in spirit to Gandhi's thought due to Galtung's emphasis on social justice, although his utilitarian streak is poorly aligned with the Gandhian thought. Gandhian nonviolence cannot and should not have peace or conflict resolution as its objective, since, as we shall see, nonviolence cannot be thought, let alone acted upon, outside of conflict. If there is peace to be found in nonviolence, it will be inner peace, but insofar as the world is beset with social inequalities, the politics of nonviolence will remain simultaneously adversarial and transformative. Even the idea of civil disobedience remains contestable when measured against Gandhi – albeit the distinction is subtle – in that civil disobedience retains action as separate from Truth, notwithstanding the actor's apparent orientation towards Truth. I exposed and discussed such algorithms in the previous chapters. For Gandhi, violence is oriented towards achieving a goal and garnering a certain future (an idea somewhat reminiscent of Arendt's, although her thought would be alien to his), whereas nonviolence is not (2012, 98).

To explore these themes we need to engage thematically with Gandhi's vast and complex thought.

(a) *Origins of* ahimsa *and Truth-oriented nonviolence.* In an essay published in *Harijan* and in his autobiography, Gandhi writes that as a young
man he learned nonviolence from Kasturbai, his wife, and her gentle
and silent but firm defiance when he treated her badly (Gandhi 1983,
305; 2011, 18–19). This experience initiated his search for a comprehensive and transformative nonviolent philosophy, for which he credits
several sources of wisdom. As an inquisitive young man he had studied
many Indian and Western sources pertaining to his endless questions,
and he admits to having been influenced by the "active nonviolence"
of Christ and Christianity rather than the "passive nonviolence" of Buddhism and Jainism (Gandhi 1997, 10n8). Above all, he recollects, it was
Tolstoy (especially *The Kingdom of God Is Within You* [1894]) who "left
an abiding impression" on him (Gandhi 2011, 147, 98; 1983, 36). He
revered Tolstoy and exchanged letters with him on several occasions in
the early twentieth century. Tolstoy had read *Hind Swaraj* (1909) and
approved of Gandhi's "passive resistance" against British colonial rule in
India (Tolstoy 1909, 14). Gandhi was also profoundly influenced by the
British social thinker John Ruskin (1819–1900), in particular Ruskin's
Unto the Last (1860) – a social critique of capitalist economy – a book
Gandhi was introduced to in 1904 in London and that he translated
into Gujarati in 1908. Reading Tolstoy and Ruskin persuaded Gandhi to
found the Phoenix Settlement in 1904 in Durban, South Africa, where
he published the *Indian Opinion*. That settlement was a precursor to his
ashrams in India (Gandhi 2011, 98, 310–11, 319, 321). At Phoenix all
societal distinctions (between Hindus and Muslims, and the Untouchables and other Hindu casts) were abolished and everyone was treated
equally. Troubled by the treatment of the Untouchables (also referred
to as "'pariahs,' 'suppressed classes,' or 'scheduled classes'"), Gandhi
called them "Harijans – Children of God" in order to shed a different
light on this huge caste, and in ashrams the harijans were treated equally
(1983, 116, 118) – evidence of the social justice orientation of Gandhian
politics. In Gandhi's thought, the minority is a moral category and Truth
always resides in the minority (Devji 2012, 58, 60). The Western–modern
way of reading this is that agency resides in the oppressed.

One can trace the "elective affinity" between Tolstoy and Gandhi, and
thus the origins of Gandhi's thought in Tolstoy, in the Mahatma's search
for Truth through ceaseless purification of the soul and his sober resistance against injustice and unjust laws. "The fulfillment of Christ's teaching
consists in *moving away from self toward God*," avers Tolstoy. "It is obvious
that there cannot be definite laws and rules for this fulfillment of the

teaching. Every degree of perfection and every degree of imperfection are equal in it; *no obedience to law constitutes fulfillment of this doctrine,* and therefore for it there can be no binding rules and laws" (Tolstoy 1951, 60, emphasis added). In Tolstoy the Law of Love requires constant purification of the self and passive resistance to violence in its various manifestations: evidence of Tolstoy's spiritual–Christian anarchism – a permanent state of defiance against secular authority insofar as this authority does not accord with the spiritual principles guiding Tolstoy's envisioned egalitarian, multilateral, and loving community. Love, Tolstoy advises, stands as "the only method" through which Indians can emancipate themselves. He also warns his Indian interlocutor that the Indians have been colonized because *they submit to force as the principle of governance.* "If the English have enslaved the people of India," observes Tolstoy, "it is just because the latter recognized, and still recognize, force as the fundamental principle of the social order" (Tolstoy 1909, 7). Gandhi's future political innovations would prove that he had taken the Russian sage's advice to heart.

Gandhi lived in an incredibly diverse and complex society, one known for its religious pluralism and for its rigid, ancient caste system, which governed Hindu social relations that inevitably cast their demons over other ethno-religious communities and Indian society at large due to the Hindus' demographic majority. While it was possible for Tolstoy, who lived in a predominantly Christian society (with Russian hegemony over the empire's Muslim, Jewish, and pagan regions), to identify the untainted teachings of Christ as the source of Love and thus bypass the authority of the Russian Orthodox Church, Gandhi needed to transform the concept of God – which inevitably remains a contested notion because of India's religious diversity, especially with regard to Hindus and Muslims – into a universal concept. Besides, unlike Gandhi's, Tolstoy's teachings do not contain elements of decolonization and liberation thought. Thus through consistent equivalential signification in his discourse, the Mahatma identifies God, and its particularistic receptions, with Truth, letting Truth to emerge as the master-signifier of his envisioned anti-colonial discourse, which is for him always concomitant with creating a *new people* (eerily reminiscent of Fanon), one that would do away with factionalisms and unite the nation against the British Empire. "My uniform experience has convinced me that there is no other God than Truth," Gandhi declares. "The little fleeting glimpses ... that I have been able to have of Truth can hardly convey an idea of the indescribable lustre of Truth, a million times more intense than that of the sun we daily see with our eyes. In fact what I have caught is only the faintest glimmer of that mightily effulgence" (Gandhi 2011, 520). Because Truth is never a given or an entity, it remains to be experienced, and the deeper and more steadfast one's quest for Truth, the more one experiences it with apprehension and the more vast its transformative powers. "The purpose of life is undoubtedly to know oneself" (Gandhi 1983, 275). Truth requires self-purification – it requires us to identify with every living being, which in turn means denying unrelentingly all desires so as to "reduce myself to zero" (Gandhi 2011, 521). Therefore, with "purification being highly infectious, purification of oneself necessarily leads to the purification of one's surroundings" (2011, 520). In this way, self-purification and humility before Truth unleash outward actions akin to social movements. What Gandhi offers is deeper than nominal or social humility: the concept of *anasakti* – as profound "non-attachment" – represents selfless or non-reciprocal service (Tahmasebi-Birgani 2014, 121). Such humble existence provides a great power for changing one's unjust status quo, for its intention is not to dominate or enforce. Gandhi's concept of *ahimsa*, therefore, "was not a refusal to revolt; rather, it was a new concept of revolution" (2014, 130). New indeed: precisely because one who dwells in Truth cannot impose and overwhelm, the weapon available to one will be *ahimsa* – literally *not* (a-) to *injure* (*himsa*). But *ahimsa* should not be understood as an anthropocentric concept: following its roots in Jainism, it precludes harming any sentient life, human or non-human. Hence Gandhi's vegetarianism, which in fact was his initial gateway, as a law student in London (1888–91), to nonviolence. It must now be clear that only a life guided by *anasakti* succeeds in not injuring; it also essentially necessitates the *brahmacharya* (self-restraint) vow (Gandhi 2011, 215, 330). Gandhi admittedly took nonviolence from Christianity; that said, his concept of *ahimsa* is a borrowing from Jainism and Buddhism, which he associates with "passive resistance," such as *dharna*, taken from in the Hindu tradition (Devji 2012, 10). For Gandhi, *ahimsa* stands as the principle most intimate to Truth itself. So much so that "the only means for the realization of Truth is *Ahimsa*" (Gandhi 2011, 520). Religious doctrines that do not adhere to *ahimsa* cannot be Godly. "Truth is my God," he declares. "Non-Violence is the means of realizing Him" (Gandhi 1983, 174), and not even for the liberation of India should Truth and nonviolence be sacrificed. According to Gandhi, all religions provide "freedom from liability to kill any kind of life" (1997, 55), thereby distancing themselves from Truth. For Gandhi, "there is no room in religion for anything other than compassion" (in Tolstoy 1909, 17). *Ahimsa* is therefore "the farthest limit of humility" precisely because "a perfect vision of Truth can only follow a complete realization of *Ahimsa*" (Gandhi 2011, 521, 520). Truth, then, reveals itself in nonviolence: "My love for non-violence ... is equalled only by my love for Truth which is to me synonymous with non-violence through which and which alone I can see and reach Truth" (Gandhi 2001, 357). For Gandhi, then, Truth and nonviolence are synonymous.

As the quintessence of life, nonviolence has sustained itself throughout the ages, but as Gandhi observes, our received history is one of violence. The Gujarati word for "history" translates as "[i]t so happened," he observes, but our selective view of "what happened" had primarily focused on the "great deeds" of kings and statesmen: wars, occupations, repressions. If such had been the entire (hi)story, the world would have ended long ago. What is not seen is how soul-force and "passive resistance" have sustained the world throughout history (Gandhi 1997, 89). Yes, "evil has wings": like fire, it consumes the house in an instant. By contrast, "good travels at a snail's pace," just as building a house takes time and effort (1997, 47–8). Nonviolence is the ultimate *dharma*, acting in accord with the principle of cosmic order, and that is how it sustains us.

Clearly, Gandhi had to think these concepts through in an original way – and indeed, he did so in his own uncompromisingly idiosyncratic manner, so that his thought, as it developed through the years, grew increasingly relevant to the project of Indian liberation, both externally (freedom from British colonial rule) and internally (the emancipation of the soul). For this to happen, he needed to arrive at that which is the most compelling aspect of his thought: (collectively) *actable concepts*. During his time in England as a young lawyer, he found several essential cues in the diverse sources he studied: Christianity, vegetarianism, Tolstoy, the *Bhagavad Gita*, and nineteenth-century British social thought. He inevitably landed on an already established expanse, a pre-existing discourse, and adopted the concept of "passive resistance," a useful concept of which he nevertheless gradually grew critical. Nonviolent resistance, in Gandhi, is *expressive* and it is not "passive resistance" (Galtung 1959, 71). The concept of "passive resistance" provided Gandhi with a *shared concept* that enabled him to meditate on how to act compatibly with the principle of *ahimsa* in a life oriented towards Truth; it also allowed him entry into an emerging philosophical and political discourse; but he dwelled in that concept only to further develop his own ideas and to make new claims in a discursive field that brought him into (actual or virtual) dialogue with his nonviolent precursors and contemporaries.

His acumen, though, did not allow the passive reception of "passive resistance," and he increasingly distanced himself from the concept. In its
stead, he offered a nuanced and rather idiosyncratic concept of resistance, one he had pondered while still in South Africa.

(b) *Nonviolence and the question of acting.* We have already seen the origins of "passive resistance" – a Christian concept – in Tolstoy and have
paused on one of its associated concepts, namely "civil disobedience"
in Thoreau. Gandhi's intellectual reception of these two already existing concepts must be understood in terms of his personal experiences
through his campaign to defend Indian indentured labourers in South
Africa and his involvement in the founding of the Natal Indian Congress
(1894) and the Transvaal British Indian Association (1903). He arrived
in South Africa in 1893 and lived there, practising law, for more than
twenty years. While Gandhi generously references thinkers as sources
of inspiration, it must be acknowledged that he arrived intuitively at the
main principles of his philosophy through his own ethics and conceptual
acumen. Throughout his political career he continually negotiated with
the existing literature akin to his philosophy as a means to arrive at the
most accurate and also the most universal signifiers – ones that transcend culturally bound epistemologies. Those universal signifiers would
lead, he hoped, to the construction of a universal nonviolent theory and
praxis.

Gandhi's nonviolent tactics do enact "civil disobedience." He tells us
that he had developed those tactics on his own, before he read Thoreau
and only after his experiences in the South African Indian resistance.
After being introduced to Thoreau, he recollects, he began using that
term. This is an example of *action,* and thus *notion,* preceding the *concept.* Realizing that the term "civil disobedience" was inadequate, Gandhi
replaced it with "civil resistance" (Gandhi 1983, 76). "Thoreau was not
perhaps an out and out champion of non-violence. Probably, also, Thoreau limited his breach of statutory laws to the revenue law, i.e., payment
to taxes" (Gandhi 2001, 3). The civil resister finds the law immoral; thus
her rebellion against the unjust law renders her an outlaw (Gandhi 1983,
143). In his reinterpretation, the concept of "civil disobedience" was
gradually subsumed under "non-cooperation," referring to nonviolent
rebellion and the "capacity for unlimited suffering without the intoxi-
cating excitement of killing" (1983, 178, 143). Non-cooperation can be
practised by the masses, whereas civil disobedience – that is, intentionally
resisting the unjust laws – is a solitary practice, at least in the first instance
(Gandhi 2001, 4).

As mentioned, Gandhi's early reception of passive resistance faded away after his experience of discriminatory laws in South Africa. In 1909, while writing about Indian Home Rule in *Hind Swaraj*, Gandhi still found "passive resistance" a useful term and a guiding principle for the struggles of the Indian minority in South Africa. "Being a popular term, it easily appeals to the popular imagination" (Gandhi 1997, 146). He evoked, rather uncritically, passive resistance as equivalent to "soul-force," which was "superior to the force of arms" and thus required courage and "[c]ontrol over the mind" on the part of the passive resister (1997, 93–4). Even so, in a 1910 letter he wrote: "I admit that the term 'passive resistance' is a misnomer" (1997, 146). "I ... used the term 'passive resistance' in describing it [the movement] ... As the struggle advanced, the phrase ... gave rise to confusion, and it appeared shameful to permit this great struggle to be known only by an English name" (Gandhi 1983, 77). Through his conceptual excursions, Gandhi was moving closer to Tolstoy's understanding of passive resistance; he enunciated the key religious aspect of passive resistance, what he regarded as joining "politics and religion." This was a mode of action informed by "ethical principles" that entailed a spiritual struggle "to obtain the mastery of self" (Gandhi 1997, 146). He viewed Tolstoy's "politics" as non-confrontational – a politics of "principled withdrawal" indeed – although for Gandhi, "confrontation" meant something different from the common notion. Tolstoy's politics could not fulfil the requirement, posed by Gandhi, that Truth be the aim of life that necessitates struggles for (social) justice. These added qualifiers – in particular the joining of passive resistance to soul-force – allowed Gandhi to keep the term "passive resistance" at the arm's length; he would use the term because it was universally intelligible, but by now he was shifting to a new concept that would address both the vital spiritual components and the ethical imperatives he wished the political struggle to reflect.

His critical approach to "passive resistance" grew sharper in light of his proposed term, Satyagraha. Thus, for the inquisitive Mohandas the question was this: From a resolutely Truth-oriented life committed to the principle of *ahimsa*, what genus of action – individual or collective – can arise? As is well-known, his answer was Satyagraha. He had developed the concept in South Africa while reflecting on (indeed in reaction to) the sharp limitations imposed by the notion of "passive resistance":

When in a meeting of Europeans I found that the term "passive resistance" was too narrowly construed, that it was supposed to be a weapon of the

weak, that it could be characterized by hatred, and that it could finally manifest itself as violence, I had to demur to all these statements and explain
the real nature of the Indian movement. It was clear that a new word must
be coined by the Indians to designate their struggle. (Gandhi 2011, 330)

Employed in particular by the suffragette movement (Gandhi 2001, 3),
passive resistance's "incompleteness" caused its adherents to fail to see
that humans are endowed with the capacity to overcome their "brute
nature." This "force," embraced and cultivated by the Satyagrahi, is
to violence, tyranny, and injustice "what light is to darkness" (Gandhi
2001, 35). But this "force" is categorically different from violent force: it
is rather the "indestructible," "love-force [or] soul-force" – understood
"more popularly but less accurately [as] passive resistance" (Gandhi
1997, 85).

Faisal Devji traces the inspiration for Satyagraha back to the Second
Boer War (1899–1902). Gandhi "took the suffering of Boer women in
British concentration camps as the model for satyagraha" (2012, 55).
Having failed to suppress the resilient Boers, the British interned the
Dutch farmers *en masse* in camps under horrendous conditions. Gandhi
participated voluntarily in the Boer War as a British subject, in the division of field medical personnel, even though his sympathies lay with the
Dutch settlers (1983, 48). He adamantly believed that in order to persuade the British to lift the discriminatory laws against coloured people
in South Africa, the Indians must accept it as their duty to defend the
British Empire. Back to our discussion: Dissatisfied with the term "passive
resistance," he offered "a nominal prize through *Indian Opinion* to the
reader who made the best suggestion on the subject. As a result [Shri]
Magandal Gandhi [his second cousin] coined the word 'Sadagraha' (*Sat*=
truth, *Agraha* = firmness) and won the prize. But in order to make it
clearer I changed the word to 'Satyagraha'" (Gandhi 2011, 330). Meaning "firmness in a good cause," *Sadagraha* then bears *Satyagraha*: "Truth
(Satya) implies Love, and Firmness (Agraha) engenders and therefore
serves as a synonym for force … that is to say, the Force which is born of
Truth and Love or Non-violence" (Gandhi 1983, 77). This neologism provides him with conceptual clarity. Thus there "is a great and fundamental
difference between passive resistance and Satyagraha" (1983, 77). Passive
resistance is always the struggle of a minority against perceived injustices, and if humans were steadfast in adhering to *ahimsa* and Truth, no
struggle would occasion civil disobedience or passive resistance (Gandhi
2001, 105). Passive resisters associate their struggle with the perception

that the resisting self is "weak and helpless," Gandhi observes; in passive resistance he sees "a weapon of the weak" (1983, 78; 2001, 110). The Satyagrahis, by contrast, launch their struggle believing they are strong and that their strength comes from Truth; therefore, Satyagraha is the weapon of the strong (Gandhi 1983, 78). Passive resistance involves forcing the government to repeal the unjust law through "Body-Force," and thus it is akin to violence in that passive resistance aims to impose the resisters' will on powers that be (that is why it can be used alongside armed resistance) (see Gandhi 1983, 77–8). In contrast, Satyagraha relies on the "Soul-Force," in that it "involves sacrifice of the self" and abandons fear (Gandhi 1983, 78, 81). Because it has no conception of injuring the opponent (1983, 78; see also Gandhi 1997, 93n186), *Satyagraha is the weapon of the strong*, for because Satyagrahis have an unparalleled capacity to absorb (violent) strikes inflicted upon them – losing their lives and embracing their injuries – they need not resort to violence. That is why Gandhi considers Satyagraha and passive resistance polar opposites (Gandhi 2001, 6). The Satyagrahi, being ready to sacrifice themselves by the thousands if necessary, are akin to the dedicated cadres of militant parties, ready to sacrifice themselves for the cause. Gandhi did not hesitate to declare that Satyagrahi are militants, and he often referred to his followers as a "nonviolent army."

Two dimensions of Satyagraha are "non-violen[t] resistance to injustice and exploitation ... [and] the 'truth force,' which is the responsibility for the welfare of the other" (Tahmasebi-Birgani 2014, 123). Nonviolence steadfastly precludes breaking the opponent (Gandhi 1983, 299). The soul houses, nourishes, and safeguards life-preserving and life-bearing *ahimsa*; in this way, Satyagraha is more than a strategy against a violent adversary; it is also, emphatically, a *weapon against violence proper*, even at the cost of the Satyagrahi's life. After all, "sacrifice is the law of life" (1983, 65).

This last point is crucial: "Satyagraha postulates the conquest of the adversary by suffering in one's own person" (1983, 78). Suffering is an act of will, of individual self-purification. Suffering may achieve certain (political) objectives. However, as the very principle of nonviolence, suffering cannot be politically instrumental (Devji 2012, 147). The Satyagrahi must cultivate – individually and collectively – the capacity to absorb suffering and injury without allowing his or her suffering to reflect back in the slightest on the adversary. For Gandhi, dying was clearly preferable to killing (2012, 6). Nonviolence, for him, was a commitment involving "utter humility and goodwill even towards our

bitterest opponent" (Gandhi 2001, 130). Gandhi expected the opponent "to hit back, and to hit hard"; his hope was that the voluntary suffering of Satyagrahi, standing resolute in their struggle, would convert the
opponent (Galtung 1989, 9). Brute force and Satyagraha, apparently,
are mutually exclusive. For Gandhi, then, Satyagraha was the distilla-
tion of the act of passive resistance. Since it is violence that creates the
binary between us and them (Gandhi 1997, 78n151), Truth-oriented
Satyagraha necessitates challenging the adversary's injustice(s) not by
excluding the so-called opponent but by incorporating him. Gandhi's
unique form of politics may seem at first to have its point of departure in
the traditional adversarial politics on which Western political thought
is founded (e.g., the Schmittian political philosophy, whose persistent
currency in academia defies my understanding), but this is in fact far
from the case. Devotion to Truth, Gandhi would recount, had drawn
him to the politics given to him by his religion (2011, 520). Gandhi's is
an *ethical politics*, a politics of unrelenting *un-Othering*, especially under
oppressive conditions, precisely because his politics are informed by
his search for Truth. The oppressors are confronted so that they can be
transported, despite their intentions, into the ambit of universal love
(Galtung 1959, 73). The common denominator of all violence is threat
(Gandhi 1997, 80). Nonviolent politics does not threaten, for it cannot
mete out sanctions against the oppressor – it cannot externalize at all.
But Satyagraha can *promise* that, should Truth-oriented action take its
course (which it can never do completely, for we lack the epistemological measures for ascertaining full attainment of Truth), both Satyagrahi
and oppressor will experience new levels of Truth, each according to
his or her level of struggle. This genus of politics is an end in itself, a
mode of life.

I hope the conceptual trajectory of Gandhi's complex approach to
nonviolent politics is now clear. There is one more point, quite an essential one, actually, that I must address. In an interview, Gandhi was pressed
on the fundamental aspect of this thought: Truth. His interlocutor asked
whether his notion of Truth was not simply an assumption, a figment of
his imagination.

> Q. But may not all this be your hallucination that can never come to pass in
> this matter-of-fact world of ours?
> A. It may well be that. It is not a charge wholly unfamiliar to me. My halluci-
> nations in the past have served me well ... If my hallucination is potent to
> the authorities, my body is always at their disposal. (Gandhi 2001, 357)

Gandhi is admitting here that, when scrutinized from a sceptic's stand-point, his Truth-oriented philosophy may appear fictitious. Yet his answer proves compelling. Whether it is "real" or not (as if it matters), Truth unleashes a course of action that places the body of the Satyagrahi on a crash course with the authorities, and as such, regardless of the "real-ity" of Truth (or God), the act is factually concrete. The exposing of the Satyagrahi's body, as the locus of political action, to potential harm, proves that *praxis is the measure of Truth.* Action, then, is the quintessence of politics. To this crucial point I will return.

It should now be clear how Gandhi achieved universal status for Satya-graha, thereby incorporating the related concepts (civil disobedience and passive resistance) into this universal concept (e.g., "Civil Disobe-dience is a branch of Satyagraha which includes all non-violent resis-tance for the vindication of Truth" [2001, 4]). Through careful and unrelenting significatory–conceptual navigations within the political discourse, Gandhi succeeded in unifying all previous concepts of non-violence under the banner of his ever-growing *master-signifier,* Satyagraha. He achieved this by constructing a *chain of equivalences* between the key concepts that capture nonviolent action, transforming the uncontested universal *signifiers* of "civil disobedience" and "passive resistance" into the particular *signifieds* of his now rising universal signifier, Satyagraha. The latter term attains a polysemic presence while retaining its significatory superiority. As a result, within the emerging discourse of nonviolence in the early twentieth century, the initial significatory *parallel(s)* between the Western–Christian terms (passive resistance, civil disobedience), on the one hand, and the Indian concept of Satyagraha, on the other, were converted by Gandhi into a *hierarchy* (late Derrida would have loved this reading!). Hence this declaration: "The movement of non-violent non-cooperation has nothing in common with the historical struggles for freedom in the West" (Gandhi 1983, 174). We will see, however, that the *universalism of nonviolence* – and the long chain of equivalences within this discourse (i.e., *ahimsa, anasakti,* Truth-force, soul-force, *swadeshi,* Satya-graha) – will return with a vengeance!

To appreciate how Satyagraha and nonviolence can achieve a concep-tually universal status, we need to recognize how Gandhi changed the logic of politics. I have already alluded to the main contours of his revo-lutionary concept of politics: for him, politics was not a means to an end; nor was it about capturing power and overwhelming one's opponents. These obsolete Schmittian logics, having informed Western political theory and conventional politics for too long, had no bearing on the

Mahatma's thought. For him, a politics enabled by Truth-force and soul-force was an end in itself, leading all to Truth. Evidently, he was offering a unique motif for his envisioned nonviolence. Satyagraha is based on the principle of non-cooperation (Gandhi 1983, 146–7), since all "exploitation is based on the cooperation, willing or forced, of the exploited" (1983, 248). The withdrawal of the oppressed from oppressive relations crystallized Gandhi's interpretation of Tolstoy's "nonresistance to evil" based on the Truth of religion (in Tolstoy, 1909, 11). The Satyagrahi always separates the oppressor from the oppression (Gandhi 2001, 275). While steadfastly challenging oppression, nonviolence must not have breaking the oppressor as its aim (Gandhi 1983, 299; Galtung 1959, 78). Gandhian nonviolence does not have a term for "an external enemy," and when confronting the oppressor, the Satyagrahis show only compassion (Gandhi 2001, 93). And because obeying unjust laws is incompatible with the human soul, it is important that regardless of the laws of the land, Satiyagrahis insist on demanding what is right (Gandhi 1997, 91). They will achieve justice through unparalleled "self-discipline, self-control, [and] self-purification," and since evil is always set apart from the evildoer, the Satyagrahi "will always overcome evil by good, anger by love, untruth by truth, *himsa* by *ahimsa*" (Gandhi 2001, 77).

Here we need to pause on Gandhi's rejection of politics as a means to an end. As mentioned, Gandhi's political philosophy radically diverges from conventional politics. Being an end in itself, *nonviolence abandons the utilitarian drive of politics*. Nonviolence is not purposive and does not seek an outcome. Violence achieves; nonviolence does not. Violence ensures the achievement of desired ends, and thus it relies on certain truisms to rationalize itself. Nonviolence, by contrast, has no such preoccupation and remains non-instrumental (Devji 2012, 100). "Truth is its own proof," avers Gandhi, "and non-violence is its supreme fruit" (quoted in Devji 2012, 99), and *since nonviolence need not prove Truth, it remains negative*. In Devji's words, the "purposes" of nonviolence are "achieved in the very moment of expression rather than subsequently" (2012, 94). Western politics remains instrumental and thus violent because it aims at bringing the future in line with pregiven expectations, but "a future known ahead of time would not longer be true to itself" (Devji 2012, 94). Driven by Truth, nonviolent struggle is not intent on harnessing the future.

Emerging through concrete political action in South Africa and India over the span of several decades, and constantly radicalized through "experiments with truth," Satyagraha resolves the problem of acting in nonviolent ways. It retains the conflictual nature of politics, links action to justice, and holds Truth as the (normative) directive against which nonviolence is measured in an unending search for self-realization. For Gandhi, of course, none of the above was ever straightforward. Before attending to the complications, though, we need to briefly review nonviolence in concrete action.

(c) *Nonviolence in action.* Consistent with the hermeneutic orientation of this book, the following constructed narrative of Gandhi's major political moves is intended to represent the abstract ideas presented above and to connect to my theoretical conclusion in the section that follows. Obviously, I cannot even try to summarize the long span of Gandhi's activism and leadership. So I will be attending to the turning points of Satyagraha in India to maintain my focus. Young Gandhi in South Africa could not have fathomed becoming the leader of Indian independence, yet looking back, South Africa was indeed a dress rehearsal for India. That said, South African anti-apartheid remains important for my study, and I will be returning to it later.

When referring to British colonialism in India, Gandhi appropriately evokes the "thief" metaphor. Like a man stealing another's property, the British have robbed Indians of their independence, and they have done so by force and "in broad daylight" (Gandhi 1997, 83). Finding this expropriation unjust, Gandhi observes, the Indians can use violent means to oust and punish the thief and the occupier, but in that case they will not have achieved a significant outcome – that is, they will not have reduced the possibility of being robbed again; to put it differently, resisting the colonizer will not eradicate the conditions of possibility of colonialism. The appropriate response, teaches the Mahatma, is to appeal to the Good within and destroy the motive for stealing, instead of punishing the thief (1997, 84). But here we are dealing not with individuals but with civilizations.

Gandhi's idea of *Swaraj* or "Indian home rule," expressed in *Hind Swaraj* (published in 1909), grapples with the complexity of this issue when the task at hand is to achieve Indian home rule through nonviolence. The shining point of this treatise lies in proposing nonviolence not as a means to an end but as an end in itself. India, he observes, must build itself into a nation – it must *become* a nation – before it expels the colonist; and for that to happen, entirely new principles are required in order to drive the liberation movement ahead; otherwise, India will remain colonized even after the British are ousted. Gandhi refers to Canada and South Africa as examples of decolonization without emancipation

(Gandhi 1997, 27). In thinking of India's future, Gandhi harbours no illusions that modern, industrial civilization imported from the West will change India's destiny forever. He rejects the values that underpin Western civilizations: industrial progress has produced a hollow civilization; the parliamentary system is a sham and leads to no true freedom at all, and thus the British political system is not worth emulating; modern civilization is barbaric and inherently violent (1997, 31, 34n48, 35, 135). The British are disliked not just because they have occupied India but because they are alien to the moral signature of India, and their industrial civilization is a great corruptor of the real civilization of India, which is a village society. India must free itself from colonialism both inwardly and outwardly: the Indians gave India to Britain because they had not attended to this (1997, 39). Freedom cannot be measured against liberation from subjection by the Other; it resides in the act of resistance, and nonviolent resistance is already free (Devji 2012, 94). Therefore, India's liberation from colonialism must entail liberation from modern civilization and its value system: postcolonial India must reject material want and go back to its age-old village life, since machinery brings violence. India must reorient its struggle towards a new form of civilization, and in this regard, Gandhi draws on the Gujarati equivalent of civilization, which means "good conduct" (Gandhi 1997, 67). Thus, India must forgo the idea of national interest and liberate the world (Gandhi 1997, 130, 131, 150, 169, 87n171). India must not only end colonization but also rise above colonialism through *transformative nonviolence* so that an entirely new nation can emerge through the process of emancipation.

In January 1915, Gandhi returned to India after two decades' sojourn in South Africa. He disembarked in Bombay to a hero's reception. But he was not in a rush to enter Indian politics. Instead, at the suggestion of his political mentor, Gopal Krishna Gokhale (1866–1915), an influential leader of the Indian National Congress (the INC, est. 1885), Gandhi began his year-long journey through the mysterious and complex country he had left as a young man. This journey enabled him to properly understand India's problems first-hand and realize the depths of the transformation India needed in order to liberate itself from colonialisms, both inner and outer. On his return to politics, Gandhi continued to advocate nonviolence. Then a significant event occurred: the massacre of nonviolent protesters by British troops in Jallianwalla Bagh, Amritsar, in April 1919, which left 379 dead and 1,137 wounded (Gandhi 1983, 131). That event, which the British authorities investigated, marked a turning point in Gandhi's thought: thereafter, Gandhi abandoned the idea of cooperating with the British as a means to bring about negotiations (Losurdo 2015, 71). The massacre forced Gandhi to abandon his earlier naive faith in British civility. No longer did he identify himself a British subject who wished to be a citizen of the empire; no longer did he seek to prove to British imperialists that Indians deserve the "right to have rights" and the "freedom to be free" (Arendt 2017). In 1920, the year after the Amritsar massacre, the INC adopted Gandhi's nonviolence and reoriented its politics in the direction of a nationwide non-cooperation movement against the British. Across India, unjust laws became the targets of organized nonviolent protesters, who were regularly beaten and imprisoned for taking part in collective action. On 5 February 1922, however, a group of non-cooperation protesters turned violent at Chauri Chaura, and when the police opened fire at them, they attacked, setting the police station on fire. The Chauri Chaura incident, which left three civilians and twenty-three policemen dead, led the INC to suspend the non-cooperation movement. This incident forced Gandhi to seriously re-evaluate Satyagraha. For Gandhi, violence had to be avoided. Indians must never act like their oppressors. I shall return to the theoretical implications of this incident for the Mahatma. Although Gandhi always maintained that an entire nation could not be nonviolent (Gandhi 1983, 300), he expected the Satyagrahi to follow nonviolence teachings: "Ever since 1921 I have been reiterating two words, *self-purification* and *self-sacrifice*" (Gandhi 2001, 252; emphasis in original). Chauri Chaura was a glaring example of those two principles being transgressed.

Gandhi's travels through India taught him that nonviolence was unimaginable without social justice: "so long as the wide gulf between the rich and the hungry millions persists," he anticipated a "violent and bloody revolution" if the rich did not voluntarily dedicate their wealth to the common good (Gandhi 1983, 247). He consistently regarded possession as a crime (1983, 55–6). In 1947 he called for a social justice program based on communal unity, an end to Untouchability, the equality of men and women, official status for provincial languages, rights for peasants and labour, and the implementation of a system of prohibitions (Gandhi 1997, 170–81). The question of the Untouchables, a caste with deep roots in Hindu culture, was especially important. Gandhi objected to the proposed conversion of the Untouchables to Christianity as a way to end their oppression. In fact, he wanted to retain Untouchability in order to cultivate the conflictual politics that, if they succeeded, would result in the disappearance of Untouchability (Tahmasebi-Birgani 2014, 121). The problem of the Untouchables was part of Gandhi's struggle for "inner emancipation," and that struggle had to be waged in tandem with the fight against British colonialism. In his ashrams, Untouchability did not exist. To raise it as a national issue, Gandhi conceived and led the Vaikom Satyagraha in 1924–25. The Vaikom Temple in North Travancore in Kerala, in southern India, was the capital of Hindu orthodoxy and the caste system. The Avarnas were not allowed to enter the temple there; indeed, they were not even permitted to use the public roads around it and were thus forced to take long detours (Gandhi 2001, 177). In 1925, after a series of Satyagrahi protests, a petition calling for the roads to be accessible to all was submitted to the Kerala legislature; it was rejected by one vote. This was demoralizing for the Satyagrahi, and although the Mahatma's intervention through the Police Commissioner of Travancore had disappointing results, in the aftermath of Chauri Chaura, the Vaikum resistance showed that Satyagraha was a sustainable strategy.

The Salt March of 1930 was meant to achieve four objectives. In colonial India it was a criminal act for Indians to extract salt from nature on their own. According to Gandhi, the British monopoly over salt production "deprives the people of a valuable easy village industry, involves wanton destruction of property that nature produces in abundance, the destruction itself means more national expenditure, and fourthly, to crown this folly, an unheard of tax of more than 1,000 per cent is exacted from a starving people" (2001, 247). The Salt March followed the INC Declaration of Independence, which was publicly issued on 26 January 1930. The Salt resistance was launched on 12 March 1930, from an ashram outside Ahmadabad, when Gandhi and seventy-eight Satyagrahis began their 390-kilometre march to the coastal village of Dandi in the state of Gujarat; there they were joined by thousands, and it was there, on 6 April 1930, that Gandhi broke the British salt law by extracting and producing salt from the shore. The Salt March sparked massive acts of civil disobedience by millions of Indians in the months to come, resulting in widespread police violence against the Satyagrahis and about 60,000 arrests. In March 1931 a settlement was reached between Gandhi and Lord Irwin, the Viceroy of India, but it turned out to be disappointing to the INC, for it was seen as making too many concessions to the British in return for too little. The Salt Act remained the law. In return for suspending Salt Satyagraha, the government released the arrestees, dropped the pending charges, and returned their fines (Engler and Engler 2014). Yet Gandhi regarded the movement as having achieved a victory. Mark and Paul Engler (2014) draw on the Salt March to acknowledge the instrumental and symbolic approaches to civil disobedience: although it had failed to abolish the Salt Act, they submit, it proved that large-scale Satyagraha was feasible and that India was ready for mass nonviolent movements. While the point is taken, analysing Gandhian nonviolence in these terms clearly violates Gandhi's non-instrumental philosophy of nonviolence.

Gandhi's radical critique of modern civilization as the epitome of subjugation through mass production and endless want was principled and driven by *ahimsa*. He constantly meditated on the ways in which his economic Satyagraha could not only challenge British colonialism but also lead to a new and pure Self, guided by Truth. India, as Karl Marx had recognized in the nineteenth century, was a blessing for British industrial capitalism (Marx 1972). Long before the term "globalization" became popular, Marx had observed how the British colonization of India not only provided capitalists with cheap raw materials for industry but also created a global market beyond their dreams. British textile manufacturers, in particular, had crushed the Indian traditional market by exporting cloth to India that was cheaper and far more durable than the Indian product. Early Indian industrialists, the rising comprador bourgeoisie, played an important role in this process, and by the early twentieth century Indian textile manufacturing was on the rise.

While still in South Africa, Gandhi showed interest in producing *khadi*, the traditional Indian cloth produced on handlooms, and by 1917 he had begun producing his own *khadi* at his ashram. Resisting modern production by returning to tradition became a key component of his Swadeshi movement, a spiritual movement involving self-discipline and the avoidance of unnecessary consumption, and thus against the violence entrenched in mass production and consumption. The Swadeshi movement was part and parcel of Gandhian nonviolent and spiritual resistance, and in the Indian independence movement it targeted the heart and history of British capitalism as well as the evil of machinery. Simultaneously, the Swadeshi movement aimed at proving that Indian self-reliance, village economy, and social justice were possible. The *khadi* movement, whose purpose was to boycott British textiles, was launched in the 1920s in the context of the nationalist boycott of English merchandise since 1905. The boycott movement was growing in strength by the 1930s. Under pressure, the British had agreed in 1921 to a tariff on imported goods; in the early 1930s that tariff was increased. As expected, the movement had a measurable impact on the British economy. For instance, in 1896 "Indian mills supplied only 8 per cent of total cloth consumption; in 1913, 20 per cent; in 1936, 62 per cent; and in 1945,

76 per cent" (Maddison 2006, 57). Gandhi meant this to be a long-term movement for delinking India from the British economy, and for the spiritual growth of Indians as well, but at that time, he was not unaware of the consequences of his *khadi* movement for British workers. On the invitation of the mill-owning Davies family, Gandhi visited Darwen in East Lancashire in September 1931. The Darwen family, socialists and Quakers, wanted Gandhi to see first-hand the suffering of the mill workers. In the round table discussion that followed Gandhi's visit, he announced that the boycott would continue until Indian independence was achieved (BBC News 2011). It is significant that while touring Greenfield Mill in Spring Vale, Gandhi *apologized* to the workers for their suffering because of the boycott. The largely female workers at the factory, however, gave the Mahatma a hero's welcome and supported the Indian independence movement.

As a matter of principle, the Mahatma reassured British citizens that the independence movement would bring them no harm: "Every Englishman and Englishwoman must feel safe, not by reason of the bayonet at their disposal but by reason of our living creed of non-violence" (Gandhi 2001, 56). Yet life is always more complicated than our creeds allow. Like the other methods in Gandhi's nonviolent arsenal, the Swadeshi movement involved mass mobilization and economic Satyagraha. The *khadi* movement amounted to a mass withdrawal from participation in the colonial economy. As nonviolent resistance, though, the movement hurt not just British capitalism but its "victims" as well: workers of the metropole. This double-injury of the colonizing Other was an inevitable consequence of nonviolence, and Gandhi's apologies to the workers at Darwen represented his courageous recognition of the injury being done to the ones caught in the middle of a decolonization movement. To this point I will return.

The "Quit India" movement, announced by Gandhi in his speech, was launched in August 1942 by the All-India Congress Committee in Bombay while Japanese forces were nearing the eastern borders of India. This move was influenced by the failure of the Cripps Mission, in March 1942, an attempt by the British government to gain the full cooperation of Indian leaders in the Second World War. Cripps assured the leaders of the Indian Independence Movement that India would receive "Dominion status" (self-government) after the war, but the Indian leaders regarded the promise as too vague and as an attempt at stalling the movement and demanded immediate independence. Within days of Gandhi's announcement of the Quit India movement (8 August 1942), all leaders of the Congress were arrested and detained, extrajudicially, until the war ended in 1945. This new civil disobedience movement turned out to be divisive: it did not have the support of many key actors in the Independence Movement – most importantly, the Muslim League. After the announcement, short-lived nonviolent movements erupted across India. Sporadic violence also broke out. As a result, tens of thousands were arrested, and many of them remained in prison until the end of the war. The Quit India movement generated a new Satyagrahi mantra: "Do or die!" "We shall either free India or die in the attempt," declared Gandhi. "We shall not live to see the perpetuation of our slavery" (Gandhi 1942). At the same time, he called on his followers to uphold the distinction between British imperialism and the British people and to show no hatred towards British citizens. It was time for India to "do," to achieve independence from Britain, before the *nation* of India perished. It seems inconceivable to us (and it did to Gandhi) that India would be completely depopulated as a result of nationwide Satyagraha. Gandhi had shrewdly found in India's unique demographics an inexhaustible source of Satyagraha: "In India ... by the 1930s, 'a mere 4,000 British civil servants assisted by 60,000 soldiers and 90,000 civilians ... had billeted themselves upon a country of 300 million persons'" (Said 1993, 11). Gandhi dwelled on this unique strength of India.

This move, which invited a strong wave of colonial repression, was consistent with the Mahatma's philosophy: Gandhi was using the international situation and Britain's entanglement in the world war as means to pressure the British to quit India. Gandhi's subtle politics are reflected in a letter to the Viceroy of India more than a decade earlier in which he wrote that the Indians aimed not to compel the British but rather to "convert" them to the Indian cause. "I have deliberately used the word *conversion*. For my ambition is no less than to convert the British people through non-violence, and thus make them see the wrong they have done to India" (Gandhi 2001, 227; see 1983, 164; emphasis in original). Clearly, conversion of one's oppressor represents irreversible liberation, and Gandhi was astute enough to exploit the war so that the conversion could take place nonviolently.

These turning points of Gandhi's leadership in the nonviolent resistance movement show how he carefully chose each struggle, revolt, and call for action with utmost concern for the situation at hand and the manoeuvrability it allowed him; he intended nonviolent action to challenge both the adversary without and the enemy within. The Mahatma "was interested ... in an unprecedented moral transformation," Devji writes, "seeing in nonviolence a practice that brooked no limits and had universal application, with the movement for India's freedom providing only a site in which it might be tried out as an experiment... India's mission, therefore, was not simply to liberate herself from imperialism, but set the precedent that would free the world as a whole from violence" (Devji 2012, 2–3). But in challenging multiple adversaries – colonialism, the caste system, and social injustice – Gandhi had to tease out evil from its hideouts in common practice and daily life, expose it, and extract its violence so that evil and violence would be absorbed by nonviolence. For him, nonviolence was key to the future conversion of evil (2012, 142). In short, Gandhi made it clear that nonviolence was only possible through conflictual politics. He showed that *nonviolence could only emerge from the (potential) spheres for exercising violence.* Stated otherwise, both violence and nonviolence arise from conflict.

These points call for a closer reading and a radical rethinking of Gandhian nonviolence.

The Necessity of Violence

In offering advice to the German Jews in 1938, Gandhi did not hesitate to recommend Satyagraha as the method of Jewish resistance against the Nazis. By this time, the concept of Satyagraha had been fully developed. Gandhi did not endorse the mass flight of the Jews as a response to their persecution in Europe, and he rejected the idea of establishing a Jewish homeland in Palestine (a project already under way, with British support). "The cry for the national home for the Jews does not make much appeal to me," he observed (Gandhi 1938; 1983, 287). The Mahatma remained steadfast in reminding the Jews that their homeland was not geographical; it resided in their hearts. Palestinian displacement to make room for a Jewish state was therefore indefensible: "It is wrong and inhuman to impose the Jews on the Arabs" (1938). For Gandhi, "it is wrong to enter it [Palestine] under the shadow of the British gun," and the Jews "can settle in Palestine only by the goodwill of the Arabs. They should seek to convert the Arab heart" (1983, 288). Instead of encouraging the Jews to flee to Palestine with British military support, Gandhi called on them to make the countries of their birth their homeland. He suggested that the persecution and expulsion of the Jews in Nazi Germany, "which seems to have no parallel in history," did not constitute a pretext for their seeking out a "homeland" elsewhere by displacing the native Arab population. It was indeed possible to resist the Nazis. Gandhi averred that if he were a Jew, "I would claim Germany as my home even as the tallest gentile German may, and challenge him [Hitler] to shoot me or cast me in the dungeon; I would refuse to be expelled or to submit to discriminating treatment" (1983, 287). In fact, Gandhi advised European nations *not* to resist the Nazis by force of arms and to let Hitler into their countries so that they could challenge and defeat the Nazis through nonviolence (Devji 2012, 128–9). After the nonviolent experiment of the Salt March, he observed in a statement on 26 November 1938, two weeks after *Kristallnacht* of 9 November 1938 (when he could not have known about the Final Solution), that the voluntary suffering of the Jews might result in their mass execution, but that this was precisely the point. *The Satyagrahi is not afraid of death.* He pointed out that the Jews were far better placed and "more gifted" than the South African Indians to challenge the Nazis (a point Arendt indirectly mocked some thirty years later). "And they have organised world opinion behind them" (Gandhi 1938).

One need not be reminded of the outcome of the multiple holocausts in Europe – Jewish, Romani, gay, communist, the disabled – all committed by the Nazis. The Jews whom Gandhi persuaded to take part in in Satyagraha perished in sadly great numbers, having been fed into a monstrously effective machinery of genocide with few parallels in history. As mentioned, Gandhi himself acknowledged that "the German persecution of the Jews seems to have no parallel in history" (1938; 1983, 287). But except for some sporadic Jewish uprisings – and Devji believes that Gandhi would have endorsed the Warsaw Ghetto Uprising of 1943 (Devji 2012, 144) – the Jewish prisoners did not die acting as Satyagrahis. This is why Gandhi described the historical suffering of the Jews as admirable but as the "nonviolence of the weak." It involved "the acceptance of victimization," which for Gandhi "was more conducive to violence than violence itself" (2012, 134).

In this respect, it is appropriate to revisit Arendt's sardonic reference to the success of Gandhian nonviolence: she offers a relevant lesson but entirely misses a crucial point. "If Gandhi's enormously powerful and successful strategy of nonviolent resistance had met with a different enemy – Stalin's Russia, Hitler's Germany, even prewar Japan, instead of England – the outcome would not have been decolonization, but massacre and submission," Arendt observed. "England in India and France in Algeria had good reasons for their restraint. Rule by sheer violence comes into play where power is being lost" (Arendt 1970, 53). "Restraint"? Should we simply ignore her alarming term "restraint," which she ascribes to centuries of atrocities and exploitation committed by British and French colonialists in India and Algeria (and elsewhere)? Having begun to colonize India in 1612 through the Mughal Emperor Jahangir (and the British East India Company), then having placed India under the British Raj in 1858, by 1947 the war-stricken, exhausted, and economically bankrupt British Empire had lost the economic strength to maintain its largest colony and had no choice but to withdraw from India, thereby submitting to the Indian Independence Movement. Arendt failed to grasp that this process had nothing to do with British liberal democracy. But speaking of "restraint": perhaps the two-year brutal repression of the Indian Mutiny in 1857 by the British (during which they virtually razed the city of Delhi) was too remote or too insignificant for the European collective memory that Arendt had internalized. But she must have remembered first-hand the Algerian War of Independence (1954–62), during which between 1 and 1.5 million Algerians were killed by the rabidly brutal French Army. Had she not read about the massacre of 17 October 1961 in Paris, when French police opened fire on a peaceful pro-FLN rally, killing at least two hundred protesters? Are we expected to believe that French democracy and German Nazism were somehow inherently different when they dealt with what they perceived as a radically unassimilable Other? Gandhi was assassinated in 1948, long before the Algerian Revolution, but his point that the difference between liberalism and fascism is a matter of degree, not kind, is better understood from his standpoint as a colonized person. Arendt's "credit" lies with the democratic systems of Britain and France. For the Mahatma, however, "Fascism and Nazism are a revised edition of so-called democracies if they are not an answer to the latter's misdeeds" and their differences were matters of degree (quoted in Devji 2012, 130, 131). Fascism and liberal democracy are contraries from the privileged European point of view (and for understandably good reasons), but from the standpoint of the colonized, to echo the Mahatma, not too different. One is reminded of Fanon, when Gandhi writes: "It would be a thousand times better for us to be ruled by a military dictator than to have the dictatorship concealed under sham councils and assemblies" (Gandhi 1983, 150). Naturally, Gandhi's lived experience under colonial rule could not entertain Arendt's (privileged) conception of politics. In reflecting on Arendt's comment, let us remember that the decolonization of India and Algeria had little or nothing to do with the "goodwill" of democracy. Rather it was the outcome of long historical-structural processes that culminated in the collapse of the colonial system and the emergence of a new, postcolonial world after the Second World War. Gandhi had rightly intuited that the

British Empire would come to an end soon after that war. Observers often exaggerate the role the nonviolent movement played in Indian independence by overlooking other factors. Had it not been for Britain's economic collapse and postwar political exhaustion, India would probably not have been granted independence in 1947 and the movement would have continued. Gandhi never viewed the nonviolent movement as a putsch. Of course, it was easy for Arendt to judge Indian independence after the fact. What she missed entirely was that understanding politics in terms of its outcomes could not have been farther from the Mahatma's vision. According to Gandhi, the low-entropy nonviolence movement should have persevered until it had exhausted the high-entropy empire. The war had been an extra burden on the empire and a blessed gift for the Swaraj movement. And yes, Gandhi probably would not have survived fascism. Yet Arendt missed the point that *Gandhian politics resided in the movement.* Which, ironically, brings us full circle, relating to the point inadvertently suggested by Arendt: with no movement to embody it, the politics of nonviolence dies away. Consistent with my reading of her (see chapter 4), it seems that Arendt is questioning the universal applicability of nonviolence and implying that some systems need to be defeated by force of arms. Once again, and somewhat ironically, this is the point raised (but not promoted) in Gandhi's second letter to Hitler (24 December 1940): "If not the British, some other power will certainly improve upon your method and beat you with your own weapon" (1940).

So at this point we need to have a more focused reading of Gandhi and revisit the concept of self-sacrifice and its importance, especially in light of a persuasive study by Faisal Devji (2012).

What links all of Gandhi's aforementioned strategies in India is that each was carefully chosen to provoke the British to use unambiguous violence (not "restraint," Arendt!) to repress the Satyagraha movement. Gandhi's tactics proved to be effective. He never withdrew from political participation, as in passive resistance (Tolstoy), and he never offered himself or the Satyagrahi as helpless albeit principled subjects of unjust laws. Nor did he simply resist unjust laws, as in civil disobedience (Thoreau), without challenging the entire system behind those laws. True, he efficiently used tactics contiguous with passive resistance or civil disobedience. But the bottom line is that *Gandhian nonviolence could not be passive.* To the contrary, he confronted the adversary, forcing the latter to exercise violence on the Satyagrahis, who had been trained spiritually to accept and endure suffering. Only by teasing out violence from its hideouts could nonviolence thrive. In brief, Gandhi's concept of nonviolence *depended* on violence. *Truth requires perpetual search for evil.* Devji has astutely observed that Gandhi invited violence and suffering in order to exhaust and transform violence (2012, 7).

The Mahatma advocated nonviolence not of the weak but of the strong. Dying was preferable to killing, he held, but for him this was no moral edict. Those who use violence, be they oppressors or armed rebels, agonize about and show cowardice towards death. Interestingly, Gandhi called himself "an anarchist, but of another type" (Gandhi quoted in Devji 2012, 152), a "Godly anarchist" who, because he was not afraid of suffering, refused the tactics of "worldly terrorists," by whom he meant the advocates of armed uprising against British colonialism. The brave, the Satyagrahi, never feared death, and in welcoming suffering and death while challenging oppression, they embraced Truth. The goal of politics is to avoid death: therein lay Gandhi's sweeping critique of Western politics (and the common denominator of fascism and liberal democracies) and their *inherent* relationship with violence. Western politics is based on the preservation and prolongation of life, something that was entirely alien to Gandhi's intentional "display [of] a certain lack of concern with death and defeat as political facts" (2012, 145). And this took Gandhi beyond the politics of the past, towards a civilizational critique of the West:

> But the West attaches an exaggerated importance to prolonging man's earthly existence. Until the man's last moment on earth you go on drugging him even by injecting. That, I think, is inconsistent with the recklessness with which they will shed their lives in war. Though I am opposed to war, there is no doubt that war induces reckless courage. Well, without ever having to engage in a war I want to learn from you the art of throwing away my life for a noble cause. But I do not want that excessive desire of living that Western medicine seems to encourage in man even at the cost of tenderness for subhuman life. (quoted in Devji 2012, 185)

As Devji observes, no moral principles can arise from such a staunch (civilizational) obsession with the prolongation of human life (2012, 187). Paradoxically, it is this profound drive to preserve life – or to invert the expression, the *inability* to embrace mortality – that leads to violence. Suffering is the source of rising; "Life comes out of Death" (Gandhi 2001, 112); for "the godfearing, death has no terror" (Gandhi 1938). The preservation and prolongation of human life whatever the cost – even, paradoxically, at the cost of sacrificing it in wars – in fact goes against the life-principle, Truth, and the *ahimsa* dwelling within each of us that underlies nonviolence. In other words, the deeply internalized value attached to human life, and attempts at prolonging life *whatever the cost*, nourish violence and endanger human (and non-human) life. This is key to understanding Gandhi: by relinquishing love of life, we can thwart the urge to kill (Devji 2012, 186). Out of this, Truth-driven nonviolence, Satyagraha, or soul-force will emerge.

While Arendtian critiques of Gandhian politics (i.e., nonviolent methods are inefficient when they face totalitarian systems) resonate even with many advocates of nonviolence, in light of Gandhi's upholding mortality as the bearer of power of Truth, Devji's observation shows how, paradoxically, Gandhian nonviolence contains its proof *within* it: "while a politics dedicated to the preservation of life had proven its hollowness by placing humanity itself under threat, the morality of nonviolence had made such life possible by disregarding it altogether. And so the vindication that fascism's potential victory could not give Gandhi's theory of nonviolence was in this paradoxical way assured by its defeat" (2012, 150). Fascism, therefore, provided Gandhi with the most formidable test of his philosophy of nonviolence, a trial from which, the Mahatma deeply believed, Satyagraha would emerge ever more triumphantly, with its inner Truth revealed, simultaneously despite and indeed *because of* the enormous human cost. "Indeed it was precisely in violence that Gandhi claimed to discover the possibility of its overcoming, something that the great revolutionary figures of the past two centuries had always maintained, though none in his intensely moral if also idiosyncratic way" (Devji 2012, 190). *Nonviolence can only emerge through violence and can only survive through sacrifice.* The Satyagrahi embodies the most radical revolutionary figure, for she achieves, unlike the armed revolutionary, dying without killing. And this remains Gandhi's ultimate discovery: what I call the *ontological dependency of nonviolence on violence*, which is consistent with the thesis of this book.

Turning to history in light of the aforesaid discovery, we now clearly see why Gandhi suspended the non-cooperation movement in 1922 after the violence committed by his followers at Chauri Chaura. The non-cooperation participants had been expected to bring out the violence of the police; they would then absorb the strike and thereby put it out of operation. With their raging, spontaneous violence, the Satyagrahis defeated their purpose both tactically and philosophically. "For if Gandhi was horrified by the violence exercised from time to time by his followers, he longed to provoke it from those who had to be opposed by their nonviolence" (2012, 3–4). Nonviolence's expressive power can only reside with the violence that represses the movement.

The above argument is consistent with Gandhi's conflictual thought, and nowhere is his conflictual thought more evident than in his unwavering affirmation of the "nonviolence of the strong" or "nonviolence of the brave" as opposed to the "nonviolence of the weak," for which he expressed disdain. "Non-violence is not a cover for cowardice, but it is the supreme virtue of the brave ... Cowardice is wholly inconsistent with non-violence ... Non-violence presupposes the ability to strike" (Gandhi quoted in Merton 2007, 50). Cowardice harbours violence because it is consistent with the tendency to preserve life: "My own experience but confirms the opinion that the Mussulman as a rule is a bully, and the Hindu as a rule is a coward ... But I as a Hindu am more ashamed of Hindu cowardice than I am angry at Mussulman bullying ... As a coward, which I was for years, I harboured violence. I began to prize non-violence only when I began to shed cowardice" (quoted in Devji 2012, 59). Non-violence, therefore, has nothing to do with enduring oppression or with inaction in the face of an overwhelming oppressor. The Mahatma famously preferred violence to cowardice.

> I do believe that *where there is a choice only between cowardice and violence, I would advise violence.* Thus when my eldest son asked me what he should have done had he been present when I was almost fatally assaulted in 1908 [by an Indian extremist opposed to Gandhi's agreement with General Smuts in South Africa], whether he should have run away and seen me killed or whether he should have used his physical force which he could and wanted to use, and defend me, *I told him it was his duty to defend me even by using violence.* Hence it was that I took part in the Boer War, the so-called Zulu Rebellion and [the First World War]. Hence also do I advocate training in arms for those who believe in the method of violence. I would rather have India resort to arms in order to defend her honor than that she should in a cowardly manner become or remain a helpless witness to her own dishonor. (Gandhi 1983, 137, emphasis added)

Violence is preferable to cowardice because it can be liberatory. As a means of liberation, violence is not ideal, for it will ultimately produce the seeds of destruction of what it achieves. The use of force to protect someone who is in danger or incapable of defending himself (in his example of a child) does not qualify as violence, for this kind of force belongs to a different order (Gandhi 1997, 86). If dignity and justice can only be maintained through violence, and if that violence brings out bravery in the Self, the courage of the kind upheld by adherents to "nonviolence of the strong," then *emancipatory violence* is preferable to submission, bravery to weakness and cowardice, and self-sacrifice to the preservation of life. As well, *defensive violence* is endorsed only when it leads to liberation – although nonviolent literature euphemistically calls such violence "force" (e.g., Rosenberg 2003) for the purpose of "consolation of the soul" (Schürmann). However, the Mahatma resolutely held nonviolence superior to violence. To challenge one's oppressors nonviolently, one must have garnered the power – within and without – to engage the opponent. Consistent with the principle of *ahimsa*, Gandhi held that while it is preferable to forgive one's oppressor, in order to properly forgive, the oppressed must already have the power to punish (1983, 137). In other words, *nonviolence is superior to violence because the nonviolent actor must already have achieved the means and power to implement violence against an adversary and then withhold the means and uphold the power.* There shines, accordingly, the Gandhian idea of converting one's opponent:

> Gandhi himself had always been clear about the fact that *his movement had nothing to do with avoiding violence,* but was meant rather to invite and in so doing convert it. For it was evident to him that unlike nonviolence, which possessed only a *negative* meaning, violence enjoyed a *positive* existence and was implied in all action, including the everyday processes of living that wore down the body and eventually destroyed it. Nonviolence, therefore, was meant not to provide some alternative to violence but instead to appropriate and ... to sublimate it. (Devji 2012, 7–8, emphasis added)

It is now clear that *nonviolence's dependence on violence is irrefutable* and that *the presumed opposition of the two concepts is a phantasm.* It means that nonviolence, as a negative concept, cannot exist, be conceived, or be enacted on its own. This point escapes the misdirected gazes of rationalists – those fascinated by reified concepts and those who measure practice in terms of its degree of conformity to theory. Such approaches miss the occasion for observing, behind the concept, "the things themselves." Referring to the many apparent "inconsistencies" in Gandhian thought as "contradiction" (Losurdo 2015) fails to appreciate that Gandhian nonviolence results from what systems theorist Niklas Luhmann (1989) calls a paradox: the conditions of the possibility of nonviolence are simultaneously the conditions of its impossibility (violence). As "it is impossible for us to realize perfect Truth so long as we are imprisoned in this mortal frame" (Gandhi 2001, 40), one only arrives at, and immerses oneself deeper in, Truth as one continually *experiments* with it (hence the subtitle of Gandhi's autobiography: *The Story of My Experiments with Truth*), each time in a more radical way, summoning and challenging fiercer modes of violence, facing increasingly perilous circumstances, under ever more impossible conditions. The Satyagrahi will only laugh at this challenge: facing violence, he seeks Truth. Gandhian Truth is not Tolstoy's "Law of Love," an unshakable absolute. Gandhian Truth-enabled Satyagraha is not the Kantian "categorical imperative" either: Truth is achieved only by approximation; it appears only relative to the depth of one's adherence to Satyagraha and to the extent of injury one allows oneself to bear, in peace and laughter, while preventing one's opponent from undergoing the same painful experience (2001, 20). Thus, while one acts in accordance with Truth, one can never act as if her act has become the universal moral principle of future action (Kant). The Satyagrahi will only become purer through greater suffering as a result of nonviolence's ceaseless conflictual politics. She has only an earthly life to lose. Detachment is her greatest weapon.

By illustrating the conceptual and practical dependency of nonviolence on violence – consistent with my hypothesis of the ontological primacy of violence but certainly irreducible to it – Gandhi collapses the primarily religiously enabled binary opposition of violence and nonviolence, a binary that prevails over our age and among diverse thinkers. The greatest philosopher of nonviolence and the noblest architect of Truth-force proves it to be entirely possible to steadfastly and uncompromisingly adhere to *ahimsa* and defend nonviolence without algorithmically subscribing to a mutually exclusive understanding of (non)violence, an understanding whose only possible use remains to (feebly) console the soul in tension. The Mahatma embraces no self-righteous peace of mind.

On Acting and Its Issues

This study is primarily a conceptual phenomenology: I am investigating the historical and contextual conditions of the emergence of (non)violence in order to discover whether the conceptual distinction between violence and nonviolence is sustainable. I am therefore reading theories and ideas regardless of their authors' intentions. As such, to call the Mahatma a "phenomenologist" may amount to a slur! Nevertheless, a close reading of the principal components of his thought shows a certain "phenomenological attitude" in his approach towards nonviolence, in that his thought time and again "suspends" the received constructs (e.g., passive resistance and civil disobedience) in relation to which nonviolence had been hitherto perceived. Let us pause on this.

(a) *Inciting violence.* I argued earlier that for Gandhi, nonviolence was not an autarkic concept, because first, it depends on violence for its emergence, and second, it is driven by the search for Truth, through the search for the evil within and the oppression without. I have shown that Gandhi refused to adhere to a binary opposition between violence and nonviolence, with the result that he refrained from identifying the Other with Evil and the Self with Good; in this way he sought and exposed evil both in the adversary and in oneself. His fundamental binary division rested not in violence versus nonviolence but in the brave or the strong versus the meek or the weak. For him, nonviolence's dependency on violence was not a mere abstraction. The Salt March and Quit India campaigns concretized this dependency. Through careful planning and organization, the Mahatma provoked the British into massively repressing his movement, detaining him and other leaders (in India alone, Gandhi spent six years and ten months in prison in the span of thirty-five years) and arresting, imprisoning, beating, killing, and fining tens of thousands of Satyagrahi. Only by confronting such rampant and unrestrained violence can nonviolence prove its fidelity to Truth. Only thus can a new nation emerge. If there is a distinction between nonviolence and violence, it will be revealed only through perpetual confrontation through which violence meets its *negation* in nonviolent action, a modality of action distinct from enactments of violence. In short, *nonviolence has no existence without violence,* and its appearance as a mode of action distinct from violence stems from the latter. I will return to this point, which is consistent with this book's thesis.

(b) *Lessons of war.* Later in life, Gandhi looked back solemnly on his *voluntary* participation in wars as a British subject (if not as a Satyagrahi than at least as a passive resister) who nonetheless had challenged the British Empire in South Africa and later in India. While in South Africa, during the Boer War (1899–1902), Gandhi gathered volunteers from the Indian community to support the British in their efforts to repress the South African Dutch population. He led a non-combatant unit called the Natal Indian Ambulance Corps comprised of 1,100 volunteers. Gandhi confesses that during this war his sympathies "were all with the Boers" (1983, 48; 2011, 188), yet he would write in his autobiography: "I felt that, if I demanded rights as a British citizen, it was also my duty, as such, to participate in the defense of the British Empire" (2011, 225). Soon after, based on the same line of reasoning, Gandhi offered his services (for six weeks) to the British in the Zulu "rebellion" in Natal (Gandhi 1983, 61). The fact that as a person of colour he did not identify with the Zulus is rather disturbing and points to his prejudicial attitude towards Africans, compared to whom the Indians were deemed closer to Europeans. The Zulu Rebellion, he would write, was no more than suppression of poorly equipped Zulus by modern machinery of massacre. Gandhi's support of the British military extended even to the First World War. Again, he supported the British by actively recruiting Indian volunteers to serve in their army, first in 1914 as non-combatants and later in April 1918 as combatants. He is said to have helped recruit 500,000 men for the British army (Losurdo 2015, 28). During this time, he suspended anti-British activities. His motto, "Partnership in the Empire is our definite goal" (Gandhi 1983, 109), suggests how he viewed Indian support for British military at this point, though he would abandon this view after the Amritsar Massacre of 1919. Mobilizing fellow Indians to join the empire's wars was a component of Gandhi's fermenting independence movement. Thus to contend that in Gandhi's engagement in wars "what was completely absent was any project of general emancipation" (Losurdo 2015, 34) represents a serious misunderstanding of the Mahatma's complex thought. The algorithmic critiques of Gandhi that try to measure his actions against abstract concepts similarly fail: an example is stating that his involvement in imperial wars "cannot be defined exclusively by reference to the category of non-violence" (Losurdo 2015, 34). That category does not precede action but emerges from it. From the reference point of *ahimsa*, yes, Gandhi's decision remains unintelligible, even though politically and pragmatically astute. But the phenomenon as the "thing in itself" is revealed precisely in the fissure between concept and practice. A phenomenologist dwells in such fissures, never wishing to measure action in logical, deductive, or algorithmic terms.

Gandhi had no illusions about his repeated involvements in British war efforts. He never tried to hide the violence he took part in as an adherent to nonviolence, notwithstanding the non-combatant roles: "I make no distinction, from the point of view of *ahimsa*, between combatants and non-combatants ... In the same way those who confine themselves to attending to the wounded in battle cannot be absolved from the guilt of war" (Gandhi 2011, 362). He did not exempt himself from responsibility for contributing to violence. The duty to take part in war is in fact consistent with one's duty – adhered to by those believing in *ahimsa* – "to free himself, his nation and the world from war" (2011, 362). Participating in the master's war allows the colonized and oppressed to show their power to the colonizer. Only in this way can the colonized demand rights. There is also a "pedagogical value" to war (Losurdo 2015, 29). War teaches a sense of duty and discipline. It brings out the exalted values of courage and self-sacrifice. The most crucial value of unity of life in *ahimsa*, the principle from which the practice of nonviolence is extracted, cannot be upheld without these values: duty, discipline, courage, and self-sacrifice. These values are revealed through nonviolence just as they are cultivated through war as the most imposing manifestation of violence. In fact, they constitute the qualities sought in a devoted Satyagrahi. The nonviolence of the brave is unthinkable without such qualities. Thus, the seemingly opposing forces of violence and nonviolence share the terrain of highest values. Stated precisely, these exalted values constitute the *shared terrain* from which the divergent forces of violence and nonviolence arise. *The mutual exclusivity of the two concepts, therefore, seems to become even harder to maintain.*

(c) *Universality of nonviolence.* Indeed because of its dependence on violence, nonviolence emerges as a universal claim. This statement defies logic: dialectically, violence is to be regarded as the positive, objective Universal (which is consistent with my proposed ontological primacy of violence), with nonviolence being its particular negation, and only thus persisting. Gandhi always disturbs logical algorithms, and understanding him through Western theories or by approximating his teachings to Western cultural (largely Christian) epistemologies has led today to the dilution of his thought. His conceiving of *ahimsa* as universal stems from the fact that as a negative concept, nonviolence has no essence. As a signifier without a commonly agreed or historically received referent, first, nonviolence depends on violent repression and injustice so that it can emerge concretely in historic movements, and second, nonviolence cannot be understood in its own terms, but only in terms of its proximity to Truth – as universal yet desubstantiated – and its strength to confront oppression, absorb the strike, and put violence out of operation. Precisely because nonviolence has no essence, it needs to reaffirm its steadfast refusal of violence by adhering to the normative yet motile standard-bearer called Truth.

"*Ahimsa* is a comprehensive principle" (Gandhi 2011, 361). The universal reach of *ahimsa* appears in Gandhi's advice for the Jews under Nazism. For the Mahatma it did not matter that the condition of possibility of his strand of nonviolent politics was the absence of total domination, and that as such popular, mass nonviolence against the Nazis would only accelerate the Holocaust. His version of nonviolence would therefore not have been applicable in Germany, despite his insistence. But for him, the inapplicability of his Satyagraha would probably not have been as disturbing as its tangential application and the irresoluteness of Satyagrahi. The comprehensive principle of *ahimsa* explains why the Mahatma trembled at the news of Chauri Chaura in 1922 when the Satyagrahi turned violent and attacked and killed police officers. Just one infringement of nonviolence would have raised radical doubts about the universality of his Truth-force, leading to the latter's relativization. The Mahatma could not allow this to happen, and that is why he called off Satyagraha after the Chauri Chaura incident. The "Mahatma was voicing his support for morality as a universal enterprise, one that could not be shunted aside in the supposedly exceptional circumstances of war without losing its credibility. For he realized that allowing exceptions to the moral rule only ended up making morality itself into an exception, one whose limited scope was henceforth to be determined by the immorality of war" (Davji 2012, 129). If in common sense and public view, nonviolent action cannot appear clearly as distinct from violent acts, then nonviolence has no existence. To borrow the Mahatma's analogy, nonviolence is the new life born out of the pain and suffering of birth. So for him, *pain and suffering register violence*, this primordial, tacit, *epistemic experience*, which is linked to the principle of life in every sentient living being. Suffering is thus the measure of violence. Satyagrahi suffering, however, also gives birth to liberation. "There is no such thing as slow freedom. Freedom is like a birth. Till we are fully free we are slaves. All birth takes place in a moment" (Gandhi 1983, 150).

Therefore, the universality of nonviolence is derived from Truth: only by adhering to Truth can nonviolence claim universality. Any action (committed by Satyagrahi) that undermines such universality has to be immediately taken out; no exceptions are allowed in the craft of Satyagraha. Paradoxically, preferring violence to cowardice serves this purpose, as it brings out courage in the meek and gives birth to the resister who will in due time discover the power of true courage: Satyagraha self-sacrifice.

(d) *Uses of violence.* Gandhi was devoted to confronting the oppressor, not to defeat or repress but to convert him. Conversion of the adversary is key to Gandhian nonviolence. However, when circumstances allowed, Gandhi brilliantly used third-party violence against his adversary to advance his nonviolent resistance. The best example of this is his timing in launching the Quit India movement. In March 1942, the British, stretched to near exhaustion on many fronts during the European war, watched the Japanese advancing to the gates of their easternmost colony. Gandhi's decision to launch Quit India in August 1942 stands in stark contrast to his aforementioned active support for the British in South Africa and in the First World War, when he had declared: "I thought that England's need should not be turned into our opportunity" (Gandhi 2011, 359). Of course, Gandhi would not have known in 1914 that a second European war would engulf the world within a couple of decades. But to read Gandhi backward, had it not been for his recruitment efforts in the First World War, the British probably would not have tried to persuade him and the Indian leadership to support the war effort in the Second World War. As such, Gandhi's earlier endorsement of the first European war inadvertently nourished the soil for the fecund Grand Refusal in the second. Gandhi said, "I do not wish Japan to win the war. I do not want the Axis to win. But I am sure that Britain cannot win unless the Indian people become free" (Gandhi 1983, 296). In fact, he further averred, "whether Britain wins or loses, imperialism has to die" (1983, 303). Declaring that the Japanese had no quarrels with India, Gandhi at this critical moment, in 1942, made what turned out to be his final brilliant move in the campaign for Indian independence: he used Japanese military aggression as leverage to pressure Britain to submit to the Quit India Satyagraha.

Put another way, to strengthen his nonviolent movement, Gandhi converted the high entropy of Japanese military force into low-entropy nonviolence. In this way, the threat of Japanese military violence – which Satyagraha must avoid at all costs – was strategically realigned with Indian nonviolent action to maximize the latter's impact. The British imperial power was thereby coerced to submit to the demands of Indian *Swaraj*. This represented the *coercion* of the adversary, not its *conversion*. Gandhian politics of nonviolence was unimaginable without the coercive force of Satyagraha and the violent force he harnessed and redirected for the purpose of his nonviolence. However saintly his image is today, *Gandhian nonviolence did not claim to be pure*. In fact, if we measure coercion as a manifestation of violence as such, then it is always difficult to separate coercive force (i.e., violence) from nonviolent conversion in the Mahatma's strategic (non-punishing) nonviolence. Thus, *coercion is the common denominator of both violent and nonviolent politics*; the two are not mutually exclusive. Notwithstanding that Satyagraha is based on the principle of *ahimsa* – indeed, perhaps precisely *because* this is so – its degree of coercion is largely a function of the voluntary diversion of harm towards Satyagrahi. This is why I believe Gandhi must be studied and probed mainly under the analytical category "politics of nonviolence" instead of "ethics of nonviolence." His religious ethics always served his politics, not vice versa.

(e) Unwilling casualties of nonviolence. Ahimsa proscribes bringing suffering to others, just as Satyagraha is meant to absorb the strike and contain the injury. But since human action remains incapable of harnessing its consequences (Arendt), nonviolence has the potential to *unintentionally* bring harm to others. The clearest example of this was the plight of British textile workers as a result of the economic boycott of English textiles and the Swadeshi movement. Gandhi's visit to the mill workers at Darwen in East Lancashire in September 1931 represented his recognition of the injury he had inadvertently caused these workers. It is important to read this event phenomenologically and according to our tripartite concept of violence: his nonviolent Swadeshi movement had produced *hubristic* violence – that is, it had imposed the will of the Indian independence movement on a sector of the British working class, making a victim of the latter. In the context of capitalist production, this had in turn imposed *structural* violence on the workers, who suffered as a result of this complex chain of effects originating in Swadeshi action. Gandhi's humble apology to those workers was a remarkable example of taking responsibility for the *violent consequences of one's nonviolent action* and acknowledging that one can never fully control the consequences of one's actions (recall Arendt's point?). In other words, as conflictual action, principled nonviolence may inadvertently produce violent excesses that it cannot control. In this case, the workers were caught and harmed in the crossfire between a liberation movement and a hubristic colonial force. Gandhi's apology did not alleviate the hardships those workers had to endure, but by acknowledging the Other's pain and taking responsibility for it, Gandhi brilliantly *converted* these otherwise passive, injured bystanders (workers) into active supporters of his cause, thereby *transforming their unwilling suffering into conscientious self-sacrifice.* Thanks to the Mahatma's apology – which transposed their suffering onto the realm of British imperialist violence – these English workers joined, as Satyagrahi, the Indian liberation.

Gandhian philosophy of nonviolence persists by *not* algorithmically anchoring nonviolence to some higher pregiven value or pre-existing objective, from which the potential conflict with the adversary arises. It endures by maintaining the tension between nonviolence and violence across the shifting fields of conflict. To a large extent, it is on those fields that adherents to nonviolence take transformative initiatives, thereby staying on top of the political game in which they tease violence out of its hideouts in order to confront it. Nonviolence persists by refusing any conciliation between the antagonistic positions that mark the distinction between violence and nonviolence. This is how Gandhi brilliantly overcame the various algorithms that rationalized nonviolence. For him, nonviolence was not ancillary to some greater good or value or grand project; nonviolence was an end in itself.

A central thesis of this book is that violence and nonviolence are both originally revealed in (individual or collective) human actions and that over time, human actions give rise to institutional procedures bound by the epochal constellations of Truth, which produce and are produced by the structural signatures specific to civilizational zones and their modes of rationality and implementations of violence. In response to the radical negativity of nonviolence, various algorithmic conceptualizations have attempted to determine (the *being* of) (non)violence by conceptually mooring the two interlocked concepts to (presumably) firm and identifiable objectives, grounds, values, or various (Kantian) categorical imperatives. These algorithms are then expected to govern the field of human action by proscribing certain acts and promoting certain others. Tolstoy's mutually exclusive Laws and Butler's recognition of the injurability of the Other provide clear examples. By virtue of his entrance into an already established but by no means settled field of nonviolence (e.g., passive resistance and civil disobedience), Gandhi inherited these algorithms and had to work with and through them in order to arrive at an authentic understanding of nonviolence that was true to his Indian experience. His concept of Truth (God/religion) at first sounded like Tolstoy's axiomatic absolutism: a rigid, normative imposition on action. But as his ideas developed, he transformed Truth from a positively pregiven field of (non-)sanctioned activity into a normative guidepost. He recognized that violence is about controlling the future and securing the desired outcome in the perceivable future through instrumental action – a thesis reminiscent of Arendt's (differences noted).

Gandhi seems to be suggesting that as a negative term, nonviolence cannot entail such a promise: precisely because action's potential outcomes are radically indiscernible, Satyagrahi need to bring the violence-induced injury onto themselves – and each time, they need to summon the more rabidly unhindered forms of violence (e.g., Nazism) so that they can control violence by containing its ripple effects, nullifying its instrumentality, and crippling its effectiveness. And in so doing, they look into Truth as the powerfully vivid standard-bearer in relation to which they reposition themselves. By absorbing the strike of the oppressor, the Satyagrahi deprive violence of its claim to the future (hence the concept of "excess"). Gandhian nonviolence is therefore a struggle for a future devoid of violence: if the Satyagrahi can absorb the violent strike, nothing will be left of violence. The condition of possibility of such a radical engagement is abandoning cowardice in favour of courage, even while knowing that by depriving high-entropy violence of its claim to the future, by stripping it of its instrumentality, the low-entropy action of the Satyagrahi may deny them a future as well. When I give up all passion for hubristic self-impositions, justice requires me to be a humble, trivial being, a being that does not overshadow the beings of others. That is how my humble existence will fully accord with the harmony of the universe, and of life itself, since everything in the universe has its place, and change will only come from my resistance to the oppression that denies this life-enabled order. "Be the change you wish to see in the world," said the Mahatma famously. So my struggle for justice cannot lead to the imposition of yet another social order on the existing order. Precisely because of its "control mechanism," which restricts the "disorder" of violence, nonviolence provides a low-entropy system. From the Gandhian point of view, the sacrifice is well worth it: death is precisely the condition of possibility of the movement, as nonviolence is born out of life itself. The paradox persists, and any attempt at overcoming this paradox must take a detour through various seemingly reassuring but factually ineffectual algorithms.

The Receding Signified

I made a number of observations in the previous passage. Let me pause on their theoretical significance. I referred to the Gandhian transformation of Truth from a positively ascertainable concept to a normative guidepost. Consistent with his engagement with the discourse of nonviolence discussed above, what Gandhi achieves here is to dwell in Truth as a *floating signifier*, a signifier whose meaning is derived from the discourse within which it is evoked and from the modes of articulation available within the general field of discursivity. As a floating signifier, Truth (God/religion) served Gandhi to subvert the structural totality of the already constituted discursive fields – passive resistance and civil disobedience – that we retrospectively call "nonviolence." Gandhi's initial dwelling in, and continued solicitation of, the concepts he had inevitably inherited (Tolstoy's passive resistance and Thoreau's civil disobedience) served him to destabilize the signifier/signified pair within the established discursive fields of nonviolence philosophy. Above all, while Gandhian nonviolence hinges on integral, ethical principles, his politics are by no means "moral," if we understand morality in rigid fashion. As such, his concept of Truth as it emerges is just as idiosyncratic as his politics. Truth as a solid, moral principle is transformed into a normative standard-bearer. But this notion of Truth only reveals itself to one in proportion to one's submission to *ahimsa* and engagement in Satyagraha. The more closely one embraces the life of a Satyagrahi, and the more one suffers while fighting for justice, the more one nears Truth. Stated differently, Truth reveals itself relative to the extent of suffering we are willing to absorb in our struggles for justice, even unto death, and as such, we can never positively arrive at the *essence* of Truth. For Gandhi, nonviolence is never axiomatic or rigid; it is, rather, an unending trial, a process of re-examining one's actions (indeed one's life) as well as the purification of the soul. These observations suggest that there is a need for better concept than "floating signifier" to capture the essence of Gandhi's adherence to Truth, primarily because with respect to Truth we are not moving across discourses as much as we are within a specific discourse. If Truth remains our normative standard-bearer, and if we can never fully embrace Truth except by dying for the cause, then the signified attached to the signifier "Truth" is a "receding signified." I developed the concept of "receding signified" in earlier works and primarily through the study of Iranian literary modernity (Vahabzadeh 2004), which I also applied to my study of social movements (Vahabzadeh 2003, 86–94). Gandhian rearticulation of Truth as an ultimately unattainable horizon (who, as a mortal, can grasp God's essence, after all?) of one's adherence to *ahimsa* allows for the convergence of a multiplicity of personal beliefs, ethical sensibilities, and political leanings within the Indian independence movement, under the banner of a signifier whose signified, by virtue of receding, allows for the incorporation of potentially multiversal conceptions under the signifier "Truth." A receding signified captures the articulation of the diverse experiences of those engaged in a discursive field as actors. It thus enables meaningful concepts attached to the actor's identity. Stated in Rumi's words, "Each befriended me out of her own surmise." Unified action in multiversal India was a requirement for Gandhi's greatest ambition: to liberate India not just from British colonialism but also, more importantly, from the evils of India – Untouchability, industrialism, and submission to liberal democracy. Just as for Fanon, for the Mahatma as well, liberation from colonialism was inconceivable without the colonized's *self-authentication*. Only in confronting an ever more ferocious adversary, as the Satyagrahi nullifies the adversary's hubristic violence by absorbing it, can she search deeper for her inner evils and extract them. This is how for the Mahatma *liberation from oppression and authentication of the Self* were to be achieved through *ahimsa* and unwavering adherence to nonviolent resistance. Self-authentication is an unending process that precedes the liberation of the collective: hence Gandhi's fasts, vegetarianism, ashram dwelling, use of *khadi*, and rejection of earthly possessions. But one cannot truly authenticate oneself unless one stands up to the oppressor, suffers, and liberates the collective. Gandhi was indeed an outstanding revolutionary.

The prodigious discovery by Gandhi of a concept of nonviolence that is confrontational and conflictual but not moral – one that promotes a specific modality of action (Truth-force) through certain *negative ethics* (*a-himsa*: *not* to harm) consistent with the radical negativity of *non*-violence – now helps us understand more clearly one of the main propositions of this book. Recall my previous propositions: (a) nonviolence depends on violence for its manifestation in human action; (b) the condition of possibility of nonviolent action rests in its provoking violence and bringing it out of its hideouts to the confrontational public arena; (c) consequently, violence and nonviolence can no longer be understood as mutually exclusive. This leads me to the next proposition: as a negative term that has no existence outside of its manifestation in resistance/subversive action against injustice, *nonviolence can only appear in the excess of violence*, when violence, confronting the Satyagrahi who is willing to suffer indefinitely and unto death, must exert itself and exceed its instrumental efficiency. The more violence tries to force the Satyagrahi to conform to violence's objectives and submit to or take part in it, the more it is confronted by a *defiant sufferer* whose refusal to submit to the instrumental essence of violence will only lead to exhausting violence. Excess refers to the field of action in which the instrumental rationality of violence is lost; when that happens, instead of being a means to an end, violence becomes vicious, random, and confused, indeed a high-entropy system pushing itself to its eventual collapse in the face of a low-entropy system of nonviolence.

Perhaps not even an ocean of ink will settle the disagreements surrounding the multiversality of Gandhi's thought. I hope this humble interpretation of his life and works will only add to the convolutions, however necessary.

Once More ... Pausing on Liberation

Shining atop the many "world-historical" applications of Gandhian nonviolence stands the American Civil Rights Movement of the 1960s (and later) led by Martin Luther King Jr. King's Christian message is akin to Gandhi's eclectic philosophy; King's vision and movement occupy a prominent place in the history of nonviolent activism in terms of his unwavering adherence to the principles of nonviolent resistance and in the strategies and tactics the civil rights movement adopted. That movement was not revolutionary in the Gandhian sense: it did not intend to liberate America from outer imperialism and inner colonialism in the manner that informed the Black Panthers (with their opposing methods). Spatial limitations prevent details, but King's nonviolence was nonetheless far less rigid than often acknowledged. Also belonging to the history of Gandhian nonviolence is the movement led by Aung San Suu Kyi and her National League for Democracy (NLD), which aimed to democratize politics in Myanmar. Suu Kyi, having emerged in 2010 from her fifteen-year house arrest, led the NLD to electoral victory in November 2015 in Myanmar's first free election in twenty-five years, and her party's rule was not without controversy, in particular as it relates to the ongoing genocide and forced displacement of the country's Muslim Rohingya minority. These cases are meant to register the "universal" applicability of Gandhian nonviolence but not its universal duplicability. What distinguishes Gandhi's movement from most movements fashioned after him is the convergence of liberation and authentication.

As discussed in the Introduction, the Iranian Revolution of the 1979 provides a historic case of nonviolent revolution. The revolutionary action – may I say, instinctively – turned out to be fairly Gandhian, as it engaged in nonviolent self-sacrifice and called for the emergence of a new spiritual nation unencumbered by the plagues of materialism and "westoxification" (*gharbzadegi*). However, the Shiʻi post-revolutionary ideology from whose universe of tropes the revolution, despite the diversity of actors, eventually built its predominant image was anything but Gandhian. From January 1978 to February 1979, protesters poured into the streets, shouted for justice and change, and were crushed, killed, and arrested by the military, only to re-emerge in another round of protests, each time in greater numbers and in more and more cities and

towns. They gave long-stem carnations to soldiers, calling them "our military brothers," while receiving bullets and batons. But the key slogan of
the Revolution, taken from the Shi'i tradition of martyrdom, prevailed:
"Blood is victorious over the Sword." The peaceful transition of power
was in the final stages of being brokered when a turn of events sealed
the fate of the Shah's regime: an air force personnel mutiny and a then
leftist-led armed revolt launched a two-day armed popular uprising. Neither this short-lived armed uprising nor the brutal, intolerant, repressive,
and unspiritual regime that arose from the revolution can conceal the
fact that the 1979 Revolution was one of the greatest popular nonviolent
movements of the twentieth century. The revolution combined Gandhi's
nonviolence with Fanon's liberation by targeting, *contra* Gandhi, the
state. The revolution failed in the end to offer a new, liberated nation
that adhered to exalted values; nonetheless it showed how collective
action is possible. And an entirely new, post-revolutionary generation
would try out the nonviolence of their parents, *sans* Fanon, in those critical days between the summer of 2009 and the winter of 2010.

Reading Gandhi Backwards

To an untrained gaze, certain ethics always *precede* nonviolence. This is
partly due to the historic emergence of the concept in the West through
Christian pacifism. Reading about how Gandhi dwelt in the principles
of *ahimsa, anasakti,* and vegetarianism (adopted from Buddhism and
Jainism) in order to arrive at the concept of Satyagraha certainly leaves
this impression. Phenomenologically, though, the ethics of nonviolence
is not the condition of possibility of nonviolent action but its outcome,
although the contrary *seems* to be the case, as mentioned, because ethics always prescribes certain modalities of action and proscribes certain
others. A phenomenologically enabled "backward reading" overcomes
this commonly held view, which presupposes principles as *a priori* of
action. Only the *outcome* of action can be measured as ethical or unethical, whereas action itself, *stricto sensu*, remains *a*-ethical. Stated differently, the outcome of action relates to the tacit or explicit epistemological criteria under ethics, thereby enabling a comprehension of
action as ethical or unethical. Gandhi's concept of Truth and unwavering adherence to life becomes an ethical guidepost dissimilar to *a
priori* principles. Once we understand this, the many "inconsistencies"
in the Mahatma's nonviolence appear differently. Phenomenological
"backward reading," as a hermeneutical strategy, enables an approach

that neither justifies nor shuns the "inconsistencies" in Gandhi's experiments. Had ethical principles grounded his nonviolence, Gandhi
would simply have preached nonviolence to his followers, in the manner of Tolstoy of yesteryear or the Dalai Lama today. He would not have
incited violence in order to confront and nullify it, nor would he have
had to resort to force – Truth-force – to resist violence or to redirect
(Japanese) external violence against (British) colonial violence. The
ethics of nonviolence, I hope I have shown, were a *guidepost* for Gandhi,
the outcome of the suffering that defined Satyagraha: a principle only
thus persisting and self-validating. Phenomenology allows these "inconsistencies" – these apparent contradictions – to cohere to a certain
Gestalt, to an overall course of action that in India culminated in the
country's independence. Gandhi shows us that the *politics of nonviolence*
requires careful navigation through "forces of circumstance" (Arendt)
and possibilities for acting (Schürmann), as well as ceaseless negotiations over the often-incompatible, even contradictory, acts afforded
by ethics in the context of imposed political exigencies. That is why
I focused in this chapter about the "politics of nonviolence" solely on
Gandhi, even though others (such as Sharp) would also fall within
"politics." Unlike Sharp's, Gandhi's politics do not invite a calculative
and utilitarian approach based on reified and supposedly universal values (democracy). Gandhian navigation through the forces that ground
us and the possibilities that release us renders his theory *political par
excellence* in that he aims at nothing less than civilizational refoundation. The politics of nonviolence is an *irreducibly generative politics*, oriented towards founding politics anew. One cannot understand Gandhi
and his "inconsistencies" without paying close heed to his perpetual
attempts to yank violence from its hideouts and test his transformative
nonviolence against it until a new, liberated nation is born out of this
struggle. That is the only way we can expose, challenge, and convert
violence. Gandhi asserted time and again that nonviolence was actually the supreme, ethical principle of life, although life always emerges
through pain and suffering (humanity's signs of violence). Because of
this, I cannot claim that the Gandhian approach is compatible with my
proposed hypothesis of the "ontological primacy of violence." Even so,
I can argue that Gandhi's philosophy is energized by an unmistakable
"phenomenological attitude," best revealed in this endless search for
ever-new manifestations of violence, due to the "protean quality" of
violence (Bernstein, 2013, 177) that contains, steers, and shapes us in
every single aspect of our lives, from food to politics.

Reading Gandhi as the supreme architect of nonviolence affords us a number of key observations consistent with the arguments in this book. Gandhi shows how political nonviolence can only emerge as the excess of violence. That is why he was always seeking out the more formidable and extreme forms of violence. He did not believe in Kantian "radical evil." Nonviolence incites and exposes violence in order to convert it, and thus the former *needs* the latter to exert itself with full force against the Satyagrahi. The more violent the adversary, the more transformative our Satyagraha. The more excessive the violence, the more universal the reach and the more wide-ranging the applicability of nonviolence. Viewed from my phenomenological gaze and from a broader perspective, Gandhian thinking paves the way for the concluding hypothesis of this book (see the next, concluding chapter).

Allowing myself to use analytical terms, I believe Gandhi held a notion similar to mine: that *violence and nonviolence are only intelligible within a (social) systemic containment.* This proposition will have significant implications for our conclusions. It is within a *contained* (totalizing but not never total) social system that one can exercise force that achieves results. Recall that Arendt distinguished violence by its hallmark instrumentality. Because of the non-totality, openness, integrity, and generative power of life (captured in the broader meaning of the term *ahimsa*), a contained social system can never be entirely totalized. Thus, there can neither be fully assimilating and homogenizing violence nor a violence that ends all violence. If we agree with my first proposition (that life is open but it is contained by systems), then we can fully appreciate the source of Gandhi's hope that nonviolence will prevail. This invites my second proposition: *violence is bound by the (civilizational) ecology of a contained social system.* In exerting its energy and depleting its resources, high-entropy violence produces an excess, a field of "wasted" violent energy that does not contribute to violence's totalizing reach or to its efficacy or instrumentality. Low-entropy nonviolence resides in this "wasteland" of violence – a field from which ever-renewable life grows – and as such, it constitutes the violent system's "disorder." To suppress this disorder, violence needs to exert its energy and diminish its non-renewable resources even further. Stated differently, in order to maintain order and reassert itself, violence must exceed its own limits, reshape itself into a field for which it was not originally intended or within which it loses its instrumentality. In other words, a contained social system is never fully totalized, yet violence aims at totalizing it by expanding (as in colonialism) because of its desperate need – given that it is high-entropy – for resources and energy.

At some point, once all non-renewable energy and resources within the existing social-civilizational system are depleted, violence withers away. Gandhian Satyagraha is an attempt to accelerate the rate at which violence depletes itself. Violence falls prey to its own "logic of excess" (an antinomy indeed!) acting as its own gravedigger in the hands of nonviolence. And this is how nonviolence *detotalizes* violence, depriving it of its potentially global reach. As violence destroys, regulates, and/or oppresses life, nonviolence absorbs it through selfless acts of voluntary suffering, rendering violence nothing.

In this regard, Satyagrahi suffering represents the movement of those without rights, the banned and the bandits. *Contra* Agamben's sacrificial bare life, the self-sacrificial Satyagrahi is the potential author of (individual and collective) self-authentication, one who confronts violence with mere physical (animal) body, the absorbent of all pain. Gandhi, we saw, recommended Satyagraha to the Jews in 1938. In envisioning the suffering and self-sacrifice involved in Satyagraha, Gandhi assumes that the movement will continue even if every activist is willing to die. He does not consider that the movement may perish under ruthless, genocidal machinery. Smaller peoples certainly do not have the luxury of overwhelming numbers (e.g., India). Historically, small and even nationwide movements have been decimated by systematic massacres. One is immediately reminded of the Indonesian genocide of 1965–66 – a purging of communists that reportedly claimed one million lives. So it is possible that nonviolent movements against brutal regimes will die out, leaving no legacy. But such calculations are alien to Gandhian philosophy. Even so, Gandhi believes that regardless of its scale and machinery, violence is structurally limited in its reach, and that in exerting itself it only exhausts itself. By inciting violence, Satyagraha intends to take it to its eventual demise.

In the context of dominant revolutionary violence – from Sorel to Fanon – Gandhi was trying to build a road to emancipation – just like Sorel and Fanon – without crossing the hitherto accepted fields of violence. *He connected, in thought and praxis, nonviolence to emancipation.* Possibly he was the first ever to do so. This is a great discovery: the Mahatma brought violence on himself by refusing to submit to the "force of circumstance" from which violence or counter-violence (neither of which was unacceptable to him) so often emanated; he embraced suffering and self-sacrifice as a means to end the cycle of violence. He did not submit to the dictates of situations: faced with totally adverse circumstances, he suspended his movement instead of allowing it to slip into (counter-)violence, even though such violence was preferable to submissive cowardice. For Gandhi, to justify violence by stating that it was "imposed" was the same as refusing to accept full responsibility for one's actions. Yet when the force of circumstance could work in favour of the movement (which is not the same as saying the circumstance was "favourable"), he was willing to engage with violence not only through the nonviolence of Truth-force but also by redirecting external violence or forces of circumstance against colonial violence.

In understanding Gandhi as a theorist *and* practitioner of liberation and emancipation, we arrive at a conception of liberation akin to Fanon's. Note that Fanon targeted the colonial state directly whereas Gandhi never did. This is a fundamental difference between them. But recall how Fanon understood the nonviolent transition of Algerian society through the violent war of liberation. Gandhi's *ahimsa* and Truth-oriented practice aimed at the birth of a new nation through structural changes – changes that started from the soul and that held the key to a transformative power that expressed itself from the inside out. By transforming the individual through the purifying act of self-sacrifice, Gandhian emancipatory theory forces the structures against which nonviolent resistance is launched through a process of transformation as well. His emancipatory theory and practice, therefore, is based on *transformative nonviolence* – through *double conversion* – and holds that the change in the Self – specifically, *self-authentication* – is the watershed down which flow transformative changes in violent relations and structures. To put the idea in the Mahatma's words, "Be the change you wish to see in the world."

As noted earlier, Gandhi's thought suspends the rigid opposition of violence and nonviolence. *Ahimsa* sustains life as such, yet we continue living in a world strongly permeated by violence, from the way we eat to the way we exploit nature, treat one another, order our economy, organize politics, and uphold values (especially in overvaluing human life). Gandhian philosophy, I surmise, relies on the *ontological dependency of nonviolence on violence through our action*, above all by confronting powers-that-be through voluntary suffering. The most nonviolent act of suffering thus reveals its two aspects. On the one hand, suffering allows us to challenge the tripartite phenomenalization of violence – hubristic (individual, personal, familial), institutional (colonial, political, familial), and structural (class, caste). On the other hand, suffering allows excesses of violence to impact the Satyagrahi in such a way that he can absorb that violence and prevent it from spreading further, thus ending the cycle of violence. This suggests that there are both *avoidable sufferings* revealed through social injustices, sufferings that stand as objects to rectify (such as social inequality and systemic and cultural discrimination), and *unavoidable sufferings*, which manifest themselves through acts of resistance and emancipation (when the resister is punished and suppressed). Only the second modality of suffering – sufferings one voluntarily brings on oneself – qualifies for a means of liberation, as it allows for self-authentication; by challenging oppression and injustice, we purify our souls. "Resister" suffering, then, is where violence and nonviolence encounter each other. *For the uncompromisingly nonviolent suffering that ends all suffering, violence is the condition of possibility.*

Conclusion:
Not Opposites, Concentric!

There is always a world already interpreted, already organized in its basic relations, into which experience steps as something new, upsetting what has led our expectations and undergoing reorganization itself in the upheaval ... Only the support of familiar and common understanding makes possible the venture into the alien, the lifting up of something out of the alien, and thus the broadening and enrichment of our own experience of the world.

Gadamer, *Philosophical Hermeneutics* (1976, 15)

This little man is at home in distorted life; he will disappear with the coming of the Messiah, of whom a great rabbi once said that he did not wish to change the world by force, but would only make a slight adjustment to it.

Benjamin, "Franz Kafka" (1968, 134)

In chemistry, a "catalyst" refers to a substance that spurs or enhances the rate of a chemical reaction between other elements without itself undergoing permanent chemical change. My proposed radical phenomenology of (non)violence and its methods, as deployed in this book, resemble a catalyst in relation to the two concepts of violence and nonviolence that have traditionally been posed as mutually exclusive due to the substantiations and algorithms attached to each. Algorithms render intelligible what would otherwise not be – in our case, the radically privative in *non*violence. The phenomenological method is informed by a certain attitude, not an ideological lens. As a *method*, the phenomenological gaze is always diverted "towards the things themselves," and thus from the outset it offers no fundamental predicates of its own. It yields nothing that is not already in the "thing itself"; the theoretical postulates of phenomenology are simply gifts delivered to the gaze through the epochal modalities of revealing(s) of the phenomenon in question. In other words, phenomenology is not intent on providing proof: it reveals that which has already revealed itself to attentive and inattentive gazes alike. Seen as such, the phenomenological method is congruent with the thesis of this book and with my particular advocacy of nonviolence. It allows a critical–projective gaze into possible common futures. As such, phenomenology enables, among other things, a "cultural critique" – in this case a critique of the uncritical distinctions between violence and nonviolence, even by critical thinkers! Because it adds nothing to the world, phenomenology allows new propositions to come to the fore and reveal their potentials, as does a catalyst in a chemical reaction. These propositions already exist in a state of having potential for self-realization, but they have been buried under age-old sediments of common notions, tacit knowledge, epistemic hegemonies, and value-laden prejudices. The conceptual product of phenomenology is thus no more than what is already there but hidden from our gaze – the possibilities concealed by actuality and by the common sense attached to it. This is how phenomenology allows my new and enhanced conceptual propositions regarding violence and nonviolence to shine forth without being hindered by theoretical expectations, teleological norms, and moral proscriptions – all of which constitute algorithmic equations – and notably, without impacting the phenomenological gaze itself (just like the catalyst!). This latter characteristic allows phenomenology to retain its "critical" stance – critical in the sense of not submitting to matter-of-fact, tacit, or accepted knowledge. In this study, the phenomenological approach showed me how every gesture towards revolutionary violence contains nonviolence; it also allowed me to detach nonviolence from metaphysical ultimacies – political interests and moral values in their various alignments – that hold on the concept in a puritan fashion.

Let us borrow further metaphors from chemistry. Radical phenomenology has affinities with the alchemists' dictum *solve et coagula,* "resolve and coagulate" – that is the attitude of the phenomenologist as well (Schmidt 1998; Schürmann 2003, 278–83). I aimed at resolving and dismantling the operational, epistemic, and algorithmic *conceptual* equivalences in the works of both defenders of emancipatory violence and the diverse (strategic, ethical, moral, utilitarian, political) advocates of nonviolence. This move led to conceptual coagulations by allowing the key concepts across different approaches to be rearranged in terms that are *not* enabled by such algorithms. Accordingly, in the process of phenomenological gazing at (non)violence, we achieve something that my borrowed metaphors from chemistry cannot accommodate: in an age in which we can no longer (deductively) fasten our knowledge onto seemingly unshakeable foundations, in these times of Being's diminishment leading to *il pensiero debole* (Vattimo) and "thinking without banisters" (Arendt), we learn to act in entirely new ways because we are now granted a fresh and enlivening *actable* knowledge, not in the old, metaphysical sense of *theōria* preceding *praxis* but rather in the sense that *acting and thinking become one*.

The knowledge component is key here. As mentioned, just like a catalyst, a radical phenomenology of (non)violence, through its deconstructions and interpretations, can give the reader nothing other than what has already been contained within the theoretical postulates and conceptual figurations that have been closely read and interpreted in this book. Just like the alchemist, the radical phenomenologist (hopes to) offer(s) the new and the novel by allowing the existing components (concepts, propositions, premises) of these theories to be fundamentally rearranged, thereby creating a new understanding and achieving a certain "discovery" of the potentials of these theories – potentials that had been hidden from these theorists (akin to Husserlian *Urstiftung*) behind their fundamental presuppositions. Equally to the dismay of puritanical defenders of nonviolence, on the one hand, and zealous advocates of the sacred, revolutionary violence, on the other, my submitting the idea of abolishing the epistemologically enabled Manichaean, oppositional identity of violence and nonviolence can only be understood as the outcome of my phenomenological intervention. A phenomenology of (non)violence enables an epistemology that does away with the tacit knowledge rooted in the "natural attitude," as matter-of-fact, and with the garden-variety axiomatic algorithms intended to sort out the confusions and challenges that the very concept(s) of (non)violence pose(s) for thought.

In relation to our study of (non)violence, the "thing in itself" is *action*. To borrow a term from Ian Angus (2000), the "primal scene" of (non)violence is action. Whether a determination of structural violence, a procedural activity of institutional violence, or a manifestation of hubristic violence (these are not mutually exclusive), it is acting alone that brings out possibilities for both violent and nonviolent actions. It is solely in the aftermath of action – an aftermath received by a hegemonic–epistemic community and through our prejudices as "deep common accord" (Gadamer 1976, 7) – that we epistemologically assign the act to the tacit or explicit but always changing *a priori* categories (from *katégorein*, "to accuse" – that is, to "make explicit") of violent and nonviolent. *Action acts having humans as its enactors and executors*, as the physical embodiments of the act. The outcome of action is then received, assessed, and acknowledged in terms of existing and sanctioned (and overlapping) notional, conceptual, and legal definitions of violence or nonviolence. Thus, strictly speaking, as potential categories of human action, *violence and nonviolence are primarily facts of knowledge* and are thereby linked to the principles of intelligibility and doability of an epoch revealed through structural, historical, and ontic determinations. "Epochal principles are always ontic givens" (Schürmann 1990, 81). This is precisely why we should acknowledge and embrace, with Richard Bernstein, the *protean character of violence*. Violence changes its shape because our changing sensibilities lead to the discovery of new manifestations of violence hitherto concealed to us because of our tacit acceptance of the normal and the necessary, matters of fact and matters of course. As our epochs change, as the hegemonic universals governing an epoch change, so do the matters of fact and the values that are in the air we breathe. Thus the "nature" of violence also changes in our views. What was valued as dutiful parents' disciplining of a child in yesteryear becomes child abuse today; nonconsensual marital sex is now legally codified as rape; child labour becomes punishable by law; public expressions of prejudices potentially become discriminatory liabilities and hate crimes; irresponsible or objectionable treatment of captive non-human sentient species (euphemistically called "pets") legally constitute cruelty against animals; and in addition to sexism, colonialism, and homophobia, today ageism, ableism, and speciesism are widely contested by emerging publics, foreshadowing new prejudices ("deep common accords") that will reveal themselves to us down the road from today's political correctness. In all of these examples, the *hubristic act* remains "the same," but the outcome of the act has shifted *epistemologically* from the category of the tacitly and morally acceptable – thus implicitly "nonviolent" – to the opposite category of unacceptable and potentially "violent," thereby punishable by law. The shift in the epochal modes of pregivenness "disallows" – culturally, socially, and/or legally, but always *collectively* (though not universally) – certain acts. The realm of enactment of violence, interestingly, expands with the spreading notions of what constitutes violence. It becomes harder and harder to live nonviolently when one considers one's (inadvertent) complicity in the staggering exploitation (and impoverishment) of fellow humans (through the products we purchase), the viciously ruthless treatment of sentient beings (through the food we consume), the massive destruction of natural habitats and resources (through the many webs that link us to products, warm our homes, fuel our engines, make our health care possible, and even pay our age old pensions). To a phenomenological gaze, these ontic conditions and our changing sensibilities towards them point to our need to have (i.e., in this book) the hypothesis of the ontological primacy of violence as a conceptual and epistemological guidepost. To be sure, *the ontological primacy of violence is not a hypothesis to be tested in a positivist manner*. Naturally, only a historical study of the origins of concepts of violence and nonviolence (a completely different study indeed) would substantiate my proposed hypothesis and even (unnecessarily!) gesture towards solid, positivist findings. But this book's task and approach have been different. My guiding hypothesis is certainly an abstract one, but it enables the *hermeneutics* of the facticity of life in our technological era in which, a là Heidegger, everything, humans included, remains "standing-reserve." The hypothesis has provided me with a standpoint from which to launch my conceptual phenomenology, and I will have to conclude my conceptual excursions in the same manner.

In the end, I think, I can claim that although the two volatile elements of violence and nonviolence have been methodically kept in separate containers in the sterilized chemistry labs of moral axioms and utilitarian algorithms, they have never in fact been apart. This phenomenological alchemist knows that the two elements remain *indistinct* from each other. The radical negativity of *non*-violence, its dependence on violence, and violence's ontological primacy all point in the same direction. To echo Gadamer in the epigraph to this chapter, I am indebted to all traditions of nonviolence – Christian, Eastern, humanist, moral, utilitarian, political – for creating a common notion, for generating a tradition that envisioned the possibility of nonviolence (albeit algorithmically), a tradition that provides me with the context for this study and with the ability to deconstruct the opposition between violence and nonviolence and phenomenologically reduce the distinction to its *Urstiftung*, to its originary moment and primal scene, in human action. Living in this age of drone warfare, state-sanctioned mass murder, colonial and denizen appropriation (often called development), and ecological genocide, I acknowledge my debt to the very tradition that I deconstruct and disavow for having introduced to our common understanding the otherwise "alien" concept of nonviolence, and for thereby broadening and enriching our experience of possibilities for acting and thinking.

I now need to further explore the consequences of this study.

Not Opposites, Concentric!

Nonviolence is our *koiné*, generally speaking, the common idiom of our age, and a sort of standard-bearer of collective action in our post-1960s era, an age being strangled by the oppression and exploitation of humans and non-humans alike that have sadly become normalized. In light of the rampant and abhorrent violence that surrounds, animates, and consumes us, citizens often choose to refrain from inflicting violence on their abusers. When they do, the counter-violence to which Schür-mann refers as an inadvertent reproduction of institutional (and other) violence is put out of operation ... for the time being. So in every non-violent act, regardless of its intentions and rationalizations, there is the potential for disrupting the cycle of violence. Gandhi must be credited for having introduced the (political) *concept* of nonviolence – and I stress "concept," not received or religiously sanctioned notions – to the twentieth century, although related notions (non-resistance, pacifism, non-cooperation, civil disobedience) long pre-existed "nonviolence," some as common notions, others as more developed concepts.

Phenomenology seeks to unearth that which is concealed through that which is revealed. The "ontological primacy of violence," already established by Heidegger and post-Heideggerian philosophers, grants me that which is revealed, a framework that allows me to bring together a diversity of approaches to violence and nonviolence and subject them equally to phenomenological probing. But this hypothesis also enables another hypothesis that has been concealed by it. In fact, my proposed "hypothesis of ontological primacy of violence" in conjunction with the "radical negativity of nonviolence," and in addition to my *interpretation* of Gandhian Satyagraha that led to the idea of "nonviolence's dependence on violence," should by now have clarified that *nonviolence cannot have an existence of its own.* This is why understanding violence and nonviolence in oppositional or mutually exclusive terms is untenable. Even their conceptual distinctiveness is often problematic. The emancipatory impulse in human action shows that neither violence nor nonviolence can be theorized as a pure concept. As such, *I propose that the relationship between violence and nonviolence is best understood as concentric.* The reader may be interested in knowing that the idea of concentricity did not dawn on me until I was writing the last chapter of this book. The idea literally *phenom-enalized* itself. In any case, concentricity renders (non)violence *indivisible.* Arising from action, *the conditions of possibility of nonviolence are always already the condition of possibility of violence. Stated differently, the conditions of possibility of violence and nonviolence are at the same time the conditions of impossibility of them both.* The concentric conception of (non)violence also clarifies why nonviolence is the *excess* of violence (see chapter 4): concentricity suggests that violence and nonviolence arise from a shared field of action, occupying changing, even alternating, radiuses and circumfer- ences and covering over, permeating, and exchanging different regions of presence, at one time or another, in relation to each other (as this book's front cover visualizes it, however abstractly).

Concentricity, moreover, achieves the dereification of the two con- cepts. Violence and nonviolence are no longer grasped outside of my experience, as seemingly *a priori*, objectified, freestanding concepts detached from the socialized relations and social constructions of real- ity through which they first emerged. Concentric propositional relations between violence and nonviolence reveal that the two concepts can only be understood within my ontic and particular experience precisely at the moment when the possibility of partaking in liberatory action appears within my reach, at the moment when it is possible for me to stand, however transiently, outside the realm of the experiential hegemony that imparts to me an idea of freedom. Liberation as the marker of action (as opposed to activity or agency) offers me a certain open horizon, thanks to the singularization-to-come in whose prospect I can deconstruct (and destroy) my governing biopolitical regimes and their concomitant regimes of knowledge. My gateway to nonviolence is *liberation* in that it negates the established terms of universals. At this moment, *when I par- take in liberatory action, I am taken back through my action to the primal scene where the distinction between violence and nonviolence – an epistemic–epochal construct – has yet to emerge (from my act).* Concentricity disturbs the (popu- larly) acclaimed distinctness of violence and nonviolence.

Every primordial act, every original decision, every claim to life certainly contains the seeds of violence within it, and as these seeds germinate and grow, as they maximize and appropriate, they dictate the laws governing the geometry of violence within their (expanding) field of reach. But that originary violence also grants the possibility of singularizing and expro- priating nonviolent resistance to these laws. Just like concentric geomet- ric shapes, violence and nonviolence can always be traced back to a single original (central) act, a primordial act, an act at variance with itself. As mentioned in the introduction and shown through my close readings, nonviolence arises as a possibility in the shadow of violence's far-reaching vigour. What they share, however, is their attempts to exclude the other from the always already *shared* and *contested* field of action.

Chapter 1 aimed to show, among other things, how seemingly age-less structural violence contains hubristic and institutional modalities of violence. Yet since every structural violence must also have arisen from a humble, originary act in time immemorial, our view today must always be diverted towards hubristic violence from which the potential primordial violence of future maximized and hegemonized structural or institutional violence may arise. Stated differently, approaching hubristic violence as potential primordial violence is important because of the connection of hubris with acting, before an action is maximized, before it is institutionalized or ritualized into a structure.

With the concentric concept of (non)violence a new mode of knowledge – indeed an epistemic shift – appears apropos the further maximization of violence in its tripartite manifestations. Let us recall that about 160 years ago in the United States most European settlers (if they so chose) could legally own slaves of African origin before slavery became a crime (although discrimination did not end there). A century ago, physical punishment of children was viewed as necessary discipline; today it constitutes child abuse punishable by law. Half a century ago, the species living on this earth appeared by and large as soulless resources to be extracted to extinction, while today there is increasing awareness that such practices are acts of ruthless violence committed against sentient and vegetal beings. Beyond any doubt, these moments indicate epistemic and epistemological shifts. Thanks to Michel Foucault's splendid works, today I can trace violence in the disciplinary practices within schools and hospitals. These shifts have enabled us to recognize violence in the otherwise or hitherto matter-of-course practices of child labour, verbal abuse, spousal rape, and cruelty against animals. The sphere of violence expands due to our epistemological shifts that in the current epochal reach (Heidegger's technological Enframing in the context of global capitalism) lead us to what Schürmann calls "arch-violence" (2003, 9). Concentricity also suggests that neither violence nor nonviolence can be thought outside of relations of power. This is the essential lesson of Gandhi. Now it must be clear why I required the hypothesis of "ontological primacy of violence" as my conceptual springboard: as violence's concentric outer ring, as its expanding circumferential perimeter, nonviolence arises from the excess of violence: nonviolent resistance against violence becomes possible as violence maximizes its reach, for in so doing, it is gradually annulled through its own implementation, allowing itself to be spread so thin that it cannot recover from its necessary high-entropy system. *High entropy is the enabler of violence as well as that which depletes it.*

The high-entropy ontological centre called violence produces the excess from which arises low-entropy nonviolence as a trace, residue, memory, and expanding container of violence. As violence expends itself, low-entropy nonviolence remains vital and linked to life. In response to its own weakening, violence changes its shape, permeating new fields, tapping into new resources for its vitality. Bernstein referred to this as violence's *protean* character; Galtung called it violence's cross-breeding. At the same time, as nonviolence expands it provides new knowledge about the structures, institutions, and hubristic acts of violence. Such an epistemology is not extracted from Reason; its pillar rests on practical knowledge of our age and within our action.

I hope it is not presumptuous to state that the above, including my "ontological concentricity of (nonviolence)" constitutes an important conceptual proposition.

I owe this "discovery" to the conceptual phenomenological deconstruction that has taken us back to the *primal scenes* of distinctions between violence and nonviolence and that has shamelessly exposed their age-old, hidden contradictions. The word "discovery" denotes that I have not invented anything new. To borrow terms from Husserl, I simply have unearthed, so as to reactivate, concentricity from underneath thick historical layers of Manichaean sediment. Concentricity has always already existed, but it has been obscured from our view due to our positivist epistemic regimes (often in radical guises). Every time I make an effort to set the two concepts apart, I am forced to revisit the primal scene, but the insecure metaphysician in me – the powerful and mysterious inner drive that anchors my conceptual anxieties to seemingly unshakeable grounds and reified concepts – forces me to simply ignore the unsettling experience of conjoined (non)violence. My tacit, inner metaphysician therefore reassures me that I am the bearer of exalted universal values. For that transient moment, I shed my fear of death. I am welcomed by my colleagues to one school of metaphysical security or another, my analytical sociology becomes descriptive sociography (despite my denial!), and I now have a erudite community I can present my ideas to, colleagues who respect me, highly regarded peer reviewed journals I can publish in, and a career of repeating others' ideas after applying personalized touches. The rewards are handsome. So I forget I am abandoning an exciting but perilous life of the mind with nimble motility in favour of garnering a life of sedentary security, thanks to the discipline's expectations.

In my case, though, radical phenomenology reappears as the ice-cold shattering of such lukewarm dreams. With the once-solid ground now quaking under my feet, I feel myself sliding gently back into the abyss.

Violence in Our Technological Age

Given that this work has been inspired by Schürmann and his "backward" reading of Heidegger, I must offer some final words about my use of the term "excess" in phenomenological terms. The term "excess" (*Übermaß*) in later Heidegger refers to the "excess of presence" in the age of technology. "*But where danger is, grows / The saving power also,*" Heidegger famously quotes Hölderlin (Heidegger 1977, 28; emphasis in original). In other words, the "reduction" of the world to "standing-reserve" – of beings to resources – involves an excess, thanks to *Ereignis* (Event of Appropriation, enowning), that allows the "saving power" to grow (see Heidegger 2012, xii–xiii). We live in an age in which the depletion of Being (Vattimo), as the accomplishment of metaphysics through technological Enframing, has taken the form of digitization. As early as 1938, Heidegger showed how the specifically modern, scientific, mathematized, and mechanistic "world picture" (*Weltbild*) offers a form of representation (duplicate) of the world such that the world is reduced to a picture (Heidegger 1977, 129). What is alarming is that this "picture of the world" substitutes for the worldview (*Weltanschauung*) of humans, a view that can only arise from humans' lived experiences. As a result, it "seems as though man everywhere and always encounters only himself" (1977, 27). In having become a resource, humans see in the picture of the world only themselves, blithely going down with the depletion of Being. It is in the context of *technology's global reach* – evidenced by the capitalist onslaught – that I can apply a Heideggerian phenomenology of epoch (which Heidegger reserved exclusively for the West) to diverse cultures and traditions. In our age, digitization has enabled the infinite duplication of beings and the endless substitution of worlds. The abstraction of the corporeal has reduced concrete worldviews to only those aspects that can be represented digitally through binary platforms. Digital representation has led to the replacement of worldviews – which are by definition concrete and linked to personal perspectives and experiences – by streaming images, and it prevents humans from acting based on their shared lifeworld experiences, since I can only resist by virtue of this *body* that is capable of striking back, occupying space, and acting in concert. Now that wealth has become abstract

and transactions virtually invisible, it is becoming impossible to fathom
the amount of wealth concentrated in the hands of the few. Poverty is
now "experienced" through documentaries; deprived of the means to
represent themselves, those who actually suffer from dispossession only
appear in the "picture" provided by the corporate media that wrap these
images in various ideological discourses. These cases attest to the calculative–
digital reduction of the world to that which is "manageable."

Here the digital depletion of Being transforms the actor into a hegemonized subject or loyal agent of the world picture. Collective action
can now only be endured through "social movement organizations"
(SMOs); humanitarian aid, human rights, and responses to crises and
poverty have been NGOized. These institutions attract and recruit actors
and activists for their own technological–utilitarian ends – ends that in
the final analysis are more about preserving the status quo than reaching out for the "saving power." But even when there is a genuine interest in changing the world, "slacktivism" strongly impacts activism: activists hook up to their social media platforms, encouraged to participate
digitally and virtually in causes by posting and reposting their social and
political preferences rather than actually getting involved in the dirty
and dangerous work of organization. And everyone knows that their IP
addresses are unrelentingly under surveillance (even as they seek ano-
nymity by means of their commercial VPNs). Yet the tendency is to prefer
surveillance, in the course of which absent participation (a paradox, I
know!) is subjected to the forms of activism that involve bodily presence
that exposes individuals to potential harm, arrest, trial, or other threats
of violence (for which our states use the shorthand "law enforcement").
This is a sad fact that African American protesters in the United States
know all too well. Social networks provide fantastic, unparalleled means
for disseminating ideas, but they also replace the lived experience of
activism and the *Weltanschauung* attached to it with digital *Weltbild*.

Increasingly, the legally enacted language of "human rights" is being
substituted for the originary rights of rightless humans (and non-humans)
to fight back. We live in an age in which human life is viewed through a
certain "economy of presence" that hinges on the concept of rights and
the legal enactments of them. This new regime of human rights is the
ontic manifestation of the ontological conditions of our time in that the
concept of rights contains within itself an attempt to reduce – through
protective measures – hubristic, violent harm brought upon humans by
humans. The Universal Declaration of Human Rights (1948) captures
one such attempt. But this mode of revealing that allows nonviolence

to emerge in terms of protection of inalienable, universal human rights also conceals the legal reduction of plurality of life to those aspects that can be subject to legal protection. This new regime of human rights has largely hegemonized the anarchic actors, turning them into the subjects of state protection by transforming their visions and struggles into legal battles for the expansion or restriction of rights. The state – one of the most violent institutions on earth – emerges as the exclusive, privileged grantor of rights that grants its protection only to those who fall within the technological–administrative categories of its calculative and teleological management strategies and institutional regulations (Vahabzadeh 2003, 103–40). The Kafkaesque reduction of humans to resources is made clear through this liberal-democratic conception of rights: the image of hegemonized humans being fed as docile, rights-bearing subjects into the machinery of state that provides them with a "world" through digitized realities evokes the motion picture trilogy *The Matrix*. Clearly, the mode of disclosure (*alethēia*) in the age of technicity's reach enables this hegemonic subject to thrive while concealing (*lēthē*) the genuine actor's path-breaking experiments within the epistemic–hegemonic frame of the age.

In this context, genuine and innovative collective actions such as the Zapatista liberated zone in Chiapas, Mexico, the communist village of Marinaleda, Spain, Rojava democratic confederalism in northern Syria, and the Occupy Wall Street movement have been severely marginalized, forced into a civil war, or were short-lived. What makes movements like these genuine is that they try to detach collective action from the signature instrumentality of our system of states and capitalism. These movements foster openness to the future, in defiance of the teleological rationality that rivets the future to the self-serving logic of technology. The real danger in the way in which (metaphysical) violence and technology – now fully globalized – are connected today is that the "excess of presence" leaves very little room for genuine, transformative nonviolent resistance against the calculative rationality and digitization of experience. Clearly, this subject requires a separate study.

Seeing as Unseeing

To avoid contradictions (and to reiterate), a nuanced distinction is in order. Phenomenologically, action is the cusp of violence and nonviolence. Primordially, both violence and nonviolence arise from an act. In civilizational terms – and thus from the point of view of the hegemonic

truisms that capture our experiences that constitute, *stricto sensu*, an
"epoch" both tacitly and explicitly – action in our age is bound to violence
in its hubristic, institutional, and structural manifestations. These modes
of violence shape us into and contain us within forms of biopolitics, productive bodies, and standing-reserve. Far from being the often mystified
and celebrated reservoir for resistance, our lived experiences are vastly
hegemonized experiences, since for the most part we cannot escape living
under (epochal) epistemic hegemonies that shape our world-knowledge
(Vahabzadeh 2003, 97). An experience can be "genuine" (roughly: non-
hegemonic) insofar as it dwells in the *openings* within hegemonic–
epistemic constellations – openings that are the by-products of hegemony
itself (Vahabzadeh 2003, 41–71). The possibility of resisting colonization
and oppression through genuine experience – and thus in terms other
than colonial and oppressive epistemic truisms – resides within the very
system to be resisted and subverted. This is the moment of unseeing
the seen and seeing the unseen (both being in fact one experience),
indeed the moment of "phenomenological attitude," when the "natural
attitude" is suspended while we are still immersed in it. As with the gaze
of Italo Calvino's fictional character, Mr. Palomar, only *the gaze that unsees,
instead of seeing, enters a new world.* Let me quote Calvino's description of
phenomenological gazing, which unsees through seeing, at length:

> And so the wave continues to grow and gain strength until the clash with
> contrary waves gradually dulls it and makes it disappear, or else twists it
> until it is confused in one of the many dynasties of oblique waves slammed
> against the shore.
>
> Concentrating the attention on one aspect makes it leap into the fore-
> ground and occupy the square, just as, with certain drawings, you have only
> to close your eyes and when you open them the perspective has changed.
> Now, in the overlapping of crests moving in various directions, the general
> pattern seems broken down into sections that rise and vanish. In addition,
> the reflux of every wave also has a power of its own that hinders the oncom-
> ing waves. And if you concentrate your attention on these backward thrusts,
> it seems that the true movement is the one that begins from the shore and
> goes out to the sea. (Calvino 1985, 7).

A new world thus appears from out of the ordinary, and I experience
it elated, exhilarated, breathless.

Within the ontological primacy of violence there always exists the
possibility of nonviolence precisely because of the phenomenological

moment, in the concrete experience, that always walks beside me. Phenomenology is not just an abstract and esoteric method; it is enlivened by concrete experience as well, in our moments of awakening to our sad realities, when we realize that we cannot breathe anymore. In "what is most its own phenomenology is not a school. It is the possibility of thinking, at times changing and only thus persisting, of corresponding to the claim of what is to be thought" (Heidegger 1972, 82). In this spirit, I need to unsee and thereby elaborate on some of the key conceptual consequences of this study. Each point enumerated and explained below invites a dedicated study. But I am going to leave things as they are for now. From this point onwards, I can no longer seek comfort in the illusory "we" in which I have sometimes immersed myself in this book in the hope of turning my observations into some collective experience. This "we" inevitably contains metaphysical anthropologism and humanism. The "we" must therefore be abandoned at the end of this study, and I return to the "I." This "I" is not the transcendental ego (although it inexorably risks being that), and clearly it cannot be solipsistic. The "I" is rather the *vulnerable and exposed being*, experienced through *topoi* on a perilous journey, the "I" that is implied in every knowledge-claim but that remains concealed – as in the so-called "universalisms" of the like of Kant's "categorical imperative" and Hegel's universal history, both of which are *inherently* racist and imperialist philosophies of the privileged European men of the Enlightenment (Dussel 1993; Eze 1997), whose experiences could not have been farther from this injured exile and refugee from Iran. Bringing the "I" out in the open and leaving it there as vulnerable is therefore a necessary move to avoid similar (epistemic–colonial) gestures. The "I" always has a personal biography, a location, and a mother tongue that gives the I's reality its particular *accent*. Only in this way does the enunciator reveal his or her singularity (Mignolo 2009, 163). At this moment, I am the one who can see and unsee simultaneously. This journey takes place in solitude, involving reflections through silent dialogue with myself (Arendt), but since the gift of this journey is presented to me by the *diremptive* times in which I live as a permanent (political and epistemic) exile, and thereby through the "things themselves" thus shining forth possibly in a new light, I look forward to being reunited with a community of fellow travellers following these reflections.

I hope the reader will forgive me for reiterating several key points below. It is necessary to go back to some key concepts or arguments time and again so that I can identify and explore their various threads.

(a) *Nonviolence as a genuine possibility.* This book offers the hypothesis, *inter alia,* that "violence" and "nonviolence" – the way we understand them – have been specifically *conceptualized* as opposites in the twentieth century. Clearly, it is absurd to claim that these concepts did not exist prior to the twentieth century or did not have other conceptualizations attached to them. What I am asserting, though – and this is an episte-mological claim – is that contemporary understandings of them, be they notional or conceptual, are holdovers from the (early to mid-) twentieth century. At least one (very different) study has tried to substantiate a similar claim (Losurdo 2015), and I have already mentioned that this conceptual book needs future historical substantiations. This claim is located in the *anticipatory trajectory* of my work. I submit that the historic moment for the conceptualization of (non)violence during the turn of the twentieth century created an epistemological vacuum in regard to understanding the violent essence of modern life: politically, in both democratic and authoritarian regimes; socially, in the rise of labour and later other subaltern classes as formidable social forces challenging the status quo; ecologically, through the continued relentless exploitation of the planet, which has been reduced to a resource for short-term profit; and globally, through the integration of the world under the gigantic economic system of capitalism and the universal technicity reigning over our everyday affairs. At their nascent moments in the early twentieth century, these processes were crystallized as the concepts of *emancipatory violence* (the *necessary* violence that ends all violence, theorized by Sorel) and *nonviolence* (through Satyagraha, conflictual self-sacrifice that renders violence obsolete, theorized by Gandhi). I place these theoretical moments in the context of the epochal structure of my argument (à la Schürmann's hypothesis of metaphysical closure) in conjunction with my hypothesis of the ontological primacy of violence. Within the radical or temporal phenomenological framework of my arguments, these historical–conceptual observations enable a new view of *nonviolence as an epochal possibility* through the historical and current, ontic and concrete, enactments and manifestations of violence that have become part of our everyday knowledge in these first decades of the twenty-first century.

Calling nonviolence a "genuine possibility" (*genuine* means "of its own genus") denotes this: violence, due to its instrumentality and its tremen-dous ability to deliver results, fixes the future in that a certain *arché*, through its process and machinery, becomes the referent of an entire subsequent course of action. As such, violence imposes foreclosures on an otherwise open future. Phenomenologically, my violent acts or my being a component of the violent machinery due to my thoughtlessness will inevitably tie me to a certain forthcoming responsibility (responding-to) in my future and thus to the victims of my violent acts or to the machinery of procedural violence. Thus violence imposes an *existential closure* on the future me, and through me, if such applies, it imposes a closure on the future of the collective to which I likely belong. By contrast, nonviolence leaves the future open because the nonviolent act disallows the consequences of my actions when it comes to determining the future. I suffer today, as a Satyagrahi, in order to disavow the future and thereby impede the expansion of the violent act to which I sacrifice myself into the future of my fellow communitarians, a future I may not see myself due to my suffering today. This is why, in my reading, Gandhi insists that we voluntarily accept the suffering today – it is so that we *deprive violence of its futurity*. Against the backdrop of the hegemonic Western–liberal mirage of human rights, Gandhi proved that there is no Philosopher's Stone capable of transforming violence into nonviolence without – referring to alchemy once more – giving up something of equal value first. To achieve nonviolence, therefore, human suffering, even death, is to be offered. For far too long humans have thrived by subjecting Others (humans and non-humans) to suffering. But there is more: violence involves the prohibition and proscription of future life, whereas nonviolence affirms a pluralistic future of potentially unassimilable singularities. If readers read this last statement as binary, they are already forgetting the concentricity of (non)violence! This conceptual distinction is meant to remind us that the future will always be a historic configuration of both violence and nonviolence, and given our epochal awareness, we may have the opportunity to envision and thus act, inasmuch as structured phenomenalizations allow it, in ways that have a growing affinity to the *open futurity that defines nonviolence*.

Let me put it in concrete, existential terms: supposing that an act is pure, from the moment I commit an act of hubristic violence – whether it arises from my willed imposition or from structurally sanctioned and/ or institutionally enabled activities – I am chained to my violent act. My violent act, therefore, imposes a potential course of action in my futurity that at every point awaits its self-actualization and that takes me back to my (past) violent act, to the victims of my action (as an actor) or my activity (as a subject and agent), and to my responsibility for the act. In short, I am tied forever to the course of action, which will always be tied to my life history, even after my death. By contrast, again supposing an act is pure, nonviolent action releases me from future entanglements because I do not owe anything to the future of my act, and my act now allows me to embrace my futurity as open and enter into relations with others that are not informed by a previous hubristic act of life against life (me against them). Here *archic violence meets an-archic nonviolence*.

The introduction of the concept of *liberation* disturbs this neat violence–nonviolence binary to which we are so accustomed. Liberation zigzags and criss-crosses along the link of violence and nonviolence to futurity. To liberate myself I have to release myself from that which, and the terms under which, I am violated. But I could not have thought of my liberation without the experience of violence. Yes, nonviolence is life-affirming because just as it allows me an open future, so it allows others to emerge in the open. Another term for nonviolence may be *an-archic phenomenalization*. But liberation also means that I force that which violates me into its reluctant deworldedness, which leads to the condition of possibility of my reworlding as a new, liberated being. *To force my hubristic antagonist into deworldedness may be a manifestation of (social) justice but it is no less an act of violence*, regardless of the nonviolent nature of my struggle. But from out of this inevitable "divine violence" – the "violence that ends all violence" – there will be born the conditions of liberating my antagonist from its hubristic relations to me as well. Now the future will be open for us both. Liberation, therefore, also shines forth in the threefold sense of (a) being liberated from oppression, (b) being liberated from the course of action that chains me to my past acts, and (c) releasing, by force if necessary, my oppressor from his oppressiveness.

In short, epochally and epistemologically, it has become possible for us – the children of this age – to think of violence as a civilizational trait, formulate it, respond to it, and offer nonviolent ways of overcoming (*Überwindung*) the violent civilization by actually going through and distorting (*Verwindung*) it. This is primarily the gift of our time, certainly not our acumen. Since (non)violence arises from action, our acting and thinking at this possible historic juncture may lead to a future different from our past. Thus, *my advocacy of nonviolence in this work does not arise from ethical subjectivity, moral principles, instrumental or strategic reason*, or a *utilitarian approach to social justice*, as these are all vestiges of responses to a history of violence that I hope to transcend. But transcending violence and leaving it behind is wishful thinking, not to mention implausible; as Vattimo says, my action must be diverted towards distorting violence and healing from it, certainly not avoiding it. Whether civilizations can be built on nonviolence remains to be seen. Certainly new *relationalities* are to be practised and envisioned, not only through human-to-human communication but also and more importantly through human-to-non-human communities. These relations always reveal themselves at points in history where I encounter others, human or non-human. To stay relational, this encounter cannot be understood from the point of view of the Self or the subject. In fact, relationality overturns the subject and his or her ethical gestures. Hence *topology* constitutes the mode of knowledge proper to (non)violence. Topology constitutes the phenomenological attunement to the places (*topoi*) in which (non)violence manifests itself in myriad forms. It involves acute attentiveness to the relationality of the world and an exploration of how an act could hold the world together without the inevitable violent manifestations of the process of deworlding/reworlding. This requires attunement to the mode of clearing-away in which "[p]lace always opens a region in which it gathers the things in their belonging together" (Heidegger 1973, 6).

The marker for such a transformative nonviolence is *liberation* – that is, being released into the open where the confluence of words, actions, and things phenomenalizes in the singularizing undertow that shatters universal hegemonies from within and in terms other than predicative–normative–legislative. Liberation now means being liberated from the ontic forms of oppression that impose themselves through structural, institutional, and hubristic modes of violence as well as being liberated from the ontological conditions that have begotten the history of violence in this time of the depletion of Being and the twilight of the idols. As regards liberated human life, Fanon's famous statement, read in epochal terms, now makes perfect sense: "He [the colonized] went from one way of life to another, but not from one life to another" (1967, 220). Not just one life to another, but an entirely new life, indeed.

(b) *Towards aethical nonviolence.* Within the scope of this study I have consistently implied that every conceptualization of violence and nonviolence by advocates of nonviolence is based on the tacit, collective agreement to demonize violence – a legacy of the Christian as well as Jainist and Buddhist teachings of "nonviolence" – a moral idea often disguised within the utilitarian discourse that claims to disavow violence due to its human costs or long-term ineffectiveness. Conversely, in the many arguments I have deconstructed in this book there has been the tacit, collective agreement (concomitant with the above) that nonviolence is morally superior or preferable to violence. This argument proceeds by anchoring violence not only to moral principles or ethical responsibility but also to social justice, utility, or the strategic necessities of the oppressed to challenge tyranny and injustice. These moralizations, whether straightforward or veiled, simply report the value judgments that are relative to our worldviews, upbringing, religious beliefs, or ideology. Such judgments presuppose one's belonging or conversion to one (or more) of the above. *Insofar as I envision nonviolence as the gift of our epochal turn* – a possible civilizational turn beyond the existing structural, institutional, and hubristic modalities and manifestations of violence (consistent with Schürmann's hypothesis of metaphysical closure) – my advocacy of nonviolence cannot dwell in any pregiven moral principles, algorithmic epistemologies, or rationalistic truisms. Civilizations have risen and reigned by maximizing violence. The primal modes of violence shared by the *conquering and expanding* civilizations are dispossession and rape. In my introductory remarks I tried to show that our present-day world runs on highly efficient (and, ironically, waste-generating) structural violence from whose existing parameters we can hardly escape. The ethics of nonviolence may be the response to this awareness of the violent fabric of contemporary life, but it is certainly inadequate, misleading, and reformist. Above all, ethics bears within itself a normative drive, a signature of potential violence in that an ethics – regardless of its shade and origins – functions through isomorphism. A phenomenological deconstruction suspends ethics in the same manner that it suspends all claims to knowledge, all epistemic attachments to the "things themselves." This violent world we have inherited cannot be reformed. We need to be liberated from it, and on terms other than normative, predicative, or legislative.

An *a*-ethical advocacy of *non*violence, therefore, exposes ethical and moral principles that proscribe certain acts and prescribe others. The negative (*a*-) in this ethics corresponds to the privative in *non*violence. Strictly speaking, "action" dies with moral or ethical principles; what remains is rather "activity" according to the normative expectations of pregiven principles. Whatever their intentions, which are often noble, moral and ethical expectations impose a closure on the world and on the futurity and potentials of my actions. A phenomenology of nonviolence refuses the lure of ethics both as a religious teaching and as a tantalizing emerging discourse in Continental philosophy. Such approaches to (non)violence indicate the seduction of gaining the moral or ethical high ground, an attempt by the religious figure and secular philosopher alike to disavow the rampant violence that embraces us all. Such attempts are informed by certain liberal notions of respect and recognition, which in fact amount to the colonization of the mind, as Fanon declared. I cannot reproduce some immutable principles, now under the fashionable guise of nonviolence, this *koiné* of our age. This strategy sounds too easy. Moralization of (non)violence indicates a deep misunderstanding. Nonviolent liberation is within my reach because its possibility has been granted to me at this point in history. I am therefore only a respondent to the summoning of nonviolence, which is *simply* a possible modality of action that is not *easy* to partake in. In advocating nonviolence, I am not making a choice, I am not claiming moral superiority, I am not gesturing towards exalted purity. I cannot be praised for advocating nonviolence, and for that matter, I cannot even condemn violence as radically evil. Violence and nonviolence are both intimately connected to life, and I understand them in terms of deworlding/reworlding in relation to liberation (see below). Ethics is the *effect* of the emancipated actor. Echoing Werner Marx (1987), the actor receives her ethics from the phenomenalization of the existents. I can only retain the concept of ethics after my phenomenological *epoché* under the proviso that what is deemed to be the ethical approach to the Other in fact stems from the opening of the possibility of receiving and treating the Other in such and such a manner – a mode of action indeed – that has already presented itself to me. Let us recall Vattimo's declaration that "ethics can never speak the language of hard proof" (2004, 48). Mine will be an "ethics" without the subject – in fact, an "ethics" possible through the dissolution of the "ethical subject." The apparent mutual exclusivity between violence and nonviolence (e.g., Tolstoy's laws of violence and love) now lead to an epistemologically cross-positioned dialectics without *Aufhebung*.

The conceptual consequences for *aethical* nonviolence are many. Let me state them briefly: I do not uphold the view that "human nature" is peaceful, caring, cooperative, or loving because I avow no philosophical anthropology. Nor do I subscribe to the notion that moral and civic education (whatever that term means) will cultivate nonviolence and respect for others. As long as I live under a state characterized by a monopoly over the (hegemonized and constructed) legitimate use of *Gewalt*, a state obsessed with enforceable laws, I hold very little hope in nonviolent change through civic engagement. Furthermore, I do not rationalize crime or violence as responses to poverty, desperation, or oppression. These are all sedimented knowledge claims that can only prevent me from seeing "the things themselves." Just as Joseph Boyden states (chapter 7), humans are "prone to fits of great generosity and even greater meting out of pain" (2013, 153). I hold this observation as the most matter-of-fact truth. A phenomenology of violence proposes to abandon the anthropocentric idea that the survival of humanity constitutes the ultimate measure of violence and nonviolence, yet humans are the only ones with incredible power to inflict unimaginable pain on or to care lovingly for one another as well as non-humans.

Along with ethics, I say farewell to all algorithms of nonviolence. It is true that nonviolence has been advanced through algorithmic thinking that evaded nonviolence's epistemic–subversive privative character and secured it to a (seemingly) positive moorage: utility, peace, social justice, and politics. These algorithms have safely transported the concept to me after many perilous journeys through shifting epistemic sands and chaotic theoretical regions. I am indebted to these algorithms. They have served their purpose as useful epistemological tools that have allowed me to concretize the outcome of nonviolence. These algorithms paved the road, as it were, for nonviolence, a once alien notion, to become a common idiom of our age. Algorithms will remain useful sociological tools for policy and strategy. But alas, however operational, algorithms are no longer sustainable theoretically or conceptually. The reader recognizes that, à la Vattimo, my defence of nonviolence is a *weak* one, as no higher justifications, no instrumental or utilitarian rationality, no moral or ethical teachings can justify my advocacy of nonviolence. The attentive reader knows by now that I have refused the language of hard proof in this book; instead, working through hypotheses, I have offered *interpretations* that invite rethinking of long-held but phantom opposites, interpretations that I hope are compelling and path-breaking. In fact, it is no longer *my* advocacy: nonviolence advocates *itself* through my discourse. This is because the possibility of nonviolence emanates from Being nihilating itself, providing me with the clearing in which I can grasp and articulate this possibility.

(c) *No act is pure.* Violence and nonviolence are notions *relative* to the *koiné* of an age, to its operational tacit knowledge *and* epistemic hegemonies. These two concepts are not free-standing, rather, they are braided together: neither can be conceptualized outside of the historic context in which it arises from individual or collective action. On the one hand, ontic-wise they both can be riveted to some absolute value or Truth-claim (political, logistical, or moral) and may therefore be rationalized or rendered intelligible through some algorithm, in which case, as I have argued, both violence and nonviolence become instrumental. It is here that most of the advocates of nonviolence (Gandhi being the exception) disregard the violence their nonviolence inflicts on the enemy, however just the struggle may be. On the other hand, both violence and nonviolence can lead to liberation, in the sense discussed above, in which case they become ontologically congruent. When Gandhi prefers violence to cowardice, he cannot be any clearer about liberation as the horizon of struggle. This is precisely where we find congruity between two seemingly incongruous figures of twentieth-century decolonization: Gandhi and Fanon. The rebel-figure who does not aim at bringing the liberated under yet another biopolitical regime (in which case the struggle will prove to be violent regardless of the methods) and who instead leaves the liberated out in the open to the irreducible plurality of life as such: this constitutes the figure of transformative nonviolence. No act is pure, since I have no access to the futures my act opens up and closes down. I am epistemologically bound to the present, and as such, to echo Berger and Luckmann, I am walking at night in the dark in the forest, guided by my memory of the trail and where it could lead, as well as to the glowing, finite spike of my flashlight (Berger and Luckmann 1966, 59).

(d) *Liminality, interstitiality, motility*. Grasping (non)violence in non-binary terms requires radically rethinking the privative character of *non*-violence. The "non-" in nonviolence is commonly taken as a negation of violence, which is more or less correct, but the "non-" also signifies a deferred difference – *différance* (Derrida) – rendering "nonviolence" to denote *something other than violence*. Here is where the presumed mutual exteriority of violence and nonviolence is suspended (a phenomenological experience). Thus, the presupposed conceptual boundary between the two no longer holds two realms of action exterior to each other; it signifies how acting always problematizes the distinction. A new dimension is thus revealed before our thinking: insofar as an act embodies liberation, it remains liminal, situated inevitably at the threshold of the supposedly distinct realms of violence and nonviolence, standing at the mercy of the appropriative–integrative, hegemonic–epistemic grip of either realm or both, which imposes on an act such designations as "violent" or "nonviolent," claiming it and giving the act a certain identity. (Non)violence arises from an act, as I have submitted, while *liminality* constitutes action.

Any act therefore permeates the small spaces not fully claimed within the binary conceptual cartography of (non)violence, and only thus can action's liminality be properly thought. In other words, the occupation of seemingly uncontested terrains across the borderline that (presumably) marks off violence and nonviolence from each other inevitably leaves (apparently) insignificant patches of *terra nullius*. Action can be perceived as liminal due to these interstices that open up action potentially to both violence and nonviolence. Hence action's *interstitiality* links it to the topology of Being. Lastly, an act without energy and momentum cannot be characterized by liminality and interstitiality. An act that is already totalized by violence or nonviolence, an act whose identity is fully constituted, an act that is not symbolic or polysemic – supposing such an act exists at all – does not, properly speaking, constitute an action: it can only qualify for the preordained "activity" performed by an institution's agent. If action can lend itself to both violence and nonviolence, then *action always remains at variance with itself* due to its *motility*. This is why the ontologically genuine form of action is *liberation*: action alone is given the gift of stepping out of normative–legislative–predicative universalizations, for in acting, properly speaking, one lets-be, thereby liberating action from (universal) expectations of Reason, utility, ethics, morality, instrumentality, and so on, and letting the actor experience, in the open, the possibility of deworlding/reworlding outside of hubristic terms. Every modality of action (as opposed to activity) other than liberatory–emancipatory is always potentially a partial manifestation of liberatory motility. Thus, "motile nonviolence" arises from the *excess* of violence as the ground whence the conflict between violence and nonviolence arises. This concept stands contrary to many of the dominant conceptions of nonviolence – what I call "sedentary nonviolence," which involves the lack of epistemological access to (indeed ignorance about) the excess of violence; it amounts to politics of rights, withdrawal, or model communities, all of which represent nonviolence in rigid terms.

(e) *Perpetuity of epistemological obscurities.* Concentricity is unsettling: it unravels the epistemological obscurities that permeate every *genuine* understanding of (non)violence. Leaving philosophical–moral truisms and algorithms of nonviolence behind, I am left with the frightening prospect of *abyssal experience.* Concentricity means that it is never fully clear whether, despite my intentions, my action lends itself to violence and nonviolence in its outcome, for the Manichaean categorization of that which action yields, and the conditions under which such seemingly distinct categories become possible, are imposed by the *epistemic hegemonies* that determine from the outset into which distinct category an act should fall. A by-product of these epistemic hegemonies is the consolation of the self-righteous soul and the removal of cultural anxieties. These by-products enable the hegemonized subject to partake in matter-of-course manifestations of structural–institutional–hubristic violence with a clean conscience. Acknowledging concentricity exposes the actor to these anxieties, and such exposition constitutes the *transformative* journey through which the hegemonized activist or agent re-emerges as the *genuine* actor. Liminality, interstitiality, and motility all point in the same conceptual direction.

It is due to the reigning epistemic hegemony in the privileged West that a (rather naive and disturbing) hegemonic experience has guided thinkers and activists alike with a shared sense of guilt regarding revolutionary violence, and thus a perpetual distancing from it, to the extent that endless, debilitating reflections have replaced partaking in liberatory action. This is how dissent is co-opted, allowing the modern state with its monopoly of the legitimate use *of Gewalt* (Weber) to re-emerge as the "liberal democratic state today," one that enjoys "*uncontested monopoly over the legitimate distribution of rights*" (Vahabzadeh 2003, 122; emphasis in original), thus concealing its violent character. The epistemic obscurity that permeates the dreamed-of distinction within (non)violence does not justify revolutionary violence. Properly understood, nonviolence reveals the strife within acting: an act always potentially lends itself to violence and nonviolence at every moment and at every decision. This is due to what Schürmann calls the untameable phenomenalization of life (Schürmann 2003, 625). Liberation may remove the guilt associated with the violence necessary to end oppression, but it inevitably leaves me responsible for it.

In terms of the reworlding/deworlding that each act inevitably represents (however partially), *genuine* action, *stricto sensu*, dwells in *Zwischenwelt*, the "between-world." This is consistent with my rejection of rigid conceptions that uphold *a priori* mutually exclusive acts of violence or nonviolence. The perpetuity of epistemological obscurities simultaneously yields *two diverging directions*. On the one hand, it enables acts of violence to be concealed under epistemic–hegemonic matters of course and thus feign nonviolence. On the other, it allows me to uncover the age-old manifestations of violence arising from my changing existential sensibilities – a reference to the flip side of the protean character of violence.

The epistemological obscurity assigns the discovery of violence to lived experience. Here it seems appropriate to expand on Vattimo's association of metaphysics and violence, and pain as the marker of violence. For Vattimo, post-metaphysical public life requires the reduction of pain. Here pain stands out as the factual–existential marker of violence, not necessarily as a form of knowledge, and thus not as an algorithm or truism, although as is well-known, pain is a social construct; thus the "deep common accord" (Gadamer's "prejudice") regarding what constitutes pain can be used as the raw material for constructing the subject of

epistemic–hegemonic regimes, as well as the soothing ender of menacing epistemological obscurities. What I mean by pain here is rather
different: a *primordial experience*, an experience innate to humans and
non-humans (thus potentially connecting me to my fellow non-humans)
but recognized and received through particular cultural knowledge and
practices. A phenomenological gaze, of course, takes the cultural constructs and rituals of pain only as a point of departure, bracketing them
in order to arrive at the primordial experience. Existentially, pain constitutes the most radical exilic experience in the sense that it allows, prior
to theorizing and conceptions, for the physical and emotional experience of being thrown out of one's world. As the experiential referent of
violence, pain contains both the denial of existence and the destruction
of life, on the one hand, and the possibility of the new and the birth of a
new life, on the other. In the first case – destruction of life – pain signifies
radical deworlding without the prospect of reworlding (at least for the time
being). In this case, the existential horizons darken. This is how the experience of pain marks off violence from nonviolence. In the second case –
birth of new life – pain stands as the suffering of going through. Here
pain *suspends the world*, and the deworldedness of pain is transformed into
the *stepping stone towards the reworlding to come*. Childbirth (thus becoming
mother), healing from injury, overcoming an illness, going through the
agony inflicted by interrogators without giving up comrades, and peace-
making and reconciling with an enemy, occupier, or abuser all exemplify
potential modes of reworlding through pain. Although opaque from
moment to moment, the existential horizons nonetheless leave us faint
glimmerings of hope. The astute reader knows that these are not distinct
cases: their common denominator is *injury*.

Epistemologically, what links pain to (non)violence is the intermediary concept of *injury*, of becoming the subject who is experiencing
suffering. Phenomenologically, in order to posit pain as a primordial
concept, I need an observable and measurable concept that leads
me, the observer, to the subject's pain. This concept is "suffering," a
mode of public manifestation of personal–primordial pain, which in
turn exposes an injury. Stated differently, suffering is the intermediary (socially constructed) concept between primordial pain and factual
injury. As Gandhi shows, however, pain and suffering can be embraced,
and their spectre of radical deworldedness acknowledged. As such, suffering and pain can be used to give birth to the new. One can overcome
being the subject of injury through voluntary suffering. This is how the
Satyagrahi invites injury, embraces pain, and brings the nonviolent new

into this world: the liberation within and without. *When suffering becomes voluntary, injury becomes impossible. Without injury, violence cannot express itself, for injury is articulated violence.* This is how pain leads to defeating the oppressor.

The agent of violence inflicts pain, suffering, and injury on others to keep them within a predefined distance so that the receivers of pain and injury stay within a specific place in the agent's stable but illusory world. This allows the agent to reside within a certain world fit for him or her and the institution he or she represents. *For the tormenter, the suffering of the other is the marker of the stable world of the agent of violence.* Yet the world of the violator is an ever-shrinking world despite the violator's ever-growing reach (hence the excess). Insofar as I embrace, love, and respect my pain, within my trivial existence, pain can bring me together with my fellow human beings at the most primordial level of solidarity, just as it joins me to other sentient beings. But this solidarity remains precarious and abyssal, and no universalism will arise from it. Furthermore, I embrace my scars as the inscriptions of pain on the artefacts of my memory – a memory of enduring, healing, and overcoming that links me to my past while guiding me to an open future.

Arendt and Schürmann have linked evil to thoughtlessness (chapter 1), thereby linking nonviolence to reflective thinking and "thoughtfulness of present and future actors" (Schürmann 1990, 208). In both these philosophers, references to thoughtlessness when accounting for and reflecting on evil and violence are vestiges of Kantian philosophy that need to be abandoned. Exposing thoughtlessness, while absolutely necessary, is totally inadequate to prevent violence. This concept has gained the status of a truism, having been repeated so long and so often without critical reflection. I hope I have shown that reflecting on the consequences of one's actions does not exclude or prevent banal, rampant violence. In fact, it is completely possible to kill, rape, and abuse willingly, soberly, and with a clean conscience, having reflected deeply on the hurtful outcomes of one's actions whether the latter are justified or not. Rapturous violence (Foucault) is a fact of life. The aesthetics of violence that feed Hollywood movies are both tantalizing and entertaining. If we still entertain doubts about thoughtful, reflective violence, let us remember, among a thousand other cases, the 2008 economic collapse in the United States, the Narmada Valley project in India, and even water privatization plans in our cities. The latter two examples involved rational choices approved by developers and officials who were fully aware of the destruction and devastation they would inflict on others' lives. In this world of

rampant violence, of the violence of life against life, from time to time,
I am beckoned by the guideposts that are meant to draw me away from
evil. But as I try to find my way out of violence, epistemological obscurities deprive me of such relics of metaphysical thinking as thoughtfulness.
Thoughtfulness may provide a signpost but it certainly does not mark
the passage.

Phenomenology's attunement to that which *is* proves its "epistemological" compatibility with nonviolence, a compatibility that stems not
from its normative expectation of theory but from the fact that phenomenology stands out as the study of appearances; thus it is possible
for phenomena to world themselves in their own terms. On this perilous journey from violence as our common epochal signature towards
nonviolence as an epochal possibility, I need to acknowledge that the
various appeals to epistemological grounds (reason, utility, morals, ethics, humanism), and the algorithms thus constructed remain at best
provisional, if not failures. No such appeals can guarantee the precarious passage between violence and nonviolence. Of course, violence is
indispensible to all utilitarian pursuits, whether revolutionary or institutional. Hidden structural and institutional violence does in fact inform
many "nonviolent" aspects of our lives today. Appealing to the inevitability and efficiency of revolutionary violence is epistemologically just
as invalid as advocating (self-acclaimed universal) moral imperatives
of nonviolence: both involve epistemic imperialisms based on universals that have no concrete reality attached to them, to borrow an idea
from Herbert Marcuse (1964, 203–5). These appeals intend merely to
soothe the angst of the metaphysician within us. *I can neither fabulate
nor unconditionally and unqualifiedly condone nonviolence.* This is when I
realize that my scars, injuries, sufferings, pains, and above all memories
of violence, which are simultaneously personal and collective, are my
most intimate and genuine guides, and when I know that the journey
will remain perilous. Genuine actors, therefore, cannot avoid abyssal
acting and thinking.

Out in the Open

Here I stand, at the end of this journey through perilous conceptual
passages, seeking "the thing itself." I am confronted with an imposing question: Why is it that in this age in which I am inserted, partaking in hubristic, institutional, and structural modalities of violence has
become a matter of fact but adhering to nonviolence requires a Grand

Refusal, an act of volition, a resistance against the matter-of-factness of commonplace violating? I know that by virtue of the garments I wear, the food I consume, the objects I use, the votes I cast, the pension I build, the rules I make, the courses I teach, and more, I am ancillary to the rampant violence which enfolds me. Given the state of permanent deworldedness and with the coming ecological disaster that is looming large over our age, I wish to step out of the economies of violence and wash my hands of the blood of my fellow humans and non-humans who are paying the price for my (supposed) enjoyment of life. It is clear that the impending collapse of global civilization will bring about catastrophic deworldings over the course of which hubristic violence will overtake the other two modalities. It is also clear that such deworlding contains the seeds for a new reworlding, possibly unlike the past. I know, however, that stepping out of these economies of violence cannot be the solitary act of an individual deluded by the comfort of an anarchistic, anti-system lifestyle. Nor can it flow from the collective sense of proud self-righteousness that arises from necessary struggles against the injustices that breed violence. I know that I can do better than appeal to some fantasmic ground – often disguised by the *koiné* of an age – that holds me tied to communities of activists, whose sensibilities, although necessary for challenging violent injustices of our time, are nonetheless rooted in the epistemic hegemonies of the time. Therefore, what baffles me most is why, in trying to advocate nonviolence, I must always justify myself through algorithmic – albeit principled – strategic, calculative, ethical, moral, or political justifications. In questioning violence, I wonder, why should I adhere to the existing value-communities that posit their struggle for justice as universal? All I am asking from my reader here is to look violence in the eye and see it for what it is, without the consolation provided by self-righteous moral high grounds.

The concentric concept of (non)violence shows that there is no "divine violence" (Benjamin), no violence to end all violence (by which violence turns into nonviolence), no shifting historic moment epitomized by revolution, overthrow, rebellion, or *coup d'état*. Theory is fascinated with these tropes of radical break due to their (seeming) power to provide epistemological demarcations. Liberation must by definition be *total*, but it never is, due to the epistemic obscurities that block my view of the *genuinely new*. That is why, with Franz Kafka, the Messiah will *radically* change the world by making slight adjustments to it. Concentricity does away with the representation of such historic breaks as *epistemological markers.* Phenomenologically, *(non)violence is relational:* thus understood, violence of life against life always encounters nonviolent preservation of life, even as (Satyagrahi) relinquishing the right to preservation of one's life. Gandhi recognized that the *preservation of human life at all costs was the source of violence.* Through the phenomenological gaze we began to see that *archic violence encounters an-archic nonviolence.* Nonviolence remains dependent on violence (attesting to my hypothesis of the ontological primacy of violence), which means that I have not yet genuinely experienced the *caesura* between the *actual,* current epoch of violence and the *possible* future age of nonviolence. Awareness of *Verwindung* I may be experiencing in an ontic way at this time (the thought behind this book) may allow in turn a radical epistemic departure from the ontological primacy of violence. This ontology leads me to conceive of nonviolence in terms other than algorithmic, for which I cannot constitute the knowledge beyond the epistemic–hegemonic truisms of my epoch. That is why I need to prepare for the deontologization of nonviolence into *a*violence. As mentioned, the "non-" in *non-*violence connotes both the *negation* of violence – *not-being* violence – and the signifier of a difference – *other-than* violence. The mode of revealing of radical departure from violence will then have to be *a*violence – living in a future age when violence will be committed to memory, myth, fable, an ineffable experience for which our predicative languages will allow no expression. To rethink deworlding and reworlding in terms other than violence remains baffling and monstrous; the experience of *Verwindung,* though, suggests a certain gentle slippage through one to the next. This view suggests that, phenomenologically, *we will have to exit violence the way we entered it.*

The experience of violence is always gendered, racial, geographic, class-based, ecological, sexually shaded, mentally conditioned, and/or linguistic – to name the obvious. These are the structured loci of categorical–existential manifestations of violence according to which life is normatively aligned with some imposed principles. There is no universal, not even common, experience of violence, and any such universal claims basically represent some dominant particulars – that is, the reflections of certain sensibilities of an age. A phenomenology of violence steps back from these diverse and concrete experiences in order to reveal the *economies of violence.* In so doing, though, phenomenology allows something interesting to show forth: oppressive (i.e., "pressing-near") reworlding yields to the *dispersion of life* across diverse terrains of (human and non-human) existence as well as different, even diverging, modes of experiencing the world without a unifying ground.

◎

Thinking through the dispersion of life will enable a modality of acting that brings beings out into the open and leaves them there without normative–legislative–predicative impositions. A perilous journey into the abyss: the thought remains monstrous. Epistemologically, one thing is certain: until such time when the experience of "not-being" and "being other than" violence – the very experience my metaphysical language forces me to neologize into *aviolence* – becomes possible, until such time that this experience finds a proper expression, that *non*violence finally releases itself from being simultaneously an appendage and a negation of violence as a dominant logos of civilizational history, until such time that *a*violence makes its appearance, we have not learned to live in dispersive mode of deworlding/reworlding. The experience of aviolent deworlding from current violent state and reworlding into an-archic existence – living without normative principles – cannot be without a "certain disinterest in mankind's future" (Schürmann 1990, 273). This study has shown that every time theorists and thinkers have attempted to distinguish violence from nonviolence and vice versa through some positively ascertainable ground, they have only alluded to and invited the supposed opposite. Such a failure in building an epistemic firewall between the two arises from the lack of knowledge of the *ontological concentricity of (non)violence* that enfolds every (individual and collective) human act. Precisely because of such a critique, this book shows that the *logos* of violence as a mode of revealing entails also a *physis*, a springing forth, of a possible economy of presence that brings thought to terms with its abyssal being just as it lets beings spring forth in myriad manifestations out in the open.

As far as acting within this caesura is concerned, my acting is diverted to letting-be. In releasing things from my normative expectations I also release myself. The normative–legislative–predicative holds, however, linger on, drawing me, with force if necessary, back into their laws. I am left with *two possibilities*: I can let-be and thus release beings and myself from the sway of metaphysical holds, or I can take beings and myself, as their anarchic custodian, out of that sway, by force if necessary, and release them into the open. These two possibilities, as can be expected, remain concentric.

The experience of living in a world without violence will inevitably be an ineffable experience. The institutive gestures vehemently conceal their future destitutive orientations. If nothing else, I hope my meditations in this book have shown that *my genealogy of violence is also always already its necrology.* "From our mother(s) we are born for death," said the classical Persian poet Ferdowsi in his epic *The Book of Kings* (*Shahnameh*). Lost for words in grasping and sharing this ineffable experience, I turn, one last time, to Leo Tolstoy:

> Ivan Ilych lived only with memories of the past. One after another images of his past came to mind.
>   ...
> "Resistance is impossible," he said to himself. "But if only I could understand the reason for this agony. Yet even that is impossible. It would make sense if one could say I had not lived as I should have. But such an admission is impossible," he uttered inwardly, remembering how his life had conformed to all the laws, rules, and proprieties.
>   ...
> At that very moment Ivan Ilych fell through and saw a light, and it was revealed to him that his life had not been what it should have but that he could still rectify the situation. "But what *is* the real thing?" he asked himself, and grew quite, listening.
>   ...
> He searched for his accustomed fear of death and could not find it. Where was death? What death? There was no fear because there was no death.
> Instead of death there was light.
> "So that's it!" he exclaimed. "What bliss!"
> All this happened in a single moment, but the significance of that moment was lasting.
>   ...
> "It is all over," said someone standing beside him.
> He heard these words and repeated them in his soul.
> "Death is over," he said to himself. "There is no more death."

He drew in a breath, broke off in the middle of it, stretched himself out, and died. (Tolstoy, 2004, 104, 105, 112, 113, original emphasis)

It has been announced; it has been uttered; it remains ineffable. It is now a possibility.

Bound to our ontological constitution, we have gone through a history of violence. Now we may stand at the disjunction where we can see the light at our violent history's possible end, its possible terminal depletion. I am the child of this unenviable history, have lived its agonizing collective (and personal) memory, and have participated in this history simultaneously as an agent of violence and a nonviolent actor: I need to constantly remind myself, therefore, that once violence is no more, I will blissfully be no more either. And this is the moment I impatiently await.

Bibliography

Abbott, Mathew. 2008. "The Creature Before the Law: Notes on Walter Benjamin's *Critique of Violence*." *Colloquy* 16: 80–96.

Ackerman, Peter, and Jack Duvall. 2000. *A Force More Powerful: A Century of Nonviolent Conflict*. New York: Palgrave.

Agamben, Georgio. 1998. *Homo Sacer: Sovereign Power and Bare Life*. Trans. D. Heller-Roazen. Stanford: Stanford University Press.

– 2005. *State of Exception*. Trans. K. Attell. Chicago: University of Chicago Press. https://doi.org/10.1215/9780822386735-013.

– 2007. *The Coming Community*. Trans. M. Hardt. Minneapolis: University of Minnesota Press.

Aljazeera. 2011. "Q&A: Gene Sharp." *Aljazeera Opinion*, 6 December 2011. https://www.aljazeera.com/indepth/opinion/2011/12/201112113179492201.html, accessed 25 February 2015.

Alther, Gretchen. 2006. "Colombian Peace Communities: The Role of NGOs in Supporting Resistance to Violence and Oppression." *Development in Practice* 16(3–4): 278–91. https://doi.org/10.1080/09614520600694828

American Friends Service Committee. 1955. *Speak Truth to Power: A Quaker Search for an Alternative to Violence*. Philadelphia: American Friends Service Committee.

Angus, Ian. 2000. *Primal Scenes of Communication: Communication, Consumerism, and Social Movements*. Albany: SUNY Press.

– 2001. *Emergent Publics: An Essay on Social Movements and Democracy*. Winnipeg: Arbeiter Ring.

Arendt, Hannah. 1958a. *The Human Condition*. Chicago: University of Chicago Press.

– 1958b. *The Origins of Totalitarianism*. Orlando: Harcourt Brace.

– 1963. *On Revolution*. New York: Penguin Books.

– 1965. *Eichmann in Jerusalem: A Report on the Banality of Evil.* New York: Penguin Books.

– 1969. *Between Past and Future.* New York: Penguin Books.

– 1970. *On Violence.* Orlando: Harcourt.

– 1972. *Crisis of the Republic.* New York: Harvest Books.

– 1990. "Philosophy and Politics." *Social Research* 57(1): 73–103.

– 2003. *Responsibility and Judgment.* Ed. J. Kohn. New York: Schocken Books.

– 2007. *The Jewish Writings.* Ed. J. Kohn and R.H. Feldman. New York: Schocken Books.

– 2017. "The Freedom to Be Free." *New England Review* 38(2): 56–69.

Arrow, Ruaridh. 2011. "Gene Sharp: Author of the Nonviolent Revolution Rulebook." *BBC News Middle East,* 21 February 2011. http://www.bbc.co.uk /news/world-middle-east-12522848, accessed 25 February 2015.

Baghi, Emadedin. n.d. "Amar-e qorbanian-e enqelab" [Statistical Figures of the Revolution's Casualties]. *100 Years.* http://100years.site90.com/naamian/ baaghi/baaghi.htm, accessed 21 December 2013.

BBC News. 2011. "When Gandhi Met Darwen's Mill Workers." 23 September 2011. http://www.bbc.com/news/uk-england-lancashire-15020097, accessed 26 October 2015.

Benjamin, Walter. 1968. *Illuminations.* Ed. H. Arendt. New York: Schocken Books.

– 1996. "Critique of Violence." In *Selected Writings,* vol. 1: *1913–1926.* Ed. M. Bullock and M.W. Jennings. Cambridge, MA: Belknap Press of Harvard University Press. 236–52.

Bernstein, Richard. 2002. *Radical Evil: A Philosophical Interrogation.* Cambridge: Polity Press.

– 2013. *Violence: Thinking without Banisters.* Cambridge: Polity Press.

Berger, Peter L., and Thomas Luckmann. 1966. *The Social Construction of Reality: A Treatise in the Sociology of Knowledge.* New York: Anchor Books.

Bouvier, Virginia M. 2006. *Harbingers of Hope: Peace Initiatives in Colombia.* Special Report 169. Washington, DC: US Institute of Peace.

Boyden, Joseph. 2013. *The Orenda.* Toronto: Penguin Books.

Brocke, Edna. 2007. "Afterword: 'Big Hannah' – My Aunt," in Arendt, *The Jewish Writings,* 512–21.

Bruyn, S., and P. Rayman, eds. 1979. *Nonviolent Action and Social Change.* New York: Irvington.

Butler, Judith. 2004. *Precarious Life: The Powers of Mourning and Violence.* London: Verso.

– 2007. "I merely belong to them." *London Review of Books* 29(9) (10 May): 26–8. http://www.lrb.co.uk/v29/n09/judith-butler/i-merely-belong-to-them, accessed 7 November 2014.

– 2009. *Frames of War: When Is Life Grievable?* London: Verso.

Calvino, Italo. 1985. *Mr. Palomar.* Trans. W. Weaver. Toronto: Lester & Orpen Dennys.

Coates, Ta-Nehisi. 2015. "Nonviolence as Compliance." *The Atlantic,* 27 April 2015. https://www.theatlantic.com/politics/archive/2015/04/nonviolence-as-compliance/391640, accessed 28 April 2015.

Coulthard, Glen Sean. 2014. *Red Skin, White Masks.* Minneapolis: University of Minnesota Press. https://doi.org/10.5749/minnesota/9780816679645.001.0001.

Critchley, Simon. 1999. *The Ethics of Deconstruction: Derrida and Levinas.* Edinburgh: Edinburgh University Press.

Crow, Ralph E., Philip Grant, and Saad E. Ibrahim, eds. 1990. *Arab Nonviolent Political Struggle in the Middle East.* Boulder: Lynne Rienner.

Dabashi, Hamid. 2007. *Iran: A People Interrupted.* New York: New Press.

– 2012. *Corpus Anarchicum: Political Protest, Suicidal Violence, and the Making of the Posthuman Body.* New York: Palgrave Macmillan. https://doi.org/10.1057/9781137264138.

– 2016. *Iran without Borders: Towards a Critique of the Postcolonial Nation.* London: Verso.

Debray, Régis. July–August 1996. "A Guerrilla with a Difference." *New Left Review* 218: 128–37.

– July–August 2007. "Socialism: A Life-Cycle." *New Left Review* 46: 5–28.

de las Casas, Bartolomé. 2004. *A Short Account of the Destruction of the Indies.* London and New York: Penguin Books.

Derrida, Jacques. 1982. *Margins of Philosophy.* Chicago: University of Chicago Press.

– 1992. "Force of Law: The 'Mystical Foundation of Authority'." In *Deconstruction and the Possibility of Justice.* Ed. D. Cornell, M. Rosenfeld, and D.G. Carlson. London and New York: Routledge. 3–67.

– 2001. *On Cosmopolitanism and Forgiveness.* Trans. M. Dooley and M. Hughes. London and New York: Routledge.

Devji, Faisal. 2012. *The Impossible Indian: Gandhi and the Temptation of Violence.* Cambridge, MA: Harvard University Press. https://doi.org/10.4159/harvard.9780674068100.

Duménil, Gérard, and Dominique Lévy. 2004. *Capital Resurgent: Roots of the Neoliberal Revolution.* Trans. D.Jeffers. Cambridge, MA: Harvard University Press.

Dussel, Enrique. 1993. "Eurocentrism and Modernity." *Boundary* 2/20(3): 65–76. https://doi.org/10.2307/303341.

Elliot, Larry. 2017. "World's Eight Richest People Have Same Wealth as Poorest 50%." *The Guardian,* 16 January 2017. https://www.theguardian.com/global-development/2017/jan/16/worlds-eight-richest-people-have-same-wealth-as-poorest-50, aaccessed 23 June 2017.

Engler, Mark, and Paul Engler. "How Did Gandhi Win?" *Waging Nonviolence*, 8 October 2014. https://wagingnonviolence.org/feature/gandhi-win, accessed October 14, 2014.

Escobar, Arturo. 1995. *Encountering Development: The Making and Unmaking of the Third World*. Princeton: Princeton University Press.

Eze, Emmanuel Chukwudi. 1997. "The Color of Reason: The Idea of 'Race' in Kant's Anthropology." In *Postcolonial African Philosophy: A Critical Reader*. Ed. E.C. Eze. Cambridge: Blackwell. 103–31.

Fanon, Frantz. 1967. *Black Skin, White Masks*. Trans. C.L. Markmann. New York: Grove Weidenfeld.

– 1991. *A Dying Colonialism*. Trans. H. Chevalier. New York: Grove Press.

– 1994. *Toward the African Revolution*. Trans. H. Chevalier. New York: Grove Press.

– 2004. *The Wretched of the Earth*. Trans. R. Philcox. New York: Grove Press.

Fazeli, Hossein (director/writer). 2013. *The Legacy of Nonviolent Movements in Iran (1978–79 | 2009-Present)*. https://vimeo.com/27549444, accessed 21 December 2013.

Foucault, Michel. 1979. *Discipline and Punish: The Birth of the Prison*. Trans. A. Sheridan. New York: Vintage Books.

– 1990. *The History of Sexuality: An Introduction*. Trans. R. Hurley. New York: Vintage Books.

Foucault, Michel, and James Bernauer. 1981. "Is It Useless to Revolt?" *Philosophy and Social Criticism* 8(1): 1–9. https://doi.org/10.1177/019145378100800101.

Freedom House. 2016. "Our Supporters." https://freedomhouse.org/content/our-supporters, accessed 5 November 2016.

Fukuyama, Francis. 1992. *The End of History and the Last Man*. New York: Avon Books.

Gadamer, Hans-Georg. 1976. *Philosophical Hermeneutics*. Berkeley: University of California Press.

Galtung, Johan. 1959. "Pacifism from a Sociological Point of View." *Journal of Conflict Resolution* 3(1): 67–84. https://doi.org/10.1177/002200275 900300105.

– 1965. "On the Meaning of Nonviolence." *Journal of Peace Research* 2(3): 228–57. https://doi.org/10.1177/002234336500200303.

– 1969. "Violence, Peace, and Peace Research." *Journal of Peace Research* 6(3): 167–91. https://doi.org/10.1177/002234336900600301.

– 1989. *Nonviolence and Israel/Palestine*. Honolulu: University of Hawai'i, Institute for Peace.

Gandhi, Mahatma. 1938. "Gandhi & Zionism: 'The Jews'" (26 November 1938). http://www.jewishvirtuallibrary.org/jsource/History/JewsGandhi.html, accessed 10 October 2015.

– 1940. "Letter to Adolf Hitler" (24 December 1940). http://www.mkgandhi
.org/letters/hitler_ltr1.htm, accessed 1 November 2015.

– 1942. "Quit India Speeches" (8 August 1942). http://www.gandhi-manibhavan
.org/gandhicomesalive/speech6.htm, accessed 20 November 2015.

– 1983. *The Essential Gandhi: An Anthology of His Writings on His Life, Work, and Ideas.* Ed. L. Fischer. New York: Vintage Books.

– 1997. *Hind Swaraj and Other Writings.* Ed. A.J. Parel. Cambridge: Cambridge University Press. https://doi.org/10.1017/CBO9780511558696.

– 2001. *Non-Violent Resistance (Satyagraha).* Mineola, NY: Dover.

– 2011. *An Autobiography: The Story of My Experiments with Truth.* Trans. M. Desai. Markham, ON: Fitzhenry and Whiteside.

– 2016. "Between Cowardice and Violence." http://www.mkgandhi.org/
nonviolence/phil8.htm, accessed 20 January 2016.

García-Durán, Mauricio, ed. 2004. "Alternatives to War – Colombia's Peace Processes." *Accord* 14. http://www.c-r.org, accessed 16 February 2014.

Gramsci, Antonio. 1971. *Selections from the Prison Notebooks.* Trans. Q. Hoare and G. Novell Smith. New York: International.

Gregg, Richard. 1984. *The Power of Nonviolence,* 3rd ed. Canton, ME: Greenleaf Books.

Haraway, Donna. 1991. "A Cyborg Manifesto: Science, Technology, and Socialist-Feminism in the Late Twentieth Century." In *Simians, Cyborgs, and Women: The Reinvention of Nature.* New York: Routledge. 149–81.

Hashemi, Nader, and Danny Postel, eds. 2010. *The People Reloaded: The Green Movement and the Struggle for Iran's Future.* New York: Melville House.

Heaven, Pamela. 2014. "Oxfam: 85 Richest People on Earth Have as Much Money as Half the World's Population." *Financial Post,* 20 January. http://
business.financialpost.com/2014/01/20/oxfam-85-richest-people-on-earth
-have-as-much-money-as-half-the-worlds-population, accessed 7 February 2014.

Hegel, G.W.F. 1977. *Phenomenology of Spirit.* Trans. A.V. Miller. New York: Oxford University Press.

– 1991. *The Philosophy of History.* Trans. J. Sibree. Buffalo: Prometheus Books.

Heidegger, Martin. 1966. *Discourse on Thinking.* Trans. J.H. Anderson and E.H. Freund. New York: Harper Torchbooks.

– 1971. *Poetry Language Thought.* Trans. S. Hofstadter. New York: Harper Colophon Books.

– 1972. *On Time and Being.* Trans. J. Stambaugh. New York: Harper and Row.

– 1973. "Art and Space." *Man and World* 6(1): 3–8. https://doi.org/10.1007/
BF01252779.

– 1977. *The Question Concerning Technology and Other Essays.* Trans. W. Lovitt. New York: Harper Torchbooks.

– 1996. *Being and Time.* Trans. J. Stambaugh. Albany: SUNY Press.
– 2000. *Introduction to Metaphysics.* Trans. G. Fried and R. Polt. New Haven, CT: Yale University Press.
– 2012. *Four Seminars.* Trans. A. Mitchell and F. Raffoul. Bloomington: Indiana University Press.
Hochschild, Adam. 1998. *King Leopold's Ghost: A Story of Greed, Terror, and Heroism in Colonial Africa.* New York: Mariner Books.
Holloway, John. 1998. "Dignity's Revolt." In *Zapatista! Reinventing Revolution in Mexico.* Ed. J. Holloway and E. Peláez. London: Pluto Press. 159–198.
Honneth, Axel. 1996. *The Struggle for Recognition: The Moral Grammar of Social Conflicts.* Cambridge, MA: MIT Press.
Huntington, Samuel P. 1996. *The Clash of Civilizations and the Remaking of World Order.* New York: Simon and Schuster.
Husserl, Edmund. 1970. *The Crisis of European Sciences and Transcendental Phenomenology.* Trans. D. Carr. Evanston, IL: Northwestern University Press.
Iranian Intelligence Ministry. 2008. *Iranian Intelligence Ministry Public Service Broadcast* (YouTube title: *Iranian Propaganda Video featuring John McCain, George Soros, and Gene Sharp*). 5 February 2008; uploaded to YouTube by kkamizadeh 8 August 2010. https://www.youtube.com/watch?v=OTCuB FuhikM, accessed 25 February 2015.
Jacoby, Russell. 2005. *Picture Imperfect: Utopian Thought for an Anti-Utopian Age.* New York: Columbia University Press.
Jahanbegloo, Ramin. 2014. *An Introduction to Nonviolence.* New York: Palgrave Macmillan. https://doi.org/10.1007/978-1-137-31426-0.
Jameson, Fredric. 1988. *The Ideologies of Theory: Essays 1971–1986*, vol. 2. Minneapolis: University of Minnesota Press.
Katsiaficas, George. 1987. *The Ideology of the New Left: A Global Analysis of 1968.* Boston: South End Press.
Keddie, Nikki. 1981. *Roots of Revolution: An Interpretive History of Modern Iran.* New Haven: Yale University Press.
Kishwar, Madhu. 1990. "Why I Do Not Call Myself a Feminist." *Manushi* 61 (November–December): 2–8.
Laclau, Ernesto. 1979. *Politics and Ideology in Marxist Theory: Capitalism, Fascism, Populism.* London and New York: Verso.
– 1996. *Emancipation(s).* London: Verso.
– 2014. *The Rhetorical Foundations of Society.* London: Verso.
Laclau, Ernesto, and Chantal Mouffe. 1985. *Hegemony and Socialist Strategy: Towards a Radical Democratic Politics.* London: Verso.
Le Bon, Gustave. 2002. *The Crowd: A Study of Popular Mind.* Mineola, NY: Dover.

Losurdo, Domenico. 2015. *Non-Violence: A History beyond the Myth*. Trans. G. Elliott. Lanham: Lexington Books.

Luhmann, Niklas. 1989. *Ecological Communication*. Trans. J. Bednarz. Chicago: University of Chicago Press.

Lukács, Georg. 1971. *History and Class Consciousness: Studies in Marxist Dialectics*. Trans. R. Livingstone. Cambridge, MA: MIT Press.

Luxemburg, Rosa. 2005. *The Mass Strike*. London: Bookmarks.

Mackay, Mairi. 2012. "Gene Sharp: A Dictator's Worst Nightmare." *CNN Profile*, 25 June 2012. http://www.cnn.com/2012/06/23/world/gene-sharp -revolutionary, accessed 25 February 2015.

Maddison, Angus. 2006. *Class Structure and Economic Growth: India and Pakistan Since the Moghuls*. New York: Routledge.

Mannheim, Karl. 1969. *Ideology and Utopia*. London: Routledge and Kegan Paul.

Marcuse, Herbert. 1964. *One-Dimensional Man: Studies in the Ideology of Advanced Industrial Societies*. Boston: Beacon Press.

– 1969. *An Essay on Liberation*. Boston: Beacon Press.

Marder, Michael. 2013. *Plant-Thinking: A Philosophy of Vegetal Life*. New York: Columbia University Press.

Marx, Karl. 1963. *The Eighteenth Brumaire of Louis Bonaparte*. New York: International Publishers.

– 1972. "On British Imperialism in India" [1853]. In *The Marx–Engels Reader*. Ed. R.C. Tucker. New York: Norton and Norton. 653–64.

Marx, Werner. 1971. *Heidegger and the Tradition*. Trans. T. Kisiel and M. Greene. Evanston, IL: Northwestern University Press.

– 1987. *Is There a Measure on Earth? Foundations for a Postmetaphysical Ethics*. Trans. T.J. Nenon and R. Lilly. Chicago: University of Chicago Press.

Matin, Kamran. 2013. *Recasting Iranian Modernity: International Relations and Social Change*. London and New York: Routledge.

Mentinis, Mihalis. 2006. *Zapatistas: The Chiapas Revolt and What It Means for Radical Politics*. London: Pluto Press.

Mertes, Tom, ed. 2004. *A Movement of Movements: Is Another World Really Possible?* London and New York: Verso.

– ed. 2007. *Gandhi on Non-Violence*. New York: New Directions.

Mignolo, Walter. 2006. "Epistemic Disobedience, Independent Thought, and Decolonial Freedom." *Theory, Culture and Society* 26(7–8): 159–81.

Mouffe, Chantal. 1993. *The Return of the Political*. London: Verso.

– 2000. *The Democratic Paradox*. London: Verso.

– 2005. *On the Political*. London, New York: Routledge.

Nazemi, Akbar. 2005. *Unsent Dispatches: From the Iranian Revolution, 1978–1979*. North Vancouver: Presentation House.

Nietzsche, Friedrich. 1967. *The Genealogy of Morals* and *Ecce Homo*. Ed. and trans. W. Kaufmann. New York: Vintage Books.

Peterson, Scott. 2009. "Iran Protesters: The Harvard Professor behind Their Tactics." *Christian Science Monitor*, 29 December 2009. https://www.csmonitor.com/World/Middle-East/2009/1229/Iran-protesters-the-Harvard-professor-behind-their-tactics, accessed 25 February 2015.

Popović, Srdja, Andrej Milivojević, and Slobodan Djinović. 2006. *Nonviolent Struggle: 50 Crucial Points: A Strategic Approach to Everyday Tactics*. Belgrade: Centre for Applied Nonviolent Action and Strategies. (CANVAS).

Rakhmanova, Tania (dir.). 2006. *The Democratic Revolutionary Handbook* (Icarus Films).

Rosenberg, Marshal B. 2003. *Nonviolent Communication: A Language of Life*. Encinitas: Puddle Dancer Press.

Rousseau, Jean-Jacques. 1968. *The Social Contract*. Trans. M. Cranston. London and New York: Penguin Books.

Russia Today News. 2013. "Drone-spotting: Survival guide informs on new breed of aerial predators." https://rt.com/news/drone-survival-guide-published-774, accessed 25 December 2013.

Said, Edward. 1993. *Culture and Imperialism*. New York: Vintage Books.

Schmidt, Dennis J. 1998. "*Solve et Coagula*: Something Other than an Exercise in Dialectic." *Research in Phenomenology* 28(1): 259–71. https://doi.org/10.1163/156916498X00155.

Schürmann, Reiner. 1981. "Principles Precarious: On the Origin of the Political in Heidegger." In *Heidegger: The Man and the Thinker*. Ed. Thomas Sheehan. Chicago: Precedent. 245–56.

– 1983a. "Neoplatonic Henology as an Overcoming of Metaphysics." *Research in Phenomenology* 8(1): 25–41. https://doi.org/10.1163/156916483X00025.

– 1983b. "'What Must I Do?' At the End of Metaphysics: Ethical Norms and the Hypothesis of a Historical Closure." In *Phenomenology in a Pluralistic Context*. Ed. W.L. McBride and C.O. Schrag. Albany: SUNY Press. 49–64

– 1984. "Deconstruction Is Not Enough: On Gianni Vattimo's Call for 'Weak Thinking.'" *Graduate Faculty Philosophy Journal* 10(1): 165–77. https://doi.org/10.5840/gfpj198410113.

– 1990. *Heidegger on Being and Acting: From Principles to Anarchy*. Trans. C.-M. Gros. Indianapolis: Indiana University Press.

– 1991. "Ultimate Double Binds." *Graduate Faculty Philosophy Journal* 14(2): 213–36. https://doi.org/10.5840/gfpj199114/152/123.

– 1993. "Technicity, Topology, Tragedy: Heidegger on 'That Which Saves' in the Global Reach." In *Technology in the Western Political Tradition*. Ed. A.M. Melzer, J. Weinberger, and M.R. Zinman. Ithaca, NY: Cornell Universtiy Press. 190–213.

– 2003. *Broken Hegemonies.* Trans. R. Lilly. Indianapolis: Indiana University Press.
Schutz, Alfred. 1967. *The Phenomenology of the Social World.* Evanston, IL: Northwestern University Press.
Seigneurie, Ken. 2012. "Discourses of the 2011 Arab Revolutions." *Journal of Arabic Literature* 43(2–3): 484–509. https://doi.org/10.1163/157006 4x-12341243.
– 2015. Personal communication with the author. Vancouver, 13 March 2015.
Sharp, Gene. 1959. "The Meanings of Non-Violence: A Typology." *Journal of Conflict Resolution* 3(1): 41–66. https://doi.org/10.1177/002200275900300104.
– 1973a. *The Politics of Nonviolent Action, Part One: Power and Struggle.* Boston: Extending Horizons Books.
– 1973b. *The Politics of Nonviolent Action, Part Two: The Methods of Nonviolent Action.* Boston: Extending Horizons Books.
– 1973c. *The Politics of Nonviolent Action, Part Three: The Dynamics of Nonviolent Action.* Boston: Extending Horizons Books.
– 1990. *The Role of Power in Nonviolent Struggle.* Monograph series no. 3. Boston: Albert Einstein Institution.
– 2002. *From Dictatorship to Democracy: A Conceptual Framework for Liberation.* Boston: Albert Einstein Institution.
– 2003. *There Are Realistic Alternatives.* Boston: Albert Einstein Institution.
– 2009. *Self-Liberation: A Guide to Strategic Planning for Action to End a Dictatorship or Other Oppression.* Boston: Albert Einstein Institution.
Sorel, George. 2004. *Reflections on Violence.* Trans. T.E. Hulme and J. Roth. Mineola, NY: Dover.
Strangers in a Tangled Wilderness. 2015. *The Rojava Revolution: A Small Key Can Open a Large Door.* Combustion Books.
Marcos, Subcommandante. 2001. *Our Word Is Our Weapon.* Ed. J. Ponce de Leon. New York: Seven Stories Press.
Tahmasebi-Birgani, Victoria. 2014. *Emmanuel Levinas and the Politics of Non-Violence.* Toronto: University of Toronto Press.
Taylor, Charles. 1994. *Multiculturalism.* Ed. A. Gutmann. Princeton: Princeton University Press.
Thoreau, Henry David. 1993. *Civil Disobedience and Other Essays.* New York: Dover.
Tolstoy, Leo. 1909. "A Letter to a Hindu: The Subjection of India – Its Cause and Cure." http://www.nonresistance.org/docs_pdf/Tolstoy/Correspondence _with_Gandhi.pdf, accessed 5 May 2015.
– 1951. *The Kingdom of God Is Within You.* Trans. C. Garnett. New York: Watchmaker.
– 1962. *Fables and Fairy Tales.* Trans. A. Dunnigan. New York: New American Library.
– 2004. *The Death of Ivan Ilych.* Trans. L. Solotaroff. New York: Bantam Classic.

– 2010. *The Law of Love and the Law of Violence.* Trans. M. Koutouzow Tolstoy. Mineola, NY: Dover.

Vahabzadeh, Peyman. 2003. *Articulated Experiences: Toward a Radical Phenomenology of Contemporary Social Movements.* Albany: SUNY Press.

– 2004. "The Space between Voices: Nima Yushij and the 'Receding Signified.'" In *Essays on Nima Yushij: Animating Modernism in Persian Poetry.* Ed. Ahmad Karimi-Hakkak and Kamran Talattof. Leiden: Brill. 193–219

– 2005. "The Secular Good in Denial: The Lesser Evil and the Politics of Fright." *Journal for Cultural and Religious Theory* 6(2): 117–29.

– 2006. "Reflections on a Diremptive Experience and Four Theses on Origins and Exile." *Journal for Interdisciplinary Crossroads* 3(1): 163–81.

– 2007. "Measure and Democracy in the Age of Politics of Fright." *Journal for Cultural and Religious Theory* 8(2): 8–27.

– 2009. "Ultimate Referentiality: Radical Phenomenology and the New Interpretive Sociology." *Philosophy and Social Criticism* 35(4): 447–65. https://doi .org/10.1177/0191453708102095.

– 2010. *A Guerrilla Odyssey: Modernization, Secularism, Democracy, and the Fadai Period of National Liberation in Iran, 1971–1979.* Syracuse: Syracuse University Press.

– 2012a. *Exilic Mediations: Essays on a Displaced Life.* H&S Media.

– 2012b. "Oblivion of Origins: Of Hegemonic Universals and Hybrid Civilizations." In *Towards the Dignity of Difference: Neither "End of History" nor "Clash of Civilizations."* Ed. W. Andy Knight and Mojtaba Mahdavi. London: Ashgate Publishing. 43–53.

– 2014. "Suggestion, Translation, Transposition: Reflections on the Affinities of Movements in the Middle East and Beyond." *Sociology of Islam* 2(3–4): 111–26. https://doi.org/10.1163/22131418-00204002.

– 2015. "A Generation's Myth: Armed Struggle and the Creation of Social Epic in the 1970s Iran." In *Iran in the Middle East: Transnational Encounters and Social History.* Ed. Houchang Chehabi, Peyman Jafari, and Maral Jefroudi. London: I.B. Tauris. 183–98.

Vattimo, Gianni. 1991. *The End of Modernity.* Trans. J.R. Snyder. Baltimore: Johns Hopkins University Press.

– 1997. *Beyond Interpretation.* Trans. D. Webb. Stanford: Stanford University Press.

– 2004. *Nihilism and Emancipation: Ethics, Politics, and Law.* Ed. S. Zabala, trans. W. McCuaig. New York: Columbia University Press.

– 2007. "Conclusion: Metaphysics and Violence." In *Weakening Philosophy: Essays in Honour of Gianni Vattimo.* Ed. S. Zabala. Montreal and Kingston: McGill-Queen's University Press. 400–21.

Veron, Jeremy. 2004. *Bringing the War Home: The Weather Underground, the Red Army Faction, and Revolutionary Violence in the Sixties and Seventies*. Berkeley: University of California Press.

Villa, Dana. 1996. *Arendt and Heidegger: The Fate of the Political*. Princeton: Princeton University Press.

Weber, Max. 1946. *From Max Weber: Essays in Sociology*. Trans. H.H. Gerth and C. Wright Mills. New York: Oxford University Press.

Wise, Christopher. 2009. *Derrida, Africa, and the Middle East*. New York: Palgrave Macmillan. https://doi.org/10.1057/9780230619531.

Wohlfarth, Irving. 2008. "*Entsetzen*: Walter Benjamin and the Red Army Faction, Part One." *Radical Philosophy* 152: 7–19.

– 2009a. "Critique of Violence: The Deposing of the Law: Walter Benjamin and the Red Army Faction, Part 2." *Radical Philosophy* 153: 13–26.

– 2009b. "Specters of Anarchy: Walter Benjamin and the Red Army Faction, Part Three." *Radical Philosophy* 154: 9–24.

World Bank. 2013. "Global GDP Rates." *World Bank Open Data*. https://data.worldbank.org/indicator/NY.GDP.MKTP.KD.ZG, accessed 5 April 2013.

Zaslove, Jerry. 2015a. Email to author, 14 March 2015.

– 2015b. "Alienation Effect – a Story from Herr Keuner, a Short Organum from an Archival Memory of 'Mother Courage.'" Personal letter to author, 11 June 2015.

Žižek, Slavoj. 2008. *In Defense of Lost Causes*. London: Verso.

Index